Fourth edition

New Headway

Intermediate Teacher's Book

Liz and John Soars
Amanda Maris

OXFORD
UNIVERSITY PRESS

Contents

Introduction

The *Headway* series

Headway has made a significant contribution to English Language Teaching for over 20 years.

The *Headway* series has always championed a blend of methodologies:

- **traditional methodology:** a grammatical syllabus with controlled practice; systematic vocabulary work, and reading and writing activities
- **a more communicative approach:** a functional/situational syllabus; personalized practice; real language work in real situations; activities to encourage genuine communication inside and outside the classroom; development of all four skills – especially listening and speaking

This blend of approaches has proved an excellent combination for English language learning, and has now become standard, and indeed expected of today's ELT course books.

New Headway Intermediate is the first of the now six-level *Headway*, from Beginner to Advanced, to be in its fourth edition.

Why a fourth edition of *New Headway Intermediate*?

Throughout the 20+ years of writing *Headway*, the authors, Liz and John Soars, have been constantly re-evaluating and seeking to improve their work. New approaches to teaching, changes in the English language, and indeed changes in the world we live in, all impact on the material they write. It is because of this ever-changing world that they have chosen to scrutinize every aspect of *Headway Intermediate* in its previous three editions, and write this brand new fourth edition.

The intermediate level

The intermediate level is an interesting one for both student and teacher.

From the student's point of view, they have been introduced to many basic aspects of the English language. However, with the exception of the most able, they are still making mistakes of grammar, wrong word choice, collocation, pronunciation, or sentence stress. There might well be an element of frustration, as they become more fully aware of what is still to be mastered, and how much more there is to learn.

For teachers, the task at this level is to revise and extend without making students feel they are doing the same areas again – one step back and two steps forward.

New Headway Intermediate, Fourth edition, helps students reflect on, analyse, solidify, and build on what they already 'know', paving the way for increased fluency and more advanced structures to come in higher levels.

Key features of the *New Headway Intermediate, Fourth edition* Student's Book

Starter

Each unit begins with a *Starter* section, which launches the grammar and/or the theme of the unit.

Grammar

The upfront, systematic, and effective treatment of grammar is a hallmark of *Headway*.

At the intermediate level, we increase students' awareness of grammar by comparing and contrasting structures with similar items, and placing them in the context of the language as a whole. The syllabus covers present, past, and future tenses; simple, continuous, and perfect aspect; modal verbs; the passive voice; verb patterns; reported speech and thought; adjectives and adverbs; the structure of the noun phrase.

Grammar spots

There are Grammar Spots in the body of the unit, which give essential rules of form, use, and pronunciation. These have cross-references to the Grammar Reference at the back of the book, where students and teachers will find more in-depth explanations.

Practice

Each unit has a wide variety of practice activities, both controlled and free, mechanical and information gap. Students are encouraged to analyse the target language and use it communicatively.

Reading texts, and listening scripts

Texts and scripts are sourced from popular and serious newspapers and magazines, literature, biographies, and reference works such as encyclopaedias, and interviews with people from a range of backgrounds, ages, professions, experiences, and nationalities. Reading and listening material therefore has broad appeal designed to engage people with a certain curiosity about the world.

Speaking, Listening, and Everyday English

The communicative emphasis in *New Headway Intermediate, Fourth edition* gives students plenty of opportunities to put language into practice.

Grammar, Reading, Vocabulary, and Writing sections are always combined with speaking and/or listening activities to encourage genuine communication using target language.

Communicative skills are also given special treatment in their own sections, with *Everyday English* pages at the end of each unit presenting and practising areas such as social expressions, giving opinions, making suggestions, requests and offers, responding, and making small talk.

Spoken English and music of English boxes

These add to the emphasis on activating language by focusing on particular phrases, expressions, or grammatical structures used in everyday communicative situations such as short answers, making a comment softer or stronger, ways of agreeing and disagreeing, expressing emphasis, and the use of items such as *just, pretty, I don't care/I don't mind,* and *as well* or *too*. Intonation is particularly important with this aspect of language, so there are clear models with controlled practice of stress and intonation.

Vocabulary

Headway has always attached great importance to the acquisition of vocabulary. Its approach can broadly be divided into three areas: the encouragement of good learning habits (using dictionaries; keeping records, reading, working out meaning from context); an examination of the systems of vocabulary (collocation, compounds, antonyms, synonyms, homophones, homonyms, word building, spelling and pronunciation); and the teaching of new items in lexical sets (sport; leisure activities; the body; phrasal verbs).

Writing

The development of the writing skill continues to be in a separate section at the back of the Student's Book. This comprises twelve complete writing lessons cued from the unit, which can be used at the teacher's discretion. The writing syllabus provides models for students to analyse and imitate.

Teacher's Book

The Teacher's Book offers the teacher full support both for lesson preparation and in the classroom.

- **Full teaching notes** for each section, with answers and tapescripts in the main body of the notes.
  There are plenty of suggestions with ideas for exploiting the material with weaker students and/or mixed ability classes, for extending the Student's Book material, and for encouraging students to use English outside the classroom.
- **Background notes** for the *Reading* and *Listening* sections with information about the people profiled in the texts, historical and geographical notes, and brief explanations about features of the English-speaking world.
- **Cross references** to relevant exercises in the Workbook.
- **Photocopiable materials** to accompany units with extra pairwork, group work, vocabulary revision, and songs.
- **Answers to photocopiable materials** are on TB pp158–9.

Teacher's Resource Disc

The Teacher's Book is now accompanied by a Teacher's Resource Disc with photocopiable, and audio resources. Some resources are available as print-ready PDFs, others are Word documents, which can be customized by the teacher. The Teacher's Resource Disc contains:

- **Introduction:** information about the disc and how to customize documents.
- **Grammar Reference practice exercises** to accompany the Student's Book Grammar Reference. With answers.
- **Complete tests, with answers and audio:**
  - *Entry test* revising key grammar from *Headway Pre-Intermediate.*
  - *Unit tests 1–12,* in two versions covering the main grammar, vocabulary and everyday English syllabus for each Student's Book unit.
  - *Stop and check tests,* in two versions, revising Units 1–4, 5–8, and 9–12.
  - *Progress tests* for mid-year and end-of-year assessment.
  - *Skills tests* covering the four skills of reading, listening, writing and speaking.
  - *Optional listening tests* 1–12.
- **Tapescripts** from the Student's Book and Workbook with ideas on how to use for further practice.
- **Wordlists** from the Student's Book with write-in lines for translations.
- **An introduction to oxfordenglishtesting.com** with details of how to access a PET practice test via the student's Interactive Practice CD-ROM.

Class audio CDs

The Class Audio CDs contain all the listening resources essential for practising listening in class.

Workbook and Student's Workbook CD

The Workbook is an important component as it practises, revises, and reinforces the language presented in the Student's Book. There is a strong element of progressing from exercises that practise recognition to those that encourage production of the target items. There are reading texts and vocabulary exercises, as well as pronunciation work, and a syllabus for phrasal verbs and prepositions.

Many of the exercises are on the Student's Workbook CD.

Interactive Practice CD-ROM

The Interactive Practice CD-ROM offers students further interactive practice for self study. There is access to a free PET practice test at **oxfordenglishtesting.com** via the CD-ROM.

Teacher's Resource Book

The Teacher's Resource Book contains photocopiable games and activities to supplement the main course material.

Headway online

There is a Teacher's Website with a comprehensive range of materials at www.oup.com/elt/teacher/headway

There is a also a student's site with interactive practice exercises and games at www.oup.com/elt/headway

Finally!

We hope you and your students enjoy using this book, and find it not only useful to learn and practise your language skills, but enjoyable and thought-provoking.

Good luck!

John and Liz Soars

1

Tenses • Auxiliary verbs
What's in a word?
Everyday situations

A world of difference

Introduction to the unit

As you begin *New Headway Intermediate*, fourth edition, you may be at the start of a new course with a new group of students. If so, try to establish a good classroom atmosphere over the first few lessons and give students opportunities to get to know you and each other.

One warm-up idea is to put students in pairs or small groups and ask them to interview each other and find three things they have in common. Then ask some students to report back about their partner/people in their group, e.g. *I'm Rosa and this is Marek. We're both university students, and we both like going to the cinema and spending time with friends.* You can also use this as an opportunity to listen to the students and assess their use of tenses and question formation, but don't give any feedback on these, as this activity is intended as an informal 'ice-breaker'.

The *Starter* section of the unit contains personalized questions that will help students to get to know more about each other, while also revising question formation and the use of auxiliary verbs.

The theme of the unit is 'our world'. The grammar review of tenses and auxiliary verbs is presented via a general knowledge quiz. The *Reading and speaking* section is a jigsaw reading on families from different parts of the world, and the *Listening and speaking* is an interview with a man from a family with different nationalities. There is an *Everyday English* section on language used in different social situations, and the *Writing* syllabus starts with an introduction to symbols commonly used to point out errors in written work.

Language aims

As part of your general lesson preparation, you can refer to the *Grammar Reference* on SB pp133–146 for an overview of the target structures in each unit.

Grammar – tenses and auxiliary verbs Unit 1 provides a global review of the auxiliary verbs that are needed to form different tenses. This allows you to assess students' knowledge of tenses and verb forms covered at earlier levels. These include Present Simple and Continuous, Past Simple and Continuous, Present Perfect Simple and Continuous, *going to*, and active and passive forms. Students should be familiar with these tenses and verb forms, but they are probably not using them completely accurately. All key tenses and verb forms are revisited in later units, where differences in meaning are explored and there is further practice and consolidation. At this stage in the course, be prepared for students to make mistakes in both tense formation and use, and don't attempt to correct every error.

Question forms The secondary grammatical aim of Unit 1 is the revision of question forms and short answers. Students often find question forms difficult because of the need for an auxiliary in the correct form and the inversion of subject and verb. Unit 1 also highlights the importance of short answers in sounding both polite and natural in English.

Common mistakes

**Where you work?*	**What you do last night?*
**Where do he live?*	**Did it stopped raining yet?*
**Where he studying now?*	**Where did you been?*

Vocabulary The exercises in the *Vocabulary* section are designed to help students think about how they learn vocabulary. The section includes exercises on guessing meaning, pronunciation, word formation, collocation, and keeping vocabulary records.

Everyday English This section contains a range of expressions, both formal and informal, used in different everyday situations. Students may come across these expressions when shopping, travelling, dealing with problems, etc. and some will also be useful in the classroom, e.g. *I'm sorry I can't make the class. / I'm sorry I'm late. I was stuck in traffic.*

Notes on the unit

STARTER (SB p6)

This section focuses on common mistakes in question formation, and gives students the opportunity to decide on the correct forms in a controlled way. Students then go on to ask and answer questions in a personalization stage, and so get to know each other a little better.

1 Focus attention on the example and the missing word *come*. Ask students to work individually to add in the missing words in the rest of the questions. Students check their answers in pairs before a whole-class check.

Answers
2 When and where **were** you born?
3 **Do** you live in a house or a flat?
4 Why **are** you studying English?
5 Which foreign countries have you been **to**?
6 What **did** you do yesterday evening?
7 What are you going **to** do after this lesson?

2 To help students in the question and answer stage, practise the pronunciation first. Get students to listen and repeat, paying attention to the intonation of the questions. Point out that *Wh*-questions start high and then fall, e.g.

Where do you come from?

Get various students to ask you the questions and answer them so that they can learn about *you*, too. As the students form the questions, check for accuracy and pronunciation. Encourage the students to self-correct by not answering a question that is not formed accurately. Indicate the part of the question that isn't correct and be prepared to drill the pronunciation of the questions again if necessary.

Students ask and answer the questions in pairs. Monitor and help as necessary.

3 Remind students that they need to use *he* or *she* and third person singular verb forms for this stage. Ask a confident student to report back about his/her partner, or give an example about one of the students yourself. Elicit more examples from a range of students across the class. Allow students to give the information, and don't over-correct at this stage. Make sure you elicit at least one answer for each of the questions. In larger classes, there won't be time to hear from everyone, so make sure that students who don't contribute this time have an opportunity to do so later in the lesson, or in a subsequent lesson.

As an optional follow-up activity, ask students to write a short biography of their partner.

I DIDN'T KNOW THAT! (SB p6)

Tenses and auxiliary verbs

The quiz contains questions on different subjects, and it is a fun way to contextualize question forms across a range of tenses. If appropriate, get students to use a dictionary to look up new words before they complete the quiz. Alternatively, pre-teach/check the following vocabulary items: *population, oil, seven wonders of the world, extinct, to sink (sank, sunk).*

At the end of the section, students get to write questions for their own quiz. This involves them doing some research, so bring in encyclopaedias and other reference books for students to use. If your school has Internet access for students, they can do the research online. Alternatively, ask them to each prepare some questions for homework and then collaborate with classmates to decide on which questions to use.

NOTES ON THE QUESTIONS

5: The seven wonders of the world were structures considered to be the most impressive things built by ancient people.

7: The *Titanic* was a large passenger ship which was considered impossible to sink but which was hit by an iceberg on its first voyage in 1912.

9: The Nobel prizes are named after Alfred Nobel, the Swedish inventor of dynamite, who left much of his fortune for the establishment of a system of prizes.

1 Give students time to read the quiz and select their answers, working individually. Then put students into pairs to compare their answers. Encourage students to exchange knowledge and to make guesses where they are not sure.

2 **T 1.1** **[CD 1: Track 2]** Play the recording, pausing at the end of each section, and let students check their answers. Remind them to make notes on any extra information for each question.

Elicit any extra information that students have understood from the recording. With a large class, students can work in groups to do the information exchange.

Answers and tapescript
1 a 2 b 3 a 4 b 5 b 6 b 7 c 8 a 9 c 10 a 11 b 12 c

T 1.1
One World Quiz

1 **A** In which country do men and women live the longest?
B Women and men live longest in Japan. Women live on average 86 years and men 79. The average life expectancy in Japan is 81.25. In the USA it's 77.8 and in Germany 78.8.

2 **A** In which year did the world population reach 6 billion?
B The world population reached 6 billion in 1999. There are now over 6.8 billion people in the world.

3 **A** If you are standing on the equator, how many hours of daylight do you have?
B If you are standing on the equator you have 12 hours of daylight every day of the year. You also experience the fastest sunrise and sunset in the world, between 128 and 142 seconds depending on the time of year.

4 **A** Where does most of the world's oil come from?
B Most of the world's oil comes from Saudi Arabia. It produces 10.9 million barrels per day. Russia produces 9.4 million, and Iran 4.3 million.

5 **A** Which of these seven wonders of the world is still standing?
B Of the seven wonders of the ancient world, only the pyramids of Egypt are still standing. The Colossus of Rhodes and the Lighthouse of Alexandria were destroyed by earthquakes hundreds of years ago.

6 **A** Why didn't dinosaurs attack humans?
B Dinosaurs didn't attack humans because they became extinct 65 million years ago. Human beings didn't appear on earth until 130,000 years ago.

7 **A** Where was the *Titanic* sailing to when it sank?
B The *Titanic* was sailing to New York from Southampton when it hit an iceberg on April 14th 1912.
8 **A** How long has Elizabeth II been Queen of England?
B Elizabeth II has been Queen of England since 1952. She was on holiday in Kenya when her father, King George VI, died.
9 **A** How many people have won the Nobel Peace prize since it started in 1901?
B 94 people have won the Nobel Peace prize since it started in 1901. These include Nelson Mandela in 1993, and Mother Teresa in 1979.*
10 **A** How long have people been using the Internet?
B People have been using the Internet since 1969. It was invented by the US Department of Defense as a means of communication. It first went live in October 1969, with communications between the University of California and the Stanford Research Institute.
11 **A** How many languages are spoken in Switzerland?
B Four languages are spoken in Switzerland: German, French, Italian, and Romansch. German is the most widely spoken. 63.7% speak German, 19.2% French, 7.6% Italian, and 0.6% Romansch.
12 **A** In which country were women first given the vote?
B New Zealand was the first country in the world to give women the vote in 1893. Canadian women were given the vote in 1917, but women in Liechtenstein weren't allowed to vote until 1984.
* These figures are correct up to 2008.

GRAMMAR SPOT (SB p6)

The *Grammar Spot* in each unit aims to get students to think about the language they have just seen in the presentation.

1 Refer students to the tenses in bold in the quiz questions, and elicit the names of the tenses in questions 1 and 2 as examples. Students then identify the remaining tenses. Check the answers with the class, eliciting that questions 11 and 12 contain passive forms.

1 Present Simple
2 Past Simple
3 Present Continuous
4 Present Simple
5 Present Continuous
6 Past Simple
7 Past Continuous
8 Present Perfect Simple
9 Present Perfect Simple
10 Present Perfect Continuous
11 Present Simple passive
12 Past Simple passive

2 With weaker classes, or if you want to review the use of auxiliaries as a class, you could build in the stage in the *Suggestion* box below before exercise 2.
Ask students to find and underline the auxiliary verbs in the quiz. Then put them in pairs to discuss the questions. Check the answers with the class, eliciting examples for each category.

Answers
The Present Simple and Past Simple use *do/does/did* to form questions and negatives.
The Present Continuous and Past Continuous use the verb *to be*. We also use *to be* in passive forms.
The Present Perfect Simple and Continuous use *have/has.*

Refer students to Grammar Reference 1.1–1.5 on SB p133.

SUGGESTION

Before you do exercise 2 in the *Grammar Spot*, you could write seven sentences on the board with the auxiliaries underlined:

We are working hard.
English is spoken all over the world.
I don't watch TV very often.
Do you drink wine?
Why didn't you come to the cinema?
Paper was invented in China.
I haven't spoken to my friend today.

Elicit that the underlined words are auxiliary verbs and that they help to form tenses and add meaning to the main verb.

Write your own quiz

3 Divide the class into two groups. With larger classes, you will need to create more teams. If students are doing the research in class, give them reference materials or set them up on computers if they are working online. If students are doing the preparation for homework, brainstorm topics that they could research, e.g. inventions, Olympic athletes, famous buildings, interesting writers/painters, dates of famous songs/films, etc. Remind students that they need questions that contain both present and past tenses. Check their questions at the start of the next class. Monitor and help each group with their research, and check for accuracy of the question formation.
Groups or teams then compete against each other, asking and answering their questions. Remind students to keep score and decide which team is the winner.

SUGGESTION

If your students enjoy this activity, you could get them to prepare more questions on a range of different topics as you work through the units. You could have a regular 'quiz time' as often as you think appropriate and keep ongoing scores, with the winner being declared at the end of term. You could even set up a quiz league with students in other classes!

PRACTICE (SB p7)

You're so wrong!

1 Read the examples as a class. Point out that students will need to change the form from affirmative to negative (as in sentence 1) or from negative to affirmative (as in sentence 2). Give students time to correct the sentences, working individually. Monitor and help, focusing mainly on the verb forms at this stage. Students will go on to practise the intonation in exercise 2.

2 **T 1.2** **[CD 1: Track 3]** Play the recording and get students to check their answers. Ask them to note down any additional information they get from the recording. Write sentences 1 and 2 on the board. Say the sentences or play the recording of the sentences again and get students to mark the main stresses.

He doesn't live in Madrid! He lives in Rome!
You're wrong! He wrote hundreds of poems.

Exaggerate the stress patterns and encourage students to copy you. Play the recording of the remaining sentences and get students to mark the stress, and then repeat.

Put the students in pairs or groups of three to practise saying the sentences. Monitor and check for accurate stress and intonation. Be prepared to drill the sentences again if students have problems.

Answers and tapescript

T 1.2

1 **A** The Pope lives in Madrid.
  B He doesn't live in Madrid! He lives in Rome! In the Vatican!
2 **A** Shakespeare didn't write poems.
  B You're wrong! He wrote hundreds of poems, not just plays.
3 **A** Vegetarians eat meat.
  B Of course they don't eat meat. They only eat vegetables and sometimes fish.
4 **A** The Internet doesn't provide much information.
  B Rubbish! It provides lots. Sometimes I think that it provides too much!
5 **A** The world is getting colder.
  B It isn't getting colder, it's getting hotter. Haven't you heard of global warming?
6 **A** Princess Diana was travelling by plane when she was killed.
  B No, you're wrong. She wasn't travelling by plane. She was travelling by car, in Paris.
7 **A** England has never won the World Cup.
  B England *has* won it, just once. I think it was in 1966. My dad goes on about it all the time.
8 **A** The 2008 Olympics were held in Tokyo.
  B No, they weren't held in Tokyo. They were held in China, in Beijing.

's = *is* or *has*?

3 Remind students that the contracted form *'s* can stand for *is* or *has*. Focus attention on the example and then get students to complete the task, working individually. Check the answers with the class. If students have problems distinguishing the forms, or need more practice in recognizing tenses, elicit the tense or form used in each sentence (see bracketed answers below).

Answers

1 is (Present Continuous)	4 has (Present Perfect)
2 has (Present Perfect)	5 is (Present Continuous)
3 is (Present Simple passive)	6 is (Present Simple passive)

4 **T 1.3** **[CD 1: Track 4]** Tell students that there are a further six sentences on the recording. Play the first one as an example and elicit the answer (*has*). Play the rest of the recording, pausing at the end of each sentence to give students time to decide on their answers. Play the recording again to check, asking students to name each tense or form as in exercise 3 if necessary.

Answers and tapescript

1 has (Present Perfect)	4 is (Present Continuous)
2 is (Present Continuous)	5 has (Present Perfect)
3 has (Present Perfect)	6 is (Present Simple passive)

T 1.3

1 My brother's just got a new job.
2 He's working in South America.
3 He's been there 3 months.
4 He's having a great time.
5 He's never worked overseas before.
6 His company's called *Intext Worldwide*.

Talking about you

5 Focus attention on sentence 1 and elicit the answer as an example (*do* – Present Simple). Ask students to work in pairs to complete the questions and name the tenses. Point out that they will need a negative form in sentences 7 and 8, and that sentence 10 requires a passive form. Monitor and help. Then check the answers with the whole class. Drill the pronunciation if necessary, reminding students that *Wh-* questions start high and need falling intonation.

Put students into new pairs to ask and answer the questions. Monitor and check for accurate question formation and intonation. Be prepared to drill the questions again if students have problems.

Answers

1 do (Present Simple)	6 were (Past Continuous)
2 did (Past Simple)	7 don't (Present Simple)
3 does (Present Simple)	8 didn't (Past Simple)
4 is ... is (Present Continuous)	9 have (Present Perfect)
5 have (Present Perfect)	10 were (Past Simple passive)

ADDITIONAL MATERIAL

Workbook Unit 1
Exercises 1–3 Tenses
Exercises 4–7 Auxiliary Verbs

MAKING CONVERSATION (SB p8)

Short answers

The aim of this section is to remind students of the importance of short answers in natural, spoken English. Students will be familiar with the form of short answers from their earlier learning, but are unlikely to be using them spontaneously, even at the end of this section! Be prepared to remind students to use short answers at any time they are doing question and answer work. Over time, this feature of spoken English should become more and more familiar to students and so they will start to use short answers as part of their own communicative repertoire.

1 **T 1.4** **[CD 1: Track 5]** Focus attention on the photo. Ask *Who are the people?* (a mother and her children) *Where are they?* (outside the children's school) *Is it the beginning or the end of the school day?* (the end).

Pre-teach/Check *kids* (informal for *children*), *loads* (informal for *lots/a lot*), *football kit*, *rubbish* (in this context, informal for *not very good*).

Play the recording and get students to complete the conversation individually. Give them time to compare answers in pairs, and elicit which child is more polite and why (see *Answer* below).

Play the recording again if necessary to allow students to complete their answers. Check the answers with the class.

Answer and tapescript
Lily sounds more polite because she uses short answers rather than saying just *yes* or *no*.

T 1.4
R = **Ruth** **N** = **Nick** **L** = **Lily**
R So, kids! **Did** you have a good day at school?
N No.
L Yes, I **did**. We **were** practising for the school concert.
R Oh, lovely. **Do** you have much homework?
L Ugh! Yes, I **do**. Loads. I've got Geography, French, and Maths! **Have** you got a lot Nick?
N Yeah.
R Nick, **have** you remembered your football kit?
N Er ...
L No, he **hasn't**. He's forgotten it again.
R Oh, Nick you know it needs washing. **Are** you playing football tomorrow?
N No.
R Lily, **do** you need *your* sports kit tomorrow?
L Yes, I **do**. I've got a hockey match after school. We're playing the High School.
R **Didn't** they beat you last time?
L Yes, they **did**. But we'll to beat them tomorrow.
N No, you **won't**! Your team's rubbish.
R OK, that's enough, children. Do up your seatbelts! Let's go!

SPOKEN ENGLISH – Sounding polite

1/2 Focus attention on the *Spoken English* box, and give students time to read the notes. Point out that the auxiliary verb in the short answer must match the tense in the question. Drill the intonation of the questions and answers. Point out that *yes/no* questions start high and end with a fall-rise, and that the short answers have falling intonation:

Did you have a good day? *Yes, I did.*

Ask pairs of students to read the questions and answers.

3 Elicit possible answers to question 1. Make sure students use the correct falling intonation in the answer and that they add some information. Students ask and answer the questions in pairs. Monitor and check for correct formation of the short answers, and for correct intonation on the questions and answers. Be prepared to drill the intonation again if necessary.

Possible answers
1 Yes, I did. It was really good fun!
2 Yes, I do. I often eat pizza.
3 No, I didn't. I thought it was boring.
4 Yes, it has. It's lovely and sunny now.

Refer students to Grammar Reference 1.6 on SB p133.

2 Tell students they are going to rewrite Nick's lines in exercise 1 to make him sound more polite. Elicit an example for the first line, pointing out that there are several possible answers, but they should all start *No, I didn't.* Give students time to rewrite the lines, working in pairs. Monitor and help, feeding in new vocabulary items as necessary and checking students are forming the short answers correctly.

T 1.5 **[CD 1: Track 6]** Play the recording and get students to compare their versions with the wording on the CD. Elicit a range of possible answers from the class, correcting any mistakes in the short answers carefully.

T 1.5
R = **Ruth** **N** = **Nick** **L** = **Lily**
R So, kids! Did you have a good day at school?
N No, I didn't. Not really. We didn't have *any* of my favourite subjects.
L I did. I had a brilliant day. We were practising for the school concert.
R Oh, lovely. Do you have much homework?
L Ugh! Yes, I do. Loads. I've got Geography, French, and Maths! Have you got a lot Nick?
N Yes, I have. Loads of it. I have to write a Geography essay on Antarctica. 1,500 words!
R Oh Nick, have you remembered your football kit?
N Oh no, I haven't – sorry, mum.
R Oh, Nick you know it needs washing. Are you playing football tomorrow?
N No, I'm not, thank goodness. The match was cancelled.
R Lily, do you need your sports kit tomorrow?
L Yes, I do. I've got a hockey match after school. We're playing the High School.
R Didn't they beat you last time?
L Yes, they did. But we'll beat them tomorrow.
N Mmm – I'm not so sure about that.
R OK, that's enough, children. Do up your seatbelts! Let's go!

3 Divide the class into groups of three. Refer them to the tapescripts on SB p118. Let students choose their own role for **T 1.4** and then get them to change roles for **T 1.5**. Give them time to practise the conversations. If students sound rather flat or inexpressive, play key lines of the recording again or model the intonation yourself. Be prepared to exaggerate the intonation to help students imitate the voice range in the 'polite' version.

PRACTICE (SB p9)

1 Focus attention on the example and get a pair of students to read out the conversation. Students work individually to match the lines of the remaining conversations.

T 1.6 **[CD 1: Track 7]** Play the recording through once so that students can check their answers. Divide students into pairs to practise the conversations. If necessary, play the recording again as a pronunciation model.

Answers and tapescript

T 1.6
1 **A** Did you hear that noise?
B Yes, I did. I think it was thunder.
2 **A** Are you doing anything tonight?
B No, I'm not. Do you want to come round?
3 **A** Have you seen my mobile phone anywhere?
B No, I haven't. Have you lost it again?

4 **A** Did you get those shoes you liked?
B No, I didn't. They didn't have my size.
5 **A** Is it time for a break?
B Yes, it is. Thank goodness!

A class survey

Tell students they are going to do a class survey to find out more information about their classmates.

2 Give students time to read through the survey and think of their answers to the questions. Deal with any vocabulary queries. Elicit ideas for the two additional questions, reminding students they can ask questions in the Present Simple, Present Continuous, Past Simple, or Present Perfect.

Possible additional questions
Have you got any brothers or sisters?
Do you see your family every week?
Does anyone in your family speak English?
Are you working very hard at the moment?
Did you go on holiday last year?
Have you ever been skiing?

Monitor and help as students write their questions.

3 Get a pair of students to read out the example question and answer. With weaker classes, read through the survey questions as a class and elicit possible answers. Students then ask and answer the questions in pairs. If possible, get students to interview a new partner that they don't usually work with so that they are asking and answering genuine questions.

4 Remind students that they are going to need *he/she* and third person singular forms when reporting back about their partner. Elicit examples from the class. With bigger groups, get students to work with a new partner to talk about the classmate that they interviewed. Note down any common errors to review in a later lesson but do not over-correct during the feedback stage.

5 Elicit a range of general statements that apply to all the class. If necessary, feed in/review quantifiers like *nearly everyone, most of, all of, some of, none of.* Elicit which quantifiers are followed by a singular verb (*everyone, none of*) and which by a plural (*most of, some of*).

Check it

6 This exercise brings together the target structures of the unit in an error correction task.

Give students time to correct the sentences, working individually. Students who finish quickly can check their answers in pairs. Then check the answers with the class.

Answers
1 Rae comes from Canada and he **speaks** French and English.
2 Which subjects **is Susan** studying at university?
3 'Do you like football?' 'Yes, I **do**.'
4 Did you **watch** the match last night?
5 What **do** you parents do at the weekend?
6 I think **it's** going to rain.
7 What **were** you talking to the teacher about?
8 I don't think John's **arrived** yet.

ADDITIONAL MATERIAL

Workbook Unit 1
Exercise 8 Short answers

READING AND SPEAKING (SB p10)

Worlds apart

ABOUT THE TEXT
This section integrates reading and speaking with a jigsaw reading task based on descriptions of two families from different parts of the world. Group A reads about the Kamau family from Kenya and group B reads about the Qu family from China. They then exchange information with a student from the other group to compare the two families.

There are a number of new words and phrases in the texts. Some of these are covered in the *Vocabulary work* in exercise 6 in an understanding from context task. They are highlighted in each text and should not be pre-taught. Students may query the following vocabulary items. Encourage them to use the context to guess the meaning and/or allow them to use dictionaries if appropriate. With weaker classes, be prepared to pre-teach/check the items to lighten the overall reading load:

The Kamaus: *200,000 miles on the clock* (the number of miles a car has driven), *take home* (in this context *earn*), *his salary doesn't go far* (he doesn't earn enough to cover all his family's needs), *school fees, raise a family, suburbs, spare* (in this context, *extra*).

The Qus: *childhood, noticeable, put someone's needs first, prestigious, propaganda, yuan* (the unit of currency in China), *hospitality, elderly, out of step* (in this context, *not fitting in*), *to rush around, headquarters* (in this context, *the main place or home*), *policy, well-balanced.*

1 Answer the questions in this exercise about your own family. Make sure students understand the difference between *immediate* and *extended family*. Put the students into groups of three or four to discuss the questions. Monitor and help but do not correct errors or interrupt the students' flow too much. Elicit one or two examples of interesting family profiles in a short feedback session.

2 Focus attention on the photos and on the profiles of each of the families. Elicit the two countries the students are going to read about (Kenya and China) and any information or ideas that students may have about them.

3 Divide the class into two groups, A and B. With larger classes, you will need to sub-divide the students into more than one group A and more than one group B. Ask all the A students to read about the Kamaus and all the B students to read about the Qus. Monitor and be prepared to deal with new vocabulary (see *About the text* above), but do not give away the meaning of the highlighted words covered in exercise 6.

4 Students work together in their A or B groups to answer the questions about their text. Check the answers with each group, but don't check the answers with the whole class at this stage.

Answers

The Kamaus

1 In a small town called Ongata Rongai near Nairobi, in a two-bedroom apartment.
2 Since 1996.
3 Boniface is a taxi driver and Pauline is a dressmaker. They don't earn much money.
4 Rent, helping parents and brothers and sisters, school fees.
5 Joyce is in her third year of school. Sharon will start preschool next year. They often only see their father at weekends. Joyce wants to be a doctor.
6 They've known each other since 1994.
7 Boniface's parents don't work. He is more successful than his brothers and sisters and so he has to help them out financially.
8 They want to give their children a good education. Pauline wants to start her own dressmaking business. Boniface wants to build a house in the suburbs of Nairobi.

The Qus

1 In a house in central Beijing, in one of the ancient Hutong alleyways.
2 The family has lived there for 70 years.
3 Qu is a propaganda officer at the municipal services bureau and Liu works at the No. 3 computer factory. They don't earn much money.
4 They are saving it to pay for their daughter's education.
5 Chen is an only child and she is lonely. She is also bright and well-balanced. She is trying for a place at the prestigious Beijing University. She wants to study archaeology.
6 They have known each other since childhood.
7 Qu's father is the centre of the family. He lives with Qu and Liu. Qu's brothers and their families visit most weekends. They are very close.
8 They want to give their child a good education and so they live frugally. Qu wants to support the traditional way of life and hospitality of families who live in the alleyways.

5 Ask students to work in pairs, with one in each pair from group A and one from group B. Elicit one similarity and one difference between the two families as examples (both families want to give their child/children a good education; the Kamaus have two children but the Qus have only one). Give students time to exchange their information and answer the questions. Monitor and help as necessary. Make sure students are exchanging the information to help them answer the questions and not simply reading from the text. Check the answers with the class.

Possible answers

1 **Similarities:** Both families want to give their child/children a good education. Neither family earns much money. Both have to support other members of their family.

Differences: The Kamaus have two children but the Qus have only one. Both parents work in the Qu family, but only Boniface works at the moment in the Kamau family. The Kamau family want to get away from the area where they live, but the Qus would like to stay.

2 The Kamaus have moved from a slum to a better area. Boniface won some money which allowed him to learn to drive and become a taxi driver.

In China, the size of the families has become much smaller due to the one-child policy. Much of the traditional housing where the Qus live has been demolished. The relaxed routine of the area is changing as the whole of China is experiencing rapid change. The traditional family structure is disappearing.

3 The Kamaus are often stressed about money. They want to raise their children in better conditions.

The Qus regret having only one child. They are concerned about having enough money for their daughter's education. Qu is concerned about the changes in Chinese society and the family.

Vocabulary work

6 Refer the students back to their texts and get them to look at the highlighted words. Remind them to use the context to help them work out the meaning. Then ask them to match the words to the meanings in the chart. Monitor and help as necessary. Check the answers.

Answers

The Kamaus	The Qus
1 dressmaker	1 cherished
2 single-storey	2 frail
3 slum	3 alleyways
4 communal	4 demolition
5 cracked	5 close-knit
6 stressed	6 frugally

7 Put students into new A/B pairs and get them to exchange the new words and expressions and their definitions. Remind them to pronounce and spell the new words correctly to help their partner.

What do you think?

Give students time to read through the questions and think about their answers. Elicit a range of responses in a whole-class discussion. In larger classes, students can work in groups and then report back.

EXTRA IDEA

Understanding meaning from context TB p145–6

You can provide additional practice in understanding vocabulary from context with this photocopiable worksheet. You will need one sheet for each student. Ask students to do the tasks without using dictionaries. The answers are on TB p158.

LISTENING AND SPEAKING (SB p12)

A world in one family

This section continues the theme of 'our world' and brings in the concepts of nationality and heritage via two interviews, one with a young man called Xabier and the other with his mother, Ana.

The following vocabulary may be new, so pre-teach/check the items before students listen, especially with weaker classes:

T 1.7 *background* (a person's past family life and experience), *to end up doing something, to support* (e.g. a football team), *neutral* (not supporting one team or another), *heritage, to influence someone, ultimately, to settle down.*

T 1.8 *to offer someone a lift, to refuse, cosmopolitan, keep in touch, the Foreign Office* (the British government department that deals with foreign affairs), *to sum up, pros and cons, tricky* (difficult).

1 Give an example of a mixed-nationality marriage that you know of. Elicit further examples from the class.

2 Focus attention on the photos of the family. Check pronunciation of Xabier /xæbɪe(r)/ and Teo /teɪjeʊ/. Elicit ideas as to how there are three nationalities in the same family. Accept a range of ideas but do not confirm or reject any of them at this stage.

3 **T 1.7** **[CD 1: Track 8]** See above note about pre-teaching/checking vocabulary. Play the recording as far as Xabier's line ending … *she still has her Spanish passport.* Elicit the answer to the question in exercise 2 (Xabier is British but his dad is Bolivian and his mum is Spanish). Give students time to read through the questions in exercise 3. Explain that some of the information to answer the questions is contained in this recording and the remainder is in the recording with the following exercise.

Play the recording again from the start and get students to note the answers to as many questions as possible. Tell them to underline any that they cannot answer at this stage. Allow students to check their answers in pairs/groups of three, but do not do a whole-class check until after exercise 4.

T 1.7

I = Interviewer X = Xabier

I So, Xabier – how old are you?
X I'm 21.
I And I know you have an interesting background, what nationality are you?
X Well, I've got a British passport …
I … so you're British, but your parents – what nationality are your parents?
X Well, my dad's Bolivian, he was born in Bolivia, in South America, but he's had a British passport for the last 20 years. My mum was born in Spain, in the Basque country, and she still has her Spanish passport.
I So how did they meet and end up having children in England?
X Erm … They met when they were both studying English in England erm … and er … and about three years after that they got married and here I am, and then my brother.
I And what was it like growing up in England with a Spanish mother and a Bolivian father?
X I don't think I actually noticed nationality for years – er … probably the first time I really noticed a difference was at secondary school, England were playing Spain in Euro '96 and my classmates made me choose which country to support.
I So which country did you support?
X I stayed neutral. Actually I didn't mind which team won.
I And which nationality do you feel now?
X I'd say I was English, rather than British – erm… but I'm also very proud of my parents' heritage, half Basque and half Bolivian. I like that.
I What contact have you had with your family abroad?
X Well, I've only actually been to Bolivia once – er… when I was a baby. I've had more contact on my mum's side. My Spanish grandparents visit us in England and when I was growing up we always went to Spain in the summer, and …
I Very nice
X … and if I'm at home I speak to them – er… to my grandparents, on the phone – er… maybe once a week.
I And do you think that your Spanish heritage has influenced you at all?
X Well, yes, I think so. I think it influenced my degree choice. I'm studying modern languages at Durham University, Spanish and French. I'm in my third year, I have one more year to do.
I And what are you hoping to do in the future?
X Erm … That's a very good question. Hopefully, a job that offers some kind of opportunity to travel, but ultimately I want to settle down for good in England. I've always been interested in my background, but I think that I realize England is my home and it's where I see myself living.
I Thank you very much, Xabier.
X You're welcome.

4 **T 1.8** **[CD 1: Track 9]** See above note about pre-teaching/checking vocabulary. Remind students to listen for the missing information from exercise 3. Play the recording through once and get students to answer the underlined questions. Play the recording again, if necessary, to allow students to complete their answers. Check the answers with the class.

Answers and tapescript

1 Xabier is British, Ana is Spanish, and Teo is Bolivian. They live in Oxford.
2 They met in the street on the way to the college where they were both studying. Teo offered Ana a lift but she refused. They ended up in the same class at the college. They decided to live in England because Teo had a job there and they wanted a place between Spain and Bolivia.
3 Xabier noticed his nationality when he was at secondary school. England were playing Spain in Euro '96 and his classmates made him choose which country to support. He stayed neutral.
4 When they were children, even though their parents spoke to them in Spanish, they always replied in English.
5 Xabier has been to Bolivia once. He went there when he was 18 months old. James has never been to Bolivia.
6 Xabier's grandparents visit them in England and he used to go to Spain in the summer for two or three weeks. He speaks to his grandparents about once a week.
7 Xabier is studying Spanish and French. James is going to study biology.
8 Xabier is hoping to work in the Foreign Office. He's planning to live in England.
9 James has just finished school. He's been working in a restaurant saving money to go travelling. He's going to travel to Bolivia before starting university.
10 It's good because you can take the best things from both cultures but her sons will never feel 100% English because their parents aren't English. It's quite tricky.

T 1.8

I = Interviewer A = Ana

I Ana, you're Spanish, aren't you?
A Yes, I am. I'm from Bilbao, in the Basque country.
I And how long have you lived here in Oxford?
A – er… 23 years.
I And how did that happen?
A Well, I wanted to improve my English so I came to England, to study. Originally, I came for six months but – er… I met my husband – er… we met at the college – actually, we met on the way to the college, in the street.
I You met in the street?
A Yes, it was my first day and I was walking up the hill to the college and Teo, that's my husband, was driving up the hill and he stopped and offered me a lift, which I refused.

I You refused?
A Yes, but we ended up in the same class. I went into the class and there he was.
I And your husband's from Bolivia, isn't he?
A Yes, he is.
I So that means you speak the same language.
A Yes, Spanish.
I So why did you decide to live in England?
A Well, mainly because my husband had a job here and erm ... we kind of decided we wanted a place in the middle, between Spain and Bolivia.
I A nice idea. And you have two sons.
A Yes, I do. Er... Xabier is 21, nearly 22, and James is 19.
I So, what's it been like for them growing up in England with parents of different nationality?
A Well, I think because we live in Oxford, a cosmopolitan city, they didn't notice it too much.
I They are both bilingual presumably?
A No, not really. Because, when they were children, even though we spoke to them in Spanish they always replied in English.
I Interesting. Tell me, how much contact has your family here had with the families in Spain and Bolivia?
A I think more with my family in Spain because it's closer. We always spent summer there – er – two or three weeks usually.
I And the Bolivian side?
A Well, my husband keeps in touch all the time but his family have never been here.
I Never?
A Never. We went to Bolivia once when Xabier was 18 months old. James has never been.
I So what are the children doing now?
A Xabier's at university and James has just finished school. He's been working in a restaurant saving money to travel.
I And what do they want to do in the future?
A Well, James. He's going to travel to Bolivia, at last! Then he's going to university to study Biology.
I And Xabier?
A I think he wants to work in the Foreign Office.
I Ana, is it possible to sum up the pros and cons of bringing up a family in another country not your own.
A Well, I think in a way it's good because you can take the best things from both cultures, but I don't think my sons will ever feel 100% English because their parents aren't English. It's quite tricky.

What do you think?

Elicit further examples of the pros and cons and write them up on the board. Students continue discussing the questions in pairs or small groups. Elicit different ideas from the class in a feedback stage. Decide if the students think that there are more advantages than disadvantages to bringing up a family in another country.

Sample answers
Pros: You and your children can learn another language.
You get to experience a different way of life.
People learn to be more open-minded and cosmopolitan.
Cons: It can be hard for people to fully belong to a culture.
You lose contact with family in the other country.
People in the new country may not accept you.

VOCABULARY (SB p12)

What's in a word?

The aim of this section is to encourage students to think about how they learn vocabulary. As a lead-in to the section, ask students how they record and remember new vocabulary. List their ideas on the board or on an OHT. Add your own ideas, or use the *Suggestions* below. Collate all the ideas onto one sheet to make a useful handout for students.

RECORDING VOCABULARY
- Don't just translate words – try to use a range of other techniques to make your vocabulary learning fun.
- Guess the meaning of words from context. Decide the part of speech (verb, noun, adjective, etc.) and what it probably means.
- Draw pictures to illustrate words and the meanings of prepositions of place and direction.
- Record words in groups under topic headings like *Sport* or *Adjectives of character.*
- Write contexts/personalized examples for new words to help you remember them, e.g. *I'd like to settle down in my home town*, rather than just *to settle down.*
- Record collocations (words that go together), e.g. *an interesting background.*
- Learn and use phonetic symbols to help you record the pronunciation of new words. Don't forget to mark the stress, e.g. cosmopolitan.
- Do everyday tasks in English to help you to recycle vocabulary, e.g. write shopping lists, write 'to-do' lists, etc.
- Design vocabulary tests for other students. Find ten words or phrases that you have seen in class in the last two weeks. Prepare definitions/clues that will help your classmate guess the word, e.g. *You do this when you phone or text someone regularly (= keep in touch).*

Meaning

1 Start by writing a sentence with *uggy* on the board, e.g.
I always have an uggy for lunch. Ask:
Is 'uggy' a real word? (no)
Is it a noun, adjective, or verb? (a noun)
How do you know? (it has the article *an*)
Is it countable or uncountable? (countable because of the article *an*)
What could it mean? (probably a type of food).

Ask students to read the sentences and decide on the part of speech. Give them time to compare their answers with a partner before checking with the class. Ask students to guess the meaning of each use of *uggy*, using the context to help them. Elicit a range of possible answers. Finally, get students to match the real words with the uses of *uggy*. Check the answers with the class.

Answers

Parts of speech

1 adjective (describing *grandmother*)
2 verb (infinitive without *to* after modal *will*)
3 noun (plural ending *-ies*)
4 adverb (describing living; adverb ending *-ly*)

Meaning

1 frail 2 cherish 3 slums 4 frugally

Pronunciation

2 This exercise helps students to distinguish vowel sounds and diphthongs in words that have similar spellings. Read out the words in number 1 or play the recording and ask students to say which one has a different vowel sound (*does*). Refer students to the phonetic symbols chart on SB p159 to help them with the sounds. Get them to work in pairs to compete the task

T 1.9 **[CD 1: Track 10]** Play the recording and get students to check their answers. If students have problems, drill the pronunciation by giving a model yourself or playing the recording again.

Answers and tapescript

T 1.9

1 rose	goes	does	toes
2 meat	beat	great	street
3 paid	made	played	said
4 done	phone	son	won

3 Try saying some of the students' names with the wrong stress to highlight the importance of correct stress to overall comprehension. Elicit the stress on *mother* and then get students to complete the task.

T 1.10 **[CD 1: Track 11]** Play the recording and get students to check their answers.

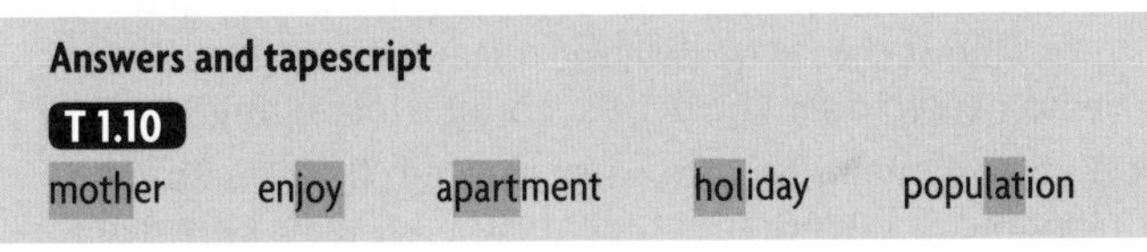

Answers and tapescript

T 1.10

mother enjoy apartment holiday population

Word formation

4 Focus attention on the example and the use of the suffix *-ive*. Students work individually to complete the sentences. Then check the answers with the class.

Answers

2 actress 3 Acting 4 action 5 activities

SUGGESTION

Encourage students to increase their vocabulary by thinking of how other words can be formed with prefixes and suffixes. You could extend this activity by getting students to look up other verbs and checking how many other words can be formed, e.g. *present, succeed, advertise.*

Words that go together

5 Remind students of the concept of collocation by writing the following gapped examples on the board:

______ *your homework* / ______ *the bed.*

Ask students: *make or do?* and elicit the answers (do your homework / make the bed).

Focus attention on the example in the Student's Book and then get students to match the other words. Check the answers with the class.

Answers

well-paid job	drive carelessly	win a race
close-knit family	fall in love	

As an extension, ask students to look back at the reading text on p10 and the scripts for this unit on SB pp118–9 and underline other collocations, e.g. *raise a family, cost a great deal of money.*

Keeping vocabulary records

6 The aim of this brief class discussion is to share ideas on how to record vocabulary. Put students into small groups to discuss the questions. If they have a vocabulary notebook, encourage students to show their classmates how they record vocabulary. Write a list of ideas on the board during the feedback stage (see *Suggestions* below) and ask students which they think work best. Again, you can collate all the ideas onto one sheet to make a useful handout for students.

ORGANIZING VOCABULARY RECORDS

- Find the way of keeping vocabulary records that best suits you, either electronically or in a special notebook.
- Leave space at the bottom of each section/page so that you can add new words and phrases.
- Set up a regular time to update your records. Be selective and include words you need to remember, but not those you need to just recognize.
- Try to organize words visually, rather than just using translation. Use pictures and diagrams and label them. Use word spiders to show the connection between words.
- Make your vocabulary records interesting and the words memorable by using different colours, images, and diagrams.
- Decide how best to record each entry including the meaning, use, and pronunciation. Include definitions, related words, example sentences, or collocations.

Look at these examples:

demolition (n) = knocking down a building; demolish (v) (*definition with part of speech and related word*)

heritage = patrimonio (*translation into Student's L1*)

cosy = warm and comfortable, e.g. a cosy room, bed, sofa (*definition with synonyms and collocations*)

end up = We lived in lots of different places but we ended up going back to our home town. (*example sentence to show meaning in context and following -ing form*)

ADDITIONAL MATERIAL

Workbook Unit 1

Exercise 9 Pronunciation – Phonetic symbols – vowel sounds
Exercise 10 Pronunciation – Word stress
Exercise 11 Vocabulary – Grammar words
Exercise 12 Vocabulary – Word formation
Exercise 13 Vocabulary – Words that go together
Exercise 14 Vocabulary – Different meanings

WRITING (SB p103)

An Informal letter – Correcting mistakes (1)

This section introduces students to symbols commonly used to point out errors in written work. The aim of using such symbols is to pinpoint errors in a piece of work and prompt students to self-correct. This section should get students to think about the sort of errors they make, and should encourage them to take responsibility for editing and correcting their own work.

1 Focus on the symbols in the box and give students an example of a mistake with a tense, e.g. **The sun shines at the moment* (*is shining*). Elicit examples of mistakes for the remaining symbols.
2 Get students to read the letter and correct the mistakes. Get them to check in pairs before checking with the whole class. You may wish to copy the answers below onto an OHT or handout.

Answers

23 St Mary's Road,
Dublin 4,
Ireland

Tuesday, 10 May

Dear Stephanie

How are you? I'm very well. I came **to** Dublin two weeks ago **to** study at a language school. I want **to** learn **English** because **it** is a very important language. I'm **staying** with **an** Irish family. They've got two **sons** and a **daughter**. Mr Kendall is **a** teacher, and Mrs Kendall **works** in a hospital. The Irish **are** very kind, but they speak very quickly!

I study in the morning. My **teacher's** name is Ann. She **told** me that my English is OK, but I **make** a lot of mistakes. Ann **doesn't** give us too much homework, so in the afternoons I **always go** sightseeing. Dublin is much **bigger** than my town. I like **painting very much**, and I'm very **interested in** modern art, so I visit galleries and museums. I've met a girl named Martina. She **comes** from Spain, and **goes** to Trinity College. Last night we **went** to the cinema, but the film wasn't very **exciting**.

Would you like to visit me? Why don't you come for a weekend?

I'd love to see you.
Write to me soon.

Love,
Kati

P.S. Here's my new email address:
Katik@intermail.hu

3 Get students to answer the questions in pairs.

Answers

1 She is in Dublin. She is staying with the Kendalls, an Irish family.
2 She is studying English at a language school.
3 She studies in the morning, and goes sightseeing in the afternoon.
4 She goes sightseeing, and she visits galleries and museums.
5 She has met Martina.

4 Prepare the students for the writing task in exercise 5 by asking them to imagine that they are a student in another town. Get them to answer the questions in exercise 3, working individually. Make sure they write full sentences, which they can use when they write their letter.
5 Refer students back to the model letter, and ask them to write a similar letter to a friend back home. This exercise could be set up in class and done for homework.

SUGGESTION

Sometimes, before students hand in homework, ask them to swap their work with a partner. They should try and find mistakes in their partner's work and use the correction symbols if they can. Ask them to write in pencil rather than pen, as they might make another mistake!

EVERYDAY ENGLISH (SB p13)

Everyday situations

In this section, students match lines of conversations from everyday situations such as travelling, ordering things, and making a phone call.

1 Focus attention on the photo and ask what the person is doing (making an appointment over the phone). Students look at sentence 1 and ask *Where?* (on the phone or possibly at the dentist's surgery) and *Who?* (a patient who needs to see the dentist about a lost filling).

Put students in pairs to work through the remaining sentences. Encourage students to pool their knowledge and use the context to help them understand new vocabulary items. Monitor and help as necessary. Check the answers.

Answers

1 On the phone or possibly at the dentist's surgery; a patient who needs to see the dentist about a lost filling.
2 In a coffee shop/café; a customer giving their order for coffee and cake.
3 In an office/from a mobile; an employee calling a colleague/secretary to say they will be late for/miss a meeting.
4 In a shop/petrol station; a shop assistant asking a customer to put in their PIN number to complete a transaction.
5 In a bar/restaurant/on a flight; a bar worker/waiter/flight attendant asking a person what sort of water they want to drink.
6 In an office; an office worker introducing a colleague about a new member of staff.
7 At the check-in desk of an airport; the check-in assistant talking to a passenger about their luggage.
8 In a hotel; the receptionist telling a guest how to get to their room.

9 On the phone; a recorded message to a customer who is held in a queue.
10 In a theatre/cinema; an assistant talking to a customer about the availability of tickets.

2 **T 1.11** [**CD 1: Track 12**] Focus attention on the example answer. Then get students to match the remaining lines, working in their pairs.

Play the recording and get students to check their answers. Ask students to focus on the ending of each conversation.

Answers and tapescript

a 7 b 3 c 6 d 8 e 10 f 2 g 4 h 9 i 5 j 1

T 1.11

1 **A** I need to make an appointment. It's quite urgent. I've lost a filling.
B We have a cancellation this afternoon. 2.45, if that's OK?
A That's great. I'll be there.

2 **A** A medium latte and a muffin, please.
B Have here or take away?
A Here, please.
B That'll be £3.90 please.

3 **A** I can't make the meeting. I'm stuck in traffic.
B Never mind. We'll start without you and brief you later.
A Oh, hang on! We're moving again. I should be there in about an hour.

4 **A** Can you put in your pin number and press 'Enter'?
B Oh, no! I can't remember my number for this card. Oh, what is it?
A Have you got another card you could use?

5 **A** Sparkling or still? And do you want ice and lemon in it?
B Sparkling, please. Ice but no lemon.
A No problem. Is that all?

6 **A** I don't think you've met Greg. He's joining us from our New York office.
B Hello. Good to meet you. I've heard a lot about you.
A Yeah, at last we meet. I'm looking forward to working together.

7 **A** How many bags are you checking in?
B Just the one.
A And did you pack it yourself?
B Yes, I did.

8 **A** The lift's on your right. Would you like someone to help you with your luggage?
B No, thank you. I'll manage.
A OK. If you're sure. Here's your key. Enjoy your stay.

9 **A** Please hold. Your call *is* important to us. All our operators are busy at the moment, but one of them will be with you shortly.
B If I have to listen to that again, I'll go mad!
C Can I help you?
B At last, a real person! Do you know how long I've been waiting?

10 **A** There are still tickets for the 5.45 performance, but the 8.45 performance is sold out, I'm afraid.
B That's fine. We'll have two, please, one adult, one child.
A Right. Two for 5.45. The doors open at 5.

3 **T 1.11** [**CD 1: Track 12**] Play the recordings again, getting students to focus on the stress and intonation. Pause at the end of each line and get students to repeat. Alternatively, play the lines for speaker A and get students to take the role of B in each conversation.

Put students into new pairs to practise the conversations. If students have problems, drill the lines again.

Roleplay

4 **T 1.12** [**CD 1: Track 13**] Refer students to the situations on SB p147. Allow students time to read through the situations, and deal with any vocabulary difficulties. Remind students to think about stress and intonation, then get students to act out the situations in pairs. Play the recording and allow students to compare. If necessary, drill some of the lines with the whole class. Remind students to use the expressions in this section as often as possible in real situations.

T 1.12

1 **A** Maria, this is my friend, Peter. We came to England together. We come from the same town in Germany.
B Hello, Peter. Nice to meet you. I hope you're having a good time.

2 **A** Excuse me. I don't think this is mine. I ordered a medium latte and a muffin.
B Oh, sorry. My mistake. This is for the next table.

3 **A** Good evening. Reception? I'm in room 216 and my TV isn't working. Can you send someone to fix it?
B Of course, sir. I'll send someone immediately.

4 **A** Excuse me. Can you tell me which is the check-in desk for Prague? I can't see my flight on the screen.
B Oh dear. You're at the wrong terminal. Flights to Prague go from Terminal 5. You can get a bus to the terminal over there.

5 **A** OK everyone. The meal's ready! Can you all come to the table? Bring your drinks and just help yourselves to the food.
B/C/D Mmm. It smells good. Can we sit where we like?

Don't forget!

Workbook Unit 1

Exercise 15 Verb + preposition

Exercise 16 Listening – The world of work

Word list

Refer students to the Word list for Unit 1 (SB p152). They could translate the words, learn them at home, or transfer some of them to their vocabulary notebook.

2

Present tenses • Passive
Free time activities
Making small talk

The working week

Introduction to the unit

This unit focuses on the working week and profiles a range of people and their study/work routines. The topic provides the context for the main language focus: the present tenses. The focus is not only on the difference between Present Simple and Continuous, but also on state verbs, which are rarely used in continuous tenses. The topic of jobs and money allows for practice of Present Simple active and passive.

The reading text profiles the life of Charles, Prince of Wales, providing an insight into his working and personal life. The *Listening and speaking* section focuses on comparisons of salaries in different jobs. This leads into a *Spoken English* section on giving opinions. The *Vocabulary and speaking* section covers the language of free time activities – what people do when they are not working. The *Everyday English* syllabus continues with a focus on *Making small talk*. This highlights features of spoken English including adding information and softening negative comments. There are photocopiable role cards that can be used with this section on TB p148. The *Writing* syllabus continues with practice of formal and informal letters and emails.

Language aims

Grammar – present states and activities At intermediate level, students should be familiar with the form and most of the uses of the Present Simple and Continuous. They may still make mistakes in the use of the tenses, but should not require a complete remedial presentation. Therefore, the approach taken in the language review is one of contrasting the tenses, distinguishing states from activities, and reviewing state verbs and frequency adverbs. The basic rules of Present Simple for states, facts, and habits, and Present Continuous for activities happening now or around now are consolidated via a range of contexts. The exceptions presented when using state verbs are given complete coverage in the unit. There are several opportunities for personalization in the *Practice* section, to encourage students' ownership of the target language.

Active and passive The language syllabus is further developed with a focus on active and passive forms, presented via a set of statistics. Students are given opportunities to distinguish the correct use and to produce appropriate passive forms.

POSSIBLE PROBLEMS

Present tenses Intermediate students often feel they already 'know' the present tenses, but, in practice, they still make frequent mistakes when trying to use them. Some students may continue to have problems with the form of the tenses, confusing the use of the auxiliaries *am/is/are* and *do/does*. The pronunciation of the weak form of *do/does* in questions may need drilling and practising. The spelling of the *-ing* form may also need revising. In terms of use, the choice of tense may present problems. Students are probably familiar with the basic differences in use between Present Simple and Continuous, but will need help to understand the use of state verbs, especially with verbs such as *think* that can be both state and activity verbs.

I think it's beautiful. (state verb)
I'm thinking about my holiday. (activity verb)

The word order with frequency adverbs can also present problems. This and all other aspects of the form and use are covered in Grammar Reference 2.1–2.4 on SB pp134–5.

Active and passive Some students may have problems manipulating the form of the passive, so this may require a short review. The main problems, however, are with deciding when to use a passive form. This is covered in Grammar Reference 2.5–2.6 on SB p135.

Vocabulary The exercises in the *Vocabulary and speaking* section focus on the language of free time activities. There is a series of lexical exercises along with a listening task and personalized group work.

Everyday English This section focuses on making small talk, and highlights features of spoken English including adding additional information and softening negative comments. Students do a controlled speaking task and then go on to do a roleplay at the end of the section.

Notes on the unit

STARTER (SB p14)

T 2.1 [**CD 1: Track 14**] The topic of the working week is introduced via the song *Blue Monday* by the rhythm and blues singer and pianist, Fats Domino.

Briefly review the days of the week. With weaker students, pre-teach/check the following words from the song: *a slave*, *honey* (in this context, *girlfriend*), *out on the town* (out enjoying yourself), *my head is bad* (my head hurts), *it's worth it*, and *amen* (the word said at the end of a prayer).

Give students time to read the questions, then play the song through once. Elicit the answers, playing the song a second time if students need to hear it again.

Answers and tapescript

His favourite day is Saturday. The other days are not so good because he has to work. Friday is OK because he gets paid, and on Sunday he has a hangover but he doesn't mind because he has had some fun the evening before.

T 2.1

Blue Monday, by Fats Domino

Blue Monday, how I hate Blue Monday
Got to work like a slave all day
Here come(s) Tuesday, oh hard Tuesday
I'm so tired (I've) got no time to play

On Wednesday, (I) work twelve hours, then
Go home, fall into bed at ten,
'Cos Thursday is a hard working day
And Friday I get my pay

Saturday morning, oh Saturday morning
All my tiredness has gone away
Got my money and my honey
And I'm out on the town to play

Sunday morning my head is bad
But it's worth it for the fun that I had
Sunday evening it's goodnight and amen
'Cos on Monday I start again

MY FAVOURITE DAY OF THE WEEK (SB p14)

Present tenses – states and activities

1 Focus attention on the photos. Elicit the job that each person does (see *Answers* below). Focus attention on the example questions about Vicky. Get two students to ask and answer them across the class. If necessary, drill the weak form *does* /dəz/ in the Present Simple question.

Put students in pairs to ask and answer the questions about the other people. Monitor and check for accurate formation of the tenses and pronunciation. If necessary, drill the question forms across the class.

Answers

2 What does Terry do? He's a waiter.
What's he doing? He's taking an order.
3 What does Dave do? He's a police officer.
What's he doing? He's talking to a child.
4 What do Jenny and Mike do? They are farmers.
What are they doing? They're feeding the sheep.

2 **T 2.2** [**CD 1: Track 15**] Tell students they are going to hear the people in the photos talking about their favourite day. For photo 4, they will hear Mike's wife, Jenny, talking. Pre-teach/check *mates* (informal for *friends*), *time flies*, *have a day off*, *lambing* (looking after sheep when they give birth), and *go hunting*. Play Vicky's extract as an example and elicit the answers to the questions (see *Answers* below). Then play the rest of the recording and allow students time to answer the questions for the remaining people.

Answers

1 Vicky's favourite day of the week is Monday because she only has two lessons on a Monday.
2 Terry's favourite day of the week is Friday because his friends come into the restaurant and they have a laugh.
3 Dave's favourite day of the week is Sunday because he spends the day on the beach.
4 Mike and Jenny's favourite day of the week is Wednesday because that is the day they go hunting.

3 **T 2.2** Give students time to read through the gapped sentences so that they know what to listen for. Play the recording again and get students to complete the sentences. Pause the recording as necessary to give students time to complete each sentence.

Check the answers with the class. Then elicit any further information that students can remember about the characters (see tapescript below).

Answers and tapescript

1 I **don't live** with my parents during term-time.
2 **I'm having a very bad** day today.
3 ... it **doesn't feel like** work at all. Time **just flies** by.
4 The restaurant**'s being** redecorated at the moment ...
5 I **like my job** because it's challenging, but I **live for** surfing.
6 The boards **are made** in South Africa.
7 We rarely **have a day off** at the weekend or Christmas Day ...
8 Now we're lambing, so we **aren't getting any sleep**, either.

T 2.2

Vicky

I go to a boarding school, so I don't live with my parents during term-time. Erm..., what I like is being with my friends all the time. Whether we're working or just chatting, it's great to know that there's always someone there. There's also a lot of freedom. I don't have to tell my parents where I'm going, who I'm going with, you know ... (Normally) Monday is my favourite day because I only have two lessons on a Monday, but I'm having a very bad day today because I have homework from every one of my teachers, and I HAVE TO DO IT NOW!

Terry

I work in a restaurant in Manchester. I have two days off a week, (usually) Monday and Wednesday, but my favourite day of the week is in fact Friday, even though I work that day. It's the best night because all my mates come into the restaurant and we have a great laugh. There's a real buzz to the place, and it doesn't feel like work at all. Time just flies by. The restaurant's being redecorated at the moment, so everything's a bit crazy.

Dave

I'm a police officer. I like my job because it's challenging, but I live for surfing. I go as (often) as I can. I'm opening two shops that sell surfboards in the next few months. The boards are made in South Africa.

Sunday is my favourite day of the week. I get up as early as I can, and spend the day on the beach.

Jenny
Mike and I live on a farm in beautiful countryside. I know we're very lucky, but it's hard work. We (rarely) have a day off at the weekend or Christmas Day, or any day of the year. We have to feed the sheep. Now we're lambing, so we aren't getting any sleep, either. But I suppose our favourite day is Wednesday because that's the day we (generally) go hunting. We go on the moors with about twenty friends.

4 Give an example of your own favourite and least favourite day, and the reasons why. Put students into pairs to discuss the questions. Elicit a few examples in a short feedback stage. Establish if there is a general favourite/ least favourite day for the class.

GRAMMAR SPOT (SB p15)

1 Focus attention on the sentences and elicit the names of the tenses. Ask students to explain why each tense is used. Allow weaker students to use their own language if appropriate.

Answers
I **have** two lessons on a Monday. (Present Simple, used to express an action that happens regularly – a habit.)
I'm having a bad day today. (Present Continuous, used to express an action that is happening now or a situation that is true now.)

Refer students to **T 2.2** on SB p119. Elicit the examples from Vicky's tapescript. Then get students to underline the other examples in the rest of the tapescript. Point out that they will also find Present Continuous used to refer to the future and they should also underline any examples of this.

Answers
See underlining in **T 2.2** above.

2 Focus attention on the sentences and elicit the correct verb forms and the reason why they are correct and the other form is wrong.

Answers
I **like** my job.
I **know** we're very lucky.
The above verbs are in the simple form, even though they refer to a situation which is true now. This is because they are state verbs (verbs which are not normally used in the continuous).

Refer students to the verbs in the box and allow them time to underline the five state verbs. Check answers and elicit any other examples students are aware of (*imagine*, *remember*, *wish*, etc.)

Answers
The five state verbs are: love, understand, want, cost, need.

NOTE
There is a growing trend in spoken English to use *like/ love* as activity verbs in the continuous form (e.g. *This is great – I'm loving it!*). Point out that students may hear these forms, but in order to be correct, they should stick to the non-continuous forms for these verbs.

3 Elicit further examples of adverbs of frequency (*sometimes*, *often*, *usually*, etc.). Then refer students to **T 2.2** on SB p119. Get them to circle the examples of the adverbs of frequency in the script.

Answers
See circling in **T 2.2** above.

Refer students to Grammar Reference 2.1–2.4 on SB pp134–5.

PRACTICE (SB p15)

Questions and answers

This section consolidates the form and use of the present tenses in a series of accuracy-based activities.

1 **T 2.3** **[CD 1: Track 16]** This reading text profiles the life of Dave, the police officer shown on SB p14. Ask students what they can remember about him. Set a time limit of about three minutes for them to read the text. Encourage students to use the context to help them understand new vocabulary, but be prepared to deal with queries about individual words. Give students time to match the questions to the paragraphs in the text.

Play the recording and get students to check their answers.

Answers and tapescript
T 2.3
Dave Telford, police officer and surfer

(1) What's your background?
I'm 46, and I'm divorced. I have two kids, who I see once a fortnight. I live in Devon, in the south-west of England. I'm a police officer. I've been in the police force for over twenty years. I love my job, but my passion is surfing.

(2) What hours do you work?
I work different shifts. The morning shift starts at 5.00, and I can't stand that because I have to get up at 4.30. My favourite shift is 2.00 in the afternoon till midnight because I get home about 12.30. What's good is that I work ten hours a day for four days, then have three days off.

(3) What do you think of your job?
My job is extremely busy and very hard. But I like it because it's challenging, and I never know what's going to happen. I like working in a team. We look after each other and work together.

(4) Why do you like surfing?
My work is very stressful, so I surf to get away from it all. It's just me and the sea, and my mind switches off. I concentrate so hard on what I'm doing that I don't think about anything else.

(5) How often do you go surfing?
I go surfing whenever I'm not working. Sometimes I'm on the beach before 7.00 in the morning. I go all over the world surfing. Next month I'm going to Costa Rica, and in the autumn I'm going to Thailand.

(6) Do you have a business?
I've got a surf school. I teach all ages, from kids to pensioners. The business is doing well. I'm also opening two shops that sell surfboards. The boards are made in South Africa. They're the best.

(7) What's your favourite day of the week?
I like Sundays best of all. I work as a lifeguard all day, then around 6.00 me and my mates barbecue some fish and have a few beers. Fantastic! I've been all round the world, but when I look around me, I think there's nowhere else I'd rather be.

2 **T 2.4** [CD 1: **Track 17**] Ask students to complete the questions, working individually. Monitor and help with the question formation. Students then ask and answer the questions in pairs. Monitor and check for accurate question formation and also focus on students' pronunciation. If necessary, drill the weak form /dəzɪ/ in the questions with *does he* and the falling intonation in the *wh*-questions. If students have particular problems, drill the questions across the class and then get students to continue asking and answering in pairs.

Play the recording and get students to check their answers.

Answers and tapescript

T 2.4

1 **A** Has he got any children?
B Yes, two.
2 **A** How often **does he** see them?
B Once a fortnight.
3 **A** Why **doesn't he like** the morning shift?
B Because he has to get up at 4.30.
4 **A** How many hours **a day does he work**?
B Ten.
5 **A** What **does he** like about his job?
B He likes it because it's challenging, and he likes working in a team.
6 **A** What **does he** think **about** while **he's** surfing?
B He only thinks about surfing, nothing else.
7 **A** Where**'s he going** next month?
B Costa Rica.
8 **A** **Is his** business doing well?
B Yes, it is. He's opening two shops.
9 **A** What **do he and his friends do** on Sunday evenings?
B They eat barbecued fish and drink beer.

Talking about you

3 The practice now moves from the third person to the first person in a personalization stage. Read the example sentence with the class and elicit some examples using other expressions in the box. Allow students time to prepare their own sentences individually.

4 Explain to students that they are going to use their sentences from exercise 3 to talk to a partner about themselves. Model the activity by asking a confident student to talk about him/herself. Put the students into pairs to exchange their information. Students then report back about their partner. Elicit a range of information about the class, making sure you hear from students who haven't said much up to now. Note down any common errors in the formation and use of the present tenses for feed back in a later lesson. Don't correct too many errors here as the main focus is on fluency.

Simple and continuous

1 **T 2.5** [CD 1: **Track 18**] The practice in a work-related context continues with a focus on people who work in the same office. Drill the pronunciation of the names of the people in the box and check comprehension of the jobs. Make sure students know how to say the abbreviations *HR* /eɪtʃɑː/, *IT* /aɪtiː/, *MD* /emdiː/, and *PA* /piːeɪ/.

Explain that students need to identify the people in the picture from the conversation in the recording. Play the first six lines of the conversation, as far as … *the man in charge*. Ask students to identify Simon (d) and his job (the managing director). Play the rest of the recording and get students to complete the task. Allow students to check their answers in pairs. Play the recording again if students have missed any of the information. With weaker classes, play the recording once for students to identify the people and a second time for them to match the people to the correct jobs.

Check the answers with the class.

Answers and tapescript

Simon (d) – Managing Director
Edward (b) – Sales Director
Anna (c) – Accountant
Jenny (f) – Human Resources Manager
Matthew (e) – IT Manager (e)
Christina (a) – Simon's PA

T 2.5

The office

A Gosh! I don't know anybody! Can you help me? Who *are* all these people?
B Uh, well, that's Simon. He's sitting at the top of the table reading something.
A He's the one with glasses, wearing a jumper, right?
B Yeah, that's it.
A And what does he do?
B He's the Managing Director. He's the man in charge.
A The boss, in other words.
B Uh huh. He shouts a lot, but he listens as well. Then there's Edward. He's wearing a suit. He's standing up talking to Anna. Edward's the Sales Director. He's charming. He always has a nice word to say to everyone. Anna's standing next to him. She's drinking a coffee. She's wearing a jacket and she's got a scarf round her neck.
A And Anna is the …?
B Anna's the Accountant. Money, money, money. Very bright, very quick.
A Ah, OK. And who's that talking on her phone?
B In the white blouse and blue skirt? That's Jenny, she's the Human Resources Manager, HR Manager. She looks after all the personnel. She's a sweetheart. Everyone loves her. Then there's Matthew. He's the IT Manager. He's only working here for a few months. He's from our New York office. I don't really know him very well.
A He's the guy working on his laptop?
B That's him. Wearing a shirt, no tie. He knows everything about technology. And finally, that's Christina talking to Simon. She's his PA. She …
A Sorry. What was that?
B She's Simon's PA, Personal Assistant. She organizes his diary, but she helps all of us, really. We couldn't cope without her. She runs the whole place, actually. She's wearing a black suit and has fabulous earrings. Very smart.
A Right. I think I've got that …

2 Focus attention on the example answers saying what Simon is doing and what he is wearing. Elicit examples for Edward (see *Answers* below). Students work in pairs to continue discussing what the people are doing and wearing. Check the answers with the class.

Answers
Edward's standing up talking to Anna. He's wearing a suit.
Anna's standing next to Edward. She's drinking a coffee. She's wearing a jacket and she's got a scarf round her neck.
Jenny's talking on her phone. She's wearing a white blouse and blue skirt.
Matthew's working on his laptop. He's wearing a shirt, but no tie.
Christina's talking to Simon. She's wearing a black suit and fabulous earrings.

T 2.5 [CD 1: Track 18] Focus attention on the example comment about Simon. Pre-teach/check the following words: *charming, bright* (intelligent), *a sweetheart* (a very nice person), *to run a place*. Play the recording again and get students to note down the comments about each person. If students have problems, or with weaker students, pause the recording after each comment. Check the answers.

Answers
Edward is charming. He always has a nice word to say to everyone.
Anna is very bright, very quick.
Jenny is a sweetheart. Everyone loves her.
Matthew knows everything about technology.
Christina runs the whole place.

See above for the full version of **T 2.5**.

3 This task contains a range of vocabulary related to the workplace. Complete the example about the Managing Director as a class. If appropriate, allow students to use dictionaries to look up new items or check/explain any items that students query.

Check the answers.

Answers
The Managing Director is responsible for running the whole company. Currently, he is discussing plans and targets with the Board.
The PA makes appointments and arrangements making bookings for a conference.
The Sales Director negotiates prices and contracts. Currently, he is visiting new customers in China.
The IT Manager runs an IT support team. Currently, he is buying new hardware.
The Accountant is in charge of budget and cash flow. Currently, she is preparing a financial report.
The HR Manager looks after employees. Currently, she is recruiting new staff.

4 Choose two confident students to read the conversation aloud. Drill the pronunciation as necessary and get students to mark the main stresses on each line. Students practise the conversation in pairs.

5 With weaker students, elicit another model conversation and write it up on the board. Students make similar conversations in their pairs, using the jobs from exercise 1 and the information in exercise 3. Allow students in their pairs to then choose another job to talk about. Students prepare their conversations and practise in their pairs. Monitor and check for accurate tenses and question formation, and correct any errors carefully. You could ask some pairs to perform their conversations for the class.

Project

This section provides personalized practice in the form of an extended interview. Students interview a person that they know about their job. Wherever possible, the interviewee should speak English (though not necessarily be a native speaker), so that students get practice of the questions forms, and the interviews have some authenticity. If some students have problems finding an interviewee, you could set up the task with students from another class, or with some of the members of staff in your school. It's worth taking the time to set the interviews up carefully so that students don't run out of things to say. Get students to brainstorm possible questions and write them up on the board or on an OHT.

POSSIBLE QUESTIONS
What do you do?
Where do you work?
Who do you work for?
How long have you done this job?
What are your working hours?
What do you do in your job, exactly?
What are you working on at the moment?
Do you like your job? Why (not)?
What do you do on your days off?
Would you like to change anything about your job?

The questions can be adapted to people who are studying/in training, e.g. *Where do you study?*

Review/extend the language students can use to talk about jobs: *to work in (marketing/IT/publishing, etc.), to set up (meetings/contracts), to make appointments, to make arrangements, to negotiate, to run (a team/a department/a business), to train, to look after, to be in charge of, to recruit, to go to conferences, to do research, to work full/part time.*

Set the interviews for homework and give a deadline for students to work to. Remind them to make notes about the person's job, including their overall opinion of their work and whether they like it.

In a later lesson, elicit a summary of the interviews from different students in the class. With larger classes, you may need to spread these across a series of lessons, or let students give their summaries in groups. Note down any common errors as students give their summaries and feed back on them in a later lesson.

As an extension, get students to write up a profile of the person they interviewed and his/her job.

State and activity verbs

NOTE
This activity highlights common errors in the use of state verbs. If necessary, refer students back to the *Grammar Spot* on SB p15 before they do the exercise.

6 Elicit the answer to sentence 1 as an example (see *Answers* below). Give students time to do the exercise, working individually. Students who finish quickly can check their answers in pairs. Check the answers with the class.

Answers
1 **I don't want** an ice-cream.
2 **Do you understand** what I'm saying?
3 ✓
4 **I think** you're really nice.
5 ✓
6 **I don't believe** you. You're telling lies.
7 **I know** you **don't agree** with me.
8 **She has/She's got** a lot of money.
* Students may have problems with the following sentences:
3 The fact that *enjoy* is an activity verb may seem strange to students, especially as *like* is a state verb. Point out that *like* expresses an opinion (e.g. *I like learning English*.) whereas *enjoy* relates to experiences (e.g. *I'm enjoying my English course*).
4/5 *Think* can be both a state and an activity verb (state verb for opinions – *I think he's a good boss*; activity verb for thought processes – *I'm thinking about my holiday*.)
8 *Have* is a state verb when it expresses possession; it can also be an activity verb, e.g. *I'm having a bad day*.

Active and passive

7 This section reviews form, and helps students understand when to use the passive. The tense coverage is limited to the Present Simple and Continuous. Further coverage of the passive is given in Units 3 (past tenses) and 7 (Present Perfect).

Pre-teach/check the following items from the statistics: *to be involved in*, *workforce*, *the state* (the government of a country), *average* (adj.), *on average*, *household*.

Give students time to read through the statistics. Elicit the correct form for the first sentence (see *Answers* below). Students work through the sentences and decide which form is correct. Allow them to check in pairs. Check with the class and elicit a range of reactions to the figures.

Answers

1 are involved*	5 earn
2 are employed*	6 are given
3 is paid	7 spends
4 pays	8 own

* If students query the use of the plural auxiliary *are* with the singular nouns *population* and *workforce*, explain that these are collective nouns and so are often used with a plural verb. Other examples of collective nouns are *the audience, the crowd, the class*, etc.

If students have problems distinguishing when to use the active and passive forms, refer them to Grammar Reference 2.5 and 2.6 on SB p135.

SUGGESTION

You could extend this activity into a mini-project by asking students to research figures for their country and produce a set of statistics. Students could work in groups to research individual topics and display their findings on the wall or on a computer network if available. Possible topics include: transport, health, work and money, leisure, food and drink. To help students, review/feed in the language of giving statistics/figures: *... per cent, (nearly) half of ...., a third of ..., (one) in (three), the average ..., on average*.

8 This exercise consolidates the form of the present passive, simple and continuous. Get students to read the gapped sentences. Deal with any vocabulary queries. Elicit the answer to the first sentence (see *Answers* below). Then get students to complete the task, working individually. With weaker students, go through the sentences as a class first and decide which tense, simple or continuous, needs to be used each time.

Check the answers with the class.

Answers

2 are made	6 Is ... included
3 is being serviced	7 are being modernized
4 is imported	8 are paid
5 is situated	

EXTRA IDEA

Song **After T 2.5** [CD 1: Track 19]
Matthew and Son TB p147
This is intended as a fun activity, which you may like to include at the end of a lesson. Students do a pre-listening task and listen for gist. They complete a gapped version of the song and then listen and check. There is also a comprehension task and the roleplay. The answers are on TB p158.

ADDITIONAL MATERIAL

Workbook Unit 2
Exercises 1–4 Present tenses
Exercise 5 Adverbs of time and frequency
Exercise 7 Present Simple and Continuous
Exercise 8 States and activities –Present Simple or Continuous?
Exercises 9–10 Present passive

LISTENING AND SPEAKING (SB p17)

Who earns how much?

This section continues the theme of work and money with a listening task on salaries of different jobs. The *Spoken English* section provides students with useful language for giving opinions, and students have the opportunity to use this language in their own discussion task. Do not give students the answers to the matching task in exercise 1 until they have finished their discussion in exercise 3.

1 Check comprehension of the jobs in the chart. Remind students that the average annual salary in the UK is £27,000. Put students in pairs or groups of three to match the jobs with the salaries. If they have problems getting started, advise them to decide on the highest- and lowest-paid first, and then work out the others. Monitor and help, but do not correct errors as this is an interest-raising activity and so students need to be able to exchange their ideas freely. If students ask for the answers, ask them to wait until the end of this section. (The *Answers* are given on SB p147.)

2 **T 2.6** [CD 1: Track 20] Explain that students are going to hear two people discussing the chart in exercise 1. Give them time to read through the questions and predict the possible answers. With weaker classes, put students in groups of three and get them each to answer one of the questions and then exchange their answers.

Play the recording and get students to note their answers to the questions. Play the recording again if students have missed any of the information. Check the answers with the class.

Answers and tapescript

1 doctor, footballer, lawyer, senior director, pilot
footballer – £1 million, pilot – £65,000
2 £105,000; £120,000
lawyer; senior director
pilot
3 Doctors earn quite a lot. They have a lot of responsibility and training.
Footballers earn ridiculous amounts of money.
Senior directors are in charge of huge companies.
Pilots earn quite a lot. They need a lot of experience; they have people's lives in their hands.

T 2.6
Who earns how much?
Part 1

A Well, I reckon that doctors earn quite a lot.
B Yeah. I think so, too. They have a lot of responsibility and a lot of training. I'd say that doctors get about ... £105,000? What do you think?
A Could be ... or it could be even more, £120,000.
B One of those two, anyway. Shall we look at the high earners first?
A Uh huh. £750,000 ...
B There's one higher ...
A Oh, is there? Oh, yeah. A million. Mmm.
B I'd say ... that has to be the footballer.
A Yes, definitely. They do earn ridiculous amounts of money, don't they? So what about £750,000? Who earns three quarters of a million?
B Erm ... I think that's the lawyer.
A As much as that? What about the senior director? Do lawyers earn more than them?
B Maybe, maybe not. I suppose the lawyer could be £105,000, and the senior director £750,000. Senior directors are in charge of huge companies.
A OK. Now ... the pilot. Pilots earn quite a lot, don't they? They need a lot of experience, they have people's lives in their hands ... I think they get ... oh, at least a hundred, a hundred and fifty.
B Mmm. I know what you mean, but I don't think they get as much as that.
A Don't they? Oh!, anyway, there isn't 150 on this list, so ...
B I reckon pilots get about £65,000 ...
A OK. I'd say that's about right ...

3 **T 2.7** [CD 1: Track 21] Tell students they are going to hear the speakers talking about the lower-earners in Part 2 of the recording. Give students time to read the questions so that they know what to listen for.

Play the recording and get students to note their answers to the questions. Play the recording again if students have missed any of the information. Check the answers with the class.

Answers and tapescript

1 The nurse and the supermarket cashier.
2 The woman thinks £50,000 or £60,000. The man thinks £22,500.
3 No, they don't. The man thinks the police officers get more than teachers and the woman thinks the opposite.
4 Both men and women can be nurses.

T 2.7
Part 2

B Let's go on down to the bottom. What's the lowest salary?
A £11,000. I guess that's the nurse. They don't get paid much, nurses.
B I thought they earned more than that, actually. I know they don't get much, but even so ...
A Then there's £12,500, and the next up is £22,500.
B Oh, look! Supermarket cashier. I don't suppose they get much. £12,500, I'd say.
A OK. That seems about right. What about farmers? How much do they get?
B I don't know. It depends what sort of farmer. They can earn a fortune, can't they?
A I suppose so, yes ... But they're always complaining that supermarkets don't pay them enough for what they produce.
B I still reckon they get a decent salary. They own so much land! I bet they get 50 or 60 thousand.
A No, I think it's much lower. I'd say £22,500.
B Hmm. Not so sure. Then we've got ... teachers. What do they earn?
A I reckon they get ... er ... £32,000?
B But it all depends how many years they've worked and how many qualifications they've got.
A Yes, I know, but we're talking about the average.
B Don't teachers and police officers earn about the same?
A Do they? I'm not so sure. I'd say that police officers get more. What have we got? £32,000 ... £36,000.
B I think 32 for the police officer and 36 for the teacher.
A Um, well, actually I'd say the other way round. 36 for the police officer and 32 for the teacher. My mother's a teacher, and she doesn't earn anything like that!
B What does that leave? We haven't decided about the farmer or the nurse yet.
A I think the nurse gets less than the farmer. She gets the least.
B Why she? Nurses can be men, you know.
A True. Sorry. Nurses – men *and* women – earn less than farmers.
B Men *and* women.
A Absolutely.

SPOKEN ENGLISH – Giving opinions

1 Focus attention on the expressions and get students to mark the main stress:

I **reck**on ...   I'd **say** ...   I sup**pose** ...

Check they understand that *I'd say ... = I would say*. Then elicit some opinions from the class, using the expressions. Refer students to the tapescript on SB p120. Students find three more ways of expressing opinions.

Answers
I guess ...   I bet ...   I think ...

2 Get students to categorize the expressions. Then check the answers.

Answers

Agreeing: I think so **too**. **Def**initely. Absol**ute**ly.

Disagreeing: I know what you **mean** but ... I'm not so **sure**. **Ac**tually, ...

Get students to mark the main stresses (see *Answers* above). Give a series of opinions and elicit responses from different students in the class.

3 Elicit the meaning of the phrases.

Answer

I'm not sure that you are completely right.

4 Model the activity by getting two confident students to discuss the salary scale in exercise 1, using the expressions. Put students into different pairs/groups from exercise 1 and get then to talk about the salaries again. Monitor and check, noting down any common errors in grammar, vocabulary, and pronunciation.

Elicit a few opinions on the salary scale. Put students into small groups and ask them to turn to SB p147 for the correct answers on *Who earns how much in Britain?* Allow groups to have a short discussion on which salaries they think are unfair and which are surprising. Elicit feedback on students' opinions.

Answer

See SB p147.

SUGGESTION

If students are interested in this topic, get them to research salaries for their own country and draw up a scale and a matching task similar to that in exercise 1. This would be interesting in a multilingual class but could also be used as the basis for another discussion task with students of the same nationality. It is also a good way to consolidate the expressions presented in *Spoken English*. As an extension, students can decide which jobs in society *should* earn the most. This is likely to generate lively discussion!

READING AND SPEAKING (SB p18)

Charles, Prince of Wales

ABOUT THE TEXT

The text in this *Reading and speaking* section is in the form of a magazine article about Charles, the first son of Queen Elizabeth II. It profiles both his working and personal life and also gives an insight into his character. The exploitation of the article includes prediction work, detailed comprehension, vocabulary work on adjectives of character, and a discussion stage.

The lexical range in the text is fairly challenging and the vocabulary items listed below may be new to students. Students will be able to guess some of them from context, but with weaker classes be prepared to check them, or get students to check them for homework before the class.

Adjectives: *eccentric, content, royal, lavish*

Nouns/Noun phrases: *passions, rage, socializer, the height of luxury, the heir* /eə(r)/ *to the throne, monarch, public engagements, heads of state, VIP* (Very Important Person), *ambassador*

Verbs/Verb phrases: *to be portrayed as, to perform your duties, to praise, to be told off, to have tantrums, to dress for dinner* (to put on formal clothes), *to host receptions*

Staff/Jobs: *deputy (secretary), press officer, valet, butler, housekeeper, chauffeur, porter, handyman, maid*

Background notes

The following notes give information on the people, places, and institutions mentioned in the text:

Prince Charles The eldest son of the Queen and Prince Philip, he was born at Buckingham Palace on 14 November 1948. His official royal title is *The Prince of Wales* and he is formally addressed as *His Royal Highness* (HRH). He is heir to the British throne. Charles is known for his interest in the environment and architecture, and at times he has expressed strong opinions on these subjects, causing some controversy.

Camilla, the Duchess of Cornwall Formerly Camilla Parker Bowles, she was married to the Prince of Wales on 9 April 2005. After the wedding, she became known as *HRH the Duchess of Cornwall*. She will use the title *HRH the Princess Consort* when Charles becomes king.

Diana, Princess of Wales Diana was Charles's first wife and the mother of Princes William and Harry. Charles and Diana were married at St Paul's Cathedral on 29 July 1981. They were divorced in 1996, but Diana continued to have a high international profile. She died in a car accident in Paris in 1997.

Princes William and Harry Prince William is second in line to the throne and the elder son Charles and Diana. Prince Harry is third in line to throne and is William's younger brother. Both men are officers in the British armed forces.

Highgrove Highgrove House in Gloucestershire is the family home of the Prince of Wales. The house, garden, and nearby farmland, now known as Duchy Home Farm, were bought in 1980.

Sandringham Sandringham House in Norfolk has been the private home of four generations of royalty since 1862. The Queen and other members of the royal family regularly spend Christmas at Sandringham and make it their official base until February each year.

Klosters The preferred ski resort of Prince Charles and his sons, situated 150 km from Zurich in Switzerland.

Prince's Charities A group of non-profit organizations of which the Prince of Wales is President; 16 of the 18 charities were founded personally by the Prince.

The organizations cover a range of areas, including opportunity and enterprise, education, the built environment, the natural environment, and the arts.

Duchy Originals The Prince of Wales launched this food company in 1992 with its first product – a biscuit made from wheat and oats grown organically (without the use of chemicals) on the Home Farm at Highgrove. Since then, the company has grown to become a well-known producer of organic products, including food, drink, gardening tools, and furniture. Duchy Originals generates more than £1 million in profit for charity each year.

1 Focus attention on the photo of the balcony and elicit the names of the people (see *Answers* below). Check students know that Charles, Andrew, and Edward are the sons of the Queen and Prince Philip, and that Charles and Camilla are married. Pre-teach/check that students know the royal titles of Charles (*The Prince of Wales*) and Camilla (*The Duchess of Cornwall*) (see *Notes about the text* above).

Answers

From left to right, the people in the photo are : Prince Charles, Camilla (the Duchess of Cornwall), Prince Harry, Prince Andrew, the Queen, Prince Philip, and Prince Edward.

2 Focus attention on the examples in the Student's Book. Elicit any further information students may know (e.g. *He was married to Princess Diana. He has two sons.*)

Divide the class into pairs. Get them to add to the list of information. Set a time limit of about five minutes. Then get students to compare their ideas in a short whole-class feedback stage. Collate the notes on the board, adding a question mark next to any points that the students are not sure of.

SUGGESTION

If you have access to the Internet at your school, you could get students to research information about Prince Charles online.

3 Read the question with the class and check comprehension of the items in the list. Give your own ranking as an example, or ask a confident student to give his/hers. With weaker students, you could elicit the ranking from the whole class and write it up on the board. Feed in useful language as necessary, e.g. 'I put 5 next to "being with his family" because I think he spends a lot of time with his sons.' Give students time to complete the task, working individually.

4 See notes in *About the text* about pre-teaching vocabulary. Give students time to read though the questions. Deal with any queries (see *About the text* for background information on Highgrove, Sandringham, and Duchy Originals). Put students into new pairs to answer the questions. Ask them to underline key parts of the text to support their answers. Check the answers with the class.

Answers

1 He has an enormous private staff and people fulfil all his requests. He dresses for dinner, even when he's eating alone. He entertains lots of people in the height of luxury at Highgrove and Sandringham. He goes skiing every year. He has a very successful food company.

2 If they do well, they are praised in a royal memo. If they make mistakes, they are called into his office and told off.

3 He arrives at Highgrove on a Saturday afternoon in time for a Martini. He entertains his guests in the height of luxury and them sends them home before Sunday lunch, after a tour of his gardens. He entertains at Sandringham at least twice a year with picnic lunches on the beach, expeditions to local churches, or lavish dinners with food from Highgrove. There is lively conversation with the guests.

4 He is a man of great humour. He cares passionately about the state of the British nation, and is devoted to his children. He is madly in love with his wife, Camilla.

5 He attends over 500 public engagements a year. He visits hospitals, youth groups, performing artists, charities, and business conferences. He hosts receptions for heads of state and VIPs. He travels abroad as an ambassador to the UK for trade and industry.

6 He works hard to promote understanding between religions. He is President of the Prince's Charities, which promote education, business, the environment, the arts, and opportunities for young people.

7 He has a family that he loves, a supportive wife, a fortune that gives him a luxurious lifestyle, a challenging job, and the opportunity to make changes.

He doesn't have 'the top job' (being king). He doesn't have the opportunity to give his opinions freely because they might be repeated in public.

8 Duchy Originals is Charles's organic food company. It is expanding to become one of Britain's best-known and most successful organic brands. It sells food, drinks, hair and body care products.

9 She will be known as HRH The Princess Consort.

10 Prince Charles, the Prince of Wales, HRH (His Royal Highness), the Prince, Charles, the heir to the throne, the future monarch/king.

5 Get students to look back at their ranking in exercise 3 and re-assess their answers as appropriate. Feed in useful language as necessary, e.g. *I thought Charles spent most of his time travelling, but in fact he is quite hard-working. Charles spends more time with his family than I thought.*

Put students into pairs/groups of three to compare their ideas. Elicit a range of general preconceptions about Charles that are not borne out in the article.

Vocabulary work

Model the pronunciation of the words in the box and get students to mark the stress (see *Answers* below) before dividing them into positive and negative words. Then elicit examples of Charles's behaviour that illustrate each adjective, allowing students to re-read the text as necessary.

Answers

bad-tempered /bæd 'tempəd/ – negative. If his staff make mistakes, Charles can get so angry that he has a tantrum.

spoilt /spɔɪlt/ – negative. He has seven eggs boiled for breakfast so that he can find the one he likes. His toothpaste is squeezed onto his toothbrush. His towel is folded in a special way for him.

eccentric /ɪk'sentrɪk/ – negative. He talks to trees and plants. He wants to save wildlife but he enjoys hunting, shooting, and fishing. He dresses for dinner even when he's eating alone.

old-fashioned /əʊld 'fæʃnd/ – can be positive or negative. The text describes him as conservative and old-fashioned.

sociable /'səʊʃəbl/ – positive. He is a great socializer. He entertains guests in the height of luxury.

cautious /'kɔːʃəs/ – can be positive or negative. He has to be careful that people don't repeat in public what he has said in private.

passionate /'pæʃənət/ – positive. He is madly in love with his wife and devoted to his children. He cares passionately about the state of the British nation.

frustrated /frʌ'streɪtəd/ – negative. He feels frustrated because governments do little to tackle the problems that he feels strongly about.

successful /sək'sesfl/ – positive. His company, Duchy Originals, is a very successful organic brand.

well-intentioned /wel ɪn'tenʃnd/ – positive. He does a lot of charity work.

Discussion

Elicit examples of countries that have a royal family (Great Britain, Spain, the Netherlands, Japan, Saudi Arabia, Thailand, etc.). Put students into small groups to discuss the questions. With a multilingual group, put students of different nationalities together.

Give students time to discuss the questions. Monitor and help, but do not interrupt to correct. Elicit a range of examples and opinions in a whole-class feedback session.

SUGGESTION

If your students are interested in this topic, you could get them to research royal families from different countries, working in groups. Students can then give a short presentation about the family before comparing across the class.

ADDITIONAL MATERIAL

Workbook Unit 2

Exercise 11 Vocabulary – Adjectives that describe character

VOCABULARY AND SPEAKING (SB p20)

Free time activities

This section covers the vocabulary of free time activities and also includes some key words associated with cooking. Students are given the opportunity to produce a word diagram for an activity that they are interested in. There is a listening task about a man called John, whose favourite hobby is cooking. Students take notes as a model for talking about their own free time activities.

1 Focus attention on the examples in exercise 1. Tell students what you do you in your free time. Then get the students to brainstorm further examples, writing a list of their own free time activities. Elicit a range of answers and write them up on the board. Ask students who they do their free time activities with, and where.

2 Focus attention on the photos a–l. Elicit the names of the activities shown, checking the pronunciation (see *Answers* below). Then put students in pairs to answer the questions about the activities. Check the answers with the class. Elicit the activities which are most popular with the class. Establish if there is an activity that everyone does and one that no-one does.

Answers

a camping
b cooking
c DIY (do it yourself)
d painting
e gardening
f running/jogging
g yoga
h photography
i playing tennis
j playing an instrument
k cycling
l shopping

- All the activities can be done alone or with friends. Some, e.g. cooking, painting, and yoga, can also be done as part of a group or class.
- Cooking, DIY, painting, gardening, yoga, and playing an instrument can be done at home. The activities that are usually done in a special place are camping, playing tennis, and shopping.
- For a lot of the activities, special clothes can be worn but are not absolutely necessary, e.g. an apron to do cooking, a leotard for yoga. Most of the activities need some sort of special equipment, except possibly yoga and shopping.

3 Check comprehension of the items in the list and deal with any pronunciation problems. Elicit examples for the first three items in the list. Students continue matching the items, working individually. Check the answers with the class.

Answers

a drill – DIY
planting – gardening
the sales – shopping
a racket – playing tennis
a concert – playing an instrument
zoom – photography
sweating – running/jogging
wearing a helmet – cycling
sketching – painting
a recipe – cooking
serving an ace – playing tennis
a sleeping bag – camping
a screwdriver – DIY
a bargain – shopping
keeping fit – running/jogging
meditating – yoga
a torch – camping
weeding – gardening

4 Focus attention on the diagram. Explain that it shows a visual way of categorizing and recording words related to cooking. Check comprehension of the categories and examples in the diagram.

Students categorize the words, working individually. Give students time to compare in pairs before checking with the class. Point out the pronunciation of *oven* /ʌvn/.

Elicit further words to add to the diagram (see *Answers* in brackets below).

Answers

equipment: an oven, a casserole dish, a food processor (a bowl, a frying pan)

food preparation: to mix, to chop, to weigh (to wash, to stir, to slice)

ingredients: herbs and spices, olive oil, minced meat (fish, vegetables)

ways of cooking: boiling, roasting, baking (steaming, grilling)

5 Tell students they are going to create a word diagram for one of their own hobbies. With weaker classes, build an example on the board for one of your hobbies or give the following example for painting:

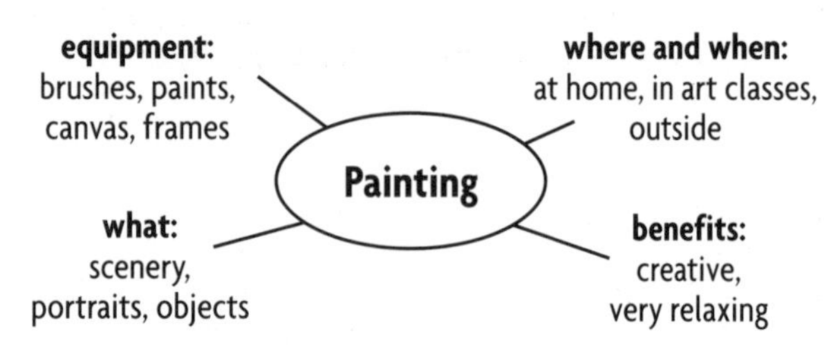

Give students a few moments to decide on their hobby. Remind them to choose the categories for the vocabulary before they start, and advise them to stick to four or five categories so that the diagram doesn't get too big and complicated. If possible, allow students to use dictionaries to look up new words and/or be prepared to feed in new vocabulary as necessary. Once students have completed their diagram, tell them to keep it to hand as they will need it in exercise 7.

SUGGESTION

If time is short, get students to produce their word diagram for homework and do the group work in exercise 7 in a subsequent lesson.

6 **T 2.8** [**CD 1: Track 22**] Focus attention on the photo and ask students what they think John's hobby will be. Play the recording as far as *cooking* and check students' answers. Give students time to copy the headings into their notebook and think about the possible answers. Play the rest of the recording and get students to complete their notes. Get students to check in pairs. Play the recording again if students have missed any of the answers.

Answers and tapescript

Favourite hobby: Cooking

Where and when he does it: At home (he cooks most days, but also enjoys eating out).

Clothes and equipment: Wears a chef's apron (to keep his clothes clean – tomatoes and spices change the colour of clothes). Very fussy about his knives (German knives, very sharp). Also uses pots and pans, casserole dishes, chopping boards, food mixers. Doesn't have a lot of gadgets.

What he likes about it: It's creative, and it's real (people have to eat every day). Also enjoys shopping, choosing what to cook.

The best bit: Seeing people enjoy his food – seeing people happy at the table and enjoying the occasion.

T 2.8

John

My favourite hobby is cooking, and that's a thing you do at home, obviously. I cook most days, though not every day. We also like eating out, you see. What clothes and equipment do I need? Well, I always wear a chef's apron to protect my clothes, because you can make a mess when you're cooking, and tomatoes and spices change the colour of your clothes forever! The most important piece of equipment is knives. I'm very fussy about my knives. They're German, and very sharp, and I really look after them. Obviously, in the kitchen you need all sorts of things like pots and pans and casserole dishes and chopping boards and food mixers, but I don't really have a lot of gadgets. I like to keep things simple. What I like about cooking is the fact that it's creative and it's real. We have to eat, and what we eat is really important, so I like to know that what I'm eating, and what my family is eating, is good. I actually like all the preparation. Going out shopping, seeing the food, feeling it, smelling it, talking to the people who are selling it, is half the fun. People often ask me what I like cooking, and I don't really have an answer. Whatever looks good, and whatever I feel like cooking that day. The best bit is of course seeing people enjoy my food, but what's also very important to me is seeing everyone happy, and enjoying being at the table. It's about the occasion as much as the food.

7 Remind students that they will need their word diagram from exercise 5. Give them a few minutes to make notes individually about their hobby under the same headings as in exercise 6. Tell students that they should just write notes, not full sentences. This is intended to be a fairly free fluency activity, with the students using their diagrams and notes as prompts. However, weaker classes may appreciate hearing a model before the group work. This one is based on the diagram for *painting* above, but you could give your own model or elicit one from a confident student:

My favourite hobby is painting. I do it at home mainly, but I also go to art classes. In the summer I also paint outside. I use brushes and paints, and also canvas and frames, of course. What do I like about it? Well, it's a creative activity and I also find it very relaxing. The best thing about it is seeing a beautiful landscape and being able to interpret it in paint. It's so exciting!

Put students in groups to exchange information about their hobbies. Remind them to use their notes.

Monitor and help as necessary but do not interrupt students' flow to correct them. Note down any common errors, particularly in tense use, and feed back on these in a later lesson. If you have time, elicit some interesting descriptions from individual students for the whole class.

EVERYDAY ENGLISH (SB p21)

Making small talk

The *Everyday English* syllabus continues with a focus on making small talk, including features of spoken English such as giving extra information and softening negative comments.

1 Discuss the questions with the class and elicit a range of answers.

Possible answers

We make small talk when we want to break the ice with a new person or to avoid an awkward silence in a conversation. We often make small talk when we meet someone for the first time. There is a range of 'safe' topics for small talk, including the weather, sport, current events, and the place in which the speakers find themselves.

2 **T 2.9** [**CD 1: Track 23**] Give students time to read the context. Play the recording and elicit answers to the questions about Lars and Ann.

Answers

They are in Liverpool. Lars is visiting Liverpool because he's attending a conference there.

3 Elicit a few examples of information that Lars adds to keep the conversation going, and comments Ann uses to show interest. Students complete the task, working in pairs. Check the answers.

Answers

For information added by Lars, see underlining in script **T 2.9** below. For comments used by Ann to show interest, see circled expressions in script **T 2.9** below.

4 **T 2.9** [**CD 1: Track 23**] Look at the example with the class, then elicit Lars's next response (see *Answers* below). Students then continue the task, working in pairs. With weaker students, elicit the tense/structure students need to use for each prompt. Monitor and help as necessary.

Get pairs of students to read aloud each question and answer from the conversation. Then play that question and answer on the recording, pausing after Lars's response. Let students compare their answers. If students have made major grammatical errors, explain the structure in the version in the recording, referring students to the tapescript on SB p120 if necessary.

Answers and tapescript

T 2.9

A = **Ann** **L** = **Lars**

A So what do you think of Liverpool, Lars?
L It's really interesting. Liverpool's such an old city, isn't it? There are some lovely buildings, and the people are so friendly!
A (Yes, they are, aren't they?) When did you get here?
L Two days ago. I got the plane from Oslo. We were a bit late landing, but it didn't matter.
A (Oh, good.) Where are you staying in Liverpool?
L At the Grand Hotel. It's very convenient for the office. My room isn't very big, but it's OK.
A (What a pity! Never mind.) Where are you from?
L Well, from Norway. I was born in Bergen, but I live in a suburb of Oslo. It's very pretty, and it's not far from the sea.
A (Really? It sounds beautiful.) Your English is very good. Where did you learn it?
L That's very kind of you, but I know I make a lot of mistakes. I learned it at school for years, and I've been to England quite a few times.
A (Oh, have you? How interesting!) And what are you doing here in Liverpool, Lars?
L I'm attending a conference. I'm here for five days, and I'm going home on the 17th.
A (Oh, so soon!) And have you managed to get around our city yet?
L I haven't seen very much. I've been for a walk along the riverside and I've taken a ferry across the Mersey, but I haven't seen the Beatles Exhibition yet.
A Well, I hope you enjoy it. Don't work too hard!
L I'll try to enjoy myself! Bye. It was nice to talk to you.

SPOKEN ENGLISH – Softening a negative comment

1 Read the notes and examples as a class.

2 Explain that to complete the task students need to use the words in brackets but will also need to modify the sentence in some cases. With weaker students, point out that they need to make some of the sentences negative. Elicit one or two examples from the class.

Students complete the task, working individually Check the answers.

Answers

1 It's a bit expensive.	4 They aren't very friendly.
2 It's quite hard.	5 I don't earn very much.
3 It isn't very warm.	6 There isn't very much to do.

Highlight the pattern *not* + *very* + the opposite adjective of what you want to say. Point out that this is a very common pattern in spoken English when we do not want to sound negative.

5 **T 2.10** [**CD 1: Track 24**] Focus attention on the example. Elicit a range of other possible answers and follow-up comments. Play the recording, pausing after each question. With weaker classes, play the recording through first and elicit possible answers and comments for each question as a class. Then get the students to repeat the task, giving their own answers in pairs.

Tapescript

T 2.10

1 Who do you work for?
2 Do you enjoy your job?
3 Where do you come from?
4 Have you been to New York?
5 What do you do when you're not working?
6 The weather's amazing at the moment, isn't it?
7 Are you having a holiday this year?
8 This city's very exciting, isn't it?
9 What's your favourite programme on television?

T 2.11 [**CD 1: Track 25**] Tell students they are going to hear the questions again, with a range of different answers. Play the recording, pausing after each answer, and get students to compare the conversations with their versions.

Play the recording again and get students to focus on the stress and intonation in the questions and answers. Highlight in particular the intonation in the question tag:

…, isn't it?

and the questions:

How about you?

Do you?

What about you?

Drill the intonation, using the recording as a model.

NOTE

There is further practice in Unit 3 on the form and intonation of question tags.

Tapescript

T 2.11

1 **A** Who do you work for?
B Siemens. I've been with them for four years. They're a good company. How about you?
2 **A** Do you enjoy your job?
B Yes, I do. It's quite hard, but I enjoy the challenge. I don't earn very much. What about you? Do you like your job?

3 **A** Where do you come from?
B I was born in Montreal, and I've lived there all my life with my parents. I'd like to live abroad some time.
4 **A** Have you been to New York?
B No, I haven't, but I'd love to. I've heard it's one of the most amazing cities in the world. Have you been there?
5 **A** What do you do when you're not working?
B Well, I like horse-riding, and I play golf. And I love music, so I often go to concerts. Do you?
6 **A** The weather's amazing at the moment, isn't it?
B Yes, it's so mild. We haven't had any really cold weather at all! Have you heard a weather forecast for the weekend? It's supposed to be good, isn't it?
7 **A** Are you having a holiday this year?
B Yes, I'm going to Mexico with some friends. I haven't been there before, so I'm really looking forward to it. What about you?
8 **A** This city's very exciting, isn't it?
B Really? Do you think so? There isn't very much to do. I get so bored here. What *do* you find to do?
9 **A** What's your favourite programme on television?
B I haven't got a favourite, but I like soaps and documentaries. And quiz shows. And the news. I suppose I like everything. What about you?

6 This activity gives students the opportunity to practise making small talk in a free and fun roleplay. Get students to read the context and give them time to invent a profile for themselves. Write the following prompts on the board to help:

name:
from (country and city):
job:
work for:
name of hotel:
arrived in city:
sights visited in the city:
opinion of city:

Alternatively, you can use the photocopiable activity described below.

EXTRA IDEA
Making small talk TB p148
If you are short of time or if you want to provide your students with profiles to do the mingle activity, you can photocopy these role cards. There are eight profiles per sheet, so photocopy enough cards for your students to have one each. With larger classes, you can divide the students into groups to do the mingle. If possible, create the correct atmosphere for the roleplay by moving the furniture to create a clear space, bringing in glasses of water to simulate drinks and playing background music.

Whichever way you do the activity, allow enough time for students to talk to four or five other people. Monitor and note down common errors, but don't interrupt or correct students during the roleplay.

Encourage students to take opportunities to make small talk with you and each other at the start of each lesson, and with English-speaking people they meet outside the class.

WRITING (SB p104)

Letters and emails – Formal and informal

Lead in by asking students a few questions about letters and emails: *How often do you email your friends? When do you write letters? What is different about writing letters and writing emails?* Check understanding of the terms *formal* and *informal.*

1 Ask students in pairs to decide which extracts are formal and which are informal. Ask them to note which words or phrases helped them decide (see underlining in *Answers* below). Check answers, then get students in pairs to look at the sentences again and decide which are beginnings and which are endings (see *Answers* in brackets below).

Answers
1 **Informal** Great to hear from you again. (Beginning)
2 **Formal** I am writing in response to your advertisement in today's Guardian for an IT consultant. (Beginning)
3 **Formal** Give my regards to Robert and all the family. (Ending)
4 **Informal** I'm sorry I haven't been in touch for so long but you know how it is. (Beginning)
5 **Formal** Thank you for your invoice of April 16th. Please find enclosed a cheque for the full amount. (Beginning)
6 **Informal** Write, or better still, email me soon. (Ending)
7 **Formal** We trust this arrangement meets with your satisfaction. (Ending)
8 **Informal** Just a note to say thank you so much for having me to stay last weekend. (Beginning)
9 **Informal** Take care. I can't wait to see you next week. (Ending)
10 **Formal** I look forward to hearing from you at your earliest convenience. (Ending)

2 Allow students time to read the beginnings of the four letters and emails, then get them in pairs to match each beginning with its next line and ending. Check answers with the class.

Answers
1 b, g   2 c, f   3 d, e   4 a, h

3 Discuss the answers as a class.

Answers
1 exchanging news
2 a formal request
3 an invitation
4 saying thank you

4 Give students a few minutes to write brief notes under the headings *personal life* and *work.* Ask which phrases from the lesson they could use in their email, then ask them to write it for homework. You could ask them to email it to you! Correct it and email it back.

Don't forget!

Workbook Unit 2

Exercise 6 Pronunciation – *-s* at the end of a word

Exercise 12 Phrasal verbs – Phrasal verb + noun

Word list

Refer students to the Word list for Unit 2 (SB p152). They could translate the words, learn them at home, or transfer some of them to their vocabulary notebook.

3

Past tenses
Spelling and pronunciation
Giving opinions

Good times, bad times

Introduction to the unit

The theme of this unit is talking about the past and past events, both good and bad. This provides the context for practising narrative tenses: Past Simple, Past Continuous, Past Perfect, and Past Simple passive. *Used to* is also introduced mainly for recognition purposes.

The *Reading* section tells the story of Shakespeare's famous lovers Romeo and Juliet, and the theme of love is carried through in the *Listening and speaking* section. The *Vocabulary* syllabus continues with a focus on spelling and pronunciation. *Everyday English* in this unit consolidates and extends the language of giving opinions from Unit 2, including ways of making opinions stronger and also the use of question tags to invite agreement. The *Writing* section practises using linking words and adding ideas to write an interesting story.

Language aims

Grammar – past tenses By intermediate level, students are familiar with both the form and uses of narrative tenses, but they are likely to still make mistakes, especially when they need to decide which tense to use. This unit reviews the Past Simple, Past Continuous, and Past Perfect in a contrastive way with a range of accuracy- and analysis-based activities, along with a pronunciation focus. The Past Simple passive is featured in the presentation text, a biography of the painter Vincent Van Gogh, and is practised, along with the Past Perfect passive, in the language work that follows. Some examples of *used to* are included in the presentation text, and students focus on it for recognition purposes in the grammar work.

POSSIBLE PROBLEMS

Narrative tenses

1 The Past Simple, not the Present Perfect, has to be used for completed actions in the past, whereas other languages can use the equivalent of the Present Perfect.
I saw Jo in town last week.   **I've seen Jo in town last week.*
The Present Perfect is covered fully in Unit 7. Until then, if students confuse these tenses, remind them that we use the Past Simple when we say *when* something happened – when we refer to a specific past time.

2 Many common verbs are irregular in the Past Simple. Refer students to the list of irregular verbs on SB p159.

3 There are three ways of pronouncing the *-ed* ending in regular Past Simple verbs and past participles: /t/ *washed*, /d/ *lived*, /ɪd/ *wanted*. This is practised in the *Pronunciation* section on SB p23.

4 Students may have problems with the use of the auxiliaries *did* and *didn't* in Past Simple questions and negatives. Point out that they are the past equivalents of *do/does, don't/doesn't* that students practised in Unit 2.

Common mistakes:

**I did see Sam yesterday.*   **I didn't went home.*
**When you saw him?*   **She no come last week.*

5 The use of the Past Continuous contrasted with the Past Simple for interrupted past actions doesn't usually present problems.
I was walking home when I saw an accident.
However, the use of the Past Continuous as a descriptive, scene-setting tense can be more difficult to grasp. It is best illustrated in context.
It was a beautiful day. The sun was shining and the birds were singing.

6 The pronunciation of *was* and *were* in the Past Continuous may need work. Students can tend to overstress them, whereas they are usually weak forms in normal context.
/wəz/   /wə/
I was working.   *They were waiting for hours.*

7 Students may confuse the contracted form of the Past Perfect *'d* (*had*) with the contracted form of *would*.
She said she'd bought the tickets. (= *had*)
She said she'd buy the tickets. (= *would*)

used to

Students may find it confusing that *used to* refers to past time, especially if they have come across *be/get used to*. Focus on getting students to recognize the form, and to understand the use of *used to* for talking about regular or repeated actions in the past.

Vocabulary This section looks at spelling and pronunciation and highlights the fact that there is often not a direct link between the two in English. The exercises focus on words that sound the same but have different spelling and meaning (homophones), words that rhyme, lost sounds, and silent letters.

Everyday English The language of giving opinions is the focus of this unit. It includes ways of making opinions stronger, and the use of question tags to ask others to agree.

Notes on the unit

STARTER (SB p22)

Explain to students that they are going to play a game in which they take turns to add a sentence, starting with *Fortunately,* [+ something positive] then *Unfortunately,* [+ something negative]. With weaker students, briefly review the irregular Past Simple forms of common verbs (see SB p159) before students play the game. Read the opening sentence, then get two students to read the examples. Check the stress and intonation on *Fortunately* and *Unfortunately*:

Fortunately, … *Unfortunately, …*

Students play the game around the class. With larger classes, students can play in groups.

VINCENT VAN GOGH (SB p22)

Past tenses and *used to*

ABOUT THE TEXT

Students are likely to know something about the life and work of Vincent Van Gogh /væn ˈɡɒf/. The texts in exercises 2 and 3 give biographical details of the artist and provide the context for the past tenses and structures (Past Simple, Past Continuous, Past Perfect, and also *used to* and Past Simple passive.)

1 Focus attention on the paintings by Van Gogh. Elicit any information and ideas from the class about the artist's life. Most students should know that he had an unhappy life and that his paintings were not successful until after his death, but confirm these details if they are unsure.

2 **T 3.1** **[CD 1: Track 26]** Pre-teach/check the names of the artists and places in the text (see *About the text* above). Also check the following vocabulary items, including the pronunciation where relevant: *art dealer, to be dismissed* (told to leave a job), *to commit suicide* /ˈsuːɪsaɪd/, *asylum* /əˈsaɪləm/ (a mental hospital), *to be buried* /ˈberɪd/.

Give students time to read the notes quickly. Then focus attention on the question prompts. Elicit the questions for the first two prompts. Tell students that they will need passive forms for some of the questions. Students complete the questions, working individually. Allow students to compare their questions in pairs, then play the recording so that they can check. With weaker students, elicit the questions as a whole-class activity and write them on the board. If necessary, briefly review the form of questions in the Past Simple, Past Continuous, and Past Simple passive. Remind students that the question *Who came to live with him?* does not need the auxiliary *did* because it is a subject question (see Grammar Reference 1.5 note 2, SB p133).

Answers and tapescript

T 3.1

1 Where was he born?
2 What **was his** job?
3 Why **was he dismissed**?
4 Why **did he try to commit suicide**?
5 Which **artists did he meet**?
6 What **was he doing** when he met them?
7 Who **came to live with him**?
8 Where **did they** first meet?
9 What **was he carrying**?
10 Why **did he cut off part of his ear**?
11 Which **paintings were completed there**?
12 What **was he** doing when he shot himself?
13 Why **did he shoot himself**?
14 Where **was he buried**?
15 Why didn't **he have any money**?

3 **T 3.2** **[CD 1: Track 27]** Set a time limit of about five minutes for students to read the full text. Deal with any vocabulary queries students may have. Demonstrate the activity by getting two confident students to ask and answer the first three questions across the class (see **T 3.2** below). Put students in pairs to continue asking and answering the questions.

Play the recording to let students hear the questions and answers in full. If students need more help with question formation, use the recording as a model and get students to listen and repeat.

Answers and tapescript

T 3.2

1 **A** Where was he born?
B In Brabant in the Netherlands.
2 **A** What was his job?
B He worked as an art dealer.
3 **A** Why was he dismissed?
B Because he'd had an argument with customers.
4 **A** Why did he try to commit suicide?
B Because he'd fallen in love with his cousin and she'd rejected him.
5 **A** Which artists did he meet?
B Degas, Pissarro, Seurat, Toulouse-Lautrec, Monet, and Renoir.
6 **A** What was he doing when he met them?
B He was studying art.
7 **A** Who came to live with him?
B Gauguin.
8 **A** Where did they first meet?
B In Paris.
9 **A** What was he carrying?
B A razor blade.
10 **A** Why did he cut off part of his ear?
B Because he'd been drinking, and he'd had an argument with Gauguin.
11 **A** Which paintings were completed there?
B *Starry Night*, *Irises*, and *Self-portrait without a beard*.
12 **A** What was he doing when he shot himself?
B He was painting outside.
13 **A** Why did he shoot himself?
B Because he was depressed.
14 **A** Where was he buried?
B In Auvers.
15 **A** Why didn't he have any money?
B Because he'd sold only one of his paintings.

GRAMMAR SPOT (SB p23)

1 Look at the three sentences as a class. Get students to identify the past forms.

Students find more examples of the forms in the text on SB p23.

Answers
He **worked** as an art dealer. – Past Simple
He **was dismissed**. – Past Simple Passive
He **was studying** art. – Past Continuous

Other examples
Past Simple: *tried, was, went, met, came, settled down, quarrelled, left, cut off, moved, included, continued, shot, died, had, took*
Past Simple passive: *was born, was dismissed, were completed, was buried, was published, was ... recognized*
Past Continuous: *was painting*

2 Students read the example, and answer the concept question. Elicit the form of the tense and write it on the board (see *Answers* below).

Students find more examples of the tense in the text on SB p23.

Answers
had argued is the first action, followed by *was dismissed*.
Past Perfect = *had* + past participle

Other examples: *had fallen in love, had rejected, had met, had been drinking* (this is the continuous form), *had had, he'd ... sold*

3 Students read the example, and answer the concept question. Highlight the form and write it on the board: *used* + *to* + infinitive. Point out that the form is the same for all persons.

Students find another example of *used to* in the text on SB p23.

Answers
Used to expresses an action that happened many times.

Another example: *used to wake up*

Refer students to Grammar Reference 3.1–3.7 on SB pp135–7.

Pronunciation

This section highlights pronunciation features connected with past tenses: the weak forms of the auxiliaries *was/were* in the Past Continuous, the contracted form of *had* in the Past Perfect and Past Perfect Continuous, and the pronunciation of the regular Past Simple *-ed* ending.

4 **T 3.3** [**CD 1: Track 28**] Give students time to read the sentences and identify the tenses. Play the recording. Students repeat chorally and individually.

T 3.3
1 What was he doing?
2 He was studying.
3 They were working ...
4 He'd had an argument.
5 They'd met in Paris.
6 He'd been drinking.

5 **T 3.4** [**CD 1: Track 29**] Elicit how we form the Past Simple of regular verbs (add *-ed*). Remind students that there are three ways to pronounce this ending. Pronounce /t/, /d/, /ɪd/ and focus attention on the example *worked*. Give students time to categorize the verbs.

Play the recording and let students check their answers. Play the recording again and get students to repeat chorally and individually.

Answers and tapescript

T 3.4
/t/ worked dismissed published
/d/ tried quarrelled moved continued died recognized
/ɪd/ rejected completed

If appropriate, give students the rules for the pronunciation of the *-ed* ending, or let students work them out:

pronounce *-ed* as /t/ after unvoiced sounds, apart from *t*.
pronounce *-ed* as /d/ after voiced sounds, apart from *d*.
pronounce *-ed* as /ɪd/ after *t* or *d*.

SUGGESTION
To give students further practice in pronunciation, get them to read aloud paragraphs 5, 7, and 8 of the text on SB p23, paying attention to the pronunciation of the past tenses.

PRACTICE (SB p24)

I didn't do much

1 **T 3.5** [**CD 1: Track 30**] Tell students to listen to the four speakers and number the lines according to who is speaking. Play the first speaker as an example and check the answer. Play the rest of the recording. Students complete the task. Check answers with the class.

Answers and tapescript
[2] I went for a drink with a couple of friends.
[4] We talked for a bit.
[1] I didn't do much.
[2] I got home about nine.
[1] I had an early night.
[3] I didn't get home till about midnight.
[4] I did some stuff on the computer.
[3] Quite a late night for me!

T 3.5
1 I didn't do much. I just had something to eat, watched telly for a while, and then had an early night. I was in bed by ten.
2 I went to my yoga class, then went for a drink with a couple of friends. I got home about nine and did a bit of housework, and that was it.
3 I went out with some people from work, so I didn't get home till about midnight. Well, after midnight, actually. Quite a late night for me!
4 I met some friends in town for a coffee, and we talked for a bit. Then I went home and did some stuff on the computer, you know, *Facebook*, then went to bed about eleven thirty.

2 Give an example of what you did last night. Elicit one or two more examples from the class. Put students into small groups to continue exchanging information.

Discussing grammar

3 This task reviews and consolidates the use of past tenses via a series of contrastive sentences. In a monolingual class, or with weaker classes, you could let students discuss the sentences in their own language. Ask students to look at the first two sentences and discuss the use of tenses in pairs. Check the answers (see *Answers* below) before students continue the task in their pairs. Monitor to help and also to assess students' ideas about the tense use. If students have problems understanding the concept of each tense, be prepared to do a remedial presentation on the board (see *Suggestion* below).

Elicit the answers from different pairs in the class.

Answers

1 sentence 1 – Past Simple for a finished action in the past
sentence 2 – Past Continuous for an action in progress at a particular time in the past

2 sentence 1 – Past Simple for a finished action in the past
sentence 2 – Past Continuous for an action in progress at a particular time in the past

3 sentence 1 – Past Continuous for an interrupted action in the past
sentence 2 – Past Simple for past actions that followed each other

4 sentence 1 – Past Continuous for an interrupted action in the past
sentence 2 – Past Simple for past actions that followed each other
sentence 3 – Past Perfect for an action completed before another action in the past

5 sentence 1 – Past Simple for past actions that followed each other
sentence 2 – Past Perfect for an action completed before another action in the past

6 sentence 1 – *used to* for repeated actions (habits) in the past
sentence 2 – Past Simple for a finished action in the past

SUGGESTION

It can be helpful to explain the use of narrative tenses in a visual way with timelines. Write the three sentences in item 4 on the board. Underline the tenses and elicit the names from the class. Also check comprehension of the contraction *we'd* (= *we had*).

1 When Bill arrived, we were having lunch.

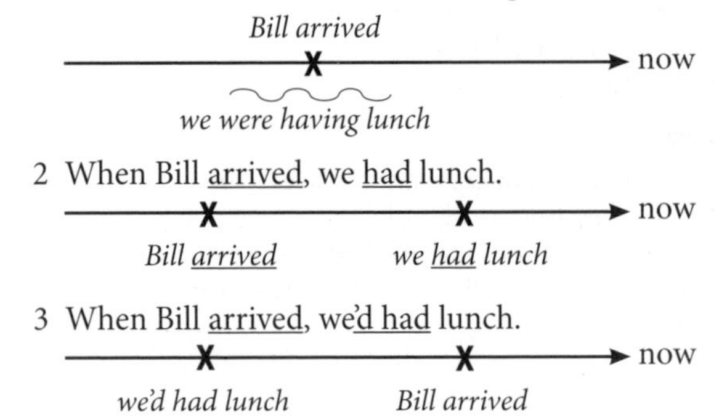

A newspaper story

This section consolidates the use of narrative tenses via a newspaper article about an accident.

ABOUT THE TEXT

The article is based on a true story that took place in the UK in January 2006 at the Fitzwilliam Museum in Cambridge. The museum contains works of art and antiquities from a wide range of centuries and civilizations. The accident involved the smashing of three priceless Chinese vases from the Qing Dynasty (1644–1911), which were on open display in the museum. There was much media coverage of the accident, but the vases have subsequently been restored and are on display again – this time in a case!

4 **T 3.6** [**CD 1: Track 31**] Get students to read the article through quickly to get a general understanding. Deal with any vocabulary queries. Elicit the answer to number 1 (*were produced*). Students then complete the task, working individually. Students who finish fast can check their answers in pairs.

Play the recording to allow students to check their answers. If necessary, pause the recording after each answer.

Answers and tapescript

T 3.6

Smash! Clumsy visitor destroys priceless vases, by Tom Ball
A clumsy visitor to a British museum has destroyed a set of priceless 300-year-old Chinese vases after slipping on the stairs.

The three vases, which (1) **were produced** during the Qing dynasty in the 17th century, (2) **had stood** on the windowsill at the Fitzwilliam Museum in Cambridge for forty years. Last Thursday they (3) **were smashed** into a million pieces. The vases, which (4) **had been donated** in 1948, (5) **were** the museum's best-known pieces.

The Fitzwilliam (6) **decided** not to identify the man who (7) **had caused** the disaster. 'It was a most unfortunate and regrettable accident,' museum director Duncan Robinson said, 'but we are glad that the visitor (8) **wasn't** seriously **injured**.'

The photograph of the accident (9) **was taken** by another visitor, Steve Baxter. 'We (10) **watched** the man fall as if in slow motion. He (11) **was flying** through the air. The vases (12) **exploded** as though they (13) **had been hit** by a bomb. The man (14) **was sitting** there stunned in the middle of a pile of porcelain when the staff (15) **arrived**.'

The museum declined to say what the vases were worth.

5 **T 3.7** [**CD 1: Track 32**] Tell students they are going to hear an interview with the man who broke the vases. Explain that they need to listen for any new information not given in the article in exercise 4. Pre-teach/check the following items from the recording: *on the mend* (informal for *getting better*), *to go head over heels* (to fall over head first), *to pay something attention*, *to ban someone*.

Play the recording through once. Allow students to exchange information. Play the recording again if necessary. Elicit the new information given in the recording (see underlining in tapescript below).

Answers and tapescript

T 3.7

I = Interviewer NF = Nick Flynn

I It's 7.45, and you're listening to the *Today* programme. The man who broke Chinese vases worth £100,000 when he fell downstairs at a museum has been named by a daily newspaper. He's Nick Flynn, and he's with us now. Are you all right, Mr Flynn? You didn't hurt yourself falling downstairs, did you?

NF I'm on the mend, which is more than I can say for the vases!

I Too true! How did it happen?

NF I was coming down the stairs, looking at the pictures, and I slipped. The stairs are very shiny, and it had been raining, so I guess my shoes were a bit wet. And I just went head over heels.

I It must have been a strange feeling, lying in the middle of all that priceless porcelain?

NF I was surprised that these incredibly valuable vases were left just standing on a windowsill. I'd seen them lots of times before, but I hadn't really paid them any attention.

I And I hear you've been banned from the museum? Is that right?

NF Yes, I got a letter from the director of the museum asking me not to go back. It's a shame, because I used to go twice a week. So now I've got to find somewhere else to go.

I Well, thank you, Mr Flynn, and good luck.

Dictation

6 **T 3.8** **[CD 1: Track 33]** The *Practice* section ends with a dictation activity, summarizing the interview in exercise 5. If students are not used to doing dictations, tell them not to panic, because the text is spoken at a reduced speed. They will already be familiar with the story and this should also help them.

Briefly review the names of the punctuation marks *full stop* and *comma*. Play the first three phrases (# = a pause in the dictation) and get a student to write them on the board. Play the rest of the recording stopping, where each pause is indicated and get students to write down the text. Tell them that if they miss anything, they should leave a gap and carry on.

Students compare their version with a partner. Play selected sections of the recording again as necessary. Refer students to the tapescript on SB p121 so that they can check their punctuation, including apostrophes.

Answers and tapescript

T 3.8

The man who broke # Chinese vases # worth £100,000 # when he fell downstairs # at a museum # has been named # as Nick Flynn (full stop)

He was coming # down the stairs (comma) # looking at the pictures # on the wall (comma) # when he slipped (full stop) # The stairs were shiny (comma) # and it had been raining (full stop)

He'd seen the vases # lots of times before (comma) # but hadn't # paid them any attention (full stop)

The museum has asked him # not to go back (full stop) He's disappointed because # he used to go there # twice a week (full stop)

ADDITIONAL MATERIAL

Workbook Unit 3

Exercises 1–4 Past tenses

Exercise 5 Past Simple and Continuous

Exercises 6–7 Past Perfect

Exercise 8 Tense Review – *ate*, *was eating*, or *had eaten*?

Exercise 9 Past Simple passive

Exercise 10 Questions and negatives

VOCABULARY (SB p25)

Spelling and pronunciation

The exercises is this section aim to highlight the fact that spelling is not a reliable guide to pronunciation in English because:

- some letters have more than one sound.
- the same sound may be represented by different letters.
- sometimes syllables in the spelling are not pronounced at all.
- some words contain letters that are not pronounced.

There is a chart with IPA phonetic symbols on SB p159.

1 **T 3.9** **[CD 1: Track 34]** Focus attention on the examples. Elicit the pronunciation of the words, then play the recording and get students to repeat chorally and individually. If students have problems coming to a conclusion about spelling and pronunciation, ask:

What is similar about the first three words? (They are all spelt with the vowels *-oo-*.)

What is different about them? (The pronunciation of the vowels *-oo-* is different in each word.)

Do the words rhyme? (No.)

What is similar about the second three words? (They all have the same pronunciation.)

What is different about them? (The spelling of each word.)

Do the words all sound the same? (Yes.)

Establish the key points of this introduction with the whole class:

- words with similar spelling aren't always pronounced the same.
- the same pronunciation can have different spellings.

T 3.9

good food blood road rode rowed

Words that sound the same

2 **T 3.10** **[CD 1: Track 35]** Tell students they are going to hear five simple words and that they should write them down. Play the recording. Students compare their answers. Elicit words that the students wrote down and write them on the board. They should give one of two possible answers depending on how they interpreted each word (see *Answers* below). Get students to say the pairs of words to establish that they are pronounced the same but have different spellings and meanings. If appropriate, point out that these words are known as *homophones*.

Answers and tapescript

T 3.10

see (sea)
new (knew)
wear (where)
peace (piece)
flew (flu)

3 Look at the example with the class and stress that in each case students must write another word that has the same pronunciation. Elicit the pronunciation of the remaining words aloud. Students complete the task, working individually. Get them to compare their answers in pairs before a whole-class check. Elicit the spelling of the second word in each pair and write the words on the board.

Answers

1 mail	6 weak
2 blue	7 whole
3 peace	8 pear
4 wear	9 aloud
5 court	10 wait

4 This task gives further practice in homophones and recognizing phonetic symbols. Focus attention on the example and elicit the second word (*war*). Point out that students need to use the context to help them choose the correct spelling. If necessary, refer students to the chart on SB p159 to help them with the phonetic symbols.

Students complete the task, working individually. Get them to compare their answers in pairs before a whole-class check.

Answers

1 war	4 wore; whole; week
2 allowed; wear	5 wait; caught; flu
3 pair; blue	

SUGGESTION

For homework, you could get students to invent similar sentences with homophones replaced by phonetics, using the words on the page. Students exchange their sentences and get their partner to work out the correct spelling of the words.

Spelling

5 **T 3.11** [**CD 1: Track 36**] This exercise emphasizes that words that look the same do not necessarily rhyme. Elicit the pronunciation of the three words in the example. Stress that *love* and *glove* are the only two that rhyme.

Students continue the task in pairs. Monitor to see how well they pronounce the words and recognize the rhymes.

Play the recording so that students can check their answers.

Answers and tapescript

T 3.11

1	**love**	move	**glove**
2	**some**	home	**come**
3	**dear**	**fear**	pear
4	lost	**most**	**post**
5	**meat**	**cheat**	great
6	**boot**	**shoot**	foot
7	**eight**	**weight**	height
8	**blood**	wood	**flood**
9	**flower**	**power**	lower

SUGGESTION

As an extension to exercise 5, get students to write in phonetic script the vowel sounds of the words that rhyme and the different sound of the one that doesn't. They can use the Phonetics symbols chart on SB p159 or a dictionary to help them.

6 This exercise highlights that the same sound can be spelt in different ways. Elicit the pronunciation of the four vowel sounds, or model them to the class. Elicit the spelling of the last two words with /uː/ (see *Answers* below). Point out that some of the words can have more than one spelling.

Answers

/uː/ juice through/threw
/ɔː/ court/caught dawn war/wore floor/flaw
/ɜː/ earth world burn fur/fir
/eə/ tear fair/fare square there/their

Lost sounds

7 **T 3.12** [**CD 1: Track 37**] This exercise highlights the fact that in some words not all the syllables are pronounced. Focus attention on the examples. Drill the pronunciation, counting out the number of syllables on your fingers to help students. Students complete the exercise, working individually.

Get students to check in pairs before playing the recording as a final check. If necessary, drill the pronunciation of the words, using the recording as a model.

Answers and tapescript

T 3.12

diff~~e~~rent sev~~e~~ral bus~~i~~ness rest~~au~~rant marri~~a~~ge int~~e~~resting
veg~~e~~table temp~~e~~rature secret~~a~~ry

8 **T 3.13** [**CD 1: Track 38**] This exercise gives students practice in recognizing silent letters. Focus attention on the example and elicit the pronunciation /ˈfɒrən/. Point out that the words are presented in pairs with the same silent letter in each. Students complete the task, working individually. Monitor and check.

Get students to check in pairs before playing the recording as a final check. If necessary, drill the pronunciation of the words, using the recording as a model.

Answers and tapescript

T 3.13

1 foreign sign
2 climb bomb
3 neighbour weigh
4 honest hour
5 knee knock
6 psychology psychiatrist

SUGGESTION

As an extension to exercise 8, get students to write out the words in phonetic script. They can use the chart on SB p159 or a dictionary to help them.

READING (SB p26)

A Shakespearean tragedy

ABOUT THE TEXT

The theme of the unit now changes to love and relationships, with a focus on Shakespeare's famous lovers, Romeo and Juliet. The text is in the form of a picture story, which summarizes the action of the play, and characters' speech bubbles, which give actual lines from the play. This allows students to understand the story while also getting a feel for the original language. A 'translation' of the lines into more modern English is provided at the back of the Student's Book on p148.

The tasks include pre-work about Shakespeare and the story of Romeo and Juliet, so you may find the following background notes useful. If you are not familiar with the details of the plot, read the text on SB pp26–7 before the class. Although somewhat simplified, this provides a good working summary of the plot of the play.

Shakespeare

William Shakespeare (1564–1616) was an English poet and playwright, widely regarded as the greatest writer in the English language. He is often called England's national poet. His surviving works consist of 38 plays and over 150 poems. His plays have been translated into every major living language and many well-known English sayings come from his work.

Shakespeare was born in Stratford-upon-Avon. At the age of 18 he married Anne Hathaway, with whom he had three children. Between 1585 and 1592 he began a successful career in London as an actor, writer, and part owner of a theatre company. He appears to have retired to Stratford around 1613, where he died three years later. He is buried in Stratford-upon-Avon and the houses where he lived can be visited. His plays are regularly performed by the Royal Shakespeare Company. His best known plays are: *Antony and Cleopatra*, *Hamlet*, *Julius Caesar*, *King Lear*, *Macbeth*, *Othello*, *Romeo and Juliet*, *The Merchant of Venice*, *A Midsummer Night's Dream*, *The Taming of the Shrew*, *The Tempest*, *Twelfth Night*, and *A Winter's Tale*.

The vocabulary items listed below may be new. Students will be able to guess some of them from context, but with weaker classes, be prepared to check them, or get students to check them for homework before the class. The items marked * are old-fashioned or literary, and so will be for recognition rather than active use.

**warring* (in a war/conflict), *feud* /fjuːd/, **to swear* (promise), *dawn*, *to unite*, *to be *wed* (get married), *to take revenge*, *to banish*, *exiled*, *to bear*, *nobleman*, *tomb* /tuːm/, *poison*, **weep* (*wept*, *wept*), *dagger*, *to stab*, *overwhelmed with grief*.

Students will need to be able to refer to the characters in the play, so check the pronunciation of the names:

The Montagues: Lord Montague /ˈmɒntəgjuː/, Romeo /ˈrəʊmiəʊ/, Mercutio /mɜːˈkuːʃɪəʊ/, Benvolio /benˈvəʊliəʊ/

The Capulets: Lord Capulet /ˈkæpjələt/, Juliet /ˈdʒuːliet/, Tybalt /ˈtɪbɒlt/, Paris /ˈpærɪs/

Other: Friar Laurence /fraɪə ˈlɒrens/

1 Ask the question and elicit a range of ideas from the class and the names of any plays students have heard of. Ask students if they have seen/read any Shakespeare plays, possibly in their own language.

2 Focus attention on the character lists and check the pronunciation of the names (see *About the text* above). Elicit what students know about the story and write up their ideas on the board. Ask the Student's Book questions about marriage and establish the answers.

Answers

At the time of the story of Romeo and Juliet, marriages were often a way of bringing the two families together to increase their wealth, power, and status. Marrying for love was not common, especially among wealthy families. A young person's parents, usually the father, decided who he/she would marry.

3 If students didn't prepare the vocabulary in the text for homework, pre-teach/check new items before students read (see notes in *About the text* above). Tell students they are going to read the first half of the story. Advise them not to worry about understanding everything in the speech bubbles, as the main paragraphs tell the story. Students read frames 1–6 and answer the questions in pairs. Check the answers with the class.

Answers

1 They had hated each other for so long that no one could remember how the feud had started.
2 Because Romeo was Lord Montague's son and the Capulets hated him and his family.
3 Romeo and Juliet fell instantly in love. They touched hands. They talked. They kissed. Then they discovered their families were enemies.
4 Romeo's name indicates he is a Montague and links him to the family that Juliet's family hates.
5 They had known each other for a day.
6 He wanted to unite the families.

7 Because the man Romeo's friend and cousin were fighting was Juliet's cousin, Tybalt.
8 Because Romeo had killed her cousin, and now he was exiled.

4 Students read frames 7–12 and answer the questions in their pairs. Check the answers with the class.

Answers
1 She couldn't tell her father that she had already married Romeo.
2 To give Juliet a sleeping potion to make her appear dead for 42 hours, so she couldn't marry Paris.
3 Everyone believed that Juliet was really dead.
4 Romeo never received the Friar's letter.
5 He thought Juliet had died and so he killed himself.
6 She woke up and saw Romeo dead. She couldn't stand the grief and so she stabbed herself.
7 They were overwhelmed with grief, and horrified at the pain their families' hatred had caused.

5 **T 3.14** **[CD 1: Track 39]** Explain to students that they are going to listen to some lines from Shakespeare's play. Point out that some of the English is old-fashioned, and they may not understand every single word. Focus attention on the first picture, and play the first line of the recording. Then students follow the picture story as they listen to the rest of the lines. Direct students to the lines in modern English on SB p148. Allow students time to read the lines, then direct students back to the picture story and play the recording again.

Answers and tapescript

T 3.14

Romeo and Juliet
T = Tybalt R = Romeo J = Julie N = Nurse
F = Friar P = Prince
1 **T** Peace! I hate the word ... As I hate hell, all Montagues, and thee.
2 **R** Did my heart love till now? For I ne'er saw true beauty till this night.
J My only love sprung from my only hate, ...
3 **J** O Romeo, Romeo, wherefore art thou Romeo? Deny thy father, and refuse thy name ... What's Montague? ... A rose by any other word would smell as sweet.
4 **R** My heart's dear love is set on the fair daughter of rich Capulet.
F This alliance may so happy prove, to turn your households' rancour to pure love.
5 **R** Now, Tybalt, ... Mercutio's soul is ... above our heads, either thou or I, or both, must go with him.
T Thou wretched boy ... shalt with him hence.
6 **N** I'll find Romeo to comfort you.
J O, find him ... and bid him come to take his last farewell.
7 **J** O, think'st thou we shall ever meet again?
R I doubt it not; and all these woes shall serve for sweet discourses in our times to come.
8 **F** Take thou this vial, ... and this liquor drink ... no pulse ... no breath shall testify thou livest ... two and forty hours.
J Give me! ... Love give me strength.
9 **J** Romeo, Romeo, Romeo! Here's drink – I drink to thee.
N O hateful day! Never was seen so black a day as this, O woeful day!
10 **R** Eyes, look your last. Arms, take your last embrace ... Here's to my love! O true Apothecary, thy drugs are quick. Thus with a kiss I die.
11 **J** What's here? A cup closed in my true love's hand? Poison, I see ... I will kiss thy lips ... some poison doth hang on them to make me die ... thy lips are warm! Oh happy dagger! Let me die!
12 **P** For never was a story of more woe than this of Juliet and her Romeo.

6 Explain to students that they are going to retell the story using the pictures as prompts. Focus attention on the first picture and elicit the first part of the story from the class. Emphasize that students should use their own words, and get them to cover the words in the Student's Book if you think this will help. Students then continue retelling the story in pairs, taking turns to tell each part of the story. With weaker classes, you could do this as a whole class activity. Monitor and listen for correct use of past tenses. Correct any mistakes in a short feedback session.

What do you think?

Discuss the questions with the class, or put students into small groups to exchange their ideas. Elicit a range of ideas and opinions in a short feedback session (see notes in *About the text* for the titles of Shakespeare's best-known plays).

WRITING (SB p105)

Telling a story (1) – linking ideas

Lead in by asking students to look at the first picture. What do they think the story is about?

1 Check/pre-teach the words *vineyard*, *grapes*, and *upset*. Get students to read the story of the farmer and his sons and identify the people in the picture. Ask if their predictions about the story were correct.

Answer
The picture shows the farmer and his three sons.

2 Give students time to read through the clauses. Put students into pairs and get them to read the story again and decide where the clauses go.

Answers
1 b 2 a 3 d 4 f 5 e 6 c

3 Refer students to the picture from the story of the emperor and his daughters. Students read the lines from the story and identify the people in the picture.

Answer
The picture shows the emperor with his three daughters and the three princes.

4 Focus on the linking words in the box and point out that as well as having different meanings, they are used in different ways in sentences (for example, *However* is usually used at the beginning of a sentence). Look at the first line from the story with the class and elicit the answer (see *Answers* below). Then get students to complete the exercise in pairs. Check answers with the class.

Answers

1 who
2 but
3 before
4 However
5 so
6 when
7 during
8 while
9 as soon as

5 Put students in pairs to compare the lines with the sentences in exercise 4. Elicit answers from the class.

Answers

There was once an old emperor who lived in an enormous, golden palace in the middle of the city Ping Chong. He had three beautiful daughters, but unfortunately no sons ...

The text is more interesting because there is more detail and there are more adjectives, adverbs, and adverbial phrases.

Get students to continue rewriting the story in their pairs, adding more detail and making it more interesting.

Alternatively, a nice interactive way of doing this is to put students in pairs and get them to copy the two sentences in the Student's Book onto a blank sheet of paper. Then ask them to write the next sentence, adding more detail. They then pass the sheet of paper on to the next pair. Pairs continue to write one sentence and pass the sheet on until the story is complete.

6 Tell students that they are going to write a folk tale or fairy story that they know. Emphasize that they should include details to make it interesting, and add adjectives and adverbs. Set this for homework. Collect it and mark it. You could put the marked stories on the classroom wall so that all the students can read each other's stories. Alternatively, bind the stories in an anthology, entitled *Folk Tales from around the World*, and leave it in the classroom or school library for students to read in their free time.

LISTENING AND SPEAKING (SB p28)

The first time I fell in love

The *Listening and speaking* section continues the theme of love with a series of recordings about falling in love for the first time. Students are introduced to the theme with a discussion task on quotations about love. The listening task consists of two monologues and an interview, and practises listening for specific information and note-taking. The post-listening section has an exercise on understanding figurative language from the recording.

1 Give students time to read through the quotations. Deal with any vocabulary queries. Put students into pairs/groups of three to discuss the quotations. Elicit a range of answers from the class.

Possible answers

You can't describe love, but you know it when you feel it.
Being in love can create very strong emotions.
You can't see your lover's faults.
You are nothing when you are not together, and when you are together you feel more than complete.
After the first effects of falling in love have faded, true love is what remains.
Love can bring great happiness but also great sadness and pain.

As an extension, elicit the English translation of any quotations students know about love from their own language(s).

2 **T 3.15** [CD 1: Track 40] Pre-teach/check the following vocabulary from the recording: *to go around with different people* (spend time with), *to hold hands*, *electric* (in this context, *very exciting*), *passion*, *upset* (adj.), *tummy* (informal for *stomach*), *to figure* (to think), *to hurt someone's feelings*, *to care what you look like* (to care about your appearance).

Write the names used in the recordings on the board: Max, Emma, and Ruth, and model the pronunciation. Get students to read the questions in the table so that they know what to listen for. Check comprehension of *reciprocated* (given back/returned). Remind students that when they listen they don't need to understand every word to be able to complete the chart.

Play the first two sentences of Sarah's recording and elicit the answers to questions 1 and 2. Play the recording through once and get students to complete as much of the chart as they can.

3 **T 3.15** [CD 1: Track 40] Put the students into groups of three or four to pool their answers. Play the recording again and get students to fill in any gaps, then elicit any reactions to the stories of first love from the class.

Answers and tapescript

	Sarah	Tommy	James
1 How old was he/she?	13	9	22
2 Who did he/she fall in love with?	a boy called Max (at her school)	a girl called Emma	a girl called Ruth
3 Was it a pleasurable experience?	Yes	No	Yes
4 Was the love reciprocated?	No, he didn't feel the same passion.	No, she didn't know he loved her.	Yes, she felt the same.
5 How did it end?	He went back to his friends and she went back to hers.	He thought he was too young to only love one person for the rest of his life.	They are still together after thirty years and they have four children.

T 3.15
The first time I fell in love
Sarah
The first time I fell in love was when I was 13. It was with a boy called Max. We were on a school trip, a geography trip, so a whole group of us were living together for a week. I'd never really noticed this boy before, because we used to go around with different people, but I suddenly started looking at him, and I remember thinking, 'Hmm! You're nice!' and I couldn't understand why I hadn't looked at him before. He was very quiet, and he had dark eyes that seemed to see everything, and he made me go all weak at the knees. We kind of started going out. When we held hands, it was electric! And the first time we kissed, I'd never felt anything like it in my life! Wow! I don't think he felt the same passion as me. He was very cool about everything. It only lasted a few months. Then he went back to his friends, and I went back to mine.

Tommy
T = **Tommy** **I** = **Interviewer**
T Well, I fell in love with a girl called Emma, but it didn't last very long.
I How long did it last?
T Well ... about two weeks. It all ended last Friday.
I Oh, dear! What happened last Friday?
T I decided that I'd had enough of being in love. I didn't like the feeling.
I Was Emma upset?
T Not really. She didn't know anything about it.
I What?
T No. I hadn't told her that I was in love with her, so she didn't know that it had ended.
I Was it so bad?
T Oh, yes. I couldn't sleep, I used to get this funny feeling here in my tummy when I saw her coming, and my heart went bang, bang, bang. It was horrible!
I So how did you manage to stop loving her?
T Well, I'm only 9, and I figured that I'm too young to only love one person for the rest of my life.
I Fair enough. I'm glad you didn't hurt her feelings.
T I'm glad it's all over.

James
Well, I've only been in love once in my life, and that was when I was 22. I'd had other girlfriends, of course, but it was never more than that. Just a girlfriend. And then I met this other girl, Ruth, and my whole life just turned upside down. I remember thinking at the time that I'd never felt anything like it. Nothing looked the same, felt the same, life had never been so amazing, so colourful. I wanted to do everything – climb mountains, fly like a bird, stay up all night – life was far too amazing to sleep. It's funny, I never used to care what I looked like, but suddenly I started to care. I wanted to look good for this girl in my life. I felt that I hadn't really lived until that moment, until I'd met her and fallen in love. Thank goodness she felt the same! We're still together. Thirty years and four kids later. Amazing, huh?

4 Elicit some examples of the effects of being in love, e.g. your heart beating fast. Explain that the recordings contain some figurative language used to talk about love. Refer students to **T 3.15** on Student's Book p121. Students work in pairs to find more examples.

Check answers with the class and elicit from the class the meanings of the expressions (see answers in brackets below).

Possible answers
... he made me go all weak at the knees. (He made her feel weak/ hardly able to stand because of the emotion experienced.)
... the first time we kissed, I'd never felt anything like it in my life. (Their first kiss created a new and very strong emotion.)
... I used to get this funny feeling here in my tummy. (He felt a strange reaction in his stomach.)
... my heart went bang, bang, bang. (His heart started to beat very fast.)
... my whole life just turned upside down. (His thoughts about his life changed completely and nothing was the same again.)

What do you think?

Focus attention on the *yin* and *yang* symbol. Ask students if they know what it symbolizes. (In Chinese philosophy, *yin* is the passive, dark female principle which combines with *yang*, the active, light male principle to form the whole world. There should be a balance of *yin* and *yang* in everything.)

Students work in small groups to discuss the questions. Elicit a range of students' ideas in a feedback session.

EVERYDAY ENGLISH (SB p29)

Giving opinions

This section assumes that students will be familiar with basic expressions for giving opinions, and also recycles some of the language from Unit 2, SB p17. The section extends the functional focus to include the form and intonation of question tags used to ask for agreement, and the use of adverbs to make opinions stronger. This includes a focus on voice range and is also an opportunity for students to give their own opinions on a range of people, things, and events.

1 **T 3.16** [**CD 1: Track 41**] Pre-teach/check the following items from the recording: *a sense of humour*, *to get on well together*, *that's rubbish* (a strong way of saying *I disagree*), *to adore each other*, *to fancy someone*.

Play the recording and get students to follow in their books. Elicit answers to the questions.

Get individual students to read lines of the conversation aloud. If necessary, drill the intonation of the lines, using the recording as a model. Put the students into groups of three to practise the conversation. Encourage them to read with expression and imitate the voice range of the original speakers.

Answers and tapescript
The conversation is about Meg, the speakers' friend, and her new boyfriend. A and B agree with each other; C disagrees.

T 3.16
A So, what do you think of Meg's new boyfriend? He's really great, isn't he?
B Definitely! I think he's absolutely fantastic!
A Mmm. Me too. I just love the stories he tells.
B So do I. He's very funny. I really like his sense of humour.
A They get on so well together, don't they?
C Well, maybe. He's quite nice, but I don't think that he's the one for her.
B That's rubbish! They absolutely adore each other!
C Mmm. I'm not so sure.
B Come on! You're just jealous. You've always fancied her.
C Actually, that's not true at all. But I quite like her sister.

2 **T 3.16** **[CD 1: Track 41]** Play the recording again and elicit the words A and B use to agree with each other.

Focus attention on the question tags A uses, and elicit the meaning they express. Play the sentences with the question tags again, and point out the falling intonation. Get students to practise the sentences.

Answers

1 Definitely! Me too. So do I.
2 She isn't really asking for information when using these tags; she is inviting the other speakers to agree with her.

3 **T 3.17** **[CD 1: Track 42]** Focus attention on the example. With weaker classes, elicit whether the question tags will be affirmative or negative (negative because the statements are in the affirmative). Then give students time to complete the exercise, working individually.

Play the recording and get students to check their answers. Play the recording again and elicit the intonation pattern (falling) and the reason why (the speakers aren't really asking questions, they are inviting others to agree with their opinion). Students practise saying the sentences with the correct intonation.

Answers and tapescript

T 3.17

1 We had a great time in Paris, **didn't we**?
2 The weather was lovely, **wasn't it**?
3 The French really love their food, **don't they**?
4 It's a lovely day today, **isn't it**?
5 Alice and Tom are a really lovely couple, **aren't they**?
6 Tom earns so much money, **doesn't he**?
7 They want to get married, **don't they**?

SPOKEN ENGLISH – Making an opinion stronger

1/2 Read the notes as a class. Practise the intonation of the phrases with the class, encouraging a wide voice range. Students then find more examples in the conversation in exercise 1. Check answers. Explain if necessary that *just* in *You're just jealous* has a different meaning (only) and does not have the function of making the speaker's opinion stronger.

Answers

He's absolutely fantastic.
I just love the stories ...
He's very funny.
I really like his sense of humour.
They absolutely adore each other.

4 **T 3.18** **[CD 1: Track 43]** Focus attention on the example. Then get pairs of students to read out each cue sentence and the stronger opinion. Drill the sentences as necessary, exaggerating the voice range to help students sound enthusiastic. Alternatively, let students change the sentences, working individually. Play the recording so that students can check their answers, then play the recording again and drill the sentences with the class, making sure that students use the correct intonation.

Answers and tapescript

T 3.18

1 **A** She's quite nice.
B She's absolutely wonderful!
2 **A** The film was good.
B The film was just brilliant!
3 **A** The hotel's all right.
B The hotel's really fabulous!
4 **A** I like dark chocolate.
B I absolutely adore dark chocolate.
5 **A** I quite like Peter.
B I really love Peter.
6 **A** The book wasn't very good.
B The book was absolutely awful!
7 **A** I don't like noisy bars.
B I just can't stand noisy bars!

5 This gives students the opportunity to practise giving and responding to opinions in a personalized way. Elicit an example for each of the items in the list. Remind students that they need to give sentences in the affirmative form and to include adverbs where possible to make their opinions stronger.

Possible answers

- The last film I saw was *La Vie en Rose*. The acting was absolutely amazing.
- I heard about the earthquake in Greece. It was really scary.
- It's really miserable today, isn't it?
- Karl is wearing a really nice sweater, isn't he?
- The Rolling Stones are touring again. I really think they should give up!
- I saw the new sitcom on TV. I thought it was absolutely awful.

6 Focus attention on the examples in the speech bubbles. Highlight the use of adverbs. Get students to read the example across the class. Drill the stress and intonation, encouraging a wide voice range.

Divide the class into pairs/groups of three to exchange their opinions. Remind students that they should also use question tags to invite agreement. Monitor and check for the use of question tags, adverbs to make opinions stronger, and enthusiastic-sounding intonation. If students sound rather reserved, write one or two of their examples on the board and rework them to give stronger opinions. Drill the pronunciation and then let students continue in their pairs/groups.

Don't forget!

Vocabulary revision

Units 1–3 (TB p149), with answers (TB p158)

Workbook Unit 3

Exercise 11 Vocabulary – Birth, marriage, and death
Exercise 12 Prepositions – *in* / *at* / *on* for time
Exercise 13 Pronunciation – Phonetic symbols – consonants
Exercise 14 Listening – Memories

Word list

Refer students to the Word list for Unit 3 (SB p153). They could translate the words, learn them at home, or transfer some of them to their vocabulary notebook.

4

Modal and related verbs
Phrasal verbs (1)
Polite requests and offers

Getting it right

Introduction to the unit

The theme of this unit is 'doing the right thing', and it includes a focus on giving advice, and on rules. This theme provides contexts for the modal verbs of advice, permission, and obligation. The grammar presentation includes a focus on modern dilemmas and appropriate advice.

The idea of 'rules for life' is presented in the *Listening and speaking* section, which includes a note-taking task on people's personal beliefs and a song by Ian Dury and the Blockheads. This section also contains a *Spoken English* feature on *have got to*.

The *Reading and speaking* section focuses on rules within the family, with an article on a modern family who spent two weeks living as if they were in the 1970s as part of a social experiment. There is also a language focus on understanding phrasal verbs, and this is carried through into the *Vocabulary and speaking* section, which covers both the meaning and form of common phrasal verbs.

The *Everyday English* focus is polite requests and offers, and the *Writing* syllabus continues with practice of combining sentences into paragraphs in a biography.

Language aims

Grammar – modal and related verbs Students revise and extend the modals of advice, obligation, and permission: *should/must* for advice, *must/have to* for obligation, *don't have to* for lack of obligation, *can/be allowed to* for permission.

Students should be familiar with the present form of the core modals *should, must,* and *can*. The past forms may present more of a problem, as will the subtle differences in meaning. These are clearly contrasted in the unit and students are given opportunities to practise them in controlled and freer activities.

POSSIBLE PROBLEMS

Students of different nationalities may try to express obligation and permission with phrases such as *It is necessary that you …* and *Is it possible for me to …?* They are unlikely to use modals spontaneously in these contexts and so will need plenty of practice in this language area.
If possible, find out how the concepts of advice, obligation, and permission are expressed in the students' own languages and highlight differences.

Mistakes with form can arise if the rules of regular verbs are applied to modals:

* *Do we must pay to park here?* * *Did you can stay up late as a child?*
* *You should to apologize.*

Have to can confuse. It is modal in use but follows the form rules of a full verb, with the auxiliary *do/don't*, etc. in negatives, questions, and past forms:

* *Had you to wear a uniform at school?* (rather than *Did you have to …?*)

Past and negative forms can also present problems, so these are revised in the *Starter* to the unit. You can refer students to Grammar Reference 4.3 on SB p137 for an introduction to modal verbs and the key issues of form.

Must and *have to* in the negative are often confused and so the difference needs to be carefully drawn:

You mustn't let the dog out. (It isn't allowed.)
You don't have to let the dog out. (It isn't necessary.)

Vocabulary This section focuses on phrasal verbs, both the meaning and form.

POSSIBLE PROBLEMS

Intermediate students should be familiar with a broad range of phrasal verbs, for recognition if not for active use. What may be new to them is the focus on form and the issues of word order with separable and inseparable verbs.

* *The baby doesn't take me after.* (inseparable verb: *The baby doesn't take after me.*)
* *If you don't know the meaning, look up it.* (separable verb but not when the object is a pronoun: *If you don't know the meaning, look it up.*)

Everyday English The syllabus continues with a focus on polite requests and offers. The approach taken here is functional, but Grammar Reference 4.6 on SB p138 covers the form and use of the modals used in requests and offers, and Grammar Reference 4.7 on SB p138 covers the use of *will* and *shall* for offers.

Notes on the unit

STARTER (SB p30)

This section aims to raise awareness of the key issues of form related to modal verbs.

Focus attention on the sentences and the verbs *can, must, should,* and *have to*. Ask students if they know what they are called (modal verbs). Get students to say them aloud. If necessary, highlight the weak forms in *can* and *have to*.

/kən/	/tə/
*You **can** go.*	*You have **to** go.*

Put students in pairs to work out the different forms, then elicit the answers. With weaker classes, also establish that there is no *-s* on the *he/she/it* forms.

Answers
1 You **can't** go. You **mustn't** go. You **shouldn't** go. You **don't have to** go.
2 **Can** you go? **Must** you go? **Should** you go? **Do** you **have to** go?
3 He **can** go. He **must** go. He **should** go. He **has to** go.
4 *Have to* is different. It is like a modal verb in meaning, but it is a full verb in form with an auxiliary (*do/don't*, etc.) in negatives and questions. *Can, must,* and *should* don't use an auxiliary to form negatives and questions.

If necessary, highlight the pronunciation in the following forms:

/kɑ:nt/	/kən/
*You **can't** go.*	***Can** you go?*

MODERN DILEMMAS (SB p30)

should/must/have to/be allowed to

ABOUT THE TEXT

Modern morals is a lifestyle feature in *The Times* newspaper and on *Times Online*. Contributors write in with a broad range of modern 'dilemmas', including family disputes, questions of fairness related to money, and matters of honesty and conscience. Other readers send in their replies with their opinion on the issue and often some advice.

'Crimestoppers' (in reply *a*) is an independent UK-wide charity which works to stop crime. People can call 'Crimestoppers' anonymously to give information about crimes.

1 Give students time to read the introduction about the *Modern morals* feature. With weaker classes, pre-teach/check the following vocabulary from the text: *to deal with, disagreeable, to dump, wireless network, to belong to, stepfather, disqualified, unemployment benefit* (informally known as *dole*), *to deny somebody something, a tantrum, a fuss*.

Get students to read the first text. Focus attention on the phrases in exercise 1 and elicit possible pieces of advice from the class, e.g. *I think he should ask his neighbour to stop. / I don't think he should get angry. / He must talk to his neighbour about the problem.*

Point out that to give a negative piece of advice, we usually say *I don't think (you) should*, rather than *I think (you) shouldn't*.

Put students into groups of three or four. Ask them to read the problems and discuss possible advice. Monitor and help as necessary. Also check students' use of the modal verbs and note any common errors to highlight when dealing with the *Grammar Spot*.

Ask each group to choose their favourite piece of advice for each problem. Elicit one or two examples for each problem and write them on the board or an OHT.

2 With weaker classes, pre-teach/check *to confront someone*. Focus attention on the replies a–g and get students to match them to the problems, working individually. Check the answers with the class.

Answers
1d 2c 3g 4a 5b 6e 7f

Refer students to SB p149 and ask them to read the full replies. Ask students what they think of the advice. Get them to vote for the best piece of advice for each problem, choosing between the readers' replies and their own examples on the board/OHT.

3 Elicit the question used to ask for advice in problem 1, and the verb or phrase used to give advice in reply *a* (see *Answers* below). Students work individually and continue finding the questions and verbs/phrases. Check answers with the class.

Answers
1 How should I deal with my difficult and disagreeable neighbour?
2 Is it OK to greet people you don't know with a 'how are you?' / Should I be less friendly in my greetings?
3 Is it right for me to use it?
4 Should we keep quiet or inform the police?
5 What do you think?
6 Is it wrong for me to record CDs borrowed from my local library?
7 Is it ever permissible to lie to children?

a must; don't have to
b are allowed; should
c don't have to
d 've got to; should
e are not allowed to
f should; have to
g must

GRAMMAR SPOT (SB p31)

1 Students read the sentences and question. Elicit the answer.

Answer
You must tell your neighbour.
Must is generally stronger than *should* for giving advice.

2 Students read the sentences and discuss the answers in pairs. Check the answers with the class. Point out that modals of obligation (*must/have to*) and permission (*can/be allowed to*) can also be used to make suggestions or give advice, as in the readers' replies on SB p31.

Answer
I can/I am allowed to go express permission.
I must/I have to go express obligation.

3 Students complete the sentences and then check their answers in pairs. Check the answers with the class.

Answers
Children **have to** go to school.
You **mustn't** ride your bike on the footpath.
People over 65 **don't have to** go to work.

If students, have problems distinguishing *mustn't* and *don't have to*, write two parallel sentences on the board for analysis. Elicit which means 'it isn't allowed' and which means 'it isn't necessary'.

You mustn't let the dog out. He has hurt his leg. (It isn't allowed.)

You don't have to let the dog out. I took him for a walk this morning. (It isn't necessary.)

4 Elicit the past of the two sentences.

Answer
I **had to** go.

Refer students to Grammar Reference 4.1–4.5 on SB p137–8.

PRACTICE (SB p31)

Discussing grammar

1 **T 4.1** [CD 1: Track 44] Elicit the correct verb for sentence 1 (see *Answers* below). Put students in pairs to complete the task.

Play the recording and get students to check their answers.

Answers and tapescript

T 4.1

1 I don't get on with my boss. Do you think I **should** look for another job?
2 We're giving Tom a surprise birthday party. You **mustn't** tell him about it.
3 Please Dad, **can** I go to Tom's party? It'll be great!
4 You **have to** drive on the left in Britain.
5 Do you **have to** wear a uniform in your job?
6 Are you **allowed to** take mobile phones to school?
7 I **had to** go to bed early when I was a child.
8 You **don't have to** go to England to learn English, but it's a good idea.

Giving advice

2 **T 4.2** [CD 1: Track 45] Tell students they are going to hear three conversations in which people discuss a problem and give advice. Give students time to read the questions to know what to listen for. With weaker classes, pre-teach/check *to have friends over, to clear up (after a party), embarrassing, windscreen, to pay a fine.*

Play conversation 1 as an example and elicit the answers. (See *Answers* below). Play the rest of the recording. Students answer the questions about conversations 2 and 3. Check the answers with the class.

Elicit students' opinions of the advice given in the three conversations. Ask students for alternative advice. If students make mistakes with the modal verbs, write the sentences on the board and get the whole class to correct them.

Answers and tapescript

Conversation 1
The girl is worried about going to a friend's party because her friend's parents said she wasn't allowed to have friends over. Their parents are also best friends. The boy advises her not to tell her mum and dad but to go to the party and to help to clear up after it.

Conversation 2
The woman is angry because another woman is smoking in a non-smoking restaurant. She wants to tell her to stop. The man doesn't want her to say anything because he thinks it is embarrassing.

Conversation 3
The girl got a parking ticket when she went shopping for her dad. She doesn't want to pay it. Her friend doesn't give any advice, but the girl thinks she shouldn't pay the fine.

T 4.2

Conversation 1
A Are you going to Charlotte's party?
B I don't know if I should go or not.
A What do you mean?
B Well, her parents are abroad and they told her she wasn't allowed to have friends over while they were away.
A Oh, come on! You must come. It's a party. Everyone has parties when their parents are away.
B Yeah, but her mum and dad are best friends with mine.
A Look. You don't have to tell your mum and dad. Just go to the party and help to clear up after.
B I'm not sure.

Conversation 2
A Do you see that woman over there?
B Yeah, what about her?
A She's smoking!
B So?
A You're not allowed to smoke in here.
B Well ...
A Do you think I should tell her to stop?
B No, no, you mustn't say anything. It's embarrassing. The waiter will tell her.
A No! I can't just sit here. I must say something. Er – excuse me ...

Conversation 3
A I'm so mad!
B Why?
A I've got a parking ticket. I had to go to the shops for my dad and when I got back to the car there was a ticket on the windscreen.
B Oh, that's bad luck!
A I think *he* should pay the fine.
B Who? Your dad? Why? He wasn't driving.
A Yeah, but I was doing *his* shopping.
B But he didn't tell you to park illegally.
A OK, OK so it's my fault. Er – I still think he should pay it.

3 **T 4.2** [CD 1: Track 45] Play the first two lines from conversation 1. Elicit the missing word from sentence 1 (see *Answers* below).

Play the rest of the recording and get students to complete the sentences. Check the answers by getting students to read the sentences aloud. Drill the pronunciation as necessary, using the recording as a model.

Answers
1 I don't know if I **should** go or not.
2 They told her she **wasn't allowed** to have friends over while they were away.
3 Come on! You **must** come. It's a party.
4 Look. You **don't have to** tell your mum and dad.
5 You're **not allowed** to smoke in here.
6 Do you think I **should** tell her to stop?
7 No, no, you **mustn't** say anything.
8 No! I **must** say something
9 I **had to** go to the shops for my dad.
10 I think he **should** pay the fine.

Put students in new pairs and refer them to the tapescripts on SB p122. Get them to practise the conversations in their pairs. Encourage them to read with enthusiasm, and remind them about the importance of voice range. If students sound rather flat, play the recording again and get students to repeat chorally and individually. Allow them to mark the main stresses in each line if this will help them when they practise the conversations again.

SUGGESTION

You can extend the practice on giving advice in a freer, more personalized activity. Write a series of problems/ situations on the board/an OHT, e.g.

You keep getting headaches.
Your brother always drives too fast.
Your sister is always borrowing your clothes without asking.
Your friends Jenny and Paul are only 16, but they want to get married.
Your friend can't manage to give up smoking.
Your brother keeps failing his driving test because of nerves.
A group of teenagers make a lot of noise outside your flat every evening.
You want to get fit.
You want to go abroad to practise your English.

Elicit a range of advice for the first situation. If students have problems with the pronunciation, get them to mark the main stresses and then drill the intonation.

I don't think you should work so long at your computer.

You've got to learn to relax more.

You must see a doctor.

Put students in pairs. Tell them to alternate between reading the situations and giving advice. Monitor and check for accurate use of the modals. Make a note of any common errors and feed back on them in a later lesson.

Rules present

1 This task provides some personalized fluency practice. In a multilingual class, a discussion on different laws can be interesting and informative.

Students work in pairs to read through the sentences and note whether the laws are the same or different in their country. Put students in groups of four to discuss the sentences. In multilingual groups, put students of different nationalities together. Monitor and help as necessary. Make a note of any common errors and feed back on them in a later lesson. Don't interrupt to correct during the discussion stage, as this is a fluency task.

2 Put students in groups of four to discuss the questions. In multilingual groups, put students of different nationalities together. Allow students time for discussion, then ask each group to feed back to the class on the laws they discussed.

Rules past

3 Exercises 3–5 are on the theme of schooldays and school rules and regulations. Introduce the topic by asking the class:
What are children allowed to do at school nowadays?
What mustn't they do?
What were you allowed to do when you were young?
What couldn't you do?
Elicit a range of answers.

Give students time to read the text. Deal with any vocabulary queries. Put students into pairs to choose the correct verbs in the sentences. Remind them to choose their answers according to the information in the text. Check the answers.

Answers
1 didn't have to 2 had to 3 weren't allowed to

4 This exercise sets out some school rules from Victorian schools. Check comprehension of *Ma'am* (short for *Madam*), *do woodwork*, and *do needlework*. Focus attention on the example. Then get students to discuss and complete the rules, working in their pairs.

Check the answers with the class. Ask: *What do you think of the rules? Were they sensible or just silly?* Elicit students' opinions.

Answers
2 had to
3 weren't allowed to
4 had to
5 didn't have to
6 had to; had to
7 weren't allowed to
8 weren't allowed to

5 **T 4.3** [**CD 1: Track 46**] This listening task consists of an anecdote told by a woman about her great-grandmother's schooldays. Pre-teach/check these items from the script: *great-grandma*, *bright* (intelligent), *great-great grandpa*, *domestic servant*. Play the recording through once and get students to discuss what the problem was. Check the answer.

Elicit the start of the story from a confident student. Students continue telling the story in their own words, working in pairs. With weaker students, write key words on the board as prompts.

Give an anecdote from your parents' or grandparents' schooldays as an example. Give students a few minutes to decide on their story. Feed in any vocabulary students ask for. Elicit some anecdotes from the class. In larger classes, students can exchange stories in groups.

As an optional follow-up, ask students to write up their stories. If appropriate, they can be displayed on the classroom walls for the class to read.

Answer and tapescript
Alice was very bright and when she was 11 the teacher said she had learnt everything the teacher knew and she couldn't teach her any more. She wasn't allowed to leave school and so she had to sit at the back of the room for a year. He father was angry because he wanted her to leave school to earn money.

T 4.3
Great-grandma Alice
This is a story that my great-grandma, Alice, loved telling about her schooldays. She started school when she was five and, apparently, she was very bright. Anyway, that's what she told us, and when she was 11 the teacher, Miss Fox, came to her and said: 'Alice, you've learnt everything that I know. I can't teach you any more now but you're not allowed to leave school until you're 12 years old, so you'll just have to sit at the back of the class.' So that's what great-grandma Alice did, she sat at the back for a whole year and her dad, my great-great grandpa, was really angry 'cos he wanted her to be out earning money for the family. She was a domestic servant.

ADDITIONAL MATERIAL

Workbook Unit 4
Exercise 1 Modal verbs – Recognizing verb forms
Exercises 2–7 Modal verbs – Obligation
Exercises 8–9 Modal verbs – *should* for advice
Exercise 10 Modal verbs – Permission and ability
Exercise 11 Modal verbs – Obligation and permission

LISTENING AND SPEAKING (SB p33)

Rules for Life

ABOUT THE LISTENING
This section contains two listening tasks, both on the theme of personal beliefs and philosophies. The first is a series of monologues in which three people of different ages set out their personal beliefs. The task is listening for the main ideas and note-taking, and students are given the opportunity to say if they agree with the speakers or not. This task also provides examples of *have/has got to* as part of the *Spoken English* syllabus.

The second listening task is a song called *I believe* by the British band *Ian Dury and the Blockheads*. There are some short biographical notes about Ian Dury on SB p33. The additional information below might also be useful.

Ian Dury
Ian Dury was born in 1942 in Middlesex, in the south of England. He contracted polio as a child and this left him with physical disabilities but also with a strong independent streak. He left school and studied at art college before winning a place at the Royal College of Art. He then taught art at various colleges in the south of England.

He formed his first band *Kilburn and the High Roads* in 1971 but it was with the *Blockheads* that Dury found fame and popularity with both fans and critics. Dury became well known for his lyrics, which were a clever combination of lyrical poetry, word play, observations of British everyday life, and down-to-earth humour.

Ian Dury and The Blockheads had several hit singles, including *What a Waste, Hit Me With Your Rhythm Stick* (which was a UK number one at the beginning of 1979) and *Reasons to be Cheerful, Part Three*. The song *I believe* was written by Dury and the keyboard player Mickey Gallagher. It appeared on the CD *Ten More Turnips from the Tip* which was released in 2002, two years after Dury had died from cancer. Since his death, the *Blockheads* have continued to play live, performing a mixture of old and new material.

1 **T 4.4** **[CD 1: Track 47]** Focus attention on the photos and ask students what they think each person's general attitude to life is.

Pre-teach/check the following items from the recording:

Millie: *fame, and the like* (in this context, *and people like that*), *bodyguard*, *fair enough* (in this context, *that's fine*), *scary stuff* (informal for *a scary situation/thing*).

Richard: *to get something out of life, to put something in to life, to have a part to play.*

Frank: *to look for the good in people, to go on and on about something* (to complain), *a menace.*

Play Millie's recording as far as ... *I would hate to be famous.* Elicit her first point and write it on the board in note form. Play the rest of the recording and elicit a summary of what Millie says. Complete the notes on the board (see *Answers* below).

Play the rest of the recording. Students take notes about Richard and Frank, and then compare answers in pairs.

Check the answers, playing the recording again if students have missed any of the main points.

Answers and tapescript
Millie: She would hate to be famous; it's frightening to be rich and famous; film stars, footballers etc. always followed and photographed, have to employ bodyguards; she just wants to enjoy her work; she doesn't mind if she doesn't earn lots of money; she never wants to be famous; it's too scary.

Richard: You only get out of life what you put in; you should never ask about the meaning of life, as you will never find the answer; you should give meaning to your life by what you do with your life; everyone has a place in the world, and has a part to play.

Frank: You have to look for the good in people and things; lots of older people complain all the time about traffic, danger of mobiles, etc.; they complain most about young people, saying they are loud and impolite, worse than in past; he doesn't agree; there has always been good and bad in the world; you should look for the good, and find 3 things every day to be happy about.

T 4.4
Rules for life
1 Millie (15)
Well, so many teenagers seem to think life is about just one thing, you know – money and fame, they think it will bring them happiness. Honestly, I would hate to be famous. When I read the magazines, and see all the photos of these rich, famous film stars, footballers and the like, it frightens me. They can't move without being followed and photographed. Often they've got to employ bodyguards. When I grow up I just want to enjoy my work, if I earn lots of money, fair enough, but if I don't I'll still be happy. I never want to be famous. That's scary stuff.

2 Richard (33)
My rule for life is that you only get out of life what you put in. I mean, you should never ask that question people always ask 'Why are we here? What is the meaning of life?' – you'll never find the answer. You've got to *give* meaning to your life by what you *do* with your life – er ... and I think you can do this in all kinds of ways. I mean, it doesn't matter if you are president of your country or a rubbish collector – you have a place in the world, you have a part to play.

3 Frank (65)
I believe you've got to look for the good in people and things. So many people of my age do nothing but complain about today's world – oh, on and on they go about – ooh, how bad the traffic is, or how mobile phones are such a menace. Oh, and most of all they complain – about young people – they're loud, they're impolite, not like in the 'good old days'. Well, I say 'rubbish' to all that. There's always been good and bad in the world and I think we should look for the good. The rule I try to live by is find three things every day to be happy about.

2 Give students time to think about whether they agree with the speakers and note their answers in the table. Ask students if they think the speakers are optimists or pessimists (all three seem to take a fairly optimistic view of life). Then get students to compare the speakers' opinions with their own, working in pairs/small groups.

SPOKEN ENGLISH – *have got to*

1 Focus attention on the *Spoken English* box. Give students time to read the notes and the examples. Point out that these forms are usually contracted in spoken English (*I've/he's got to*, etc.). Point out also that in the negative, we tend to say, *I don't have to*, not *I haven't got to*.

2 **T 4.5** [CD 1: Track 48] Focus attention on the example. Students complete the sentences, working individually. Play the recording so that students can check.

Elicit the extra information in the speakers' answers. Play the recording again if necessary and check the answers with the class (see underlining in the script below).

Highlight the pronunciation of *got to* /ˈgɒtə/ in the sentences. Students then practise the conversations in pairs.

Refer students to Grammar Reference 4.2 on SB p137.

Answers and tapescript

T 4.5

1 **A** Isn't your mum away at the moment?
B Yeah, so Dad's **got to** do all the cooking and I've got to do all the ironing.

2 **A** Where's my briefcase? **I've got to** go to work.
B It's where you left it when you came home. In the hall by the front door.

3 **A** Mum, why can't I go out now?
B You've **got to** tidy your room first. Your friends will just have to wait.

4 **A** Won't you be late for work?
B Oh, goodness. Look at the time **I've got to** go now. I mustn't stay here chatting. We'll catch up later. Bye!

Song – *I Believe*

3 Focus attention on the photo and get students to read the note about Ian Dury. Elicit the answer to the question and any other information students know about him and his music. (See the notes on Ian Dury above.)

4 **T 4.6** [CD 1: Track 49] Play the recording through once and ask if Ian is an optimist or pessimist (an optimist). Elicit any examples from the song of his positive attitude.

T 4.6
Song (Ian Dury and the Blockheads)
I believe
I believe in **bottle banks**
And beauty from within
I believe in saying **thanks**
And fresh **air** on the skin

I believe in healthy **walks**
As tonic for the feet
I believe in serious talks
And **just enough** to eat

Chorus
That's what I believe
Surprising as it seems
I believe that happiness
Is well within our dreams

I believe in being **nice**
In spite of what you think
I believe in good **advice**
And not too much to **drink**

I believe in being **true**
In everything you try to **do**
I believe in me and you
I hope you share my **point of view**

Chorus (*repeat*)

I believe in being **kind**
Especially when it's hard
I believe an open **mind**
Can show a fine regard

I believe that **manners** make
A person good to know
I believe in birthday **cake**
And going **with the flow**

Chorus (*repeat*)

That's what I believe
Although it seems naïve
I believe that **peace and love**
Are there to be achieved

That's what I believe ...

5 **T 4.6** [CD 1: Track 49] Refer students to SB p150.

Put students in pairs to read the song and discuss which words best fit the gaps.

Play the song again so that students can check their answers.

Answers
See bold words in **T 4.6** above.

6 **T 4.6** [CD 1: Track 49] Play the recording again and get students to check their answers. Give students time to look at the list and tick the things that Ian believes in. Check the answers with the class.

Answers
1 Recycling rubbish. ✓
2 Healthy outdoor activities. ✓
3 Having lots to eat and drink. ✗
4 Being truthful and kind. ✓
5 Having strong opinions about everything. ✗
6 Good manners. ✓
7 Putting yourself first. ✗
8 Peace not war is possible. ✓

7 Ask students which of the things in exercise 6 are important to them. Brainstorm other examples, e.g. having a close family, enjoying nature, having a worthwhile job, etc. Try to establish one or two things that are important to most of the class.

WRITING (SB p106)

A biography – Combining sentences

This section helps students understand how to combine sentences into paragraphs. The tasks are based on a biography of the missionary Mother Teresa. Students go on to research and write a short biography of a person that they admire.

The section starts with an information-sharing exercise about Mother Teresa. The texts contain fairly detailed biographical details about her, so you might want to read them before the lesson.

1 Focus attention on the photos of Mother Teresa and her work. Give students a few moments to note down ideas and information. Elicit a range of answers and collate the information on the board under headings, e.g. *early life*, *work with the poor*, etc. Feed in key vocabulary at this stage: *missionary*, *convent*, *slums*, *to be awarded the Nobel Peace Prize* (named after Alfred Nobel, the Swedish inventor of dynamite), *funeral*.

2 Focus attention on the first two facts in A and how they are combined in B (a relative clause with *who*). Students work in pairs to continue the task. Remind them to note all the ways in which the sentences combine.

Answers
The sentences combine in the following ways: relative clauses, linking place and date of birth to avoid repetition of *she was born*, a present participle clause *leaving her mother ...*

3 Give students a few moments to read through the notes in the section *Working as a teacher*. Elicit the missing information for the first gap in the paragraph in B (see *Answers* below). Students complete the paragraph, working in their pairs. Give students time to compare their version with another pair and discuss any differences or make corrections.

Check the answers with the class.

Answer
From a very young age Agnes had wanted **to become a missionary**, so in September 1928 she **left home** to join **a convent** in Ireland, where she was given **the name Teresa**. A few months later, in **January 1929**, she was sent to **India** to teach at **St Mary's High School Convent** in Calcutta. Here she worked for **over 20 years**, first as Sister **Teresa** and finally, in 1937, as Mother Teresa.

4 Follow the same procedure as exercise 3 for the section *Working with the poor*. When students have completed the text, get them to read their paragraph aloud to the class. Encourage students to discuss any differences or make corrections as each pair reads their version.

Elicit an agreed version of the wording. Then get students to underline the ways ideas and facts have been combined (see underlining in the *Answer* below). Also ask students to find examples of the Past Perfect to express an action happening before another action in the past (*she had felt*, *had spread*).

Answer
Mother Teresa finally left **St Mary's Convent** on August 17, 1948. <u>Two years earlier</u>, in **1946**, she had felt called by **God** to help **the poorest of the poor**, <u>so</u> she started visiting **families in the slums of Calcutta**, <u>looking **after**</u> sick **and dying children**. In 1950 she started **a religious community** called the Missionaries of Charity, <u>which</u> by the 1960s and 70s had spread **all over the world**. In 1979 Mother Teresa **was awarded the Nobel Peace Prize**. She continued to work **amongst the poor** <u>despite developing</u> **severe health problems**. <u>When she finally **died**</u> on September 5, 1997, thousands of people **from all over the world came to her funeral**.

5 Set the planning and research for the writing task as homework. Ask students if they need any help with their notes and then get them to write their biography. If appropriate, ask students to exchange their first drafts and make suggestions as to how to improve them. Students' final drafts can be displayed on the classroom walls and you can organize a class vote for the most interesting biography.

READING AND SPEAKING (SB p34)

Kids then and now

ABOUT THE TEXT
The overall theme of rules and behaviour is carried through with an article on children's lives in the past and present. The article describes an experiment by a TV company in which a wealthy family were taken back to the 1970s to live a much more frugal lifestyle, as the father of the family had done. The documentary, by the

UK TV company Channel 4, is representative of a type of 'reality TV' in which people learn about the past by watching others live the conditions of that period in as realistic a way as possible.

Milton Keynes /mɪltən 'ki:nz/, where the family live, is a large town in South-East England, about 45 miles (75 km) north-west of London. Leeds /li:dz/, where the father was born, is a large industrial and business centre in the north of England.

The tasks include detailed comprehension, prediction, and language work on understanding phrasal verbs in context. (This acts as a lead-in to the *Vocabulary and speaking* section that follows.)

The exploitation of the article includes language activities and dictionary work, but if you are short of time, or with weaker classes, you could pre-teach/check the following vocabulary: *cuddly (toys), hi-tech, the running of the house, discipline, thrift, to dig (the vegetable garden), to adjust* (to get used to something), *hair mousse, 'Sunday Best'* (a person's best clothes, only worn on special occasions or, traditionally, for church), *a demand.*

1 Students close their eyes and think of their childhood bedroom. Elicit examples of what it was like and what was in it. Establish if there were many electronic items.

Sample answers
Books, furniture, a lamp, a desk, toys

The number and type of electronic items will depend on your students' ages, but possible items include: a radio, a record player, a cassette player.

2 Focus attention on the introduction to the article.

See *About the text* above for notes on pre-teaching vocabulary. Set a time limit of one to two minutes for students to read the introduction. Put students into pairs to discuss the questions in exercise 2. Check the answers and elicit students' opinions in question 4.

Answers
1 It usually had some books, a few toys, and a desk.
2 Because it probably has a computer and other hi-tech toys.
3 Because it probably has electronic items and also sports equipment, designer clothes, and accessories such as watches or jewellery.
4 Do they have everything and appreciate nothing? Students' own answers to this questions.

3 See *About the text* above for notes on pre-teaching vocabulary. Focus attention on the photo of the family and ask students who they think the people in the family are. Tell students that the family members are the father, Jon, the mother, Emma, the daughter, Hannah /'hænə/, and the son, Josh /dʒɒʃ/.

Ask students to read the title and predict the type of experiment the family participated in. Elicit a range of ideas, but do not confirm or reject answers at this stage.

4 Students work individually to check the vocabulary from the text, looking up new words in a dictionary if possible. If students don't have access to dictionaries, deal with any vocabulary queries as a class. You may need to explain the significance of the reference to a *council house* in paragraph 2: this was housing built and owned by a local government authority, usually provided at a low rent and often lived in by working class people.

Give students time to predict what happened in the experiment. Put students into pairs to compare their ideas. Elicit a few predictions from individual students, but do not confirm or reject ideas at this stage.

5 Set a time limit of about three minutes for students to read paragraphs 1–5 of the text and check their ideas. Elicit any initial reactions to the experiment, and ask students if they had predicted correctly.

6 Allow students time to read the questions. Students read the text again and underline the information they need to answer the questions. Students check their answers in pairs before a whole-class check.

Answers
1 He set up his own business.
2 Jon grew up in a small council house. His childhood was very disciplined. He had to walk to school and share all the household chores. He had to do as he was told because his dad was very strict.
3 The children had to eat the food that they were given. They had to wash and iron their clothes, do all the washing up and help to dig the vegetable garden.
4 The family had to go back to the 1970s and the same childhood as Jon. All the modern gadgets and equipment were taken away.
5 They had to wash and iron their clothes, do all the washing up and help to dig the vegetable garden. Hannah wasn't allowed to buy hair mousse or to wear all her clothes. Josh had to give up watching wide-screen TV and take up the piano.
6 At first, there were tears and rows. Hannah was horrified when her clothes were taken away, and both children were embarrassed about the van. Gradually, they learned to appreciate the little things in life and understood the value of money.
7 They baked cookies and sold them to their neighbours. Hannah did extra jobs around the house.
8 You shouldn't give in to children's demands.

Vocabulary work

This exercise focuses on phrasal verbs in context. With weaker students, tell them the paragraph number where each verb appears:

1 – Introduction
2 – paragraph 1
3 – paragraph 2
4 – paragraph 4
5 – paragraph 5
6 – final paragraph

Students work individually to find the phrasal verbs. Check the answers with the class.

Answers
1 push up
2 set up
3 brought up
4 give up; take up
5 dug up
6 give in

SUGGESTION
As an extension, or for homework, get students to write personalized sentences using the phrasal verbs in *Vocabulary work*.

What do you think?

Put students in groups to discuss the question and write the list of rules. Remind them of the structures they can use for their rules:

You must (help with the chores).
You mustn't (leave the washing-up).
You have to (listen when others are talking).
You've got to (let other people watch their favourite programmes).
You're not allowed to (help yourself from the fridge).

Monitor and help as necessary.

Students read out their rules. If appropriate, get students to vote for their top 10 rules for domestic harmony!

SUGGESTION
As an extension, you can get students to write a list of rules for the classroom and for the smooth running of lessons. Students can vote for the top 10 and then write them up and display them on the classroom walls.

EXTRA IDEA
Song **After T 4.6** [CD 2: Track 2]
Our house TB p150
This is intended as a fun activity, which you may like to include at the end of a lesson. Students choose the correct words in the song, and then listen and check. There are also two comprehension/interpretation tasks. The answers are on TB p158.

VOCABULARY AND SPEAKING (SB p36)

Phrasal verbs (1)

The aim here is to help students understand that phrasal verbs can be literal or idiomatic, and to introduce them to the rules for using different types of phrasal verb.

Literal or idiomatic meanings?

1 Check comprehension of *literal* and *idiomatic*. Focus attention on the cartoons and elicit the answers to the questions. Also elicit a synonym for the idiomatic meanings.

Answers
His business has really **taken off**. – idiomatic = become successful
She **took** her boots **off**. – literal
The flight to Singapore **took off**. – idiomatic = left the ground

2 Focus attention on the first set of sentences and elicit the answers. Students work in pairs to complete the task.

Check the answers. Elicit a synonym for the idiomatic meanings (see text in brackets below).

Answers
1 a idiomatic (raised/educated)
 b literal
 c idiomatic (started to talk about)
2 a idiomatic (be successful in; pass)
 b idiomatic (get a connection)
 c literal
3 a idiomatic (isolated; made impossible to reach)
 b idiomatic (the connection has been interrupted)
 c literal
4 a idiomatic (improved)
 b literal
 c idiomatic (learned without formal training)

Separable or inseparable?

3 Write the following examples on the board to present/review the meaning of separable and inseparable:

put up (separable)	We put up the pictures. We put the pictures up.
run across (inseparable)	Don't run across the road. ~~Don't run the road across~~.

Focus attention on the examples in exercise 3. Elicit the rule for separable verbs that when the object is a pronoun it always comes *between* the verb and the particle.

Students complete the task, working individually. Check the answers.

Answers
3 He took it up when he retired.
4 We picked it up very quickly.
5 I looked them up in my dictionary.
6 They brought them up really well.
7 I've given it up at last.

4 Focus attention on the example. Students work in pairs to complete the task. Check the answers.

Answers
2 Nearly everyone got through it.
3 We looked after them.
4 He gets on well with her.
5 I'm looking for them.
6 They're looking forward to it.
7 We couldn't put up with it any longer.

Talking about you

5 **T 4.7** [CD 2: Track 3] This task gives students the opportunity to use common phrasal verbs in a personalized way. Elicit the answer to sentence 1. Students complete the task, working individually. Check the answers, but don't play the recording at this stage. With weaker classes, do a quick check of the meaning of the phrasal verbs by eliciting a synonym.

Put students in pairs to ask and answer the questions. Monitor and help as necessary. Play the recording and let students compare their answers with the recording.

Answers and tapescript

T 4.7

1 **A** Who do you take **after** in your family?
B Mmm ... I don't think I take after anyone in particular. Mind you the older I get, the more I think I'm like my mother. Humph!

2 **A** Do you get on well **with** both your parents?
B Yes, I do. Most of the time. I do a lot of stuff with my dad. Football and things.

3 **A** Have you recently taken **up** any new sports or hobbies?
B Me? No! My life's too busy already!

4 **A** Do you often look **up** words in your dictionary?
B Sometimes, if I'm really stuck.

5 **A** Are you looking forward **to** going on holiday soon?
B I wish! I've just been on holiday so I've got to wait till Christmas now.

6 **A** Do you pick **up** foreign languages easily?
B Well, I picked up Italian quite easily when I was living in Milan, but I already knew French, so I think that helped a bit.

7 **A** Have you got any bad habits that you want to give **up**?
B Yes, I bite my nails. I just can't stop and I'm a teacher so I have to hide my hands from the kids 'cos I don't want to set a bad example.

SUGGESTION

It's a good idea to get students to think about how to record phrasal verbs as part of their vocabulary learning. Refer them back to the discussion they had in Unit 1 about recording vocabulary (see SB p13 and TB p15). Elicit the information that would be useful when recording a phrasal verb, e.g. ask students to think about whether it would be better to record by verb (e.g. *Phrasal verbs with look*) or by lexical set (e.g. *Phrasal verbs to do with travelling*). Ask how they could record whether a verb is separable or inseparable, and ask whether they think it would be better to give an example sentence, especially with phrasal verbs with an idiomatic meaning, or a translation where there is a clear equivalent in their own language. You could do a few example entries for a vocabulary record as a class.

Don't forget to review phrasal verbs at regular intervals. You can do this by giving students synonyms in context and eliciting the phrasal verbs, reviewing the difference in meaning when you add a different particle to a base verb, e.g. *look for/after/up*, etc. Making flashcards is also a good way of getting students to work with phrasal verbs. They can be used in matching activities, as cues for sentence building, and in games such as pelmanism. Students can also create gapped sentences or multiple choice tasks for each other as a homework activity.

ADDITIONAL MATERIAL

Workbook Unit 4

Exercise 12 Phrasal verbs – separable or inseparable?

EVERYDAY ENGLISH (SB p37)

Polite requests and offers

Intermediate students should be familiar with a number of basic ways of making requests and offers. The activities in this section aim to extend their range, both receptively and productively. There is grammar support for the modals in this section in Grammar Reference 4.6–4.7 on SB p138. You could get students to read through this section before the lesson. The use of *will* for offers is dealt with in Grammar Reference 4.7 on SB p138, and this use of *will* is presented and practised in more detail in Unit 5.

1 **T 4.8** **[CD 2: Track 4]** Focus on the example, then put students in pairs to match the rest of the lines. Encourage them to pool their knowledge and use the context to deal with vocabulary problems, but be prepared to answer individual queries as they arise. Remind students to think about who is talking and where.

Refer students to Grammar Reference 4.6–4.7 on SB p138. If students haven't read this for homework, they could look at it after the class, if you are short of time.

Play the recording so that students can check their answers. Elicit who is talking and where (see suggested answers in brackets).

Answers and tapescript

1 g (two friends/members of same family, possibly at home)
2 f (customer talking to a shop assistant in a gift shop/department store)
3 d (driver talking to a cashier at a petrol station)
4 a (customer talking to a cashier in a fast-food restaurant/café)
5 c (caller talking to the operator)
6 h (two people at work, working on a computer)
7 e (one driver talking to another, possibly in a car park/the street)
8 b (two people talking to each other, possibly in a waiting room)

T 4.8

1 **A** I'll give you a lift into town if you like.
B That would be great. Could you drop me at the library?

2 **A** It's a present. Do you think you could gift-wrap it for me?
B Yes, of course. I'll just take the price off.

3 **A** Pump number 5. And could you give me a token for the car wash?
B I'm sorry, it's not working today.

4 **A** Two large Cokes, please.
B Diet or regular?

5 **A** Can you tell me the code for Tokyo, please?
B One moment, I'll have to look it up.

6 **A** Could you show me how you did that?
B Certainly. Just go to 'Systems Preferences' and click on 'Displays'.

7 **A** Would you mind moving your car?
B Oh, sorry, I didn't realize that you couldn't get through.

8 **A** Would you mind if I opened the window?
B Go ahead. It's very stuffy in here.

MUSIC OF ENGLISH

1 T 4.9 [CD 2: Track 5] Read the notes with the class, then play the recording and get students to repeat. Model the pronunciation yourself if necessary, exaggerating the intonation to help students reproduce it.

> **T 4.9**
> Could you show me how you did that?
> Would you mind moving your car?

2 T 4.8 [CD 2: Track 4] Play the conversations again and drill the lines individually and chorally. Students then practise the conversations in pairs. Listen and monitor, and be prepared to drill some of the lines again if necessary.

2 T 4.10 [CD 2: Track 6] Play the first conversation and elicit the topic. Play the rest of the recording and get students to write down their answers.

Check the answers with the class.

Answers and tapescript

1 two friends arranging to meet for lunch
2 two friends arranging to meet after work for a drink and watch some sport
3 a husband talking to his wife about his day at work and his wife asking him to look after the baby
4 two colleagues/friends talking about a problem with a computer

T 4.10

1 **A** Hello it's me again. I've just remembered that I have a doctor's appointment in the morning. Could we possibly make it lunch instead of coffee?
B Erm ..., no problem. I can do lunch too. How about 12.30 in the usual restaurant?

2 **A** Would you mind if we didn't go out for a drink after work? I want to watch the match on TV.
B Hey, we could have a drink at Bar Metro. They have a huge screen. We could both watch the match there.
A You're on. A great idea.

3 **A** So, anyway, there I was just finishing my report, when suddenly the boss calls me into his office and he starts ...
B Sorry darling, I really do want to hear all about it, but the baby's crying. Do you think you could go and check him? He might need changing.

4 **A** Help! Urgh ... I don't know what's gone wrong with my computer. The screen's frozen again.
B I'll try and fix it if you like. I'm quite good with computers.
A Go ahead. Be my guest. I've had it with this machine!

3 T 4.10 [CD 2: Track 6] Play the first conversation again and elicit the wording of the request. Write it on the board. Play the rest of the recording and get students to write down the wording of the request or offer from each conversation. Check the answers with the class.

Elicit as much of the exact wording from the first conversation as possible with the whole class. Play the recording again if necessary and write the key words on the board.

Students then work in pairs to remember the wording of the other conversations. Play the recording again if necessary to help them, or write key words on the board. Monitor and check for the correct use of the structures for requests and offers. Correct any mistakes carefully.

Answers

1 Could we possibly (make it lunch instead of coffee)?
2 Would you mind if (we didn't go out for a drink after work)?
3 Do you think you could (go and check him)?
4 I'll try (and fix it if you like).

See above for T 4.10.

Roleplay

Give students time to read the situations. Check the pronunciation of potentially difficult words, e.g. *dessert* /dɪˈzɜːt/, *suits* /suːts/, *bargain* /ˈbɑːgən/.

Put students in pairs to choose a situation to roleplay. With weaker students, review the structures they can use and write them on the board:

Requests	**Offers**
Could you/we ...?	*I'll ...*
Do you think you/we could ...?	*Shall I ...?*
Could you/we possibly ...?	
Would you mind ... + -ing?	
Would you mind if I/we ...?	
Can you ...?	

Give students time to prepare their ideas. Monitor and help as necessary. If possible, rearrange the furniture in the class to create a space for students to perform in and bring in simple props to add authenticity. Ask pairs to act out their conversations to the rest of the class. Discourage them from reading the lines if they have scripted the whole conversation, but be prepared to prompt a little with key words.

SUGGESTION

If you have access to a camcorder, it can be fun to record students. You can then review the roleplays and get students to comment on content, and correct errors. Archiving the recordings and viewing them a few months later also provides a valuable marker of progress.

Don't forget!

Workbook Unit 4

Exercise 13 Listening – A radio phone-in

Exercise 14 Vocabulary – Crossword 1

Word list

Refer students to the Word list for Unit 4 (SB p153). They could translate the words, learn them at home, or transfer some of them to their vocabulary notebook.

5

Future forms
may, might, could
Word building
Arranging to meet

Our changing world

Introduction to the unit

The broad theme of Unit 5 is 'the future'. In terms of target structures, this theme provides the ideal context for a review and consolidation of future forms and *may/might/could* for making predictions. These are practised in a range of controlled and freer tasks, including a section on weather forecasts.

The skills coverage continues the theme of the future with a *Listening and speaking* section on space tourism, and a *Reading and speaking* section on life in 50 years' time. This includes an article which presents scientists' predictions for 2060.

Vocabulary and pronunciation covers the use of prefixes and suffixes in word building. *Everyday English* comes back to the idea of the future with a focus on the language used for making arrangements.

The *Writing* focus is on writing for talking, and students are given the opportunity to prepare a talk on a current issue that they find worrying.

Language aims

Grammar – future forms Students, often think of *will* as 'the future tense'. In fact, English doesn't really have a future tense, but rather a range of forms that can be used to refer to the future. The choice of form is dictated by how the speaker sees the event, for example whether it is a general prediction about the future or a plan or fixed arrangement. Sometimes more than one form is possible, and the differences in meaning between different forms can be subtle.

Another factor which influences the choice of future form is when a decision about the future is made. In English, *will* is used for decisions about the future made at the time of speaking, for example in offers and promises. Students will have encountered and practised this use in Unit 4, SB p37.

The overall focus in this unit is making predictions. The key forms covered are *will*, *going to*, and *may/might/could*. The unit also revises *going to* for intentions and Present Continuous for arrangements.

POSSIBLE PROBLEMS

Students often overuse the Present Simple to refer to the future, and they tend to use *will* where *going to* or the Present Continuous would be the more natural choice. The spontaneous decision use of *will* is often incorrectly replaced by the Present Simple. When making negative predictions, students may use *I think* + *won't* rather than the more natural-sounding *I don't think* + *will*.

Common mistakes	**Corrections**
* *What do you do this weekend?*	*What are you doing/going to do …*
* *What will you do this evening?*	*What are you doing/going to do …*
A *There's someone at the door.*	
B * *I go.*	*I'll go.*
We've booked a holiday. * *We'll go to Spain.*	*We're going to Spain.*
* *I think people won't live in space.*	*I don't think people will …*

Try to get students to understand these basic rules:

- We use *will* for predictions, future facts, and promises/offers made at the time of speaking.
- We use *going to* for intentions decided on before speaking.
- We use the Present Continuous for arrangements that are unlikely to change.

Grammar Reference 5.1–5.2 on SB p139 gives further explanation.

may/might/could

The key issues of the form of modal verbs were covered in Unit 4, but if necessary refer students back to Grammar Reference 4.3 on SB p137. *May*, *might*, and *could* express possibility in the present and future. The negative forms *may/might not* express negative possibility, but *couldn't* is not used with this meaning. The continuous form *may/might/could be* + *-ing* is probably new and is worth pointing out to students.

Students are often confused by the fact that there is not a direct equivalent of *may/might/could* in their own language. They tend to use *perhaps* or *maybe* instead, sometimes as a direct translation from their own language.

Common mistakes	**Corrections**
* *I could not come tomorrow.*	*I may/might not come ...*
* *Perhaps I'll change my job.*	*I may/might change ...*
* *Maybe we see you later.*	*We may/might see ...*

Vocabulary The Vocabulary syllabus continues with a focus on using prefixes and suffixes in word building. This is integrated with a pronunciation section on changing word stress, e.g. *prefer*, *preference*.

Everyday English The use of the Present Continuous is consolidated with a focus on discussing and making arrangements. There is a *Music of English* feature on stress and intonation.

Notes on the unit

STARTER (SB p38)

ABOUT THE TOPIC

The term 'global warming' /ˌgləʊbəl wɔːmɪŋ/ refers to a general increase in the average temperature of the Earth's air and oceans. There is now strong evidence that significant global warming is occurring. It is also likely that most of the recent warming can be attributed to human activities.

Scientists generally agree that the main cause of global warming is the release of greenhouse gases (e.g. carbon dioxide and methane) from burning fossil fuels for energy and from cutting down forests.

Scientific research indicates that, because of climate change, we may experience more intense and more frequent extreme weather events. A gradual increase in temperature also has major implications for ecosystems, animals, and their habitats.

Write the phrase *global warming* on the board and elicit a definition and/or examples of it from the class (see above). Ask students if they feel their country/region is affected by global warming.

Pre-teach/check the language students may need to talk about the photos: *habitat, temperatures, sea level, to rise, Arctic, to melt, drought* /draʊt/, *flood* /flʌd/, *to become extinct, to survive, rainforest, coral reef, gorilla, jungle.*

Focus attention on the photos and elicit a few predictions for the first one, e.g. *I think temperatures will continue to rise. There will be less rainfall, so there will be more deserts.* Put students in pairs to discuss their ideas. Monitor, and feed in extra vocabulary as required. Then elicit predictions from the class about each photo.

Sample answers

I think sea levels will rise and some cities will flood.

I think people will continue to cut down trees in rainforests.

I don't think gorillas will survive. I think they will become extinct.

I think the world will become warmer and the ice at the Arctic will melt. I don't think polar bears will become extinct. I think they will move to other areas.

I think the sea will become warmer. I don't think that coral reefs will survive.

THINGS OUR GRANDCHILDREN MAY NEVER SEE (SB p38)

Making predictions

1 **T 5.1** [CD 2: Track 7] Focus attention on the photo of Hannah and Dan, and let students read the context and questions 1–5. Check comprehension of *to reassure* (to make someone feel less worried). Briefly review the use of *what ... like* when asking for a description, e.g. *What will life be like in 50 years?*

Pre-teach/check the following items from the listening: *to grow up, to get warmer, to rise, Arctic, to melt, to find solutions, to do your bit* (informal for *to do your share of the work*), *to bring up* (*a baby*). Play the recording through once and check the answers.

Answers and tapescript

1 She's worried about what life will be like when their grandchildren grow up.
2 He isn't thinking about grandchildren yet.
3 It will definitely get warmer.
4 Temperatures might rise by up to 4°C before the end of the century. If the Arctic ice melts, there will be floods and the polar bears will have nowhere to live.
5 He says that not *all* scientists think the same about global warming. Humans are clever enough to find solutions. They'll do their bit and they'll bring up the baby to do the same.

T 5.1

Things our grandchildren may never see

H = **Hannah** **D** = **Dan**

H Do you ever worry about what the world will be like when our grandchildren grow up?

D Hang on! We haven't had our baby yet. I'm not thinking about grandchildren!

H I know, but having a baby makes me wonder – what **will** the world **be** like when he or she grows up? Look at these pictures. Don't they make you worry about what **could** happen in the future?

D Mmm – OK, of course things **are going to** change a lot in the next hundred years, even in the next fifty but ...

H I know and I'm getting worried. Everyone says global warming is a fact nowadays. No one says it ***may*** get warmer or it ***might*** get warmer any more. Scientists say that it definitely ***will get*** warmer. It's going to be a very different world for our children and grandchildren.

D Look, Hannah, it's no good worrying. Not *all* scientists think the same ...

H Yes, I know but *most* do. Look. It says here over 2,500 climate scientists agree. They say temperatures **might** rise by up to 4°C before the end of the century. Dan, this is the world our son or daughter is going to grow up in.

D Hannah, you've got to take it easy, you'**re having** a baby soon and I don't ...

H I can't help being worried. If the Arctic ice melts, there'll be floods and the polar bears will have nowhere to live. Oh and look at this ... *(intake of breath)*

D Come on, Hannah. Look here, it also says humans are clever enough to find solutions. We'**ll** do our bit and we'll bring up our baby to do the same. Every little helps ...
H OK, but maybe it **won't** help. It **may be** too late already.

2 These gapped sentences contain the target structures for the lesson. Give students time to read through the sentences so that they know what to listen for.

T 5.1 **[CD 2: Track 7]** Play the first three speeches of the recording and elicit the missing words in sentences 1 and 2 (see words in bold in above script). Play the rest of the recording, pausing after the key lines as necessary. Students complete the sentences. Check the answers with the class.

Answers
See words in bold in **T 5.1** above.

GRAMMAR SPOT (SB p39)

1 Read the sentences aloud and elicit the answers to the concept questions.

Answers
Most sure: *It is going to/will change.*
Less sure: *It may/might/could change.*

2 Give students time to read the question and possible answers. Get them to discuss the concept question in pairs before checking with the class.

Answers
Correct answers: *I'm seeing/I'm going to see my grandmother.* Present Continuous and *going to* can be used to talk about arrangements and plans made before the time of speaking.

Incorrect answer: *I'll see my grandmother. Will* is used for predictions about the future and decisions made at the time of speaking, not for plans or arrangements.

3 Students match the future forms to the meanings. Check the answers with the class.

Answers
Our love will last forever. (a prediction)
I'm going to stop smoking next year. (an intention)
We're meeting James at 11.00 in the conference room. (an arrangement)

Refer students to Grammar Reference 5.1–5.3 on SB p139.

What do you think will happen?

3 **T 5.2** **[CD 2: Track 8]** This exercise gives students the opportunity to respond to a range of predictions, using *will* or the modals *may/might/could*. With weaker classes, you may prefer to do the exercises in the *Grammar Spot* before you do this exercise. Pre-teach/check the following items from prompts 1–8: *to be banned, CO_2 (carbon dioxide) emissions, source of energy, lifestyle.*

Get four students to read the examples aloud. Drill the stress and intonation:

Do you think the earth will continue to get warmer?

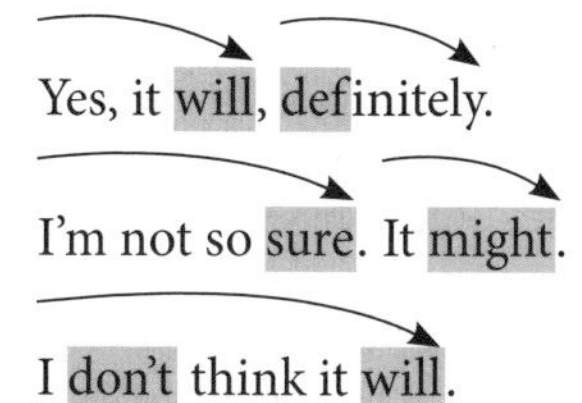

Yes, it will, definitely.

I'm not so sure. It might.

I don't think it will.

SUGGESTION

If students have problems with the intonation of the model question in exercise 3, trying building up the intonation from the end. Drill the questions in sections like this:

... to get warmer?
... will continue to get warmer?
Do you think the earth will continue to get warmer?

Elicit the question and sample answers for number 2. With weaker classes, drill all the questions students need to use and elicit a range of answers from the class. Check the question formation with the class. (See answers in bold in **T 5.2** below.)

Put the students in groups of three or four to discuss the questions. Monitor and check for accurate use of *will* and the modals. Also check the students' pronunciation and drill the questions and answers again as necessary.

Tell the students they are going to listen to some people discussing the same questions. Pre-teach/check *nuclear energy, wind farm, barrier, to recycle rubbish.* Play the recording through once and elicit students' reactions to the opinions expressed. Play it again and establish where the students agree or disagree with the opinions in the recording.

Answers and tapescript

T 5.2

What do you think will happen?

1 **A** **Do you think the earth will continue to get warmer?**
B Yes, I do. The more I read about it, the more I think it will. A few years ago I wasn't so sure.

2 **A** **Do you think all the ice will melt at the Poles?**
B Well, I don't think *all* the ice will melt, but a lot has melted already. Do you know a new island near Greenland has just appeared? They thought it was part of the mainland, but it was just an ice bridge and it melted. It's called *Warming Island*. A good name, don't you think?

3 **A** **Do you think polar bears will become extinct?**
B I think they might. They only live in the Arctic and I read that the ice there has decreased by 14% since the 1970s.

4 **A** **Do you think more people will travel by train?**
B Definitely. I think lots more people will choose train travel when they can, especially across Europe. Of course it won't always be possible to.

5 **A** **Do you think that air travel will be banned to reduce CO_2 emissions?**
B Well, I think it could become much more expensive to travel by air, but I don't think it'll be banned.
6 **A** **Do you think new sources of energy will be found?**
B I hope so. Some people say nuclear energy is the only answer, but I think this could cause more problems. Actually, I like wind farms, they look amazing. But I know some people hate them.
7 **A** **Do you think there'll be more droughts or more floods in the world?**
B I don't really know. There might be both droughts and floods. I think parts of London may be flooded – there's already a barrier across the River Thames to stop flooding.
8 **A** **Do you think our lifestyles will have to change?**
B Definitely. They're already changing. We're told all the time to do things like drive smaller cars, use cleaner petrol, and recycle our rubbish. That worries me a lot – the amount of rubbish we make.

PRACTICE (SB p39)

Discussing grammar

1 **T 5.3** [**CD 2: Track 9**] This exercise focuses on different future forms and the modals of possibility. It highlights common errors in the target grammar and gives students the opportunity to discuss the correct forms. Allow students to discuss the correct forms in their own language if appropriate.

Elicit the correct form in conversation 1. Students discuss the rest of the exercise in pairs.

Play the recording and get students to check their answers. If appropriate, elicit the reasons why the verb forms are correct (see bracketed text in the *Answers* below).

Play the recording again and get students to listen and repeat. Students then work with a new partner to practise the conversations.

Answers and tapescript

T 5.3

1 **A** Have you decided about your holiday yet?
B No, not yet. We've never been to Prague so we **might** go there. (*might* used to express a possibility – they haven't decided about the holiday yet)
2 **A** **Are you going to** take an umbrella? (*going to* used to express a plan/intention)
B No, I'm not. The forecast says it'**ll** be fine all day. (*will* used to express a prediction that the speaker feels quite sure about)
3 **A** Why are you making a list?
B Because **I'm going** shopping. Is there anything you want? (*going to* used to express a plan/intention)
4 **A** Would you like to go out for a drink tonight?
B Sorry, **I'm working** late. How about tomorrow night? **I'll call** you. (Present Continuous used to express an arrangement; *will* used to express a decision made at the time of speaking)
5 **A** What **are you doing** Saturday night? (Present Continuous used to express an arrangement)
B I'm not sure yet. I **may** go to friends' or they **may** come to me. (*may* used to express a possibility – the speaker isn't sure who will go where)
6 **A** Are you enjoying your job more now?
B No, I'm not. **I'm going to** look for another one. (*going to* used to express a plan/intention)
7 **A** Your team's rubbish! It's 2–0 to United!
B Come on. It's only half-time. I think they **could** still win. (*could* used to express a possibility – it's possible that the score will change)
8 **A** You **won't pass** your exams next month if you go out every night. (*will* used to express a prediction that the speaker feels quite sure about)
B I know, **I'll** work harder nearer the time. I promise. (*will* used to express a promise/intention made at the time of speaking)

World weather warnings

NOTE
At the end of this section, students need to talk about the weather forecast for where they are. If you think they are unlikely to know this, get them to check it on TV/in a newspaper/online before the class.

The focus of this section is extreme weather. Most intermediate students should be familiar with a range of weather words, so you could brainstorm key vocabulary as a lead-in to the section. Elicit a range of relevant words and write them on the board in groups. This can be according to season, e.g.

Winter: rain, snow, ice, storm, cool/cold, wind
Summer: sun(shine), to shine, hot, humid, to rise

2 Check pronunciation of the vocabulary: *thunderstorms* /θʌndəstɔ:mz/, *floods* /flʌdz/, *hurricane* /hʌrɪkən/, *heatwave* /hi:tweɪv/, *snowstorms* /snəʊstɔ:mz/. Then elicit definitions/examples of the types of weather. Ask students if they have ever experienced such weather conditions, where, and what happened.

3 **T 5.4** [**CD 2: Track 10**] Read the task instructions with the class. With weaker classes, play the first recording and elicit the country (see *Answers* below).

Play the recording through to the end. Students number the countries. Check the answers.

Answers and tapescript

Hungary	3
The British Isles	1
Mexico	4
Canada	2
South Africa	5

T 5.4

World weather warnings

1 The British Isles
A prolonged period of heavy rain and thunderstorms will affect parts of the country on Friday and into Saturday. Rainfall could total 20–30mm in the south, but there may be up to 60–90mm in the north and Scotland. The heavy rain might lead to flooding in some areas.

2 Canada
High winds following in the path of Hurricane Gloria will head north from the US overnight. They could reach up to 160 kilometres per

hour and may cause damage to buildings across north-west Ontario. These winds are going to bring with them high temperatures across the country and thunderstorms in many areas.

3 Hungary
The country's heatwave is going to continue. Temperatures could rise to more than 40 degrees Celsius by midday tomorrow. Budapest's city council are going to send out teams of workers to distribute 22,000 bottles of drinking water to local people. Meteorologists say that temperatures will continue to rise until the end of the week.

4 Mexico
Tropical storm Barbara is forming rapidly over the coast and will move towards land. Winds of 110 kilometres an hour are expected and they could reach the popular tourist destination of Acapulco over the next few days. Hotels and houses may have to be evacuated. Meteorologists say that the winds might even reach hurricane status.

5 South Africa
For the first time in 25 years forecasters in Johannesburg are predicting snow. Up to 10 centimetres could fall during the night and this is causing much excitement throughout the city. SABC News is reporting that some parents are going to take their children to the local parks after midnight to play in the snow. Tambo International Airport may be affected.

4 **T 5.4** [CD 2: **Track 10**] In this task, students listen for detail and make notes. Briefly review the abbreviations and symbols for giving measurements and temperature: *mm* = millimetres, *km* = kilometres, *40°* (= *degrees*) *Celsius*, *cm* = centimetres.

Tell students that they are going to listen to the recording again and they need to make notes of the key points. Pre-teach/check the following: *to affect, to lead to, following in the path of* (following close behind), *to head, to reach up to, meteorologists, to evacuate, to reach hurricane status.*

Play the first part of the recording again and elicit the key information about the weather in the British Isles. Write it in note form on the board (see *Answers* below).

Play the rest of the recording. Students take notes. With weaker classes, you could split the listening load by getting pairs of students to take notes on alternate recordings, or to listen for specific things in each one, e.g. Student A notes down figures; Student B notes down other weather conditions.

Play the recording again if necessary to allow students to complete any gaps in their answers. Don't check answers with the class at this stage.

5 Put students into new pairs to talk about the weather in the five countries. Encourage them to combine the information they have noted. Elicit descriptions of the weather in each country in a feedback session (see *Answers* below).

Elicit examples of what the weather is going to be like tomorrow. Put students in new pairs/small groups to create a weather forecast. If you have time and if your students are keen on the topic, you could get them to roleplay a weather forecast on TV. Refer them to the tapescript on SB p123 as a model for their forecast. They can underline key words and expressions to use. If possible, bring in a large map of the area/country for students to point to as they deliver their forecast.

Answers

The British Isles
Heavy rain and thunderstorms on Friday + Saturday.
Rainfall 20–30mm in south; up to 60–90mm in north and Scotland.
Flooding in some areas.

Canada
High winds after Hurricane Gloria move north from the US.
Could reach 160 km per hour; damage across north west Ontario.
Winds to bring high temperatures and thunderstorms in many areas.

Hungary
Heatwave to continue – more than 40º Celsius by midday tomorrow. Budapest's council to send out 22,000 bottles of water to local people. Temperatures continue to rise until end of week.

Mexico
Tropical storm Barbara over coast; will move towards land.
Winds of 110 km an hour expected; could reach Acapulco over next few days. Hotels/houses may be evacuated. Winds might reach hurricane status.

South Africa
First time in 25 years Johannesburg predicting snow; up to 10 cm could fall during night –much excitement in city. Some parents take children to local parks after midnight to play in snow. Airport may be affected.

I think/don't think ...

6 **T 5.5** [CD 2: **Track 11**] This exercise practises *will* for predictions. Focus attention on the prompt in A for sentence 1 and the matching line in B. Ask one student to read out the complete example. Students complete the task, working individually.

Play the recording so that students can check their answers. Highlight the silent letter in *wrap* /ræp/ and drill the contracted forms *it'll*, *I'll*, *you'll*, etc. Play the recording again and get students to repeat. Drill the stress and intonation. Students work with a partner and take turns to practise the lines.

Answers and tapescript

T 5.5
1 I think it'll be a cold night tonight. Wrap up warm if you go out.
2 I think I'll get a new computer. I want a laptop this time.
3 I think I'll do a cookery course. I can't even boil an egg.
4 I think you'll like the film. It's a great story, and really well cast.
5 I think we'll get to the airport in time. But we'd better get a move on.
6 I think you'll get the job. You've got all the right qualifications.

7 **T 5.6** [CD 2: **Track 12**] Read the instructions with the class and focus attention on the example. Remind students that we say *I don't think I will* rather than **I think I won't*. Students complete the task, working individually.

Play the recording so that students can check their answers. Play the recording again and get students to repeat. Drill the stress and intonation.

Elicit possible continuations to the first line, e.g.

... And we're not going to be staying out very late.

Students work with a partner and take turns to practise the lines and continue them. Monitor and help, feeding in any language students need.

Answers and tapescript

T 5.6

1 I don't think it'll be a cold night tonight. You won't need to take a jacket.
2 I don't think I'll get a new computer. It may seem old-fashioned to you but it's OK for me.
3 I don't think I'll do a cookery course. I'll get lessons from my mum.
4 I don't think you'll like the film. It's not really your kind of thing.
5 I don't think we'll get to the airport in time. There's too much traffic.
6 I don't think you'll get the job. You're too young, and you've got no experience.

Talking about you

8 Model the activity by giving a few sentences about yourself. These can be true or amusing, e.g. *I think I'll give you extra homework this week. We might have a test next class.* Focus attention on the examples in the Student's Book and elicit a few more examples for the prompts for sentence 2.

Put students into groups of three or four to complete the task. Monitor and help as necessary. Check for accurate use of the verb forms, and stress and intonation. Feed back on any general errors at the end of the task, but try not to interrupt students during their group work. Elicit a range of sentences from different groups or ask questions like *Who thinks it will rain tomorrow?* in a short feedback session.

SUGGESTION

You can extend this activity in a personalized way by listing further prompts on the board and getting students to make predictions. These can refer to local events, activities that are happening soon, facts that are relevant to the students, e.g.

our team/win their next match
snow/next week
Laura/get a new job soon

ADDITIONAL MATERIAL

Workbook Unit 5

Exercise 1 Future forms – Recognizing tenses
Exercises 2–4 Future forms – *will*
Exercise 5 Future forms – *going to*
Exercise 6 Future forms – *will* or *going to*?
Exercise 7 Present Continuous
Exercise 8 *will, going to*, or the Present Continuous?
Exercise 9 *may/might/could* for possibility
Exercise 10 All future forms

LISTENING AND SPEAKING (SB p41)

Rocket man

ABOUT THE LISTENING

The overall theme of the future is carried through in this section with a focus on space tourism. The listening task takes the form of a radio interview between a presenter and a rocket scientist called Steve Bennett. He is a real person whose ambition is to make space tourism a reality. The interview first appeared on BBC Radio 4's *Saturday Live* programme. This is a 'magazine-style' programme with a range of features including interviews with interesting people, a guest poet each week, music, and celebrity guests.

The X Prize referred to in the recording is a multi-million dollar prize given to the first team to achieve a specific goal, set by the X Prize Foundation. The Ansari X Prize was a space competition in which the foundation offered a multi-million dollar prize for the first non-government organization to launch a reusable manned spacecraft into space twice within two weeks. *Thunderbirds* was a children's TV programme of the 1960s with puppets playing members of 'International Rescue', an emergency response organization which covered the globe and even went into space, rescuing people in their futuristic vehicles.

The recording itself is longer than students may be used to, but they will hear it at least twice and work in pairs to do the main comprehension task.

If you are short of time, or with weaker students, pre-teach/check the items below. You can get students to check the vocabulary for homework before the class: *billionaire, trillionaire, to commission someone to do something, to go into orbit, weightlessness, curvature, to launch a rocket, struck* (impressed), *expansion, resources.*

1 Focus attention on the pictures. Ask students if they recognize the rockets. Check the answers.

Answers

a The rocket from the cartoon series *Tin Tin.*
b Apollo II, launched in 1969 and the first manned rocket to land on the moon.
c An illustration from the 1872 edition of *From the Earth to the Moon* by Jules Verne.
d The Space Shuttle Discovery, 2007.

2 Focus attention on the photo of Steve Bennett. Give students time to read the text and think about the answers to the questions. Check the answers with the class.

Answers

He is Britain's leading rocket scientist. His dream was to be a spaceman. His dream is coming true because he's building his own rocket. He's going to travel into space with two passengers. Space tourism is the new phenomenon of tourists paying for spaceflights, primarily for enjoyment and/or a sense of challenge.

3 **T 5.7** [CD 2: Track 13] See notes in *About the listening* for vocabulary that you could pre-teach. Give students time to read the pre-listening questions. Explain to students that the listening is relatively long, but they don't need to understand every word – they just need to get an impression of Steve and his work.

Ask students to close their books. Play the recording through once. Give students time to compare their answers in pairs before checking with the whole class.

Answers and tapescript

Students can give their own impression and description of Steve, but in general he sounds realistic about his dream and quite professional.

Establish who would like to travel into space with Steve and why/why not.

T 5.7

Rocket man

I = Interviewer S = Steve Bennett

I Steve Bennett's ambition was to be a rocket scientist. A few years ago he almost won a £10 million prize, the X prize. Now Steve is building a rocket that will take him and two passengers up into space. He believes that space tourism is not really that far away.

S Space tourism is just about to happen. There are quite a lot of people around the world actually putting a lot of money into space tourism. So it's simply a question of *when* not *if*. You know, just as the Internet made billionaires, well, space tourism is going to make trillionaires. And all the big names are at it – you've got Jeff Bezos, he did Amazon.com; he's building his own spaceship; you've got Richard Branson, even he's commissioning somebody to build a spaceship for him. So it really is going to happen.

I And what are you intending to take people into space in? What is your rocket?

S A rocket that can carry 3 people into space. We're not going into orbit. It's going straight up, straight down, but it will go into space, it'll give you about 3 or 4 minutes of weightlessness, you'll see the blackness of space, the curvature of the earth and you really will truly become an astronaut just like the early American astronauts.

I And you're going to be one of the people who goes up, so it's going to be you and two space tourists. Have you been up in this exact rocket before, Steve?

S No, we're still working on this one. We've launched 16 big rockets to date, but this actual space tourism rocket, called *Thunderstar*, we're still working on it; we're still building it. I was influenced as a small child watching too many episodes of *Thunderbirds*, I think.

I Were you very much struck by the first moon landings as well?

S Yup. I was about 5 years old when they landed on the moon. Erm, my parents wouldn't let me stay up to watch the actual landing, which was a bit of a shame.

I How mean!

S Yeah, yeah. Well they just didn't get it. 'Oh it's marvellous, but they should spend the money on something better' kind of attitude.

I Lots of young boys will have had exactly that kind of experience themselves but very few of them will now have a business that is making rockets. Did you always feel that eventually you would get to do it professionally?

S I kept it pretty quiet. 10, 15 years ago you start talking about space tourism and people, they think you're nuts, so you keep that kind of thing to yourself.

I Why do we really need to do that, though? I mean, is there actually any necessity to have more humans in space?

S Well, that's pretty much where the human race needs to be, you know, in terms of expansion. You know, there's enough resources in space to allow the human race to continue to grow and expand for the next ten thousand years.

I What kind of training do you have to do to in order to go up in the rocket?

S Actually, one of the most important things we do is skydiving training. We feel that if you haven't got what it takes to jump out of an airplane with a parachute, you really shouldn't be strapping yourself to the top of a 17-ton rocket.

I These two other people who've already booked their place on your *Thunderstar*, do you,know who they are?

S Absolutely. I've taken their money.

I Right.

S Well, it's a couple. It's two people that want to fly in space and they came to me a few years ago and basically they said 'Steve we want to fly in the rocket. Here's the money', and they paid me half a million pounds for it.

I And how often do you consider the possibility that something might go wrong?

S I think about it every day, you know. I've built a lot of rockets, most of them have worked really well; some haven't, and I think about that every day.

4 **T 5.7** [CD 2: Track 13] Students read the comprehension questions. Deal with any vocabulary queries. Put students into pairs to answer as many of the questions as they can. Encourage them to pool their information and underline the questions they cannot answer yet.

Play the recording again so that students can complete their answers. With weaker classes, be prepared to pause the recording at key points.

Check the answers with the class.

Answers

1 A lot of people are putting a lot of money into space tourism. Jeff Bezos and Richard Branson are called big names because they are very wealthy entrepreneurs.
2 The Internet made billionaires and space tourism is going to make trillionaires.
3 The passengers will get 3 or 4 minutes of weightlessness, and see the blackness of space and the curvature of the earth, just like the early American astronauts. They aren't going into orbit, just straight up and straight down, but they will go into space.
4 Steve was influenced by a programme called *Thunderbirds*. He called his rocket *Thunderstar*, after the programme. He wasn't allowed to watch the first moon landings.
5 They thought people should spend the money on something better.
6 Humans need to be in space to expand. There are enough resources in space to allow the human race to grow and expand for the next 10,000 years.
7 If people can't jump out of an airplane with a parachute, they really shouldn't try a rocket flight.
8 He thinks about the rockets that haven't worked.

What do you think?

If you are short of time, discuss the questions with the whole class. If not, put students into small groups. Then elicit a range of opinions from different groups in a feedback session.

SUGGESTION

If your students are interested in this topic and have expressed both positive and negative opinions, you could set up an informal debate. Students can put forward the pros and cons of space tourism and then organize a class vote to decide whether money should be spent on this, or on other things.

SPOKEN ENGLISH – *pretty*

Students will be familiar with the use of *pretty* to mean attractive, but probably won't be aware that it has other uses in spoken English.

1/2 Read the notes with the class. Then model the sentences and get students to repeat.

3 **T 5.8** [**CD 2: Track 14**] Put students in pairs. Elicit the position for *pretty* in conversation 1 (see *Answers* below). Students complete the task.

Play the recording so that students can check their answers. Students listen and repeat and then practise the conversations in their pairs.

Answers and tapescript

T 5.8

1 **A** Did your team win?
B No, but they played **pretty** well, all the same.

2 **A** You haven't lost your mobile phone again!
B Oh, no. I'm **pretty** sure it's in my bag somewhere.

3 **A** Do you enjoy skiing?
B I do, but I'm **pretty** hopeless at it.

4 **A** What do you think of my English?
B I think it's **pretty** good.

WRITING (SB p107)

Writing for talking – My cause for concern

1 This is a lead-in to the overall topic of the *Writing* section. It gives students the opportunity to discuss current news stories and share their ideas about the issues they find worrying. If possible, bring in copies of newspapers or news magazines for students to refer to. You can also ask students to listen to/read the news before the lesson.

Elicit examples of current news stories from the class and write the topics on the board. Give an example of a topic in the news that concerns you. Put students into groups of three. Ask them to add to the list of topics and also discuss the ones they feel most concerned about. Remind students to give reasons for their opinions.

Elicit examples from each group. Then get students to share their ideas on the different topics. Establish if there is a topic that most of the class is concerned about.

2 **T 5.9** [**CD 2: Track 15**] Allow students time to read the task and the questions. Play the first sentence of the recording and get students to follow in their books. Check the girl's cause for concern and then ask students to predict what she might say in her talk. Elicit a range of ideas but do not confirm or reject them at this stage. Before you play the rest of the recording, encourage students to use the context to help them understand new vocabulary. With weaker classes, you may want to check the following items: *an influence, an addict, virtual world, minority, to play truant, thumb*. Play the rest of the recording and get students to follow the text. Ask students if they were right in any of their predictions about the talk.

Put students in pairs to answer the questions. Then check with the class.

Answers and tapescript

1 The influence that video games may have on children.
2 She has a younger brother who is becoming a video game addict.
3 He was happy and fun-loving. He had many interests, he played football, he was learning judo, and he went out on his bike with his friends.
4 Forty per cent of family homes have a computer and so there is plenty of opportunity for children to use them. By the age of seven, many have developed an interest in video games.
5 No, only a small minority become addicts by the time they are teenagers, playing for at least 30 hours a week.
6 He says that some children may become so addicted that they stop doing homework, start playing truant, and steal money to buy games.
7 Violence in the games could make children more violent; sitting without exercise for so long is bad for the children's health.

T 5.9 See SB p107.

3 This exercise highlights the structure and key language used in the talk to make it coherent and easy to follow. Do question 1 with the whole class (see *Answers* below) then get students to do questions 2–4, working individually.

Give students time to compare their answers in pairs before checking with the class.

Answers

1 The thing I'm concerned about at the moment is ... (introduces the main topic)
Let me explain why. (introduces reasons for the speaker's concern)
Research shows that ... (gives support to the speaker's opinions)
I have two more concerns. (tells the listener what the speaker is going to say next)
Finally, ... (introduces the speaker's conclusion and general opinion)
2 Paragraph 2: I have a younger brother ... tell him to stop.
Paragraph 4: My brother isn't violent ... stopped from playing. Craig often plays ... bad to worse.
Paragraph 5: I don't need to read ... evidence he needs.
3 Paragraph 2: Research shows ... 30 hours a week.
4 She says that she doesn't agree that more research is needed. Meeting Craig is all the evidence that Dr Griffiths needs.

For part 5 of exercise 3, give students time to read through the paragraph to themselves, marking the main stresses and checking the pronunciation of any difficult words. Elicit the first few sentences from individual students. If they are having problems, play the paragraph again. Pause after each sentence and ask individual students to repeat.

Students take it in turns to read the whole paragraph to each other. Monitor and check their overall delivery. If it sounds rather flat, remind them of the importance of using their voice to keep the listeners interested. Be prepared to drill key sentences from the recording.

Preparing your talk

4 You will need to build in time for students to do this planning stage for their talk. If you are short of time in class, get students to do initial research and prepare their notes for homework. Remind them that their target is 200–300 words and that it's preferable to have a few well-selected personal examples and one or two quotations from research, rather than lots of background information and data.

If students prepare the notes in class, monitor and help as necessary. If they do this for homework, check if students need any help at the beginning of the following lesson.

5 Focus attention on the key language students can use to structure their talk. Elicit possible endings for each sentence from a range of students. You may need to get students to write their talk for homework. If students do the writing in class, monitor and help as necessary. In either case, remind students to keep a check on the word count and not to write too much.

6 Give students time to read their talk to themselves. Monitor and help. Check for mistakes with the key language, and other mistakes that may interfere with the success of the talk, but do not correct other errors.

Put weaker and stronger students together to do the practice stage for the talk. Monitor and help, checking for potential pronunciation problems and helping with overall delivery.

Let students who feel confident give their talks first. Insist that the rest of the class pay attention and avoid interrupting during each talk. Encourage them to note any questions they want to ask. There probably won't be time to hear every talk in a single lesson, so set up a timetable of who will give their talk in the subsequent classes. Don't let the less confident students wait until the end!

SUGGESTION

If you have access to video equipment, it's a good idea to record the students giving their talk. They usually overcome any initial shyness and will often rise to the challenge of a task if they know they are going to be on film. It is also useful to be able to feed back on the students' performance in a later lesson. It can be interesting to repeat the task at a later stage, using a different topic, and let students compare the two talks. This can provide a concrete indicator of progress and so add to students' overall motivation.

READING AND SPEAKING (SB p42)

Life fifty years from now

ABOUT THE TEXT

The theme of the future is continued in an article about life in 2060. It consists of a series of predictions made by international scientists about how life will change in the next 50 years. It isn't necessary for students to know anything about these experts to be able to do the tasks, but if they show interest in a particular person and their field, they can look for more information on the Internet.

The tasks include a pre-reading discussion to establish the main topics covered in the article. The first reading task is replacing removed lines from the article, and detailed comprehension is covered in a true/false exercise.

In line with the text genre, the article contains a certain amount of scientific/medical terminology. It's a good idea to get students to check the following terms in a bilingual dictionary or online before you start this lesson: *life expectancy, biological clock, injections, limbs* (note the silent *b* – /lɪmz/), *organs, cells, awareness, consciousness, primates, mammals, vertebrates, aliens, extra-terrestrial beings, permafrost, quantum physics, parallel universes, galaxy, sensors, cyber-*.

Dr Dolittle, referred to in paragraph 4, is a character in children's books who can communicate with animals. NASA, referred to in paragraph 5, stands for National Aeronautics and Space Administration. This is the US government organization responsible for space travel and the study of space.

1 Read the instructions and question with the class. Elicit a few examples of what life was like 50 years ago, e.g. *There were fewer cars. People didn't have mobile phones. People dressed in a more formal way. They didn't travel abroad very often*, etc.

Elicit examples of what characterizes life today, e.g. dependence on technology, especially computers and mobile phones, environmental problems, greater freedom, medical breakthroughs, etc. Ask students what things were probably not predicted 50 years ago. Elicit a range of answers. If students are short of ideas, suggest the following: access to mobile phones and computers, the importance of the Internet, space tourism, people living into their 80s and 90s.

2 See *About the text* above for suggested vocabulary for students to prepare before the lesson. Give students time to read the introduction and the headings, and deal with any vocabulary problems. Elicit students' predictions about the first topic, then put students into pairs or small groups to make predictions about the other topics.

3 Give students time to read through the sentences. Elicit the sentence that goes with paragraph 1 (d). Remind students to look at the meaning of each sentence and not to just spot similar words when they complete the matching task. Check the answers with the class.

Answers
1d 2a 3b 4g 5c 6f 7e

4 Students read the article including the missing lines in paragraphs 1–7. They can refer to dictionaries to help them, but encourage them to use the context for understanding new words wherever possible. With weaker groups, you could get students to read a paragraph at a time and deal with new vocabulary before moving on.

5 Elicit the answer to sentence 1 with reasons for choosing true or false (see *Answers* below). Put students into small groups to complete the task. Remind them to underline the key information in the text to support their answers. Check the answers by asking various groups for their conclusions. If there is disagreement, write the numbers of the relevant sentences on the board and get students to look at them again. Do a final check with the whole class.

Answers
1 ✗ (*women will give birth well into old age; their biological clocks could be extended by 10 years*) The text doesn't state they will be able to give birth aged 100.
2 ✓ (*whole-body replacement will be routine*)
3 ✗ (*organs could be grown inside animals from human cells*) The text doesn't state that doctors will transplant animal parts.
4 ✗ (*... by 2060 computers will develop their own consciousness and emotions*)
5 ✓ (*it could cause a global revulsion against eating meat*)
6 ✗ (*we may find evidence of if alien life frozen in the permafrost on Mars; there may be every chance of making the most sensational discovery ever, that is confirmation that life really does exist on Mars*)
7 ✓ (*there may be an infinite number of them*)
8 ✓ (*they will change to a colour of your choice ... whatever suits your mood*)
9 ✗ (*your house computer will perform all your everyday household tasks*)
10 ✗ (*nobody wants them. There is too much pleasure in cooking, chewing, and tasting all kinds of food.*)

What do you think?

Students read the article and underline the predictions they found most surprising. Put students into new pairs/groups to compare their answers and discuss the rest of the questions. If students are short of ideas for the last question, feed in the following prompts and/or elicit ideas with the whole class:

transport: destinations? costs? speed?
jobs: workplaces? equipment? age of retirement?
television: size of TV sets? channels? programmes?
communication: equipment? costs? speed?
the home: gadgets? housework? leisure?
food: meals? preparation? nutrition?
clothes: styles? fabrics? special features?
sport: places? people? training?

Elicit a range of predictions from the class. Establish which area of life generated the most similar predictions and which generated the most different ones.

VOCABULARY AND PRONUNCIATION (SB p44)

Word building – suffixes and prefixes

The vocabulary syllabus continues with a focus on using suffixes and prefixes to build words. Students are likely to be familiar with a range of the target words in this section, e.g. *disagree, impossible*, and with the meaning of some of the prefixes and suffixes, e.g. *un-*, *-able*. This section gives them the opportunity to extend their knowledge and generate words with a range of endings/beginnings.

1 Read the information on suffixes as a class. Focus attention on the word endings in bold in the examples. Elicit the part of speech of each word and an example of its use, e.g. *I'd love to* ***act*** *in a play* (verb). *It's an exciting film with a lot of* ***action*** (noun). *She has a very* ***active*** *lifestyle* (adjective). *He is* ***actively*** *looking for a new job* (adverb).

Focus attention on the words in the box. Elicit the part of speech for *prediction* (noun) and *shorten* (verb). Highlight the endings of the words on the board: *prediction* / *shorten*.

Put students in pairs to categorize the rest of the words. You could let them use dictionaries for this, although students should already be familiar with the majority of the words. Encourage them to pool their knowledge. Monitor and help as necessary.

Check the answers with the class. Write the words on the board, elicit the part of speech and get students to underline the word endings. Also deal with any pronunciation problems as you go.

Briefly categorize the endings to the parts of speech

noun endings: *-tion, -ment, -ness*
verb endings: *-en, -fy*
adverb ending: *-ly*
adjective endings: *-ful, -ive, -able, -less*

Answers

prediction – noun	excitement – noun
shorten – verb	creative – adjective
automatically – adverb	qualify – verb
colourful – adjective	suitable – adjective
confidently – adverb	business – noun
imagination – noun	careless – adjective

2 Read the information on prefixes as a class. Focus on the prefixes in bold in the examples. Students match the prefixes to their meanings. Check the answers. Establish which is a negative prefix and explain that negative prefixes give a negative or opposite meaning to a word.

Answers
predict – before
regrow – again
extra-terrestrial – outside
disorder – this is a negative prefix

Focus attention on the example *impossible*. Students match the prefixes to the words 1–8 to form opposites.

Check the answers with the class, dealing with any pronunciation problems as you go.

Answers

1 impossible	5 disappear
2 impatient	6 irregular
3 unlucky	7 informal
4 illegal	8 unconscious

3 This exercise gives students the opportunity to build a range of new words from common base words.

Focus attention on the words in the chart and ask *What words can be formed with un-?* (*unconscious, unhappy, unkind*). Divide the class into two groups, A and B. If you have a large class, set up multiple sets of A/B groups. Remind students that they may need to change the spelling in the base word when adding a suffix, and that they can use both a prefix and a suffix in the same word. You could set a time limit for the task, with the groups competing against each other to make the most words.

You could let students use dictionaries for this task, although they should already be familiar with the majority of the words. Monitor and help as necessary.

Check the answers with the class, dealing with any pronunciation problems as you go. Check the spelling changes in *happiness, usable,* and *expensive.*

Establish which prefixes/suffixes can make the most words (*un-* and *re-*; *-ness* and *-able*).

Answers

Prefixes

un-	unconscious, unhappy, unkind, unsuccessful
im-	impolite
in-	inexpensive
dis-	disagree
mis-	misunderstand, misuse
re-	rearrange, reuse

Suffixes

-ness	consciousness, unconsciousness, happiness, unhappiness, kindness, unkindness, politeness
-ment	agreement, disagreement, arrangement
-ion	reaction
-ful	helpful, unhelpful, useful, successful, unsuccessful
-less	helpless, useless
-able	agreeable, disagreeable, understandable, usable
-ive	expensive, inexpensive

4 **T 5.10** [CD 2: Track 16] This task consolidates some of the words from exercise 3 in context. Elicit the answer for sentence 1. Students then complete the task, working individually.

Play the recording so that students can check their answers.

Answers and tapescript

T 5.10

1 Bob and Jan don't get on at all. They **disagree** about everything.
2 Money doesn't always lead to **happiness**.
3 My aunt says today's kids are all rude and **impolite**.
4 Thanks for your advice; it was really **helpful**. I really appreciate your **kindness**.
5 My dad is **useless** at fixing his computer. I always have to help him.
6 Please don't **misunderstand** me. I didn't mean to be **unkind**. I'm really sorry.
7 Timmy fell off his bike and hit his head. He was **unconscious** for a few hours.
8 What was your wife's **reaction** when she heard you'd won the lottery?

Changing word stress

5 **T 5.11** [CD 2: Track 17] This section covers the pronunciation aspect of word building. Read the instructions to exercise 5 with the class. Ask a student to read aloud the first pair of words and draw attention to the change in stress. Students work in pairs, reading the words aloud.

Play the recording once for students to check. Play it again and get them to repeat. Drill the words if necessary.

Answers and tapescript

T 5.11

advertise	advertisement
imagine	imagination
prefer	preference
employer	employee

6 **T 5.12** [CD 2: Track 18] This task presents and practises the stress change in pairs of words in context. Play conversation 1 and elicit the pair of words with the spelling and the stress change (see *Answers* below). Play the rest of the recording and get students to complete the task. With weaker classes, give them one of each pair of words on the board in jumbled order.

Check the answers, drilling the stress change in the individual words chorally and individually. Refer students to the tapescript on SB p124, and get them to practise the conversations in pairs. Monitor and check for accurate changes in word stress. If students have problems, get them to listen and repeat the conversations, using the recording as a model.

Answers and tapescript

T 5.12

1 **A** The doctors are going to **operate** on my grandma's knee.
B Oh, dear!
A Don't worry it's not a serious **operation**.
2 **A** Did you **explain** the homework to Maria?
B I did, but I don't think she understood my **explanation**.
3 **A** I couldn't find the book I wanted in the **library**.
B Did you ask the **librarian**? She'll tell you if they have it.
4 **A** Can I have a copy of that **photograph**?
B Yes, of course. I'm not a great **photographer** but this one's OK, isn't it?
A It is. Usually I can't stand photos of me.

SUGGESTION

This is a good time to remind students to record vocabulary in word groups whenever possible, including any changes in word stress. Encourage them to record opposite adjectives in the same way.

EVERYDAY ENGLISH (SB p45)

Arranging to meet

The *Everyday English* syllabus continues with the language of arranging to meet, and making suggestions. This also consolidates the use of the Present Continuous for arrangements from the grammar section of this unit. With weaker students, you could briefly review the use of the Present Continuous for arrangements before starting this section.

Write your diary (real or imaginary) for next week on the board. Include an example of the causative *have sth done*, e.g. *have your hair cut/have your car serviced*, etc. A possible diary might look like this:

Mon. *view flat with estate agent*
Tues. *go swimming*
Weds. *have my hair cut*
Thurs. *go to German class*
Fri. *see friends for a drink*

Tell students this is your diary for next week. Say *On Monday I'm viewing a flat with the estate agent.* Elicit the question *What are you doing on ...?* Students ask you the question about each day. Reply using the Present Continuous. Students then ask and answer about their own arrangements for next week.

1 **T 5.13** [CD 2: Track 19] This listening task provides a model for the roleplay that follows. Focus attention on the photos and get students to read the context. Play the recording as far as *I could meet you in the afternoon.* Elicit why Mike can't make Friday evening (his Spanish class).

Play the rest of the recording and get students to complete the chart. Students check their answers in pairs. If students have missed any of the information, play the recording again.

Check the answers, then elicit why it is difficult to arrange a time, and where and when they agree to meet.

Answers and tapescript

	Gary	Mike
Friday		
afternoon	on train till 7 p.m.	finish work early
evening	–	Spanish class
Saturday		
morning	–	hair cut/meeting sister
afternoon	see estate agent	–
evening	–	theatre with friends
Sunday		
morning	meet Mike at station get train at 11.55	meet Gary at station

It's difficult to arrange a time because Mike and Gary are both very busy. They agree to meet at the station café at 10.30 on Sunday morning.

T 5.13

G = Gary M = Mike

G Mike, it's me, Gary.
M Gary! Long time no see. How are you doing?
G Good, thanks. Listen, I'm coming up to town next weekend and I was wondering if we could meet?
M Oh dear, I'd love to – but this weekend of all weekends – I am *so* busy.
G Look, you must have some free time.
M Yeah, I'll just get my diary. Hang on ... OK ... shoot!
G Right. What are you doing Friday evening?
M Friday evening? Er ..., that's my Spanish class. Our company's going to do a lot of work in Spain, so we're all learning Spanish. But I finish work early on Friday. I could meet you in the afternoon.
G No, I'm afraid that's no good, my train doesn't get in until 7 o'clock. Er ... have you got any free time on Saturday?
M Er, ... let me see. What about Saturday afternoon? I'm having my hair cut in the morning and then I'm meeting my sister for lunch, but I'm free in the afternoon.
G Oh no, sorry, Saturday afternoon, I can't, I've got an appointment with an estate agent. I'm going to look around one of those amazing new flats by the river. Didn't I tell you? I'm changing jobs and moving back to the big city.
M Hey, great news, Gary. I knew the small town life wasn't your thing!
G So, what about Saturday evening? Is Saturday evening any good?
M Sorry, the evening's out for me. I'm going to the theatre with friends. We've had it booked for ages. But ... hang on, what time are you leaving on Sunday?
G Late morning. I'm getting the 11.55 train.
M Hey, I've got an idea. Why don't we meet at the station?
G Good idea! We could have coffee together.
M I've got an even better idea. They do a great full English breakfast at the café. Let's meet there for breakfast. Should we say about 10 o'clock?
G Sounds good to me. But can you make it 10.30? It *is* Sunday.
M Fine. 10.30 it is. I'll see you then. Bye, Gary! Hope you like the flat.
G Fingers crossed. Bye, Mike. See you Sunday.

Making suggestions

2 **T 5.13** [CD 2: Track 19] This task highlights the language of making suggestions which is contextualized in the recording. Students should already be familiar with a number of the structures, e.g. *What about ...?, Why don't we ...?, Let's ..., Shall we ...?*

Play the first three lines of the recording and elicit the answers to sentence 1. Play the rest of the recording. Students complete the task. Check the answers.

Answers

1 I was **wondering** if we **could** meet?
2 I **could** meet you in the afternoon.
3 What **about** Saturday afternoon?
4 Is Saturday evening **any good**?
5 Why **don't** we meet at the station?
Let's meet there for breakfast.
6 **Shall** we say about 10 o'clock?
7 Can you **make** it 10.30?

MUSIC OF ENGLISH

1 **T 5.14** **[CD 2: Track 20]** This feature focuses on the stress and intonation of the suggestions. With stronger classes, you could get students to mark the stress and intonation in the sentences, and then listen and check. Otherwise, play the recording as a model and get students to repeat, chorally and individually. Encourage them to mark the main stress(es) in each sentence. If students have problems with the intonation, remind them that questions in English usually start high, questions with *wh*-words usually fall, and *yes/no* questions have a slight rise at the end.

T 5.14
1 I was wondering if we could meet?
2 I could meet you in the afternoon.
3 What about Saturday afternoon?
4 Is Saturday evening any good?
5 Why don't we meet at the station?
Let's meet there for breakfast.
6 Shall we say about 10 o'clock?
7 Can you make it 10.30?

2 Give students time to read the list of replies. Check comprehension of *appointment*, and the meaning of *the evening's out for me* (I can't make the evening) and *sounds good to me* (that's fine with me).

Model the activity by reading the completed suggestions from exercise 2 and eliciting possible replies. It's important to have a good voice range to sound enthusiastic/interested. If students sound rather 'flat', be prepared to drill the stress and intonation again.

Students work in pairs to complete the task. Monitor and check for accurate use of the language of suggestions, and for stress and intonation. Feed back on any common errors before students start the next section. If necessary, review the key structures and write them on the board:

What about + noun/*-ing*
Let's + infinitive without *to*
I/We could + infinitive without *to*
Shall I/we + infinitive without *to*

Roleplay

3 Read the context with the class. Give students time to fill in their diary. They can use real information or imagine some appointments/activities. Remind them to leave some time free on each day so that they can arrange to meet another student.

4 Focus attention on the speech bubbles and elicit a possible conversation from the class, e.g.

Are you doing anything on Saturday morning?
I'm afraid I'm going shopping.
What about the afternoon?
Let me see. No, nothing.
I was wondering if you'd like to go to the cinema?
Sounds good to me. Why don't we meet at the cinema?
OK. Shall we say 2.30?
Fine. 2.30 it is.

Students work with a partner to roleplay the situation, consulting their diaries as they go. If you have a mixed-ability class, try to put a stronger student with a weaker one. Monitor and note down any common errors. Deal with any specific requests for help, but don't interrupt or correct students during the roleplay.

Elicit examples of the arrangements students have made.

SUGGESTION
Encourage students to use the language in this section both inside and outside the classroom. For example, they could use it to make suggestions about day-to-day routines in class, to arrange to meet after class, or to make arrangements for a class outing or party, etc.

Don't forget!

Workbook Unit 5

Exercise 11 Prepositions – Adjective + preposition

Exercise 12 Listening – Friends of the earth

Word list

Refer students to the Word list for Unit 5 (SB p154). They could translate the words, learn them at home, or transfer some of them to their vocabulary notebook.

6

Information questions
Adjectives and adverbs
In a department store

What matters to me

Introduction to the unit

The title of the unit is *What matters to me* and the content covers the topics of people, places, and things that are important to us. The target language of information questions is contextualized in descriptions of people, places, and things. The *Vocabulary* section continues the theme of descriptions with a focus on adjectives and adverbs. *Reading and speaking* contains a jigsaw reading on the heart of the home – the kitchen. The topic of the *Listening and speaking* section is *My closest relative*, and there is a *Spoken English* feature on adding emphasis. The *Everyday English* syllabus continues with a situational focus: *In a department store*. The language of descriptions is consolidated in the *Writing* section for this unit – describing a place.

Language aims

Information questions This unit brings together different types of questions asking for information about people, places, and things. Intermediate students will be familiar with the majority of *Wh-* question words and will have had plenty of practice of using them. The unit also includes questions with *like*, which students often confuse, even at intermediate level. They will, of course, be familiar with *like* as a verb, but may be confused by the question *What … like?* as a way of asking for a description of something or someone, e.g. *What was the hotel like?* The presentation also covers these question patterns:

What/*Which* + noun, e.g. *What size is the battery? Which floor is your flat on?*

How + adjective/adverb, e.g. *How heavy is your case? How long does it take to drive to the station?*

POSSIBLE PROBLEMS

It's easy for students to confuse *What's she like?* and *What does she like?* especially in rapid speech. In descriptions of people, students will usually understand that *What does she look like?* asks for a physical description, but they will need help and further practice with *What's she like?*, which asks for a physical and/or character description.

Students also have problems distinguishing *What's she like?* from *How is she?*, often due to interference from their own language.

Common mistakes

A *How's your sister?*
B **She's taller than me.*
A *What's your sister like?*
B **She likes tennis and swimming.*
A *What's your new house like?*
B **Yes, we like it.*

Vocabulary The vocabulary section revises and extends students' knowledge of adjectives and adverbs. This includes *-ed* and *-ing* adjectives, adjective + noun collocations, and compound adjectives. The adverb section covers verb + adverb collocations, and adverbs that don't end in *-ly*. The section ends with a short project on *My most treasured possession*.

POSSIBLE PROBLEMS

Students often confuse *-ed* and *-ing* adjectives, e.g. *This party is awful, *I'm boring* (rather than *I'm bored*). They will probably need reminding that the *-ed* ending describes a person's feelings and the *-ing* form describes the thing/person that produces those feelings.

Some students find it difficult to distinguish between adjectives and adverbs. They may need reminding that adjectives are used with nouns, e.g. *a quick walk* whereas adverbs are used with verbs, e.g *We walked quickly*.

Everyday English This covers the language students might need in a department store.

Notes on the unit

STARTER (SB p46)

1 This is a fun way of introducing the theme of descriptions. It also allows you to assess the language that students can already use for describing clothes, hair, etc.

Model the activity with the class. Ask *Who am I thinking of?* Remember not to look at that person! Students ask a range of questions to find out who it is.

Students play the game across the class. With larger classes, they can play in groups. You can bring in an element of competition by counting the number of questions needed before students guess correctly. The lowest number of questions wins.

2 Students play the game again about famous people.

DESCRIPTIONS (SB p46)

Information questions

1 **T 6.1** [**CD 2: Track 21**] This exercise revises key information questions and aims to highlight the meaning of different questions with *like* (see *Language aims* and *Common mistakes* on TB p66).

Focus on the example question and answer, then give students time to do the matching task, working individually. Play the recording so that students can check their answers.

Model the practice activity with the class. Tell students to cover the answers column. Ask one or two of the questions in random order and elicit the answers. Then ask students to cover the questions column. Read out one or two of the answers in random order and elicit the questions. Put students into pairs to continue the activity.

Answers and tapescript

T 6.1

1e 2d 3b 4c 5g 6a 7i 8h 9f

1 **A** What's she like?
B She's really nice. Very easy-going.
2 **A** What does she look like?
B She's quite tall and pretty.
3 **A** What does she like doing?
B She likes dancing and shopping.
4 **A** How tall is she?
B Five foot eight.
5 **A** What colour eyes has she got?
B Brown.
6 **A** How old is she?
B She's in her twenties.
7 **A** What kind of clothes does she wear?
B Not smart. Casual. She has a lot of style.
8 **A** What's her hair like?
B It's sort of long, fair, and wavy.
9 **A** How is she?
B She's fine.

2 Focus attention on the vocabulary in the box. Check that students know what the sets of descriptions refer to, e.g. character, looks, height, age, hair. Highlight the use of *mid-twenties* to give an approximate age. Elicit other expressions in this pattern, e.g. *early-fifties*, *late-thirties*, *mid-forties*, etc. With weaker students, brainstorm other vocabulary that can be used to describe character, looks, height, age, and hair.

Focus attention on the examples in the speech bubbles. Check what the contracted forms mean in the question and answer (*'s = is*; *'d = would*). Students work with a partner to ask and answer questions about their relatives. Monitor and check for accurate question formation and use, especially with the questions with *like*. Correct any mistakes carefully with the class before moving on to the next activity.

3 **T 6.2** [**CD 2: Track 22**] This section focuses on the language of describing places. Elicit the correct answer to question 1 and then let students complete the task, working individually.

Play the recording so that students can check their answers. Check the pronunciation of *square* /skweə/ and *metre* /'mi:tə/. Students work in their pairs to practise the questions and answers.

Answers and tapescript

T 6.2

1 **A** What's your flat like?
B It's quite modern, but it's cosy.
2 **A** How big is it?
B About 75 sq m.
3 **A** How many rooms are there?
B A kitchen-diner, a living room, and a bedroom.
4 **A** What size is the kitchen?
B Four metres by two.
5 **A** Which floor is it on?
B The fourth.
6 **A** Which part of town is it in?
B It's south of the river.
7 **A** How far is it to the shops?
B Just a five-minute walk.

4 Check comprehension of the language in the box, then ask students to ask you the question in the speech bubble, and give your answers. Students ask and answer the questions from exercise 3 in their pairs. Monitor and help, feeding in any specific vocabulary as necessary.

5 **T 6.3** [**CD 2: Track 23**] This section focuses on the language of describing objects and gadgets, including dimensions and features such as battery life. Elicit the missing word in question 1. Make sure students understand that *make* here is the noun meaning the same as *brand*. Students complete the task, working individually.

Play the recording so that students can check their answers. Check the pronunciation of *weigh* /weɪ/, highlighting the silent letter g, and also check pronunciation of *gigabyte* /'gɪgəbaɪt/. Students work in their pairs to practise the questions and answers.

T 6.3

1 **A** What **make** is it?
B Sony.
2 **A** How **much** does it weigh?
B 1.3 kg.
3 **A** What's it made **of**?
B Carbon and titanium.
4 **A** What's this button **for**?
B It turns it on.
5 **A** **How** big is the screen?
B 13.2 inches.
6 **A** How **long** is the battery life?
B Eight hours.
7 **A** What **size** is the hard disk?
B 80 gigabytes.

6 Get students to ask you about a piece of equipment in class, or a gadget that you own. Students then work in their pairs to practise the questions and answers. If they are unsure what the gadget is made of, they can simply say *I don't know*.

GRAMMAR SPOT (SB p47)

This *Grammar spot* highlights the use of *What/Which* + nouns, *How* + adjective/adverb, and the possible confusion between *What's she like?* and *How is she?*

1/2 Focus attention on the questions in the Student's Book. Then get students to look for further examples on pp46–7.

Answers
1 What colour eyes has she got? What kind of clothes does she wear? What size is the kitchen? Which floor is it on? Which part of town is it in? What make is it? What size is the hard disk?
2 How tall is she? How old is she? How big is it? How far is it to the shops? How big is the screen? How long is the battery life?

3 Students match the questions and answers. Ask *Which question asks about health/happiness?* (How is she?) *Which question asks for a description?* (What's she like?)

Remind students that we don't use *like* in the answer to questions with *What ... like?*

Answers
What's she like? Very nice. Quite pretty.
How is she? Very well, thanks.

Refer students to Grammar Reference 6.1–6.2 on SB p140.

PRACTICE (SB p47)

Getting information

T 6.4 [CD 2: Track 24] Focus attention on the example. Elicit the alternative wording to *What sort...* (*What kind...*). Students work individually to write the questions. With weaker classes, elicit the question words students need to use for each question before they work individually (see *Answers* below).

Play the recording so that students can compare their answers (alternative answers are given in brackets).

Answers and tapescript

T 6.4
1 What sort of bread do you have?
2 What flavour ice-cream would you like? (What kind/sort ...)
3 Which way do we go?
4 What make is your camera?
5 What kind of food do you like? (What sort ...)
6 Whose top are you wearing?
7 How long does it take to get to the airport?
8 How far is your house from the beach?
9 How often do you go to the cinema?
10 How many of you want coffee?
11 What size shoes do you take?

EXTRA IDEA

Describing people and things TB p151–2

You can provide additional practice of information questions by photocopying this information gap activity. You will need one sheet for each pair of students. Review the questions students need to ask for each category in the table before they do the task. Students can compare their worksheets to check answers at the end of the activity.

ADDITIONAL MATERIAL

Workbook Unit 6
Exercise 1 Question forms
Exercises 2–6 Questions
Exercise 7 Tenses and questions

VOCABULARY (SB p48)

Adjectives

In this section, students look at adjectives in the context of short advertisements. They revise *-ed* and *-ing* adjectives, and work out adjective + noun collocations and compound adjectives.

1 Divide the class into pairs. Get students to match the advertisements to the things they are advertising.

Answers
a date – 3 something to eat – 1 a holiday destination – 2

2 Elicit one or two adjectives from the first advert. Students continue finding and underlining the adjectives in the adverts. Remind them that some adjectives consist of two words joined by a hyphen, and some may be in their comparative or superlative form. Check the answers with the class, dealing with any pronunciation problems as you go.

Answers
1 much-loved, latest, finest, organic, old-fashioned, tempting, home-made, amazed
2 world-famous, relaxed, sun-tanned, sandy, exciting, ancient, disappointed
3 pretty, slim, blue-eyed, tired, tall, dark, handsome, easy-going, charming, great, long-lasting

-ed and *-ing* adjectives

3 Students often confuse these adjective endings, especially when talking in general conversation (see *Language aims* on TB p66).

Elicit the forms used in the advertisements with the whole class. Then get students to complete the sentences with the correct adjectives, working individually.

Let students check their answers in pairs before checking with the class. If they have made a lot of mistakes, use a pair of parallel sentences and a mime or simple board drawing to highlight the difference:

I'm bored with this book (= this is how I feel).

This book is boring (= it makes me feel bored).
NOT **I'm boring.*

Answers

Advert 1	amazed
Advert 2	relaxed, exciting, disappointed
Advert 3	tired, charming

1 relaxing	4 excited
2 amazed	5 tiring
3 disappointing	6 charming

Adjectives and nouns that go together

4 **T 6.5** [CD 2: Track 25] Students will already be aware of different types of collocation, but may not use a very wide range of adjectives + nouns spontaneously when speaking or writing. Point out that using these collocations will help them to sound more natural.

Focus attention on the examples from the advertisements. Elicit a noun that goes with *fresh* (*fruit*). Then get students to complete the task, working individually. Point out that sometimes more than one answer is possible (see *Answers* in brackets below).

Play the recording so that students can check their answers. Check the pronunciation of *casual* /ˈkæʒuəl/.

Answers and tapescript

T 6.5

fresh fruit	casual clothes
latest fashions	close friend
pretty woman (clothes)	handsome man
clear sky	straight hair
fast food	cosy room (restaurant)
crowded restaurant (room)	challenging job

SUGGESTION

Remind students to record adjective + noun collocations in their vocabulary records. Encourage students to read texts of different types (short stories, advertisements, news reports, etc.) to help them become aware of common collocations.

Compound adjectives

5 Focus attention on the examples and check comprehension of the term *compound adjective* (an adjective formed from two words with a hyphen).

Students look for examples of compound adjectives in the adverts. Check the answers.

Answers

1 much-loved, old-fashioned, home-made
2 world-famous, sun-tanned
3 blue-eyed, easy-going, long-lasting

Elicit the compound adjectives with *well-* in the table. Students do the matching task, working in pairs. Check the answers, eliciting the main stress on each compound adjective (see *Answers* below). Point out that the stress falls on the second word.

Answers

well-dressed	good-looking
well-behaved	second-hand
full-time	hand-made
hard-working	brand-new

Note: well-made is also possible

Focus attention on the examples *well-behaved children/badly-behaved children*. Elicit examples for *well-dressed*, e.g. *well-dressed employees/badly-dressed employees*. Students continue the task, working in pairs. Point out that not all the opposites will be compound adjectives. Check the answers with the class, dealing with any pronunciation problems as you go.

Possible answers

well-dressed employees/badly-dressed employees
full-time job/part-time job
hard-working students/lazy students
good-looking parents/unattractive parents
second-hand car/brand-new car
hand-made clothes/shop-bought clothes
brand-new computer/second-hand computer

6 Ask two students to read the examples in the Student's Book aloud. Students continue the activity, working with a new partner.

SUGGESTION

You can revise and extend the compound adjectives in this section by getting students to write definitions/clues for a partner. This can be done in the form of crosswords, short written tasks, or as the game in exercise 6.

Adverbs

This section focuses on adverbs in the context of short advertisements. The collocation focus is continued with verbs and adverbs that go together. Most intermediate students will already be aware of the rule for forming adverbs with *-ly*, and they will be familiar with a few common exceptions such as *fast*, *hard*, etc. Students do an exercise on other adverbs that do not end in *-ly*. The section ends with a project on *My most treasured possession*.

1 Focus attention on the advertisements. Get students to match them to the products without reading the adverts in detail.

Answers

a pain killer – 6 a watch – 5 a house to rent – 4

2 Students underline the *-ly* adverbs in adverts 4 and 5. Then ask them to look for the adverbs that don't end in *-ly* in advert 6.

Check the answers with the class, dealing with any pronunciation problems as you go.

4 simply, beautifully, peacefully, fully
5 actually, merely, probably
6 just, too, fast, straight, soon, again

Adverbs and verbs that go together

3 Focus attention on the examples in the Student's Book. Elicit the adverb for *wait* (*patiently*). Then get students to complete the task, working individually. Point out that each adverb and verb should be used only once and that students should choose the best collocation if answers appear to overlap, e.g. *speak fluently* rather than *speak softly*, because we don't say **whisper fluently*.

Check the answers with the class.

Answers

wait patiently	whisper softly
love passionately	die peacefully
behave badly	rain heavily
shine brightly	dress smartly
fight bravely	speak fluently
leave suddenly	breathe deeply

4 This is an opportunity to have some fun with the language and to get students out of their seats. Focus attention on the examples. Then mime one of the verbs and adverbs and elicit the collocation. Students mime other collocations to the class. With larger classes, students can work in groups.

Adverbs that don't end in *-ly*

5 **T 6.6** [CD 2: Track 26] Remind students that not all adverbs end in *-ly* and elicit some examples, e.g. *fast, hard.* Ask students for the missing word in sentence 1. Students then complete the task, working individually.

Play the recording so that students can check their answers.

Answers and tapescript

T 6.6

1 Peter and I lived **together** at university.
2 He's a good student. He tries **hard**.
3 **A** Where's the town hall?
  B Go **straight** on.
4 Say that **again**. I didn't hear you.
5 Don't talk so **loud**! Everyone can hear you.
6 Why do you drive so **fast**? Slow down!
7 His wife's name is Sue, not Sally! Get it **right**.
8 The holiday was a disaster. Everything went **wrong**.
9 This room is cool, **even** in summer.
10 **A** Are you ready?
  B **Almost**. Give me another five minutes.

Project – My most treasured possession

This activity gives students the opportunity to use adjectives and adverbs in a fluency-based task.

1 **T 6.7** [CD 2: Track 27] Focus attention on the photos. Ask students if they would save anything similar if their home was on fire.

Tell students they will hear Amie, Jack, and Lucy talking about objects they would save from a fire. Ask *What is each object? Why would they save it?* Play the recording and elicit the answers.

Answers and tapescript

Amie – photo albums because they have photos of her kids at important times. The memories they show are irreplaceable.

Jack – his computer because it contains all the information he needs for his work and life. He couldn't live without it.

Lucy – a matching hairbrush and mirror that belonged to her grandmother. They're not particularly pretty, but they have sentimental value.

T 6.7

1 **Amie**

I would have to save my photo albums. They've got all the photos of my kids, when they were babies, their first steps, you know, when they walked for the first time, their birthday parties, their first day at school. And all the holidays we had together. All those memories are irreplaceable.

2 **Jack**

I know it sounds a bit sad, but I would have to save my computer. Not very sentimental, but very practical. It's got all my work, all my email contacts, several thousand photos, address books, and my work diary for the next year. I just couldn't live without it.

3 **Lucy**

I have a matching hairbrush and hand mirror that belonged to my grandmother. She was given them as a wedding present, and she gave them to me before she died. I don't use them, but they're always on the shelf in my bedroom, and every time I see them I think of her. They're solid silver, and they're quite heavy. They're not particularly pretty, but they have immense sentimental value.

2 Focus attention on the examples and elicit possible endings for each sentence. Ask students to prepare their talk for homework. Remind them to use adjectives and adverbs, as collocations if possible, in order to make their talk sound vivid and interesting. If appropriate, ask students to bring the object in with them to show to the class when they give their talk.

Students can give their talks in a subsequent lesson, either to the whole class or in groups. Make notes of any common errors to feed back on in a later lesson. You could record students as they give their talk (see the *Suggestion* on TB p60).

Encourage the rest of the class to ask questions about the object and what it means to the speaker. If appropriate, ask students to vote for the most interesting/touching story.

ADDITIONAL MATERIAL

Workbook Unit 6

Exercise 8 Adjectives – *-ed/-ing* adjectives

Exercise 9 Adverbs

Exercise 10 Vocabulary – Antonyms

READING AND SPEAKING (SB p50)

The heart of the home

ABOUT THE TEXT

This is the second jigsaw reading task in the book. Students work in three groups, read their text, and then exchange information. The theme of the text is the kitchen as the heart of the home and how this is true across different cultures. The text itself is in the form of interviews with three women from around the world about how they use their kitchen and how they feel about it. The format is typical of articles found in lifestyle magazines.

In terms of vocabulary, students shouldn't need much help with pre-teaching or dictionary work, but see the notes for exercise 3 about pronunciation of some of the key vocabulary. Of the food items mentioned, a *bagel* is a ring-shaped bread roll typical of Jewish cooking, and *turmeric* is a fine yellow powder used to give colour and flavour to food, especially curry.

1 This task uses a visualization technique to help students focus on the topic and picture their own kitchen in a meaningful way. Ask for quiet in the class and get students to close their eyes. Read the questions out individually, giving students time to think of their answers. Elicit a few descriptions of what students pictured in a short feedback session.

2 Students read the introduction. Give your own answers to the Student's Book questions. Then elicit examples from the students.

3 Focus attention on the photos of the three women and where they are from. Elicit students' initial ideas about how these women live and what they and their families eat.

Divide the class into three groups, **A**, **B**, and **C**, and assign the relevant text to each group: **A** Santina /sæn'tiːnə/, **B** Elizabeth, **C** Lakshmamma. Students read through their text, working in their groups. Encourage them to help each other with any new vocabulary. Monitor and help as necessary, highlighting the pronunciation of difficult words in the texts for each group:

A *cupboard* /'kʌbəd/, *vegetables* /'vedʒtəblz/, *sausages* /'sɒsɪdʒɪz/, *orchard* /'ɔːtʃəd/

B *bomb* /bɒm/, *groceries* /'grəʊsəriz/, *bagels* /'beɪglz/, *vegetables* /'vedʒtəblz/, *champagne* /ʃæm'peɪn/, *yoghurt* /'jɒgət/

C *mud hut* /mʌd 'hʌt/, *crumbling* /'krʌmblɪŋ/, *lentils* /'lentlz/, *turmeric* /'tɜːmərɪk/, *vegetables* /'vedʒtəblz/

Students answer the questions, underlining key information in their text or making brief notes to refer to when they exchange information in exercise 4. Check students in each group are confident of the answers for their text, but don't check the answers with the whole class at this stage.

4 Put the class into new groups of three, made up of one student from each of the three groups, A, B, and C. Model the activity by asking each student from a group to answer question 1. Give students time to exchange their information and answer the questions. Monitor and help as necessary. Make sure students are exchanging the information and comparing the three women, and not simply reading out the questions and giving short answers.

Check the answers with the class.

At the end of the information exchange, you may wish to draw students' attention to the irony that the best-equipped and, indeed, biggest kitchens are those in Elizabeth's house, although she and her family barely 'cook' beyond serving cereal, bagels, and reheating ready meals.

Answers

1 Both Santina and Lakshmamma are housewives. Elizabeth is a lifestyle coach.
2 Santina's husband is a mechanic, Elizabeth's is a businessman, and Lakshmamma's works on a cattle farm.
3 Santina lives in south-east Italy, Elizabeth in California, and Lakshmamma near Bangalore.
4 Santina lives in a two-bedroom farmhouse. It doesn't sound very big, but she has a garden; Elizabeth lives in a 30-room house on the beach, including two kitchens. She has a swimming pool, astronomy dome, and even a bomb shelter. The house kitchen has three ovens and a lift from the garage. Lakshmamma lives in a mud hut. It's small, dark, and in poor condition. She doesn't have running water or a fridge and there are no windows in the kitchen.
5 Santina feels that her kitchen is where she belongs, and it's the place where she's happiest. Elizabeth says she doesn't know how everything works in her kitchen, so it's a bit alien to her. Lakshmamma doesn't like her kitchen because it's so old.
6 Santina has a busy life but it isn't particularly difficult; Elizabeth has a very easy life; Lakshmamma has a very difficult life.
7 Santina's family eat chickens, rabbits, fruit, vegetables, and olives from their own garden/orchard. They also eat sausages, cheese, ham, pasta, eggs, beans, honey and jam. Elizabeth's family eat low-fat, organic prepared food/take-away meals, and fruit, vegetables, yoghurt, pâté, cheese, crisps, and cereal. Lakshmamma's family eats lentils, rice, and vegetables, cooked with spices.
8 All three women all seem to be happy, despite the difficulties of Lakshmamma's life.
9 Santina might worry about the drought and the effect on her animals and garden, Elizabeth doesn't seem to have any worries, although she might worry about her family's diet, Lakshmamma might worry about the condition of her home, her younger son's health, and lack of money.

5 This is an interpretation task based on the information about each woman's life. Elicit the answer to the first sentence. Students complete the task, working in pairs.

Answers

1 Elizabeth
2 Lakshmamma
3 Santina
4 Elizabeth
5 Santina
6 Lakshmamma

What do you think?

Put the students in groups to discuss the questions. Elicit a range of answers from the class.

Speaking

Ask a confident student to start describing their kitchen, answering some of the questions in the text, or model the activity yourself. Elicit other examples from individual students. With bigger classes, students can do the activity in pairs.

WRITING (SB p108)

Describing a place – Relative pronouns and participles

This section consolidates the work students did on adjectives in the *Vocabulary* section, and carries through the theme of the kitchen being the heart of the house from the *Reading and speaking* section.

Students work through a series of activities leading up to the final writing task of describing their favourite room. There is a *Grammar spot* feature on relative clauses and pronouns, and also on present and past participles.

1 Draw a rough plan of your favourite room on the board/OHT and describe it to the class. Include information about what happens there and why you like it, e.g. *My favourite room is my living room. I read my most treasured books and listen to music there. I like it because it's light and airy, with huge windows.*

Ask students to close their eyes and picture their favourite room. Give them a few moments to draw their plan. Students make notes about why they like the room and write down some key adjectives to describe it. Encourage students to use a range of more vivid adjectives, rather than just *big*, *nice*, etc. With weaker students, brainstorm possible adjectives and write them on the board.

Students then work in pairs to describe their room and say why they like it. Monitor and help as necessary.

2 Ask students to read the text and think about the answers to the question. Encourage them to use the context to help them with new vocabulary, but you may need to check *to gravitate* (in this context, to naturally move towards), *seldom*, *without doubt* /daʊt/.

Elicit the answer to the question.

Answer
It's the place where family and friends come together.

3 Intermediate students should have already covered relative clauses/pronouns, but if students are at all unsure, ask them to read Grammar Reference 6.3 on SB p147 and then go through the *Grammar spot* after this exercise.

Elicit the clause that goes in gap 1. Students complete the task, working individually. Let them check their answers in pairs before checking with the class.

Answers
1 I like best
2 where we cook and eat
3 where family and friends come together
4 who are cross and sleepy
5 which is the focal point of the room
6 which tells the story
7 whose family have all emigrated
8 that we're going to next Saturday
9 we haven't seen
10 which means

GRAMMAR SPOT (SB p108)

1 Elicit the relative pronoun in the first clause in exercise 3 (*which*). Students find and underline the remaining relative pronouns. Ask them to think what they refer to and when we use them. Check students' answers during feedback.

Answers
***which** tells the story* = the huge notice board
***that** we're going to next Saturday* = a wedding
***where** we cook and eat* = the kitchen
***whose** family have all emigrated* = Auntie Nancy
***which** is the focal point of the room* = the rectangular table
***which** means* = the fact that they use the back door
***who** are cross and sleepy* = the children
***where** family and friends come together* = the kitchen
We use *which/that* to refer to things.
We use *who/that* to refer to people.
We use *where* to refer to places.
We use *whose* to refer to someone's possessions or relations.

2 Students read the sentences and work out the rule. Let them compare their ideas in pairs before checking with the class.

Answers
This is the room ~~which~~ I like best.
He's a friend ~~who~~ we haven't seen for years.
When *who*, *which*, or *that* is the object of a relative clause, it can be left out.

3 Identify the participle in each sentence (*spent* – past participle; *looking* – present participle). Students rewrite the sentences with relative pronouns.

Answers
I have so many happy memories of times **that/which we spent** there.
There is a large window **that/which looks** out onto two apples trees in the garden.

Refer students to Grammar Reference 6.3 and 6.4 on SB p140.

4 Elicit the answer for sentence 1. Students complete the task, working individually.

Answers
1 The blonde lady **who/that** is wearing a black dress is Pat.
2 There's the hospital **where** my sister works.
3 The postcard **which/that** arrived this morning is from Auntie Nancy.
4 I passed all my exams, **which** made my father very proud.
5 Did you meet the girl **whose** mother teaches French?

5 Elicit the answer for sentence 1. Explain that we use *-ing* clauses when we say what someone is or was doing, and *-ed* clauses when the meaning is passive. Students complete the task, working individually.

Answers
1 I spend hours in my room, **listening** to music.
2 I have a lot of posters **stuck** on the walls
3 My brother is in his bedroom, **playing** on his computer.
4 There are photos of my family **arranged** on my shelves.
5 I also have a colour TV **given** to me on my last birthday.

6 Set the writing task for homework. Remind students to use relative pronouns and participles, and recommend a word count of about 250 words.

SUGGESTION
Students often enjoy reading each other's work, so you could ask them to exchange their descriptions before handing them in. Students can comment on the content and also help improve the writing by highlighting mistakes/suggesting changes. If you have space, you could also display the descriptions on the classroom

walls for students to read. If appropriate, ask them to choose the description(s) that made them most want to spend time in the room described.

LISTENING AND SPEAKING (SB p52)

My closest relative

The theme of *What matters to me* moves in this section to talking about people. The section starts with a discussion task on family relationships. The recording consists of five short monologues on a favourite relative, and the listening task is selecting key information and completing a chart. The *Spoken English* feature covers adding emphasis by changing word order and the use of cleft sentences, e.g. *What I like is her sense of humour*. Students focus on understanding figurative language from the recording and then discuss their own closest relatives.

1 Read the statements with the class and check comprehension of the adjectives *dominant*, *(in)secure*, and *spoilt*. Tell students where you come in your own family and give your opinions about birth order and children's character.

Students discuss the statements in small groups. Monitor and help as necessary. Elicit students' opinions and examples from their own families. Ask the class in general if they think birth order affects character.

2 **T 6.8** **[CD 2: Track 28]** With weaker classes, you could play the recording through once and get students to complete just the first row in the chart. Otherwise, give students time to look at the chart so that they know what to listen for. Make sure they understand that they might need to tick more than one reason for each person.

Play the recording, pausing after each speaker to allow students to fill in the chart. Students compare their answers in pairs. If they disagree about the answers or have missed any information, play the recording again.

Check the answers with the class. Elicit any other information students can remember about the speakers.

Answers and tapescript

	Ellie	Simon	Julia	Tessa	Chris
I feel closest to ...	my mum	my grand-mother	my father	my sister	my twin, Nick
He/She is easy to talk to.	✓		✓		
We do things together.	✓	✓	✓		✓
We have a similar character.		✓	✓		
I like the way he/she thinks.	✓	✓	✓		
We are different.				✓	✓

T 6.8

My closest relative

Ellie

The person that I'm closest to in my family is probably my mother. She's the kind of person you can talk to about anything. She's very open, my mother, and I can talk to her about boyfriends, stuff that's bothering me at work, friendships, anything. We have our ups and downs of course, but basically we have an easy relationship. We go shopping together. What I like about her is her attitude. She's quite young at heart, like me, not old-fashioned or anything like that.

Simon

I'm closest to my grandmother. Erm, my father I don't really get on with. We don't really see eye to eye about anything. My mother, uh, I hardly ever see, she's too busy. My grandmother and I like doing the same things. Erm ... we like watching TV and, uh, having a glass of wine together. We love playing cards. And I think emotionally I'm closer to her than I am to my parents ... because she and I have a similar attitude to life. I think we both like people. We're quite outgoing, sociable, and open.

Julia

The person I'm closest to in my family, I think, would be my father. We stay up late listening to music and talking a lot. What I like about him is that he's interesting and interested. He has a curiosity about life. We can talk about anything and everything. We have the same sense of humour, the same love of life. My friends all love him because he's such a good laugh. He doesn't care what people think of him, and I reckon that's great. He's pretty cool, my dad.

Tessa

I think the person that I'm probably closest to is my sister. The thing I love about her is the way everyone knows her. It doesn't matter where we go, everyone says 'Hi, Nina! How you doin'?' I'm just her little sister, so people call me 'Baby Nina', but that's fine. We're so different. We have blazing rows. She's so hyperactive and loud, she can't sit still, she has to have people around her, and everyone loves her. In many ways she drives me crazy. She just can't think straight. Me, I'm a lot quieter. I'm happy on my own. But we're so proud of each other.

Chris

I'm closest to my twin, Nick. Obviously, we have so much in common. The same friends. The same football team. The same music. We go everywhere together. But we have amazing rows about everything. We're like chalk and cheese. I'm like my Mum – calm and easy-going. Nick's like my Dad – very bad-tempered. They fight like cat and dog. But things have changed between me and Nick now we're older. We appreciate each other more. The biggest difference is probably interests. I'm into all things history and politics, and Nick's interested in science and nature. But of course we're a lot closer than just brothers and sisters. In a way we're like one. I would trust him like I would trust no one else.

3 Focus attention on the expressions and ask students if they can remember who said them. If they are not sure, refer them to the tapescript on SB p125. Elicit the meaning of the first expression. Students then complete the task, working in pairs.

Answers

1 We have our ups and downs of course. (Ellie – we have problems/disagreements sometimes.)
2 We don't really see eye to eye about anything. (Simon – we disagree about everything.)
3 In many ways she drives me crazy. (Tessa – she irritates/annoys me.)
4 We're like chalk and cheese. (Chris – we're totally different.)
5 They fight like cat and dog. (Chris – they have a lot of fierce arguments.)

SPOKEN ENGLISH – Adding emphasis

This section highlights a common feature of spoken English when the speaker wants to emphasize a part of a sentence/piece of information.

1 Read the notes and sentences with the class. Elicit the more usual word order.

Answers
My mother's very open.
My dad's pretty cool.
I don't really get on with my father.
I hardly ever see my mother.
I'm a lot quieter, myself.

2 Read the sentences aloud and get students to follow in their books. Read the sentences again with the correct stresses and get students to repeat. Encourage them to read the sentences quite quickly to get the correct rhythm.

What I like about her is her attitude.

What I like about him is that he's interesting and interested.

The thing I love about her is the way everyone knows her.

3 Elicit the first sentence with one of the expressions from exercise 2. Students re-form the sentences, working in pairs. Check the answers, getting students to say the sentences with the correct stresses.

Answers
1 What I like about Joe is his sense of humour.
The thing I love about Joe/him is the way he makes everyone laugh.
2 What I like about Tina is her kindness.
The thing I love about Tina/her is the way she makes everyone feel good.
3 What I like about Beth is her attitude to life.
The thing I like about Beth/her is the fact she doesn't care what other people think.

Give examples about people in your family, e.g. *What I like about my family is that everyone gets on so well, The thing I love about my mum is her great sense of humour.* Students work in pairs and give further examples about their own relatives. Monitor and check for accurate use of the structures and pronunciation. Drill the sentences as a class if necessary.

Discussion

Put the students in pairs to discuss their closest relatives. Then join pairs together to form groups of four. Students discuss their families and decide whose relationships are similar. Bring the class together to discuss families and decide which person most people are closest to.

EVERYDAY ENGLISH (SB p53)

In a department store

This section includes the names of different departments that students might come across in a department store. There is also a focus on understanding signs. The section ends with some gapped conversations, followed by a roleplay and personalization stage.

1 Discuss the questions with the class. Establish which students like shopping in department stores, and who prefers individual shops, or shopping online. Focus students' attention on the three department store bags at the top of the page. Elicit the names of any other famous department stores around the world, e.g. Harrods, Harvey Nicholls in London, Bloomingdale's, Macy's in New York, KaDeWe in Berlin, Galeries Lafayette in Paris, etc. Ask students what they all have in common (they are built over several floors, with different departments, and they stock designer and luxury brands).

NOTE
In American English, the floor names for buildings are different. In American English the *first floor* is the floor that is level with the street. This is always called the *ground floor* in British English, with the *first floor* being the first one above street level.

2 Focus attention on the store guide and the names of the floors. Ask:
Which floor is underground? (basement)
Which is on the same level as the street? (ground floor)
Point out that we say *on the ground floor, first floor* etc. but *in the basement.*

Check comprehension of all the items in the bulleted list. Elicit the department for the first two items. Students work in pairs to complete the task. Monitor and help as necessary.

Check the answers with the class, dealing with difficult pronunciation as you go. Students may need help with the following: *appliances* /ə'plaɪənsɪz/, *stationery* /'steiʃənri/, *jewellery* /'dʒu:wəlri/, *furniture* /'fɜ:nɪtʃə/, *accessories* /ək'sesərɪz/.

Point out the use of *-ware* to mean things used for the same purpose or things made of the same material, *-wear* used to refer to clothes, *goods* to mean things for sale, and *accessories* to mean 'extra items'.

Answers
a wallet – menswear (ground floor), or leather goods (first floor)
earrings – jewellery, on the ground floor
a saucepan – kitchenware, in the basement
a hair-dryer – electrical appliances, in the basement
shower gel – toiletries, on the ground floor
a doll – toys and babywear, on the third floor
a DVD player – TV, audio, and phones, on the third floor
women's boots – ladies' fashions, on the first floor
the Ladies' – on the second floor
a birthday card – stationery, on the ground floor
a shaving mirror – bathroom accessories, on the second floor
a lipstick – cosmetics, on the ground floor

a vase – china and glassware, in the basement
trainers – sports, on the third floor
a sofa – furniture, on the second floor
sheets – linen, on the second floor
a suitcase – luggage, on the first floor
a pair of tights – ladies' fashions, on the first floor
a light snack – Terrace Cafeteria, on the second floor

SUGGESTION

You can give students more practice with the vocabulary in exercise 2 with the following pairwork activity. Students each write a shopping list of 8–10 things that can be found in the departments in exercise 2. They roleplay a customer and assistant to find out which department they need to go to, and then they change roles.

3 Focus attention on the signs. Elicit the department for the first sign. Students continue the task, working in pairs. Check the answers.

Answers

a Hairdresser's
b Kitchenware
c Luggage
d Menswear
e Terrace Cafeteria
f Stationery

4 Allow time for students to read the signs and answer the questions. Students compare their answers in pairs before you check with the whole class.

Answers

The sign on the left is inviting you to save as you spend.
The sign on the right is telling you how to take things back.

5 **T 6.9** [CD 2: Track 29] Tell students they are going to hear six conversations in a department store. Play recording 1 and elicit the answers to the questions (see *Answers* below).

Pre-teach/check *fruit bowl* and *cashmere*. Play the rest of the recording and get students to note down their answers.

Check the answers with the class.

Answers and tapescript

1 menswear; some shoes
2 sports; a pair of football shorts
3 furniture; a sofa
4 china and glassware; a fruit bowl
5 ladies' fashions; a cashmere sweater
6 electrical appliances; a coffee maker

T 6.9

1 **A** Morning!
B Hello. I'd like to try on these shoes, please.
A Certainly, sir. **What size** do you take?
B Nine. That's 41, isn't it?
A Uh, no, **I think you'll find** 43 would be more comfortable, sir.

2 **A** Have you got these football shorts for age 10–11?
B I'm afraid **that's all we have**. We've **sold out of** that size.
A Will you **be getting** any more **in**?
B We should **be getting a delivery** by the end of the week.

3 **A** Do you have **any sofas like this in stock**?
B No, Madam. They all **have to be ordered**.
A How long does delivery take?
B It all depends, but on average about eight weeks.

4 **A** Yes, madam?
B I'd like this fruit bowl, please.
A Certainly. Is it a present?
B Yes, it is.
A Would you like me **to gift wrap it**?
B Ooh, **that would be lovely**! Thank you so much!

5 **A** I like this.
B How does it feel?
A Really good. I love the colour, but the size is wrong. It **doesn't fit me**. It's too tight.
B Shame. It **really suits you**. What's **it made** of?
A Cashmere. It's so soft.

6 **A** Yes, sir?
B I'll have this coffee maker, please.
A Certainly. Have you got a store card?
B No, just a debit card.
A That's fine. Uh ... Pin number, please.
Keep your **receipt**. That's your guarantee.
B **How long** is it **guaranteed** for?
A For a year.

6 **T 6.9** [CD 2: Track 24] Play recording 1 again and elicit the first of the missing lines. Play the rest of the recording, pausing after each conversation so that students can write their answers.

Check the answers with the class (see bold text in above script).

Refer students to the tapescript on SB p125. Ask two students to read out conversation 1 aloud across the class. Put students into pairs to practise the conversations. Monitor and check for accurate pronunciation. If students have problems, drill key lines from the recording again.

7 Put students in new pairs to roleplay two further conversations in other departments. Assign the roles of customer and assistant to each student and remind students to change roles for the second conversation. Give students time to think about what they want to buy and the department the assistant will work in. Encourage students to roleplay the conversations without scripting them first. Weaker students can model their lines very closely on **T 6.9**.

Students roleplay the conversations in pairs. Ask some pairs to perform their conversations for the class.

Don't forget!

Vocabulary revision

Units 4–6 (TB p153), with answers (TB p158)

Workbook Unit 6

Exercise 11 Pronunciation – Word stress

Exercise 12 Phrasal verbs – Phrasal verbs in context (1)

Exercise 13 Listening – My favourite room

Word list

Refer students to the Word list for Unit 6 (SB p154). They could translate the words, learn them at home, or transfer some of them to their vocabulary notebook.

7

Present Perfect – simple, continuous, passive
Making the right noises

Passions and fashions

Introduction to the unit

The title of this unit – *Passions and fashions* – summarizes the main themes: people who are passionate about something in their life, and things that are incredibly popular, including the Harry Potter books and football.

This unit marks the start of the second half of the course. The first half covered a review and extension of many of the core tenses and structures, but did not include the Present Perfect. This tense is perhaps the most difficult for students to master and so this unit offers a comprehensive study of all the main uses of the Present Perfect Simple and Continuous, as well as Present Perfect passive. The study of the Present Perfect is contextualized through a profile of the life of J.K. Rowling, author of the Harry Potter books, and of the fashion designer Calvin Klein. Students complete a series of language analysis tasks, and do controlled and freer practice activities on the Present Perfect, and the adverbs and time expressions that go with it. The focus on the passive is a continuation of the work students did in Units 1 and 2.

The *Reading and speaking* section has a text on how football developed into the modern game. *Vocabulary* is linked with the *Listening* section *Things I'm passionate about* and covers expressions for likes and dislikes. The unit ends with an *Everyday English* section on reacting with interest in conversation.

The *Writing* section continues the work students have done on descriptions with a focus on describing a person.

Language aims

Grammar – the Present Perfect Intermediate students will be familiar with the form of the Present Perfect, both Simple and Continuous, but are unlikely to have mastered all its uses or be able to integrate it accurately into natural conversation. Their own language may well have an equivalent form, but the uses will be different, thereby creating the problem of interference errors.

The key thing students need to understand is that the Present Perfect links past and present. Its main uses are:

- unfinished past – *I've been self-employed for 10 years* (= I still am). The prepositions *for* + period of time and *since* + point in time are common with this use.
- experience use – *I've lived in Paris and Milan* (= at some time in my life I did this, and I still remember it). The adverbs *ever/never/before* are common with this use.
- present importance – *I've just missed my plane* (= this is important now, as I have to book another flight). The adverbs *yet/already/just* are common with this use.

In this unit the Present Perfect is contrasted with the Past Simple, and students are also reminded that we can't use the Present Simple to refer to unfinished past (see *Common mistakes* below).

The continuous form of the Present Perfect is reviewed alongside the simple form. The key differences between the two are:

- the simple form expresses a completed action. We use the simple form if the sentence has a number or quantity: *I've written three chapters of my book.*
- the continuous form expresses an activity which has continued over a period of time and is still not finished: *I've been writing a book.*

In the *Practice* section students analyse the Present Perfect through contrasts with other tenses. They also review adverbs and time expressions used with the Present Perfect and Past Simple, and practise the use of the Present Perfect for experiences in a personalized way. Freer practice is given via a roleplay activity.

Present Perfect Simple passive The rules for when to use the Present Perfect are the same for the active and passive forms. Students practise the form of the Present Perfect Simple passive, and practise recognizing when the passive is needed.

POSSIBLE PROBLEMS

1 Students often think the Present Perfect is interchangeable with other past tenses, notably the Past Simple.
2 They think the use of tenses in their own language can be applied in English, especially with the unfinished past use, where they often use a present tense.
3 They forget that the idea of an activity continuing over a period requires the continuous form, especially if they don't have continuous forms in their own language.
4 They may use adverbs and time expressions incorrectly.
5 They may fail to recognize the need for a passive form.

Common mistakes	Corrections
**I have arrived last week.*	*I arrived last week.*
**How long do you work here?*	*How long have you worked here?*
**I live here since May.*	*I've lived here since May.*
**It's rained for hours.*	*It's been raining for hours.*
**They've been married since 10 years.*	*They've been married for 10 years.*
**The post has just delivered.*	*The post has just been delivered.*

Vocabulary In this unit, vocabulary is included as part of a *Vocabulary and listening* section. Students analyse and practise words and expressions for talking about things people love and hate.

Everyday English This covers how to respond in conversations to express agreement, sympathy, pleasure, and surprise. The *Music of English* feature is included here to help students with intonation and voice range.

Notes on the unit

STARTER (SB p54)

This activity gets students using the Present Perfect Simple in a meaningful and fun way. Get pairs of students to read out the examples in the book. Check they produce the correct stresses:

I've never been to a football match.
Me neither. I hate football.

I've never had body piercing or a tattoo.
I have. I've got a tattoo of a rose on my ankle.

I've never read a Harry Potter book.
Really? I've read them all.

Give your own examples of things you have never done and elicit responses from the class, e.g.

I've never eaten sushi. *I have. It's delicious.*
I've never been to India. *Me neither. But I'd like to.*
I've never run a marathon. *Me neither. I'm not fit enough.*

Students write their three examples. With weaker students, you could briefly review the most common irregular past participles first. Students then work in pairs to exchange their examples and react.

If students make mistakes with past participles, note them down and refer them to the list on SB p159.

300 MILLION BOOKS SOLD! (SB p54)

Present Perfect – simple, continuous, passive

ABOUT THE TEXT

The profile of J.K. Rowling on SB p55 provides the context for revising the uses of the Present Perfect (simple, continuous, and passive) and contrasting it with the Past Simple and Past Continuous. The text gives biographical information, a short summary of her early life, and information about her books and how she writes. Students who are interested in the Harry Potter series will probably have read/heard information about J.K. Rowling that they will want to share. You could read the profile before the class to provide yourself with some background information on the author.

Lead in to the topic by asking a few general questions:

Who is Harry Potter? (a boy wizard)
What's the name of his school? (Hogwarts /hɒgwɔ:ts/)
When was the first book published? (1997)
And the last book? (2007).

1 Focus attention on the book titles. Ask students if the books have been translated into their language, and if the translated names of the books/films in their language are similar to the original English, or completely different. Ask for a show of hands of who has read any of the books or seen any of the films. Find out who is the biggest Harry Potter fan, and who isn't keen on the series.

Then elicit any ideas students have about J.K. Rowling. Tell them they will find out about her later in the lesson.

2 This exercise revises the form and use of questions in the Past Simple, the Past Continuous, and the Present Perfect Simple and Continuous, both active and passive forms. The questions are divided to cover the Past Simple and Continuous forms first (1–5), and then the Present Perfect forms (6–12). Students should be able to complete the questions with the auxiliaries fairly easily, but you could point out the tense division to weaker classes before they complete the exercise.

Elicit the answer for question 1. Give students time to complete the exercise, working individually. Students check the answers in pairs. Ask if they disagree on any of the answers and deal with these as a whole class first. Then check the rest of the answers.

Answers

1 was	4 did	7 has	10 have
2 did; was	5 was	8 has	11 has
3 was	6 has	9 have	12 have

3 **T 7.1** [CD 2: Track 30] Focus attention on the text on SB p55. Play the recording and get students to follow the text in their books. Deal with any vocabulary queries and elicit what *J.K.* stands for (Joanne Kathleen). Ask why students think she uses her initials, rather than full name, as a writer (it may be because she didn't want to give her gender away).

Tapescript

T 7.1 See SB p55.

4 **T 7.2** **[CD 2: Track 31]** Put students into pairs to ask and answer the questions, re-reading parts of the text if necessary to find the answers. Play the recording and let students check.

Answers and tapescript

T 7.2

1 **A** Where and when was she born?
 B She was born near Bristol, in England, in 1965.
2 **A** When did she write her first story? What was it about?
 B She wrote her first story when she was six. It was about a rabbit with measles.
3 **A** What was she doing when she had the idea for Harry Potter?
 B She was travelling by train between Manchester and London.
4 **A** Where did she teach English?
 B In Portugal.
5 **A** When was the first Harry Potter book published?
 B In 1997.
6 **A** How long has she been writing the books?
 B For nearly twenty years.
7 **A** How many has she written?
 B Seven.
8 **A** How many children has she had?
 B Three.
9 **A** How many books have been sold?
 B Over 300 million copies.
10 **A** Which books have been made into films?
 B The first six.
11 **A** How much money has she made?
 B She's made over £600 million.
12 **A** How many authors have become billionaires?
 B Only one – her.

GRAMMAR SPOT (SB p55)

This *Grammar spot* reviews Present Simple, Past Simple, and Present Perfect (unfinished past and experience uses). It also contrasts Present Perfect Simple and Continuous, and reviews the form of the Present Perfect passive.

1 Students work in pairs to name the tenses and discuss their use. Monitor and check students' ideas. This will help you see how far students have grasped the basic tense system. Check the answers.

Answers

*She **lives** in Scotland.* (Present Simple used for a fact that is true now.)

*She **lived** in Portugal for three years.* (Past Simple used for a finished action in the past.)

*She's **lived** in Scotland since 1993.* (Present Perfect used for an action that began in the past and still continues in the present.)

*She's **lived** in England, Portugal, and Scotland.* (Present Perfect used for an experience that happened at some time in the past.)

2 Students match the rules to the questions.

Answers

*How long **has** she **been writing** Harry Potter Books?* asks about the activity.
*How many **has** she **written**?* asks about the quantity.

3 Students make the sentences passive and then check them against the text (paragraph 7).

Answers

Her books have been translated into 60 languages.
300 million copies of her books have been sold.
Six of the books have been made into films.

Refer students to Grammar Reference 7.1–7.6 on SB pp140–2.

5 **T 7.3** **[CD 2: Track 32]** The interview gives further contexts for the tenses covered in this lesson. Focus on the example, then give students time to read the questions through first. Play the recording and get students to complete the questions. Allow students to compare their answers in pairs, then check with the whole class.

Play the recording again and get students to note down Jack's answers. Let them compare in pairs. Play relevant sections of the recording again if students disagree or have missed any of the information.

Check the answers.

Answers and tapescript

Answers

1 have you been; Since he was about five. His mum read them to him.
2 have you read; All of them except one, *Harry Potter and the Half-blood Prince.*
3 did you; All of them except *Harry Potter and the Half-blood Prince.*
4 Have you seen; Did you; Yes, all of them and he liked all of them.
5 have been sold; Maybe 20 million (This is Jack's guess, the real figure is 300 million.)
6 do you know; It's J.K. Rowling and she's got two children. (This is Jack's guess, she actually has three children.)
7 Have ... read; Yes, all of them.
8 have you been playing; Since he could walk.
9 Play football.

T 7.3

I = **Interviewer** **J** = **Jack**

Jack, aged 10, talks about Harry Potter

I So Jack, I know you love Harry Potter. How long have you been a fan of the books?
J I think since I was about five but I was so small I couldn't read yet and my mum read them to me.
I How many of the books have you read?
J I've read them all – well, not all exactly.
I What do you mean?
J Well I didn't like *Harry Potter and the Half-blood Prince* so I didn't finish it.
I Which did you like best?
J I liked all the others but not that one. It was too 'samey' – it was boring 'cos it was just like the one before.
I Have you seen any of the Harry Potter films?
J Yes, I have.
I Which have you seen?
J I've seen them all, every one.
I And did you like them *all*?
J Yes, I did. I thought they were fantastic, but my brother didn't, he got scared. He didn't like *The Chamber of Secrets*, the bit where the Basilisk attacked ...
I The what?

J The Basilisk. It's kind of a huge snake and it attacked Harry Potter.
I Oh, I bet a lot of children were frightened by it.
J I wasn't.
I Jack, have you any idea how many Harry Potter books have been sold in the world?
J Er – I dunno. Er – millions, maybe 20 million.
I Er – not quite. It's 300 million.
J 300 million. Wow! That's a lot of books.
I And what do you know about the author?
J I know it's J.K. Rowling and she's got two children. I wonder if they've read their mum's books.
I She has three children, actually. Have a lot of your friends read the books?
J Yes, every single one.
I What *all* your friends?
J Yeah, definitely – all of them.
I That's amazing. Now, I know as well as Harry Potter, you have another passion.
J Yeah, football. I'm a big Blackburn Rovers fan. They're brilliant!
I Are they? And how long have you been playing football?
J Since I could walk. I'd rather play football than do anything else in the world.
I So, If I asked you – what would you rather do this afternoon? Read a Harry Potter or play football?
J You know the answer.

6 Give students a few moments to think of their favourite books/films. Model the activity by giving an example of your own favourites and getting students to ask questions. Put students into pairs to continue the activity. Monitor and check for accurate question formation and tense use. Note any common errors and feed back on them at the end of the activity or in a later lesson.

Ask a student from some of the pairs to tell the class about their partner's favourite books/films. This allows for practice of the *he/she* forms.

PRACTICE (SB p56)

Discussing grammar

1 This exercise consolidates the tense use with a series of contrastive sentences. Elicit the names of the tenses and reasons for their use in the first pair of sentences.

Students work in pairs to complete the task. In a monolingual class, you could let students use their own language, especially with weaker students.

Go through the answers with the class. If there are areas of confusion, refer students to the relevant sections of Grammar Reference 7.3–7.6 on SB pp141–2.

Answers

1 **I lived** (Past Simple used for a finished action in the past.)
I've lived (Present Perfect used for an action that began in the past and still continues in the present.)
2 **I work** (Present Simple used for a fact that is true in the present.)
I've worked (Present Perfect used for an action that began in the past and still continues in the present.)
3 **have you been working** (Present Perfect Continuous used for an action that began in the past and is still continuing in the present. The Present Perfect Simple would also be possible here.)
have you worked (Present Perfect Simple for experiences at some time in your life. The Present Perfect Simple is used when saying how many times, places, etc., and expresses completion.)
4 **Have you ever met** (Present Perfect used to ask about an experience at any time in your life.)
Did you meet (Past Simple used to ask about a finished time in the past.)
5 **I've already finished** (Present Perfect positive + *already* to say that something has happened earlier than expected.)
I haven't finished yet (Present Perfect negative + *yet* to say that something has not happened although we expect it to happen.)
6 **Who's been eating** (Present Perfect Continuous used for an action that began in the past and is still continuing = there are some chocolates left.)
Who's eaten (Present Perfect Simple to express completion = there aren't any chocolates left.)
7 **was shot** (Past Simple passive for a finished action in the past.)
's been shot (Present Perfect passive for an action in the recent past that has a present result.)
8 **How long are you here for**? (Present Simple of *be* to refer to the future.)
How long have you been here for? (Present Perfect used for an action that began in the past and still continues in the present.)

Note that the contrast in the sentences in 8 is practised again in the *Spoken English* box at the end of SB p57.

2 **T 7.4** [**CD 2: Track 33**] This exercise gives further practice in the contrasts highlighted in exercise 1.

Elicit the correct verb form in sentence 1. Students complete the task, working individually. Let students check in pairs before playing the recording.

Answers and tapescript

T 7.4

1 His plane **took off** a few minutes ago.
2 The president **has resigned** and a new president **has been elected**.
3 **I've been working** in Dubai since last March. When **did you arrive**?
4 How many emails **have you sent**?
5 What **have you been doing** in the bathroom? You**'ve been** in there for ages.
6 A huge snowstorm **has hit** New York. Over 40 cms of snow **has fallen** in the past 12 hours. People **have been advised** to stay at home.

3 This exercise practises word order with the adverbs that are often used with Present Perfect Simple and Continuous. Write the first sentence *I've read that book* on the board. Ask students where they can put the words from the box in the sentence without changing the verb form. Ask what these words add to the meaning (see *Answers* below).

Students work through the sentences individually and then compare answers with a partner. When checking with the class, elicit what these words express (see *Answers* on TB p80). Remind students that we use *yet* only in negatives and questions. Remind them also that we use *never* with a positive verb, and *ever* in questions.

Answers

1 I've **just** read that book. (= very recently)
I've **already** read that book. (= before now/before expected)
I've **never** read that book. (= not at any time)
2 I've **just** been reading an interesting book. (= very recently)
3 Has it **just** been made into a film? (= very recently)
Has it **already** been made into a film? (= before now/before expected)
Has it **ever** been made into a film? (= at any time)
4 He's **just** learned to drive. (= very recently)
He's **already** learned to drive. (= before now/before expected)
He's **never** learned to drive. (= not at any time)
5 The match hasn't finished **yet**. (= up to now)
6 Have you **just** been to Morocco? (= very recently)
Have you been to Morocco **yet**? (= up to now; it implies you expect it to happen)
Have you **already** been to Morocco? (= before now/before expected)
Have you **ever** been to Morocco? (= at any time in your life)

Calvin Klein – a passion for fashion

The aim of this section is to consolidate the use of Present Perfect Simple and Continuous to refer to indefinite past time. The context is the life and work of the fashion designer, Calvin Klein. The Coty Award, referred to in the chart about Klein on SB p56, is a prestigious award given in the world of fashion.

4 Write the name Calvin Klein on the board and elicit any information students know about him. If students are short of ideas, give them prompts, e.g. *nationality? year of birth? married? famous for?* Elicit a range of ideas/guesses. Then get students to read through the chart quickly and check their ideas. Deal with any vocabulary queries and check the pronunciation of the names of the Calvin Klein perfumes: Obsession /əbseʃən/, Eternity /ɪtɜːnəti/, and Euphoria /juːfɔːrɪə/.

Then elicit the answer about what Klein has designed.

Answer

Clothing, sportswear, jeans, underwear, perfumes, cosmetics, and make-up.

5 **T 7.5** **[CD 2: Track 34]** Put students into pairs. Get two students to ask and answer the example question across the class. Students then continue the task in their pairs. Monitor and check for correct tense use. Note any common errors and feed back on them after the listening stage of this exercise.

Tell students that they can listen and check their answers and also learn some more information about Klein's life. Encourage them to make brief notes of any extra information.

Play the recording and get students to check their answers. With weaker students, be prepared to play the recording again to let students focus on the extra information.

Elicit examples of the extra information students have learned from the recording. As students have just been practising the Present Perfect, they may try to use it to refer to the definite past, e.g. **He has met his wife when they were students*. Remind students that if we know exactly *when* something happened or if the time period has finished, we use the Past Simple (*He met his wife …*). Students continue to share the extra information they have heard. Highlight any tense mistakes and encourage the rest of the class to help with corrections.

Answers and tapescript

2 Sportswear, underwear, and jeans.
3 He's been married twice, divorced twice.
4 One.
5 Seven.
6 Since the 1980s. *Obsession*, *Eternity*, *Euphoria*, *Truth*, and *Crave*.
7 Kate Moss, Julia Roberts, Gwyneth Paltrow, Helen Hunt, and Brooke Shields.
8 Since the 1990s.

T 7.5

Calvin Klein – a passion for fashion

A How long has Calvin Klein been interested in fashion?
B Since he was about 14. When he was a teenager he spent hours sketching women's suits and dresses.
A What different kinds of clothes has he designed in his career?
B He's designed sportswear and underwear but he's possibly most famous for his jeans, which always have his name on the back pocket.
A How many times has he been married and divorced?
B He's been married twice and divorced twice. His first wife was Jayne Centre. He met her when they were both fashion students. His second wife was Kelly Rector – she was a rich New York socialite and photographer.
A How many children does he have?
B Just one. A daughter Marci, who is now a successful television producer.
A How many awards has he won?
B He's won seven fashion awards altogether. He made history because he won awards for both men's and women's fashions in the same year.
A How long has he been making his own perfumes?
B He's been making Calvin Klein perfumes since the late 80s.
A What are they called?
B His first were called *Obsession* and *Eternity*, his most recent is called *Euphoria*. His others include *Truth*, and *Crave*, which was designed for men.
A Which famous people has he worked with and designed for?
B He's worked with the model Kate Moss and designed clothes for many stars including Julia Roberts, Gwyneth Paltrow, and Helen Hunt. He's also worked with Brooke Shields, who, aged 15, modelled his jeans with the famous line 'nothing comes between me and my Calvins.'
A How long has he been selling cosmetics?
B Since the 1990s. These are only sold in the best department stores such as Harrods, in London, and Bloomingdales in New York.

Time expressions

6 This exercise reviews and consolidates time expressions used with the tenses in this unit. Refer students back to the chart about Calvin Klein and their answers in exercise 5, and elicit the missing expression from sentence 1. Students complete the exercise, working individually. Let students check in pairs before checking with the class. Deal with any answers that students disagree on first, asking the whole class to feed in.

Answers
1 when he was 14
2 while he was studying at the Fashion Institute
3 in 1972
4 four years after he got married
5 for ten years
6 until he was 44
7 since the 1970s
8 Between 1982 and 1986

Roleplay

If you are short of time, you can get students to prepare their interview questions for homework and do the roleplay in a later lesson.

Give students time to draft their questions in pairs. Monitor and help as necessary. If possible, set up the interviews to look as authentic as possible. Position chairs opposite each other and give the students props such as a microphone, the interviewer's set of questions and notes, and glasses of water. Students who enjoy roleplay can even try adopting American accents!

With smaller classes, a pair of students can do the roleplay for the rest of the class as if they are a studio audience. With larger classes, students will need to do the roleplay at the same time. Whichever format you choose, make notes on any common errors to highlight in a later lesson. The focus here is fluency and fun and so students shouldn't be interrupted. See TB p52 for notes on recording students on video.

SUGGESTION
If students enjoy the roleplay, you could ask them to research another living celebrity/public figure in pairs and repeat the activity. Make sure students who played the interviewer take the role of the celebrity this time.

WRITING (SB p109)

Describing a person – Facts and opinions

This unit continues the work on descriptions that students started in Unit 6, with a focus on describing a person. The stages that lead up to the writing task include reading a model text for gist, distinguishing facts from personal opinions, finding words for different aspects of descriptions, and looking at words that modify the meaning of adjectives.

1 Give some example sentences about someone in your own family. Students then write their sentences. Encourage them to include some of the adjectives they covered in Unit 6. Students read their sentences to the rest of the class, or in groups if you have a big class.

2 Answer the questions about your sentences. Then get students to do the same about theirs.

3 Focus attention on the photo of Joe and elicit initial impressions of him. Get students to read the text through quickly and answer the question.

Answer
The writer admires everything about Uncle Joe.

4 Read the task instructions with the class. Ask students to read the first paragraph again and mark the text accordingly. Check they have coded the text correctly (see *Answers* below) before they continue the task in pairs. Encourage them to use the context to help them with new vocabulary, or to use a dictionary if appropriate. Monitor and help as necessary.

Check the answers.

Answers
My Crazy Uncle Joe
Of all my relatives, I like my Uncle Joe the best. He's my mother's much younger brother. He was only nine when I was born, so he's been more like a big brother to me than an uncle. He is in his mid-20s now and he is always such good fun to be with.

He studied at a drama school in Liverpool, and then he moved to London a year ago to try his luck in the theatre. He shares a flat with three other would-be actors and he works as a waiter and a part-time DJ. He's passionate about his music, it's called House Music, and it's a kind of electronic dance music. When he 'deejays' he goes completely wild, waving his arms and yelling at the crowds. Everybody catches his enthusiasm. He's absolutely brilliant, I'm proud that he's my uncle.

Also, I think he is really good-looking. He's quite tall with sandy-coloured hair, and twinkly, dark brown eyes. He's had lots of girlfriends, but I don't think there is anyone particularly special at the moment. He has a great relationship with his flatmates, they are always laughing and joking together. He knows how to have fun but he's also an extremely caring person. I can talk to him about all kinds of problems that I could not discuss with my parents. He's very understanding of someone my age.

He works hard and he plays hard. He's had lots of auditions for various theatrical roles. He hasn't had much luck yet, but I'm sure that one day he'll be a highly successful actor. I think he's really talented but he says he doesn't want to be rich or famous, he just wants to prove to himself that he's a good actor.

SUGGESTION
It can be interesting for students to analyse newspaper/magazines articles in the same way as exercise 4. This helps them to see the balance between fact and opinion in the articles.

5 Students find examples of the aspects of description in the text. If you are short of time, you could put students in pairs and divide the task up so that each student does half and they then exchange answers.

Elicit the key words and lines from the class.

Answers
his physical appearance: quite tall, with sandy-coloured hair, and twinkly, dark brown eyes; really good-looking

his character: He is always such good fun to be with; absolutely brilliant. He knows how to have fun but he's also an extremely caring person.

his past life: He was only nine when I was born. He studied at a drama school in Liverpool, and then he moved to London a year ago to try his luck in the theatre. He's had lots of girlfriends … He's had lots of auditions for various theatrical roles. He hasn't had much luck yet. **his current lifestyle:** He shares a flat with three other would-be actors and he works as a waiter and a part-time DJ. He's passionate about his music. When he 'deejays' he goes completely wild, waving his arms and yelling at the crowds. Everybody catches his enthusiasm. He has a great relationship with his flatmates, they are always laughing and joking together. He works hard and he play hard.

6 Ask students to find *much* in the text and ask them how it qualifies the meaning of the adjective which follows it (it makes the adjective stronger). Students work through the other examples in pairs. Check the answers with the class.

Answer

The words all make the following adjective stronger, except *quite*, which makes it slightly less strong.

7 If you have time in class, get students to make notes for each of the points in the list. Monitor and help students with this planning stage.

Set the writing task for homework. Remind students to keep to the number of words and to check their work before handing it in.

See the *Suggestion* on TB p72 for ideas for peer checking and displaying students' work.

Have you ever ...?

7 This exercise gives students personalized practice in the experience use of the Present Perfect. With weaker students, elicit the past participles of the verbs in the list.

Focus attention on the examples in the speech bubbles. Model the intonation, stresses, and weak forms and get students to practise the two versions of the conversation across the class:

/ə/ /ə/ /ə/ /ə/ /ə/

Have you ever bought a pair of designer jeans?

No, I haven't. I can't afford them.

Yes, I have. I'm wearing them now.

Where did you buy them?

Tell students they don't need to use all the ideas in the list, but can choose four or five that interest them. Remind them to use Past Simple in their follow-up questions if they are asking *When ...?/Where ...?*

Students have conversations in pairs, using the prompts. Monitor and note any common errors in the tense use.

Students tell the class about their partner and so get some practice of the he/she forms. Feed back on any tense errors and get students to correct as a class.

SPOKEN ENGLISH – *How long ...?*

This section extends the coverage of *How long ...?* to cover present and future meaning.

1 Read the sentences with the class and elicit the two questions with *How long*. Elicit the answers to the concept questions.

Answers

1 *How long are you here for?* a period around now (past and future)
2 *How long have you been here?* past up to the present

2 **T 7.6** [CD 2: Track 35] Elicit the question for the first answer. Students complete the task, working in pairs.

Play the recording. Students check their answers and then practise the conversations in pairs.

Answers and tapescript

T 7.6

1 **A** How long are you here for?
B Four more days. We came two days ago.
2 **A** How long have you been here?
B Since Monday.
3 **A** How long are you here for?
B Until Friday. We're leaving Friday morning.
4 **A** How long have you been here?
B Over half an hour! Where have you been?
5 **A** How long are you here for?
B We're staying a month altogether.

ADDITIONAL MATERIAL

Workbook Unit 7

Exercises 1–4 Present Perfect or Past Simple?

Exercise 5 Present Perfect passive

Exercises 6–9 Present Perfect Continuous

Exercise 10 Tense review

READING AND SPEAKING (SB p58)

Football – a global passion

ABOUT THE TEXT

The theme of 'passions' is carried through with a section on one of the world's most popular sports – football. Whether students are football fans or not, they are likely to be aware of its dominance in sport, and to have an opinion about it – positive or negative!

The text outlines the development of football from its origins to the worldwide sport it is today. It is rich in facts and details to make it of interest to those who aren't necessarily football fans, but the exploitation of the text is staged so that students don't get overloaded with information.

The high-profile teams mentioned in the text are *Manchester United* /ju:naɪtɪd/, *AC Milan*, *Real*

Madrid, and *Bayern Munich*. The players are Pelé, David Beckham, George Best, and Diego Maradona.

The Football Association (FA), formed in the 1800s in London, and its international equivalent the Fédération Internationale de Football Association (FIFA), now control the modern game. The World Cup is an international competition held every four years. The text uses both the terms *football* and *soccer*. Both terms are used in British English, though *football* is more usual, but American English uses *soccer* to distinguish this game from its own sport of American football.

The text mentions the role of public schools in the development of football. You may need to explain that, despite the name, public schools in Britain are private and fee-paying. The schools mentioned in the text are Eton (one of the best-known and most expensive public schools for boys, located to the west of London) and Rugby School (a smaller public school in central England famous for developing the game of rugby).

Two vehicles are mentioned in the text: *rickshaw* (a light two-wheeled hooded vehicle drawn by one or more people, chiefly used in Asian countries) and *tuk tuk* (a motor vehicle with three wheels, used as a taxi in Thailand).

Lead in to the topic by asking students to brainstorm words and expressions connected with football, e.g. *footballer, football team/coach/fan/club/player/match/stadium/field*, etc. Also use this opportunity to pre-teach/check related words which may be new from the text: *chaos* /ˈkeɪɒs/, *half-time, rules, to kick, side* (in this context, *team*), *posts, to host/co-host (a competition), to qualify, waste ground.*

1 Ask students for a show of hands to find out who loves football and who hates it. Elicit a few reasons from the class for their opinions. Ask for the names of famous footballers and their teams. If appropriate, ask students who they think is the best player and team, but keep this brief!

2 Tell students they are going to find out how football has become so important across the world. Set a time limit of 2–3 minutes for students to read the two paragraphs. Put students in small groups to discuss the answers before checking with the class. Elicit students' reactions to the statistics.

Answers

1 1.5 million teams worldwide; 300,000 clubs; eight out of ten people watch the World Cup; 120 million regular team players.
2 The Brazilian footballer Pelé called it that.
3 All you need is a ball, a piece of ground, and two posts.
4 George Best, Diego Maradona, and Pelé. They all learned their football skills on waste ground.

3 Elicit a few suggestions about how football began. Give students about five minutes to read the relevant section of the text, check their ideas, and answer the questions. Check they understand 'sticking point' in question 8 (an area of disagreement). Students discuss the answers in pairs/small groups before checking with the class.

Answers

1 A Chinese kicking game.
2 The Romans and North American Indians played a kicking game. In the 1500s the English played 'mob football'.
3 'Mob football' was probably very fast and violent with no rules. Players did anything to get the ball and often got injuries and broken bones.
4 Each school had different rules for playing the game. At Eton, the ball was kicked high and long. At Rugby School, the boys caught the ball and ran with it.
5 Each player followed the rules that he was used to.
6 It was common to play half the match by one side's rules and the second half by the other's.
7 The men who loved football met in the London pub to sort out the chaos. They formed the Football Association and started the Book of Laws.
8 The 'sticking point' was whether you could pick up the ball and run with it. Once this was decided, rugby was also born. It was decided you couldn't pick up the ball in football, but you could in rugby.

4 Ask students to look at the first sentence in question 1 and guess the correct continent. Students read the relevant sections of the text and check their answers. Students then work in pairs to answer the rest of the questions, referring back to the text as necessary.

Check the answers with the class.

Answers

1 a Australia
  b Europe
  c Asia
  d South America; Africa
  e North America
2 Europe, South America, and Africa are most enthusiastic; Asia and Australia are the least enthusiastic.
3 It is called 'soccer' to distinguish it from the Americans' own game, American football, which is called 'football'.
4 The European clubs have a lot of money to buy the best players.
5 North America: in 1991 the US won the first Women's World Cup, and the World Cup was in Los Angeles in 1994; Asia: Japan and Korea co-hosted the World Cup in 2002; Australia: they qualified for the 2006 World Cup; Africa: having the 2010 World Cup in South Africa is very important for African football.

What do you think?

Put students in small groups to discuss the questions. Elicit a range of opinions in a feedback session. Check what students understand by 'football has totally changed the worlds of sport, media, and leisure' (football has become not only a sport but also an important source of income for the media and leisure industries, with TV programmes, magazines, fashions, etc.).

VOCABULARY AND LISTENING (SB p60)

Things I'm passionate about

ABOUT THE LISTENING

This section brings together the language of expressing feelings and opinions with a listening task on people's passions. It also consolidates the tense use (Present Perfect + *How long ...?* and Past Simple). The listening consists of five people talking about the thing they are passionate about and the reasons why they like it so much. Students read sections of each monologue, work out what the people are talking about, and listen and check. They then listen again to pick out specific information. The five monologues together make for a relatively long recording, but the task can be broken up and students only have to listen for certain information. The overall tone is conversational, and students should easily understand the gist of each recording. You can pre-teach/check the following items to help students with the more detailed comprehension: *to read aloud, a challenge, freshness, a miracle, magic, a fox.*

1 Lead in to the section by asking students to talk about their likes and dislikes without using the verb *like*! Students should be familiar with the verbs/expressions *love, hate, be keen on, can't stand.* Elicit a range of examples, e.g. *I love spending time with my friends. I'm keen on hill walking. I hate shopping in busy places. I can't stand people who use their phones in restaurants.*

Focus attention on the expressions in the box. Students work in pairs to decide which are positve, negative, and neutral.

Check the answers and the pronunciation of *loathe* /ləʊð/ and *fond* /fɒnd/. Highlight the prepositions in *keen* ***on*** and *fond* ***of***.

Answers

positive:	adore, keen on, crazy about, fond of
negative:	loathe, can't stand, can't bear
neutral:	quite like, not that keen on, don't mind

2 Focus attention on the example. Point out that some of the expressions are verbs, e.g. *quite like*, and *can't bear*, but others are adjectives and need to be preceded by a verb such as *be*, e.g. *I am keen on football.* Students continue the task, working individually. Remind them to check that they have changed the verb forms correctly and that they are using the correct prepositions.

Get students to read their answers aloud and check their main stresses and intonation (see *Answers* below). Remind them that English uses a wide voice range, especially when expressing feelings.

Answers

1 She absolutely adores ice -cream.
2 He's very keen on all water sports.
3 I can't bear opera.
4 My brother is crazy about (playing) video games.
5 My sister isn't really that keen on any sports.
6 I can't stand people who always talk about themselves.
7 My mum is very fond of (going to) musicals.
8 I don't mind green tea but I prefer English breakfast tea.
9 The thing I loathe most is tidying my room.
10 I quite like my job but it's time I applied for another one.

As a personalized extension to the exercise, get students to change the information to make the sentences true for them, e.g. *I absolutely adore Italian food. I'm very keen on jazz.* Students take it in turns to modify the sentences about themselves. Alternatively, students can give three sentences about themselves, using the expressions, one of which isn't true. Their partner or the rest of the class must guess which one isn't true.

3 Give students time to read the extracts from the recordings. Deal with any vocabulary queries and elicit possible answers about Julia.

Students work in pairs or groups of three to discuss the other extracts. Don't confirm or reject any suggestions that they have at this stage.

4 **T 7.7** [CD 2: Track 36] Play the recording and let students check their answers. Get them to write the passion next to the correct name.

Answers and tapescript

Julia – tennis
Paul – horseriding
Andrew – poetry
James – British weather
Harriet – foxhunting

T 7.7

Julia

I'm really passionate about playing tennis. I've been playing nearly 20 years. I was about 7 or 8 when I started having lessons, and I had a fantastic teacher. I think that's why I still love it – she was passionate about the sport and that influenced me. I've played in competitions, mainly when I was at school, I still do sometimes. I enjoy it, I think, because it's a very psychological game. I mean, if you're playing badly you have to push yourself to continue; it's a challenge not to give up. It's also a very sociable sport – I've made lots of friends playing doubles, and it's a game that doesn't have to be expensive – anyone can play – all you need is a tennis racket. You don't need expensive clothing or equipment, like you do for skiing, and it's a fantastic way to keep fit all year round – there's only about 3 months that you can't play. When I lived in Australia I played every week of the year. I adored that, it was brilliant.

Paul

My passion at the moment is horseriding – it's strange to hear myself say that 'cos I've only been doing it about a year and I never imagined I'd be so keen on it. It all happened because I was talking to someone who rode horses and I said that stupid thing people often say, 'Oh, I've always wanted to do that,' and she said, 'Why don't you then?' And I thought, 'why not?' I've always liked horses, they're so big and powerful but so beautiful when you see them racing round a field or on a track. It amazes me that they let people ride on their backs. Riding is very physically demanding because your body has to be in harmony ... er, it has to move with the horse, but it keeps you fit. Of course, I have fallen off a few times, but it seems that the more you fall, the less it hurts. Also, you have to try and understand your horse – they have moods, you never quite know what a ride is going to be like – a horse you had a fantastic ride on one week can be slow and miserable the next week. I really like that about horses – they have personalities.

Andrew

I'm passionate about poetry – I studied English Literature at university but it wasn't until after I graduated that I really got into poetry and I started writing some myself. And I met some other people who wrote poetry and I heard them read it aloud and that was amazing. I felt the power of the words – the thing I like so much about it is that you can say so much with just a few words, so little means a lot. Each word, each noun, adjective, preposition has to work hard. There's a poem by Simon Armitage called 'To His Lost Lover' – it's a poem of regret, about not saying the things you should have said in a relationship. It has it all for me – poetry's all about saying what often goes unsaid, and with passion. It can be such a help in your life – if you feel tired or depressed, you can always find a poem that will help – it can be short or long, it doesn't matter.

James

The thing I'm passionate about, and this may surprise many people, is -erm, British weather. I know lots of people can't stand our weather -er, they complain about it all the time, but I love it. You see, when I was a child my family lived in California for five years and we had about 365 days of sunshine every year, it was so boring. I was ten when we came back to England and I just loved all the changes in the weather. Here, you really appreciate the sunshine *and* you notice the seasons. For me one of nature's miracles is after a long, hot, sunny day there's a thunderstorm or a downpour of rain and you go out in the garden and you can smell the freshness in the air, the world has been washed clean and bright. It's magic. And you know it's a myth that it rains all the time; it doesn't. Anyway, it's the rain that gives us our green fields. You know that joke 'if you don't like English weather – wait ten minutes' – that's why it's interesting.

Harriet

Something I feel really passionately about is fox-hunting. My grandmother, mother, and uncles have always been keen on hunting and I started when I was about 6. We hunt up in the Welsh mountains, we go out from about 11 a.m. and we don't get back till after dark. And the thing I love best about it is that you are away from everything and everyone, up in the hills, and you work together with horses and dogs. And if you're following a clever fox you can see him working out how to lose the dogs – he knows the countryside so well, where the holes are, where to hide. Where we hunt in Wales – erm ... it's a sheep farming area, so the farmers contact us if they have a problem with a fox. We only hunt on their land if we are asked. I don't hunt so much now because the laws have changed.

5 **T 7.7** **[CD 2: Track 36]** Give students time to read the questions. Play the recording of Julia again and elicit the answers. Play the rest of the recording, pausing at the end of each speaker to let students record their answers. Students check their answers in pairs. Play selected sections of the recording again if students have missed the information.

Check the answers with the class.

Answers

Julia

1 Nearly 20 years.
2 Her teacher was passionate about the sport.
3 It's a challenge not to give up if you are playing badly. It's also a very sociable sport. It doesn't have to be expensive – all you need is a tennis racket. It's a fantastic way to keep fit all year round.

Paul

1 About a year.
2 He was talking to someone who rode horses. He had always wanted to do horseriding, and she suggested he should try it.
3 He's always liked horses. It keeps you fit. Horses have personalities and each time you ride it is different.

Andrew

1 Since he graduated from university.
2 He met some people who wrote poetry and he heard them read it aloud.
3 You can say so much with just a few words. Each word has to work hard. It can be a help in your life.

James

1 Since he was ten.
2 He lived in California for five years, and it was boring because it was sunny all the time. When he came back to England he loved all the changes in the weather.
3 The changes in weather are interesting. He loves the freshness in the air after a storm/rain. The rain makes everything green.

Harriet

1 Since she was six.
2 Her family has always been keen on hunting.
3 You are away from everything and everyone, and you work together with horses and dogs. A clever fox will know how to lose the dogs.

6 Elicit an example using one of the expressions from exercise 1, e.g. *James is crazy about the British weather.* Students work in pairs to talk about the five people.

What do you think?

Work through the discussion questions as a class. Establish which passion described in the listening students find most appealing, and which they aren't interested in. Elicit a range of examples of what the students feel passionate about. Encourage the rest of the class to ask questions about their passions.

SUGGESTION

Students could prepare and give a more formal presentation about their passion to the class and, if possible, bring in objects related to it. The rest of the class could then ask questions. See TB p52 for notes on recording students on video.

EXTRA IDEA

Song After T 7.7 [CD 2: Track 37]

Somewhere only we know TB p154

This is intended as a fun activity, which you may like to include at the end of the lesson. Students complete a gapped version of the song and then listen and check. There are also three comprehension/interpretation tasks. The answers are on TB p158.

EVERYDAY ENGLISH (SB p61)

Making the right noises

This section contains a number of short expressions used in spoken English when expressing agreement, sympathy, pleasure, and surprise. Although students aren't expected to use all of them immediately in natural conversation, it's good for them to be able to recognize the expressions, especially when they are talking to native speakers. Regular recycling of the expressions in class will help students build them into their productive repertoire in a natural way. The section contains a *Music of English* feature to help students with the stress and intonation in these expressions.

1 Focus attention on the boxes. Check comprehension of the headings. Elicit the heading for the first box. Students complete the task, working individually. Check the answers with the class. Point out that although the expressions in each box have the same general meaning, there are subtle differences between them, which means they are not all completely interchangeable.

Answers

Pleasure	Agreement
How fantastic! That's great! Lovely! Congratulations! Brilliant! Good for you!	Absolutely. Definitely. Of course. Fair enough. Fine. OK.
Surprise	**Sympathy**
Did you? You didn't! That's amazing! You're kidding! You did what? Really?	What a pity! That's a shame. Oh dear. That's too bad. How awful! Bad luck.

MUSIC OF ENGLISH

1 T 7.8 [CD 2: Track 38] Play the recording and get students to repeat the expressions. If they are sounding rather flat, repeat their intonation back to them and ask if it sounds interested or not. Be prepared to drill the intonation chorally and individually.

T 7.8

How fantastic! Absolutely. Did you? What a pity!

2 T 7.9 [CD 2: Track 39] Tell students they are going to listen to some more expressions. Play the recording, stopping after each expression so that students can repeat.

T 7.9

Pleasure: That's great! Lovely!
Agreement: Definitely. Fair enough. Fine.
Surprise: You didn't! You did what?
Sympathy: That's a shame. That's too bad. Bad luck.

2 T 7.10 [CD 2: Track 40] Give students time to read A's lines and think about the possible responses. Play the recording, pausing after each response to give students time to write down their answers.

Check the answers and then get students to practise in pairs. Monitor and check students' intonation. If necessary, play the recording again and get students to repeat, exaggerating the voice range.

Elicit alternative responses for B's lines (see bracketed answers below).

Answers and tapescript

T 7.10

A My grandfather hasn't been too well lately.
B **Oh dear.** (What a pity!/That's a shame./That's too bad.)
A He's 79. Don't you think at his age he should slow down a bit?
B **Absolutely.** (Definitely./Of course.)
A But he won't listen to me. He says he wants to enjoy his life to the full.
B **Fair enough.** (Of course. Absolutely.)
A Last summer he went on a two-week cycling holiday in France.
B **You're kidding!** (That's amazing!/Really?)
A We're going to give him a big party for his 80th birthday.
B **That's great.** (How fantastic!/Lovely./Brilliant./Good for you.)
A But before that, I'm going to have a word with him and tell him to take things more easy.
B **Good for you.**

3 T 7.11 [CD 2: Track 41] Elicit possible answers for conversation 1. Students complete the task, working in pairs.

Play the recording and get students to compare their responses with those on the recording. Elicit as many of B's further comments as students can remember. Play the recording again if necessary.

Check the range of responses that are suitable (see bracketed answers below).

Answers and tapescript

T 7.11

1 A My boyfriend's just asked me to marry him.
B Did he? (Really?) How fantastic! (Brilliant/Lovely./That's great.) Did you say yes?

2 A Will spaghetti bolognese be OK for dinner?
B Of course. (Absolutely./Definitely./Fine.) That's great! It's one of my favourites.

3 **A** There's a strike at the airport so my holiday's been cancelled.
B Oh dear. That's a shame. (What a pity!/That's too bad./How awful!/Bad luck.) Will you get your money back?
4 **A** I failed my driving test again.
B You didn't! (Did you?) That's too bad. (What a pity!/That's a shame./Oh dear./How awful!/Bad luck.) Better luck next time.
5 **A** We're expecting a baby.
B Are you? (That's amazing!/You're kidding!/ Really?) Congratulations! (How fantastic!/That's great./ Brilliant./Good for you.) When's it due?
6 **A** So you think I should save to buy a car, not borrow the money?
B Definitely. (Absolutely./Of course.) You've already got too many debts.
7 **A** I told him I never wanted to see him again.
B You're kidding! (Did you?/You didn't!/You're kidding!/You did what?/Really?) What a pity! (That's a shame./Oh dear./That's too bad./How awful!) I always thought the two of you were so good together.

4 Ask two students to read out conversation 1 and keep it going. Students practise and continue the conversations. Remind them to use a wide voice range on the responses. Monitor and check students' intonation.

5 Model the activity before students do the pairwork. Start a conversation with a confident student about a good or bad day, e.g.

A *I had a great day last Saturday.*
B *Really? Why? What did you do?*
A *Well, it was my birthday and my sister organized a surprise party.*
B *How fantastic! Were many people there?*
A *Yes, quite a few. And my sister had invited all my old school friends.*
B *You're kidding. That's great.*

Put students in new pairs to invent new conversations. If students seem short of ideas, feed in possible contexts:

good: you heard from an old friend/got promotion at work/had a fantastic meal/met the man/woman of your dreams

bad: you got a parking ticket/had a row with your best friend/had to take back your new computer/failed a test/ lost your wallet/purse.

Don't forget!

Workbook Unit 7

Exercise 11 Vocabulary – *be* and *have*

Exercise 12 Prepositions – Noun + preposition

Exercise 13 Pronunciation – Sentence stress

Exercise 14 Listening – Applying for a film course

Word list

Refer students to the Word list for Unit 7 (SB p155). They could translate the words, learn them at home, or transfer some of them to their vocabulary notebook.

8

Verb patterns
Body language
Travel and numbers

No fear!

Introduction to the unit

This unit takes two broad themes – facing fears, and the potential dangers of travelling. The unit starts with language work on verb patterns, which are contextualized through emails that young travellers have sent home to their parents. The *Listening and speaking* section focuses on fears and phobias. *Reading and speaking* picks up the travel theme with a jigsaw reading on dangerous journeys in history. The vocabulary syllabus continues with a focus on 'body language' (parts of the body, verbs related to them, and idioms). *Everyday English* covers the language of numbers in travel contexts, and *Writing* goes back to storytelling with the book's second focus on writing a narrative.

Language aims

Grammar – verb patterns This unit covers a range of verb patterns. Students will already be familiar with some of these patterns such as verb + *-ing* and verb + infinitive, and they are likely to use them fairly accurately, e.g. *I like going to the cinema. I want to be an architect*, etc. The aim here is to consolidate the basic forms and highlight and practise others to extend students' knowledge. This includes verbs that can be followed by both the *-ing* form and the infinitive with a change of meaning. Students may be unaware of these verbs and will need help in using them accurately:

I remember paying the bill. (= I have a memory of a past action.)

I remembered to pay the bill. (= I didn't forget.)

These pairs of verbs appear in the summary of Verb patterns on SB p158.

There are no difficult grammatical rules for students to deal with in this unit, but students are still likely to make mistakes with the range of patterns covered, especially if the patterns are different in their own language. Students are likely to need regular revision and frequent practice of the patterns in subsequent lessons.

Vocabulary In this unit, students revise the vocabulary of parts of the body, practise related verbs such as *bite*, *blow*, *clap*, etc. and practise nouns and phrases which collocate with these verbs. They are also introduced to idioms to do with parts of the body, e.g. *see eye to eye, have a sweet tooth.*

Everyday English Students review and extend their knowledge of talking about numbers with a lesson on numbers related to travel. This includes phone numbers, credit card numbers, prices, decimals, and percentages.

Notes on the unit

STARTER (SB p62)

Focus attention on the cartoons. Students match the sentences with the pictures. Elicit the difference in meaning between the two forms. Ask students if they know any other verbs which change meaning when they are followed by the infinitive or the *-ing* form (*start*, *try*, *remember*, *forget*).

Answers
1b, 2a

In sentence 1, *stopped* + infinitive means they stopped in order to talk to each other. They stopped, then they talked.

In sentence 2, *stopped* + *-ing* means that they were talking to each other, then they stopped.

DON'T WORRY MUM! (SB p62)

Verb patterns

ABOUT THE TEXT

The four emails provide a humorous context for the various verb patterns in this lesson. They are typical of the type of messages that young people might send to their parents while travelling or on a gap year (a year taken by a student as a break from education between leaving school and starting a university or college course). The style of writing is informal and contains expressions typically used by teenagers. These are explained in the glossary feature on SB p63. There are also a number of abbreviations, but students should be able to understand these from the context.

Facebook, mentioned in email 1, is a social networking website, set up in 2004 by Mark Zuckerberg, a former student at Harvard University in the US. Initially the membership of *Facebook* was restricted to students of Harvard College and other universities. Since September 11, 2006, anyone 13 or older may join. The site now has more than 62 million active users worldwide. It is the most popular website for uploading photos, with 14 million uploaded daily. Cairns, also in email 1, is a city in Queensland, Australia. Piranhas, in email 3, are South American flesh-eating river fish.

Lead in to the topic by asking some general questions about travelling and young travellers, e.g.
Have you ever been travelling for a few months?
Where did you go and what happened?
Do you know any young people who have taken a gap year and gone travelling?
Why might parents of young travellers be worried while they are away?

1 **T 8.1** **[CD 2: Track 42]** Focus attention on the photos and elicit what the situations are and what students think has just happened. Get students to read and listen to the emails and answer the two gist questions. Deal with any vocabulary queries, encouraging students to use the context to help them understand.

Ask students which scenario they think is the most dangerous, and which email is the funniest.

Answers and tapescript

1 Kate is in Cairns, Australia. She hit her head on a metal bunk bed after having a few drinks. There was a lot of blood and she had to go to hospital.
2 Dan is in Australia. He has given his mother's phone number to some Australians he has just met and said that they can stay with her next month.
3 William is in South America. He went piranha-fishing and tried to attract the fish by dropping meat into the water. He camped on the river banks without a torch and so was lucky to escape from the crocodile.
4 Sally is in Arequipa, Peru. She spent a night in a hotel but was woken by an earthquake. She fell asleep again and woke up in a room full of holes. She plans to stay there for two more days.

2 This exercise highlights key verb patterns in sentences based on the contexts of the emails. Point out that more than one answer may be possible, as in the example in number 1. Students work through the task individually.

Give students time to check their answers in pairs before checking with the class. In addition to checking the letters in the key, reinforce the focus of the lesson by getting students to say what pattern follows each verb, e.g. *want/hope* + infinitive, *love/look forward to* + *-ing*. Point out that some of the verbs, e.g. *forget* in sentence 3 and *stop* in sentence 8, can be followed by either infinitive or *-ing* form, but with a change in meaning.

Answers
2 a, b 3 b 4 c 5 a, b 6 a 7 b, c 8 b, c 9 a 10 b, c

3 **T 8.2** **[CD 2: Track 43]** Tell students they are going to hear eight lines taken from phone conversations the travellers had with one of their parents at home. Play the first sentence, and elicit the missing word and who is speaking.

Play the rest of the recording and get students to complete the task. Check the answers, eliciting who is speaking each time. Also check the meaning of *couldn't help* + *-ing* (= couldn't avoid). Check students understand that this meaning has nothing to do with the general meaning of *help*.

Answers and tapescript

T 8.2

1 When we saw the photos we **couldn't help** feeling worried. (Kate's mum/dad)
2 The photos **made it** look worse than it really was. (Kate)
3 Your friends must **promise to** keep their room tidy. (Dan's mum/dad)
4 It's really kind of you **to let** them stay. (Dan)
5 Did Victor **help you** escape from the crocodile? (William's mum/dad)
6 He warned us not **to go** swimming. (William)
7 We couldn't **help feeling** a bit scared. (Sally)
8 Have you **decided to** come home yet? (Sally's mum/dad)

GRAMMAR SPOT (SB p63)

1 Focus attention on the example. Check students understand that the abbreviation *sb* stands for *somebody*. Then get students to match the patterns with the sentences.

After checking the answers, ask students to find more examples of the patterns in the emails. Point out the additional pattern in email 1:
verb + sb + *-ing*: *I don't remember anyone taking the pics.*

Answers

verb + *-ing* He enjoyed swimming. (Hope you don't mind putting them up ... We ... enjoyed watching the sunset ...)

verb + *to* I need to warn you. (I was trying to climb up to the top bunk bed. I forgot to mention the ambulance ride to hospital. I didn't want to say anything ... They're planning to go to London ... I was sure you'd like to meet them ... ... we didn't manage to catch anything. We stopped to camp on the banks ... We'd forgotten to bring a torch ... We expected to have a good night's sleep ...)

verb + sb + *to* Victor told us to throw meat.

verb + sb + infinitive (without *to*) You'll make them feel at home. (I'll let you know our plans.)

adjective + *to* It's impossible to see the scar. (... so were lucky to escape from the crocodile. I'm pleased to say we fell asleep again immediately ...)

preposition + *-ing* We're thinking of staying two more days. (They're looking forward to meeting you.)

2 Elicit the difference in meaning in the sentences. Ask students to highlight the pattern in each one.

Answers

She remembered to email her mum. (*remember* + infinitive = she didn't forget to email her mum)
She remembered emailing her mum. (*remember* + *-ing* = she emailed her mum and she had a memory of doing it)

Refer students to Grammar Reference 8 on SB p142 and the Verb patterns on SB p158.

PRACTICE (SB p64)

Phoning home

1 Ask students what they can remember about Kate from the emails on p62 (she was travelling in Australia and she had an accident). Focus attention on the example. Put students in pairs to complete the task.

2 **T 8.3** [CD 2: Track 44] Play the recording and let students check their answers. Students practise the conversation in their pairs. If possible, get them to sit back-to-back, so that they can't see each other, as in a real phone conversation. They can also use mobile phones as props if appropriate. Monitor and check. If students need help with pronunciation, especially intonation, drill key lines from the conversation with the class.

Answers and tapescript

T 8.3

M = **Mum** **K** = **Kate**

M Kate! It's so good **to hear** from you. Are you OK?
K Oh Mum, I'm really sorry for **worrying** you so much. I really didn't mean to.
M We opened our emails and we were so delighted **to see** all your photos and then we saw that one.
K I didn't want my friends **to post** it on *Facebook*. I asked them not to.
M But Kate, all that blood, and you went to hospital. We couldn't help **feeling** worried.
K I know, but honestly Mum, my friends made me **go** to the hospital, I really didn't need to.
M How is your head now?
K Absolutely fine. Honestly. I'll email you some more photos and you can see for yourself.
M OK. Don't forget to.
K I'll call again soon and I promise **to text** regularly. Bye.
M Bye. Take care!

SPOKEN ENGLISH
Don't forget to! – the reduced infinitive

The work on infinitives and *-ing* forms is extended here to cover a common feature of spoken English – the fact that you don't have to use the full infinitive if the verb is understood from the context.

1 Read the notes and the example conversations with the class. Ask two pairs of students to read the conversations across the class. Check pronunciation, and point out if necessary that we use the weak form of *to* in a full infinitive (*I'd love to come!*), but the strong form of *to* in a reduced infinitive (*I'd love to!*):

Don't forget to /tu:/.

We'd love to /tu:/.

Drill the pronunciation with the class.

Students find the examples in Kate's conversation in exercise 1. Point out the negative form in *I asked them **not** to.*

Answers

I really didn't mean to.
I asked them not to.
I really didn't need to.

2 **T 8.4** [CD 2: Track 45] Give students time to complete the conversations individually.

Play the recording and get them to check their answers. Students practise the conversations in pairs. Monitor and check. If students need help with pronunciation, play the recording again and drill key lines with the class.

Answers and tapescript

T 8.4

1 **A** Did you post my letter?
B Oh sorry, I **forgot to**.

2 **A** I can't go out with you this evening. Sorry.
B Oh, but you **promised to.**
3 **A** Why did you email your mother again?
B Because she **asked me to.**
4 **A** Do you think you'll apply for that job?
B Yes, I've definitely **decided to.**
5 **A** Are you taking your brother to the airport?
B Well, I **offered to** but he said he **didn't want** me **to.**

Talking about you

3 This gives students the opportunity to practise the verb patterns in a personalized way. Elicit possible endings to each of the sentences, write them on the board, and underline the verb pattern in each. Point out to students that they must use a verb form rather than a noun to complete each sentence. Give students time to complete the sentences individually. Remind them to make two of them false. Monitor and help as necessary.

Possible answers
1 I really enjoy spending time with friends.
2 I'm no good at cooking.
3 I mustn't forget to book my flight.
4 I will always remember meeting my best friend.
5 I've just finished painting my flat.
6 I sometimes find it difficult to sleep.
7 My parents made me go to bed early when I was a child.
8 I'm looking forward to going out at the weekend.
9 I'd love to travel round the world.

4 Focus attention on the examples and get three students to read them aloud. Give three sentences about yourself from the list in exercise 3, including one false one. Read the sentences aloud and get students to respond to find the false sentence.

Put students in groups of three or four to do the activity. Monitor and check for accurate use of the verb patterns. Feed back on any common errors at the end of the activity, highlighting the correct verb patterns on the board.

SUGGESTION
Students will need regular practice in the verb patterns highlighted in this lesson. It's a good idea to recycle them as often as possible in different ways:
- error correction tasks
- matching sentence endings and beginnings
- changing sentences to make them true for the students
- writing short notes containing a selection of the verbs
- writing short roleplays containing a selection of the verbs

ADDITIONAL MATERIAL

Workbook Unit 8
Exercises 1–7 Verb patterns

LISTENING AND SPEAKING (SB p65)

Fears and phobias

ABOUT THE LISTENING
This section has two recordings, and continues the unit theme with a focus on fears and phobias. Students start with a general discussion on common phobias, and then match some unusual phobias with their meanings. The first recording consists of three speakers talking about their unusual phobias (buttons, fish, and balloons). Students listen to each monologue and answer a set of comprehension questions. They then retell each person's story, using a series of prompts. Students take part in a general group discussion on phobias by answering a set of general questions, and then compare their ideas against the second recording, an extract in which a psychologist answers the same questions. The section finishes with a *Language work* task which consolidates the verb patterns students covered at the start of the unit.

Pre-teach/check the following vocabulary from recording **T 8.5**:

Jodie: *cardigan, to scream, to calm sb down, belts, zips, psychotherapist* (a person who treats mental illness by encouraging the patient to talk about their problems).

Gavin: *to feel sick, psychologist* (someone who studies the human mind, emotions, and behaviour, and how these are affected by different situations), *oyster* /ˈɔɪstə/, *to conquer* /ˈkɒŋkə/ *a phobia*

Melissa: *to blow up* (*a balloon*), *to pop, rubber, to chase someone, to shake.*

Dr Lucy Atcheson is a real psychologist and an expert on phobias and relationships. She has written books on both subjects and hosted a BBC programme on phobias called *The Panic Room*. You will probably need to pre-teach/check the following items from recording **T 8.6**:
to be programmed to do something, DNA (the chemicals in cells that carries genetic information), *genes.*

Lead in to the topic by asking
Which is stronger, a fear or a phobia? (a phobia)
Can you control a phobia? (usually not)

Elicit related language and check the pronunciation, e.g. *be afraid* /əˈfreɪd/, *frightened* /ˈfraɪtnd/, *scared, terrified of, have a phobia* /ˈfəʊbiə/ *of, to panic, a panic attack.*

1 Elicit a few examples of typical phobias and write them on the board. Elicit further answers from the whole class, adding items to the list on the board and checking the pronunciation.

Give an example of something that you are afraid of, when it started, and how it affects your life, e.g. *I've got a phobia of dogs, especially big dogs like Alsatians. I was bitten as a child and I've been frightened of dogs ever since. If I see a big dog in the street, I often cross the road to avoid it. If I visit someone who has a dog, they need to keep it in another room. I could never touch or stroke a dog.*

Elicit a few more examples from the class. Wait for students to volunteer information and don't force anyone to talk about their fears if they seem uncomfortable.

Possible answers

A fear/phobia of:

spiders	bacteria/germs
dogs	needles/injections
insects	dying
snakes	drowning
flying	closed/small spaces (claustrophobia)
heights	public/open spaces (agoraphobia)
the dark	

2 Focus attention on the chart and ask students to look at the list of phobias. Check where the main stress falls in each word (on *-pho-* in each word).

Put students in pairs to discuss the meanings and do the matching task. Put students into new pairs to compare their answers before checking with the whole class.

Answers

Autophobia is the fear of being alone.
Ablutophobia is the fear of washing.
Aviophobia is the fear of flying.
Frigophobia is the fear of feeling cold.

3 **T 8.5** [CD 2: Track 46] Focus attention on the cartoon and elicit a brief description. This will introduce the words for the phobias described in the recording, but don't specify what these phobias are at this stage.

Possible answer

There's a fish standing on a hill. It's wearing a hat, and a waistcoat with big buttons and it's holding three balloons. Someone is running away in fear.

See the notes about pre-teaching/checking vocabulary in *About the listening*. Give students time to read the questions before they listen.

Play the recording of Jodie through once. Elicit the answers from the class. If students have missed any of the information, play the recording again.

Repeat the procedure for the recordings of Gavin and Melissa.

Answers and tapescript

Jodie

1 The buttons on the waistcoat.
2 It started when she was a little girl. She saw the buttons on her grandmother's cardigan and she was terrified.
3 It's difficult for her to buy clothes. She tries to find skirts and trousers with just belts and zips.
4 A button came off a colleague's jacket at work.
5 She's decided to see a psychotherapist.

Gavin

1 The fish.
2 He isn't sure when it started. His dad used to go fishing and Gavin didn't like watching him cleaning the fish. When he was about seven he started feeling afraid when he saw his dad coming home with the fish.
3 He couldn't go into supermarkets – the sight of fish made him feel sick. When he started going out with his wife, he had to ask her never to eat fish. He can't go to restaurants, so he only eats in hamburger bars now. It makes life very difficult for his family.
4 He saw someone eating an oyster.
5 He's started to see a psychologist but he hasn't succeeded in conquering the phobia yet.

Melissa

1 The balloon.
2 Her phobia started when she was five. She was trying to blow one up and it popped in her face.
3 Her friends chase her with balloons because they think it's fun to see her cry. She can't go to parties if they have balloons. She can't imagine ever blowing up a balloon. She can't look at balloons on TV without shaking.
4 Someone chased her with a balloon.
5 She wants to see a doctor/professional about it. Her teacher agrees.

T 8.5

Fears and phobias

1 Jodie

I have a really unusual phobia. It began when I was a little girl. I was staying with my grandmother and she asked me to go upstairs and get her cardigan. I opened the cupboard and saw this big, dark green cardigan with huge, black buttons hanging there – I was terrified. I started screaming. My grandmother rushed upstairs and finally managed to calm me down but from then on it was a problem, it was the buttons – all buttons made me feel uncomfortable. It's difficult for me to buy clothes – I try to find skirts and trousers with just belts and zips, but it's not easy. About a year ago a button came off a colleague's jacket at work and I had a panic attack. I've decided to see a psychotherapist, but I'm embarrassed to say 'I'm scared of buttons.' It sounds silly.

2 Gavin

I'm not sure what first started my phobia, but my dad used to go fishing and afterwards I didn't like watching him cleaning the fish in the kitchen sink. Then when I was about seven I started feeling afraid when I saw him coming home with the fish. He had to stop catching it. As I grew up the problem got worse and worse. I couldn't go into supermarkets – the sight of fish made me feel sick. When I started going out with my wife I had to ask her never to eat fish. I daren't go to restaurants because once I saw someone eating an oyster and I had a panic attack. I can only eat in hamburger bars now. It makes life very difficult for my whole family. I've started to see a psychologist but I haven't succeeded in conquering my phobia yet.

3 Melissa

I'm 13 years old and I've been terrified of balloons since I was five. I was trying to blow one up and it popped in my face. I can remember feeling the rubber on my skin – ugh, it was awful. My friends don't understand; they enjoy chasing me around with blown up balloons because they think it's fun to see me cry. Last time, we were in the school playground, and I had a panic attack. At first they refused to believe me and they didn't get the teacher but then they saw how bad it was – I was having difficulty breathing and they got frightened. The worst thing is that I can't go to parties, if I do I have to ask them not to have balloons. I can't imagine ever blowing one up. I can't even look at them on TV, I start to shake. I want to see somebody about it. My teacher says I have to.

4 Give students time to read through the prompts. Deal with any queries about pronunciation. Elicit the first two sentences of Jodie's story. Put students into groups of three

or four to retell the rest of the stories. Monitor and help. Be prepared to play relevant sections of the recordings again if students can't remember the details.

Answers
See **T 8.5** above.

What do you think?

5 Put students into new groups to discuss the questions. Encourage them to share their ideas even if they don't know very much about the subject. Explain that they will be able to compare their ideas against the information in the recording.

Elicit a range of ideas from the class about which person they think suffers most and why.

6 **T 8.6** [**CD 2: Track 47**] See the notes about pre-teaching/checking vocabulary in *About the listening*. Play the recording through once and elicit the psychologist's answers to questions 2–4. With weaker classes, you could pause the recording at key points and elicit the answer to each question.

Check the answers with the class.

Answers and tapescript
2 They get phobias as a result of a bad experience.
3 Some people get phobias and others don't because it's in their genes.
4 Dr Atcheson talks about the phobia and helps the patient to relax. She might show just a picture or cartoon of the phobia. Then she sometimes shows a film, and finally she asks the person to touch the object. In this way phobias can normally be treated in just three or four sessions.

T 8.6
The psychologist's view
Human beings are programmed to be afraid of things that can hurt them. Show a baby a picture of a snake or a big, poisonous spider and the baby will show fear. It's in our DNA. We're all afraid of some things and that's good. But a phobia causes absolute terror, with physical symptoms such as a racing heart, sickness, and panic attacks. Phobias are usually the result of a bad experience, for example a car crash can cause a fear of driving, but it's often just fear of ordinary things like balloons or a particular food. Some people are more likely to get phobias than others, it's in their genes. My job is to train people to conquer their phobia. First we just talk about it, and help the patient relax. Then we might show just a picture or cartoon of their phobia. After that we sometimes show a film and finally we ask them to touch the object. In this way phobias can normally be treated in just three or four sessions.

Language work

This task consolidates the work students did on verb patterns on pages 62–4. Refer them to the tapescript on SB p127. Elicit one or two examples of verb patterns from Jodie's story. Give students time to choose a story and underline the patterns. If you are short of time, students can do the task for homework. Check answers and point out the double *-ing* form used by Gavin: *I didn't like watching him cleaning the fish.*

Answers
See the underlining in script **T 8.5** above.

SUGGESTION
As an extension to the *Language work*, ask students to write personalized sentences using the patterns in the story they chose. Alternatively, students could write a short story/anecdote using those patterns and others covered in the unit.

READING AND SPEAKING (SB p66)

Dangerous journeys in history

ABOUT THE TEXT
This is the third jigsaw reading in the course. The theme of fear and facing problems is carried through with two texts on dangerous journeys in history. It's a good idea for you to read the texts ahead of the lesson. You may also find the following background information helpful.

Hannibal /'hænəbl/ was a general who led the army of Carthage /'kɑ:θɪdʒ/ (an ancient city in Tunisia) against the Romans between 218 and 201 BC. He is perhaps best known for crossing the Alps into Italy with a large army and 37 elephants in 218 BC.

Mao Zedong /maʊ dze'dʊŋ/ (also known as Mao Tse-tung and Chairman Mao) was a Chinese politician who helped to set up the Chinese Communist Party. He became the Party's leader during the Long March, which took place in 1934–5. In 1949 he came to power and established the People's Republic of China. He was in power during the Cultural Revolution in the mid-1960s.

Each text outlines the man's early life, the journey they each undertook, and their later years. Students start by imagining the problems they would face on a long winter journey on foot and then predict the difficulties Hannibal and Mao Zedong met by looking at maps of their route. Students work in two groups, and read their text in stages. They then exchange information, and compare the leaders and their journeys.

In terms of vocabulary, encourage students to use the context to help them with new vocabulary, or let them use a dictionary. If you are short of time, you could pre-teach/check the following items:

Hannibal: *prosperous, commander, daring, tribesmen, raft, snorkel, a (mountain) pass, to perish, to desert, defeat* (noun and verb), *resources.*

Mao Zedong: *illiterate, to found, a defeat, tough, to catapult, a bog, to swallow, an ascent, to proclaim.*

Both texts contain large numbers, distances, and dates, and students will have to use these in their answers and discussions. With weaker classes, you may want to revise how to say dates and larger numbers. Alternatively, the *Everyday English* section in this unit has a review of how to say a range of numbers and dates, and this could be done before the reading lesson.

1 Set the scene for this visualization task. Ask for quiet in the class and get students to close their eyes. Read the instructions out section by section, giving students time to imagine the scene and the likely problems. Elicit a few examples in a short feedback session.

Possible answers
Possible problems: keeping everyone together, beating the cold and hunger, crossing difficult terrain, finding suitable places to camp, keeping everyone's morale up.

2 Focus attention on the maps. Students work in pairs to discuss the difficulties presented by the route of each group. Monitor and help, feeding in any vocabulary students need. Elicit a range of answers.

Possible answers
Crossing mountains, possibly covered in snow, crossing rivers, running out of food.

3 Divide the class into two groups, A and B. Assign the relevant text to each group (A Hannibal and B Mao Zedong). With larger classes, you will need to sub-divide the students into more than one group A and more than one group B.

Working in their groups, students read through their text and answer the questions. Encourage them to help each other with any new vocabulary (see *About the text* above). Monitor and help as necessary. Remind students that they will need to refer to the dates and numbers in the text when they exchange the information, so they should make sure they are confident of how to do this. Check students in both groups are confident of the answers before moving on to exercise 4, but don't do a whole-class check.

Answers
Hannibal
1 His father was a general in the army and a bold fighter. He made Hannibal promise to hate the Romans forever. Hannibal became commander of the army and was also a fearless fighter.
2 The Romans.
3 He moved to Spain with his family.
4 He planned to march from Spain to Italy because the Romans threatened to attack. He wanted to reach Italy before the Romans declared war.

Mao Zedong
1 His father was ambitious but illiterate, and he wanted his son to have the education that he hadn't had.
2 The Nationalist Government.
3 The remote Jiangxi province.
4 They had a lot of bloody battles and so had to escape from the area.

4 Students read the text and answer the questions in their groups, underlining key information in their text or making brief notes to refer to when they do exercise 6. Again, check students in both groups are confident of the answers but don't check the answers with the whole class at this stage.

Answers
Hannibal
1 May 218 BC.
2 Hannibal and an army of 90,000 men and 37 elephants.
3 He was an inspiring leader.
4 They were attacked by local tribesmen; they had to build rafts to cross the River Rhone to get the elephants across. Some fell off but were able to swim. It started to snow and the elephants slid over the ice.
5 Five months.
6 36,000 men arrived and only one of the elephants. Over half of the men died or deserted.

Mao Zedong
1 October 16th, 1934.
2 Mao Zedong and 86,000 men and 30 women, including Mao's wife.
3 Mao became leader of the Red Army and the Communist Party during the match. He was tough but popular.
4 They weren't sure where they were going. They lost 56,000 and much of their equipment when crossing the Xiang River. Many men died from lack of oxygen when crossing the Great Snowy Mountains. They were exhausted but they couldn't stop. Many men fell off the mountains when sliding down them. There were bogs under the grasslands between the Yangtze and Yellow Rivers. Mao lost more men here than on the Snowy Mountains.
5 370 days.
6 4,000 people arrived.

5 Working in their groups, students read the last part of their text. Get them to produce a short summary in their own words of what happened to the leader they are reading about. Again, don't check the answers with the whole class at this stage.

Answers
Hannibal
He defeated the Romans in many battles at first but then they had more resources and manpower and so Hannibal couldn't beat them. He sailed back to North Africa aged 45 and committed suicide 20 years later. Although he was defeated by the Romans, he is recognized as an important military leader.

Mao Zedong
He became powerful during the Long March. In 1949 he established the People's Republic of China. The Great Cultural Revolution followed. Mao's Little Red Book was published and his ideas were taught throughout the country. He died in 1976, aged 82.

6 Ask students to work in A/B pairs, so in each pair there is one student who has read each text. As an example, read out question 1 from exercise 3 and elicit information comparing the two leaders' fathers.

Give students time to exchange their information and answer the questions. Monitor and help as necessary. Make sure students are exchanging the information to help them answer the questions and not simply giving each other facts about each journey. Check the answers with the class.

Answers
On both journeys, the people had to deal with extreme difficulties including crossing dangerous rivers and mountains, and dealing with extreme cold. Many people lost their lives during both marches. 2,152 years separate the journeys.

What do you think?

Give students time to read through the questions and think about their answers. Elicit a range of responses in a whole-class discussion. In larger classes, students can work in groups and then report back.

WRITING (SB p110)

Telling a story (2) – Organizing a text

This is the second opportunity in the course for students to write a story. The first section covered linking ideas, and this one focuses on organizing the text and producing an interesting narrative. The theme links to the topic of the *Reading and speaking* section, with pre-writing work on the story of the *Titanic*. In the writing task, students use picture and text prompts to write the story of the Trojan Horse.

NOTES

The *Titanic* was a large British passenger ship which was thought impossible to sink. It was hit by an iceberg in the Atlantic Ocean on its first voyage in 1912. It sank, and more than 1500 passengers died. There have been many books and films about the event. In 1997 an American film starring Kate Winslet and Leonardo DiCaprio was a huge box office success and won 11 Oscars.

The Trojan Horse was a wooden horse used by Greek soldiers to trick their enemies, the Trojans, during the Trojan War. The Greeks built a large wooden model of a horse and offered it to the Trojans as a gift. The Trojans accepted it, and took it into Troy, unaware that Greek soldiers were hiding inside it.

1 Focus attention on the examples. Put students in pairs/small groups to discuss the question. Elicit a range of answers from the class.

2 Pre-teach/check the following vocabulary: *to warn, to hit an iceberg, lifeboat, to sink* (*sank, sunk*). Focus attention on the pictures and elicit possible wording for the first picture, e.g. *On April the 10th, 1912, the passenger ship the 'Titanic' left Southampton to cross the Atlantic to New York.* Students tell the rest of the story in pairs.

Give students time to read Text A and match the lines with the pictures.

Answers

On April 10 ... New York.
There were ... listening to the band.
The Titanic was travelling ... the Atlantic.
Some ships nearby ... delivered.
A look-out ... too late.
The Titanic hit ... quickly.
The lifeboats ... people.
The band ... sank.
Most ... in the sea.

3 Students read Text B and compare it with A. Encourage students to use the context and what they already know about the story to help them with new vocabulary. You may need to check *maiden voyage* (first crossing), *steerage* (the part of the ship with the cheapest accommodation), *knot* /nɒt/ (the unit of speed used by ships), *SOS* (a message sent from a ship when in danger and in need of help).

Elicit which text is more interesting (B) and why.

Possible answers

Text B uses a range of vivid adjectives: *luxurious, magnificent, sumptuous*, etc.
It gives a lot of details about speed, times, etc.
It uses more interesting alternatives for 'basic' verbs, e.g. *hit – strike; die – meet their death; warn – sound the alarm.*

4 Give students time to read the questions through before they discuss texts A and B again. Elicit ideas about the general organization of the texts.

Students discuss the questions in their pairs. Elicit a range of answers from the class.

Answers

The general organization: Text A sets the scene by giving only the basic detail; B tells the reader how grand the ship was, and gives details about the number of people and lifeboats.

In Text A, the main part is quite short with basic events told one after the other; in B the main story is much longer with details of the timing of events and information about all the people involved.

In Text A, the conclusion is very short and given in very simple language; in B there is more detail and the story is brought up-to-date.

Telling the story: Text A gives only basic details of the events of the story; B tells the reader about the range of people on the ship, the atmosphere at different points, and gives a detailed narrative of the events with times.

In Text A, there is little attempt to interest the reader; in B, the setting and atmosphere are described and the events are narrated in detail.

Both texts tell the story in a roughly chronological way, using the past continuous for longer actions and the past simple for the main events. But text B links some events together in non-chronological ways, using a wider variety of tenses and structures, e.g. *... the ship sank, just two hours and forty minutes after hitting the iceberg.* (= it hit the iceberg and then sank; two events linked using *after*); *Amazingly, they had kept playing until the ship disappeared beneath the waves* (past perfect to refer back to an earlier action).

The language: Text A uses very basic descriptive language, e.g. *rich, quickly, interested*, etc.; Text B uses much richer language, e.g. *luxurious, magnificent, sumptuous, amazingly, incredibly*, etc.

Text A uses very simple sentence structure; B uses a wider range of constructions and more complex sentences, with clauses linked in different ways, e.g. *The owner of the ship was on board, encouraging the captain to go faster.* The sentences in text B also start in different ways, e.g. with *However, After all, Amazingly*, etc.

5 Elicit information about the Trojan Horse from the class. Give students time to look at the pictures in pairs and read the text prompts. Deal with any vocabulary queries.

6 Students continue working in their pairs to write the story. Remind them to try to make it interesting, and tell them they can use the questions in exercise 4 as a checklist.

7 Students read some of their stories to the class. With larger classes, they can do this in groups. Refer students to the story on SB p150–1 and get them to compare it with their own.

VOCABULARY AND IDIOM (SB p68)

Body language

This section focuses on the vocabulary of parts of the body, along with verbs that involve parts of the body, e.g. *bite*, *clap*, etc., and expressions that use these verbs. Students are also introduced to idioms based on parts of the body. The final task involves dictionary work, so make sure students have access to dictionaries in class, or set the task for homework.

1 Do the brainstorming as a class. Write the words on the board, checking spelling and pronunciation as you go. You could group words according to different areas of the body (see *Possible answers* below).

Check the irregular plurals *teeth* and *feet* and the words with silent letters: *wrist* /rɪst/, *thumb* /θʌm/, *thigh* /θaɪ/, *knee* /niː/.

Possible answers

Head: hair, face, nose, eye, ear, mouth, lips, tongue, tooth (teeth), chin, neck, throat, cheek, forehead

Main body: chest, stomach, waist, hip, back, bottom

Arms: shoulder, elbow, wrist, hand, finger, thumb, nail

Legs: thigh, knee, ankle, foot (feet), toe, heel

2 Elicit the parts of the body for *bite* and *blow*, using mime to demonstrate the verbs if necessary.

Students work in groups of three or four to continue the task. Encourage them to also use mime to teach each other the verbs as necessary.

Check the answers with the class.

Answers

bite – teeth
blow – mouth/lips
clap – hands
climb – hands and feet
hit – hands
hug – arms
kick – feet
kneel – knees
lick – tongue
march – legs and arms
point – fingers
scratch – nails
stare – eyes
whistle – lips

3 **T 8.7** [CD 2: Track 48] Elicit the verb that goes with *a ladder*. Students complete the matching task, working individually.

Play the recording so that students can check their answers. Point out that the verbs may be in different forms from the infinitive. Elicit the situation for each example, playing individual sentences again as necessary.

Answers and tapescript

T 8.7

1 The cat got up the tree easily enough but I had to **climb a ladder** to get her down.
2 Daniel, stop **staring out of the window** and get on with your work!
3 Since you **whistled that tune** I can't get it out of my head.
4 I hate it when my Aunt Mary **hugs me tight**. She wears this disgusting perfume, and I smell of it afterwards.
5 Bob's hopeless at all sports. He can't even **kick a football**.
6 You'd better **lick your ice-cream** – it's melting.
7 Do people **kneel down to pray** in all religions?
8 I keep trying to stop **biting my nails** but I can't. It's a terrible habit.
9 I'm terrified of **blowing up balloons** in case they go 'pop'.
10 Don't **scratch that insect bite**. You'll get an infection.
11 By the end of the concert we were all **clapping our hands** to the music.
12 The tourist guide **pointed at a place on the map**.
13 My dad's useless at doing DIY. He can't even **hit a nail with a hammer**.
14 My two-year-old nephew is so cute. He loves **marching** up and down **like a soldier**.

4 Read the instructions and first sentence as a class. Check students understand that the expressions in bold are not used in a literal way. Focus on the first sentence and elicit the meaning of *see eye to eye* (agree).

Students work in pairs to continue the task. Remind them to use the context to help them work out the meanings. Do not check answers until after exercise 5.

5 Students match the meanings in the box to the idioms in exercise 4. Check the answers with the class.

Students take it in turns to read the pairs of sentences aloud. Monitor and check for accurate pronunciation.

Answers

1 I don't get on with my brother. We don't **agree** about anything.
2 I saw a programme on TV about quantum physics but I'm afraid **I didn't understand a word**.
3 **It's not worth** trying to explain it to me. I'll never understand.
4 Did you hear about Millie's party? People drank too much and the whole thing **got out of control**.
5 The house was such a mess and when her parents came back they **were furious**. I don't blame them.
6 Can you help me? **I'm having trouble with** installing this program on my computer.
7 My dad keeps a stack of chocolate in his desk for while he's working. He **loves sweet things**.
8 I feel silly. I got so excited when he said I'd won the lottery, but he was only **joking**.

6 This exercise involves dictionary work. Elicit an example of an idiomatic expression with *heart*. Students look up the words and note down the related idioms.

Students pool their answers in a feedback session. Write the answers on the board or an OHT. If possible, collate them into a single document that can be printed/photocopied and given to the students.

Possible answers

heart to break someone's heart/have a change of heart/cry your heart out/have your heart in your mouth/have your heart in the right place/have a heart of gold/open your heart to someone

head to bang your head against a brick wall/bite someone's head off/bury your head in the sand/go to your head/have your head in the clouds/hit the nail on the head/keep your head above water

hand to have your hands full/have someone in the palm of your hand/know someone or somewhere like the back of your hand/take the law into your own hands/wait on someone hand and foot/lend someone a hand/live from hand to mouth

foot to fall on your feet/get cold feet/have a foot in both camps/put your foot in it/have your feet on the ground/have two left feet

hair to let your hair down/make your hair stand on end/split hairs/tear your hair out/not turn a hair

SUGGESTION

Students work in small groups to write a conversation or short sketch containing about six of the idioms. Students can perform their conversations for the rest of the class over a series of lessons.

EVERYDAY ENGLISH (SB p69)

Travel and numbers

This section focuses on the way we say a range of numbers including phone numbers, dates, amounts of money, fractions, decimals, and percentages. Some of the numbers are contextualized in two travel situations – at an airport check-in desk, and booking train tickets over the phone. Students talk about numbers that are important to them in a personalized groupwork task at the end of the lesson.

POSSIBLE PROBLEMS

Numbers in English can be read in different ways depending on their type. It's a good idea to ask students to review numbers up to 100 and ordinals up to 30th for homework before the lesson.

You may need to review/highlight the following:

- **Use of *and*** *And* is used after *hundred/thousand* when it is followed by numbers less than a hundred, e.g. *a hundred and fifty pounds, one thousand and twenty-five kilometres*. (In American English, *and* is often left out.) *And* is also used in fractions, e.g. *two and a half.*
- **Phone numbers** These are read as individual numbers; the area code is read first, then the remaining numbers, divided into groups of 3; 0 is usually read as *oh*, and repeated numbers as *double two/three*, etc. The intonation rises after each set of numbers and falls at the end:

  ↗ ↗ ↘
  01884 983 760 = *oh one double eight four, nine eight three, seven six oh*
- **Dates** These require ordinal numbers and the definite article, e.g. *the seventh of May*. With years, we divide the numbers into two sets of two, and 0 is *oh*, not *zero*, e.g. 1902 = *nineteen oh two*. Years up to 2009 are usually read as numbers, e.g. *two thousand and nine*; years from 2010 are divided into two sets of two, e.g. *twenty ten*. In American English, the month, not the day, is written or said first, e.g. 3/22 = *March twenty-second* (without *the*).
- **Prices** Prices are read like this: £1.82 = *one (pound) eighty-two*; €7.75 = *seven (euros) seventy-five*; $99.99 (*ninety-nine (dollars) ninety-nine*); 99p = *ninety-nine pence/p*.
- **Bank card numbers** Numbers on bank cards, credit cards, etc. are usually read in sets of four digits. 0 is *oh* or *zero*. The intonation rises on the first sets of numbers and falls at the end:

  ↗ ↗ ↗ ↘
  4840 8302 1953 0842 = *four eight four oh/zero, eight three oh/zero two*, etc.
- **ID/Passport numbers** These are often a combination of numbers and letters, and each number or letter is read individually.
- **Fractions** Students may need reminding of these: ½ = *a half*; 5½ = *five and a half*; ⅓ = *a third*, ¼ = *a quarter.*
- **Percentages and decimals** A written percentage is read … *per cent*, e.g. 25% = *twenty-five per cent*; in decimals, a point (.) is used, not a comma, e.g. 1.25 = *one point two five*. In numbers less than 1, 0 is *zero* or *nought* /nɔːt/, e.g. 0.25 = *zero/nought point two five*.

Note that students are unlikely to be able to say numbers spontaneously and accurately even at the end of this lesson, so be prepared to review them in a range of contexts in subsequent lessons.

1 **T 8.8** [**CD 2: Track 49**] Focus attention on the numbers. Elicit how you read the first two numbers aloud. Students work in pairs, taking it in turns to read the numbers. Monitor and check, noting down common errors.

Play the recording and get students to check their answers. Play the recording again if necessary and drill the pronunciation of numbers that students found difficult.

Read the information about points and commas with the class. Make sure students understand that commas are used to indicate thousands, and points are used for decimals. Point out that 3.14 could also be a time, in which case it would be read as *three fourteen*.

Answers and tapescript

T 8.8
fifteen
fifty
four hundred and six
seventy-two
one hundred and seventy-eight
ninety
nineteen
eight hundred and fifty
one thousand five hundred and twenty
seventeen point five
thirty-six
two hundred and forty-seven
five thousand
one hundred and eighty thousand, five hundred and seventy-five
two million

2 **T 8.9** [**CD 2: Track 50**] Give students time to read through the questions. Check comprehension of *expiry date*, and *VAT* /viː eɪ ˈtiː/ (*Value Added Tax*; a tax added

to the price of goods and services). Elicit the number for question 1. Students match the questions and answers, working in pairs. Give students time to read the questions and answers aloud, focusing on getting the numbers right. Monitor and check, noting down common errors in how the numbers are read and pronunciation problems.

Play the recording and get students to check their answers. Play the recording of the numbers students found difficult again and drill the pronunciation. Students practise the questions and answers again in new pairs.

Answers and tapescript

T 8.9

1 **A** What time does the train leave?
B 13.45.
2 **A** How far is it to Moscow?
B 1,915 km.
3 **A** How long's the flight?
B About 1½ hours.
4 **A** How much does it cost?
B £34.99.
5 **A** What's your credit card number?
B 6356 5055 5137 9904.
6 **A** What's the expiry date?
B 02/14.
7 **A** How much does it weigh?
B 27 kilos.
8 **A** What's your mobile number?
B 07700 984 361.
9 **A** What's the rate of VAT?
B 17.5%.

3 Focus attention on the pictures. Elicit the first number as an example. Students then work in pairs to find the numbers and practise saying them. Check answers with the class.

Answers

760519814	seven six oh, five one nine, eight one four
6179 500 0574	six one seven nine, five double oh, oh five seven four
692	six nine two
01/2015	oh one twenty fifteen
9.5 km	nine point five kilometres
20:25	twenty twenty-five / twenty-five past eight
20:30	twenty thirty / half past eight
3	three
12	twelve
159	one five nine (with buses we usually say the numbers individually)
453	four five three
0778 4259	oh double seven eight, four two five nine
1€ 45	one (euro) forty-five
£234,950	two hundred and thirty-four thousand, nine hundred and fifty pounds
01-FEB-03	the first of February, two thousand and three
15.00	fifteen hundred hours, three o'clock
53	fifty-three
34.50	thirty-four (pounds) fifty
50/20/10/5	fifty/twenty/ten/five euros
17%	seventeen per cent
3¾	three and three quarters
£009.99	nine (pounds) ninety-nine
009.43	nine point four three (litres)

4 **T 8.10** **[CD 3: Track 2]** Give students time to read the questions. Play the recording through once and elicit the answers to the questions.

Answers and tapescript

1 At the check-in desk of an airport.
2 A passenger and check-in clerk.
3 Dubai.
4 The man's luggage is overweight.

T 8.10

A Good morning. Where are you flying to?
B Dubai.
A And how many bags do you want to check in?
B Just this one.
A Fine. Put it on the scales please ... Oh dear.
B What's the matter?
A I'm afraid it's overweight. It's nearly 30 kilos and you're only allowed 23.
B What can I do?
A Well, you can pay for excess baggage. The rate is erm – £18.75 – that's $37 per kilo.
B So 7 times £18.75 that's –er
A That's £131.25 or $259.
B Goodness. That's a fortune but I'll just have to pay it.
A OK. And just the one piece of hand luggage?
B Yes, just this bag.
A That's fine. Here's your boarding pass. You're boarding from Gate 6 at 9.20. The gate will be open 45 minutes before the flight. Have a good journey.
B Thank you.

Focus attention on the example numbers. Play the recording again. Students note down the numbers and what they refer to. With weaker students, you could pause the recording at the end of the lines that contain the numbers, or write the numbers on the board before students listen again.

Check the answers with the class. Refer students to the tapescript on SB p127. Students practise the conversation in pairs. Monitor and check for accurate reading of the numbers. If students have problems, drill the lines and get students to repeat.

Answers and tapescript

one – bag
30 kilos – the weight of the bag
23 (kilos) – the number of kilos you are allowed
£18.75/$37 – the rate per kilo for excess baggage
7 – the number of kilos over the limit
£131.25/$259 – the fee for excess baggage
one – piece of hand luggage
6 – gate number
9.20 – the departure time
45 – number of minutes before the flight that the gate will open

T 8.10

See tapescript above.

5 **T 8.11** **[CD 3: Track 3]** Refer students back to the questions in exercise 4. Play the recording and elicit the answers for this conversation.

Play the recording again and ask students to note down the numbers and what they refer to. With weaker students, you could pause the recording at the end of the lines that contain the numbers, or write the numbers on the board before students listen.

Check the answers with the class. Refer students to the tapescript on SB p127. Students practise the conversation in pairs. Monitor and check for accurate reading of the numbers. If students have problems, drill the lines and get students to repeat.

Answers and tapescript

1 Over the phone.
2 A passenger and a booking clerk.
3 Edinburgh.
4 The online booking system doesn't work.

13th (of March) – the date of travel
30th (of March) – the return date of travel
10.30 – train departure on first journey
14.53 – train arrival on first journey
19.00 – train departure on return journey
17.30 – train departure on return journey
22.28 – train arrival on return journey
£98.20 – ticket price
0494 7865 4562 1320 – credit card number
05/12 – expiry date
15 – number of house/flat

T 8.11

A Good morning. Transport direct. Can I help you?
B Oh yes, I was trying to book rail tickets online and it didn't work.
A That's OK. Where and when do you want to travel?
B I want to go from London, King's Cross to Edinburgh on the 13th of March.
A March 30th?
B No, no, March 13th. I want to go on the 13th and return on the 30th.
A OK, the 13th to the 30th – so you want a return ticket. And do you want to travel in the morning or the afternoon?
B Well, I want to travel up mid-morning if possible, but I'd like to come back on an evening train.
A Right. There's a train at 10.30 a.m., it arrives in Edinburgh at 14.53.
B Sounds good. And returning?
A For the return, there's one at 19.00, arrives back in London just after midnight.
B Mmm ... is there an earlier one?
A There's the 17.30. It arrives back in London at 22.28.
B Er, that sounds perfect. I'll go for that. How much is that?
A It's a saver return, so that's £98.20. Is that OK?
B Fine.
A Can you give me your credit card details?
B Yes, it's a Visa card. The name on the card is Mr K Farnham. The number is 0494 7865 4562 1320.
A The expiry date?
B 05/12.
A And your address?
B 15, Kingston Road ...
A Did you say 50?
B No, 15, one, five Kingston Road ...

6 Focus attention on the examples in the Student's Book. Put students in groups of three or four to continue the activity. Monitor and help as necessary, but do not interrupt – let students to have fun with the guessing game.

SUGGESTIONS

There is a range of ways of getting students to revise numbers. They can:

- listen to/read a news story and pick out the numbers and what they refer to. Students then summarize the story to a partner, using the numbers.
- talk about the numbers they have seen/used earlier in the day before the class.
- write a roleplay in pairs using five numbers chosen by you/another pair.
- do simple class surveys that involve numbers/percentages/fractions, e.g. how students spend their time, students' journeys to work/school/university, etc.
- write questionnaires in pairs with facts containing numbers. They test the rest of the class with true/false or multiple-choice questions.

Don't forget!

Workbook Unit 8

Exercise 8 Phrasal verbs – Phrasal verb without a noun
Exercise 9 Pronunciation – Weak sounds
Exercise 10 Listening – Interview with a stuntwoman
Exercise 11 Vocabulary – Crossword 2

Word list

Refer students to the Word list for Unit 8 (SB p155). They could translate the words, learn them at home, or transfer some of them to their vocabulary notebook.

9

Conditionals
Words with similar meaning
Dealing with money

It depends how you look at it

Introduction to the unit

The unit has two main themes – looking at things from different perspectives, and dealing with bullying and crime. This provides the context for language work on conditionals and *might have done/could have done/should have done*. The *Speaking and listening* section recycles some of these forms with a questionnaire called *Do you have a social conscience?* The *Reading and speaking* section has an article on a burglary from the point of view of the victim and the burglar, and the Restorative Justice process that brought them together. *Vocabulary* covers synonyms and near-synonyms, and the *Everyday English* focus is *Dealing with money*. The *Writing* syllabus continues with a focus on organizing paragraphs in a for and against essay.

Language aims

Grammar – conditionals Students should be familiar with the form of the zero, first, and second conditionals. The language presentation in this unit covers second and third conditionals, along with the forms *might have done, could have done*, and *should have done*. The *Grammar Reference* includes an introduction to conditionals and notes on when to use first, second, and third conditionals.

The system of conditionals in English is a complex one with a range of possible forms in both the *if* clause and the result clause. We have used the common naming system of *zero, first, second*, and *third conditionals* as this provides a convenient framework for students to stage their learning, and also ties in with the wording in many grammar books.

The presentation in this unit reviews second conditionals and introduces third conditionals in a staged way, and the practice section provides opportunities for controlled practice and personalization. Further language practice is given in *Speaking and listening*, but students are still likely to make mistakes, particularly with the more complex forms in the third conditional.

POSSIBLE PROBLEMS

Students tend to confuse the tenses in the different clauses of conditional sentences, especially when moving from second conditional to third. They may also have problems remembering what the contracted form *'d* stands for, so this is highlighted in the *Grammar Spot* on SB p71. Pronunciation can be a problem, especially the weak form /əv/ for *have* in third conditional and perfect infinitive forms.

Common mistakes

Reverting to Present Simple for any time reference:

**What do you do if you win a lot of money?* (rather than *What would you do if you won …?*)

Confusing the tense use:

**If you have a lot of money, what would you do?* (rather than *If you had …*)
**I'd have told you if I would have known.* (rather than *I'd (=would) have told you if I'd (=had) known.*)

Pronunciation:
Students need practice of the contractions *I'd*, etc. They also tend to over-stress weak forms:

*/aɪ 'wʊd 'hæv/ (rather than /aɪ 'wʊdəv/ for *I would have …*)

Vocabulary The vocabulary focus in this unit is words with similar meanings. The section recycles language from across the unit and also highlights verbs which are easily confused, e.g. *win* and *beat*.

Everyday English This section focuses on the language used when dealing with money in everyday situations such as in shops, restaurants, and banks. The section ends with discussion questions on money, including exchange rates between the currency in the students' country and the US dollar and sterling. If necessary, ask students to research these rates before the lesson.

Notes on the unit

STARTER (SB p70)

The overall theme of points of view and different perspectives is introduced in the *Starter*. The exercises in this section also lead in to the profile of the troubled teenager in the presentation that follows.

Write the word *teenager* on the board and elicit the words/images students associate with it. Establish which ideas are positive and which are negative. Then read the notes and examples in the exercise as a class. Put students into groups of three to discuss the pros and cons of being a teenager.

Students compare their ideas as a class. Establish if students think there are more pros than cons, or vice versa.

Possible answers

Pros You can spend a lot of time with friends./You can do different activities and go to more places./You start to develop your own identity.

Cons You can feel under pressure at school./You can fall out with friends/find it difficult to make friends./You can feel confused about emotional and physical changes.

BILLY'S STORY (SB p70)

Conditionals

ABOUT THE TEXT

The text in this presentation takes the form of a leaflet advertising a fictitious support agency called Kidcare, which offers help and advice to young people who are being bullied. The leaflet profiles a young teenage boy and the problems he has experienced with bullying, and is directed at other young people in similar circumstances.

Students shouldn't have any problems with the vocabulary, but check the pronunciation of the following items: *bully* (noun and verb) /ˈbʊli/, *bullying* /ˈbʊliɪŋ/, *tough* /tʌf/, *truant* /ˈtruːənt/. Also elicit the passive form *to be bullied* and point out that it is often used in continuous forms, e.g. *If you are being bullied …, Billy was being bullied.*

See the *Language aims* section for an overview of possible problems with the target structures. You could also read Grammar Reference 9.1–9.6 on SB pp142–3 ahead of the lesson.

1 Ask and answer the questions with the class. Elicit a range of possible answers.

Possible answers

Children are bullied because they are different in some way; they are seen as a threat because they are talented/popular; they have problems/some sort of weakness that bullies become aware of.
Some children become bullies because they have been bullied themselves; they feel weak or inadequate in some way; they feel scared and so want to be in control.

2 Students read the leaflet. Deal with any vocabulary queries and then ask:

Who produced the leaflet? (Kidcare)
What is Kidcare? (an organization that helps children who are being bullied)
Who is the leaflet directed at? (young people like Billy)

Elicit the problems experienced by Billy.

Answers

He found studying hard.
He didn't have many friends.
His dad left the family home.
He was bullied by other kids. They called him names, took his money, sent him texts, and attacked him.
He tried to tell people but they didn't listen.
He started playing truant and he didn't know where to go for help.

3 This exercise gives students the opportunity to use the second conditional as if they were different people related to Billy's story. Students should be familiar with the second conditional, so let them try the activity without spending too long highlighting the form.

Focus attention on the examples in the speech bubbles. Ask two students to read them aloud and continue the second one. If necessary, highlight the use of the weak form /wə/ in *If I were …* and the pronunciation of *I'd* /aɪd/.

Elicit an alternative example for Billy's mum, e.g. *If I were Billy's mum, I'd talk to his teacher.*

Check comprehension of *counsellor*. Students continue the activity, working in pairs. Monitor and check for accurate use of the second conditional and for pronunciation. If necessary, highlight the form and drill examples chorally and individually:

If + Past Simple + *would* (in speaking usually contracted to *'d*)

Point out that *was* is often changed to *were* in the conditional clause, e.g. *If I were Billy's mum.* Students will have another opportunity to focus on the form of the second conditional in the *Grammar Spot* after exercise 6.

4 **T 9.1** **[CD 3: Track 4]** Focus attention on the example. Pre-teach/Check *to bang people's heads together* (to speak angrily to people to stop them behaving badly).

Play the recording and get students to note down who each person is imagining they are. Give students time to compare their answers in pairs before checking with the class (see bracketed text below for answers).

Answers and tapescript

T 9.1

1 I'd organize a school day which tried to educate everyone about bullying, and I'd invite social workers, police, and psychologists. (head teacher)
2 I'd get my dad to speak to those … if I was older, I'd speak to them myself! (Billy's sister)
3 I'd ask Billy to try to understand the bullies. I'd get all the parents to meet together. (a counsellor from Kidcare)

4 I'd move house so we could change his school and start again somewhere new. (Billy's mum)
5 I'd get really angry and bang the bullies' heads together. (Billy's dad)
6 I'd run away. (Billy)

5 **T 9.2** [CD 3: Track 5] Check comprehension of *missing* and *to suspect*. Students read the report and find the answers to the questions. Point out that the answer to the three questions is *no* and that the forms in bold in the report refer to unreal situations about the past.

This is students' first opportunity to practise these quite complex forms. Play the recording and drill the sentences chorally and individually. It can be helpful to highlight the pronunciation of the key forms on the board, especially the reduction of *have* to the weak form /əv/:

/ðeɪd/ /ˈðeɪdəv/
If they'd listened to him, they'd have understood

/ˈfɑːðərəd/ /ˈmaɪtəv/
If his father had stayed, Billy might have felt happier.

/hiːd/ /ˈkʊdəv/
If he'd talked to us, we could have helped him.

/ˈʃʊdəv/
He should have come to us a long time ago.

It is worth spending time drilling the forms to give students the confidence to reproduce them later. If students have problems, you could highlight what the contracted forms stand for:

If they'd (= had) *listened to him, they'd* (= would) *have understood.*

This is also highlighted in the *Grammar Spot* that follows exercise 6.

Answers and tapescript
Billy ran away. He's been missing for six months.
No, people didn't listen to Billy.
No, he didn't talk to Kidcare.
No, his father didn't stay.

T 9.2
If they'd listened to him, they'd have understood.
If his father had stayed, Billy might have felt happier.
If he'd talked to us, we could have helped him.
He should have come to us a long time ago.

6 **T 9.3** [CD 3: Track 6] Ask one student to read out situation 1, and ask another to read the *If* sentence in the example. Drill the pronunciation if necessary.

Students work individually and use the prompts to make the other sentences about Billy's situation. Monitor and help as necessary. Play the recording and get students to check their answers. If necessary, get students to listen again and repeat.

If you think your students need further controlled practice with these forms, write more prompts on the board, e.g.

Billy didn't get the support he needed.
got support ... wouldn't ... run away

Billy's school didn't help.
helped ... bullying might ... stopped

His father didn't take an interest in him.
taken ... in him ... might ... felt better

Billy didn't contact Kidcare.
contacted them ... would ... given ... advice

Answers and tapescript

T 9.3
1 If they'd understood, he wouldn't have run away.
2 If he'd gone to Kidcare, he could have talked about his problems.
3 If he hadn't left, Billy might have felt more secure.
4 If they hadn't threatened him, he wouldn't have run away.

GRAMMAR SPOT (SB p71)

1 Read the notes as a class. Elicit the form of the second and third conditionals. Focus on the second conditional sentence and point out that it contains past forms, but the *meaning* refers to an unreal situation in the present. Then focus on the third conditional sentence and point out that both clauses can have the contracted form *'d*: *If they'd* (= had) *known about Billy's problems, they'd* (= would) *have helped him.* Also remind students that the *if* clause can come first or second in the sentence. When the *if* clause comes first, we use a comma after it:
I'd have called you if I'd known you were in town.
If I'd known you were in town, I'd have called you.

Answer
Second conditional *If* + Past Simple + *would* (*'d*)
Third Conditional *If* + Past Perfect + *would have*

2 Read the sentences as a class. Give students time to think about the answers and then check with the class.

Answer
I might have helped you. I could have helped you.

3 Read the examples as a class. Give students time to think about the answer, then check with the class. Point out that this form often expresses criticism.

Answer
It is good advice, but it is too late.
Yes, Pete stole the money.

Refer students to Grammar Reference 9.1–9.6 on SB pp142–3.

PRACTICE (SB p72)

It all went wrong

The *Practice* section starts with a focus on crime. Students read humorous texts about three robberies that went wrong, discuss the robbers' mistakes, and then rewrite sentences using the target structures. The second part of the section provides personalized practice in which students respond to situations in which someone else did something stupid and also talk about things in their own lives that went wrong.

1 Lead in to the topic by asking what can go wrong in a robbery, e.g. the getaway car breaks down, the robbers are recorded on security cameras, etc. Pre-teach/check *to flee (fled, fled), to pose (for a photo), to take out a loan, to burst into (a bank).*

Set a time limit of about two minutes for students to read the texts. Elicit an example of a mistake from the first story (see *Answers* below). Put the students in pairs to continue discussing the robbers' mistakes. Monitor and help as necessary.

Elicit who students think was the most stupid and which was the most amusing story.

Possible answers

Easy arrest: He left an envelope in the bank with his address on.

Smile!: He took photos of himself and left the camera in the stolen car.

'Have a loan instead': They didn't take the money. They went back to the bank ten minutes later.

2 Focus attention on the example sentence. Pre-teach/check *to get away with* (*a crime*). Ask one student to read out the cue sentence and another student to read the version with *shouldn't have.*

Students continue rewriting the sentences, working in pairs. Remind weaker students that they will need to change some Past Simple forms to Past Perfect or perfect infinitive forms. Monitor and help as necessary.

Check the answers, encouraging students to get the main stresses and weak forms correct. Be prepared to drill sentences students have problems with, highlighting the main stresses by clapping out the rhythm. If students make mistakes with the form, write their answers on the board and get the rest of the class to help with the correction.

Answers

2 He should have taken the note with him.
3 If he hadn't left his address, the police wouldn't have found him.
4 He shouldn't have taken his photo.
5 If they hadn't crashed the car, they could have escaped.
6 If he hadn't left photos of himself, he might have got away with it.
7 If they hadn't been so stupid, they'd have escaped with the money.
8 If they hadn't listened to the manager, they could have stolen the money.
9 They shouldn't have gone back to the bank.
10 They should have just run away.

You're an idiot!

3 **T 9.4** [**CD 3: Track 7**] Ask students to imagine that their friend did some stupid things. Ask two students to read out the examples in the speech bubbles. If necessary, remind students of the weak form /əv/ in the pronunciation of *have.*

Put students into new pairs to continue the task. Students take it in turns to read the statements and comment on them. Monitor and check for accurate use of the target structures and pronunciation. Note down any common errors and feed back on them at the end of the activity. Correct any form mistakes carefully with the class.

As an extension, students can give their own examples of stupid behaviour (real or imaginary) and ask their partner to comment on it, using *might have* or *could have.*

Possible answers and tapescript

T 9.4

1 You're an idiot! You could have died! You could have starved to death or died of cold!
2 You're such an idiot! Your boss might have seen you. You could have got the sack.
3 That's so stupid! You could have been really ill. You should have gone to bed.
4 That was a really dumb thing to do! Sally might have seen you in the pub.
5 That's such a shame! You might have been a champion! You might even have won Wimbledon.

Speaking

4 Focus attention on the example. Check pronunciation of *row* /raʊ/. Ask students to read out the examples in the speech bubbles. Again, remind students of the weak form /əv/ in the pronunciation of *have* if they over-stress it. Give another example from your own experience (real or imaginary), e.g. *I borrowed my brother's camera without asking and I dropped it. The next time he used it, it didn't work. He had to buy a new one.*

Elicit sentences using the target structures, e.g. *I shouldn't have used the camera without asking. If I'd told my brother, he might have been able to repair the camera. I should have given him some money for a new camera.*

Give students time to think of examples of when things went wrong and sentences about the situation, using the target structures. Put students in pairs to exchange examples. Monitor and check for accurate use of the target structures and pronunciation. Note down any common errors and feed back on them at the end of the activity. Correct any mistakes carefully with the class.

As an extension, students can comment on their partner's situation/behaviour using *should have/shouldn't have*, e.g. *You should have asked permission to use the camera. You shouldn't have dropped the camera.*

ADDITIONAL MATERIAL

Workbook Unit 9

Exercise 1 Recognizing conditionals
Exercise 2 Types of conditional
Exercise 3 Possible conditions
Exercise 4 Improbable conditions
Exercises 5–6 Impossible conditions
Exercises 7–8 *should/might/could have done*
Exercise 10 Verb forms for unreal situations

SPEAKING AND LISTENING (SB p73)

A social conscience

This section gives students the opportunity to practise *would/wouldn't/might*, and *would/wouldn't have* in group tasks.

1 Check comprehension of *to have a social conscience* by eliciting relevant situations/examples, e.g. intervening if you see someone being bullied/threatened, stopping someone from making a lot of noise or damaging property, etc.

Read the situations as a class and deal with any vocabulary queries. Give your own responses to situation 1, using the language in the prompts, e.g. *I'd tell the police about the man. I wouldn't ask for my money back. I might stop giving money to people in the street.* Elicit a range of responses from the class to situation 1.

Put students in groups of three or four to discuss the situations. Monitor and check for accurate use of *would/wouldn't* and *might*. Make a note of any common errors and feed back on them at the end of the section, or in a subsequent lesson.

2 **T 9.5** [CD 3: Track 8] Tell students they are going to hear about a further five situations relevant to the idea of a social conscience. Pre-teach/Check the following vocabulary: *to wait in a queue, to make a scene, to grin, to mess around* (to behave in a silly way), *to bump into someone, to knock someone over, to turn on someone* (to attack someone suddenly without warning), *to mind your own business, to storm off* (to leave in an angry way), *to let a dog do its business* (to allow a dog to foul an area), *to stink, a bruise, to hand something over, to tremble.*

Give students time to read questions 1–6. Play the first recording and elicit the answers.

Play the rest of the recording. Students note down their answers to questions 1–6 for each situation. Students check their answers in pairs. Play the recording again if students have missed any of the key information. Check the answers with the class.

Answers and tapescript

Situation 1

1 In the bank, waiting in a queue.
2 A man in the queue.
3 The man jumped in front of the woman and said he had to ask a quick question. In fact it took a long time.
4 The woman let him because she didn't want to make a scene.
5 The man looked back at the woman and grinned. He looked pleased with himself.
6 The woman was furious but she didn't say anything.

Situation 2

1 In the park.
2 A woman with three children.
3 The woman was cross and had been shouting at the children. One of the boys bumped into his sister and knocked her over. The woman turned on the boy and hit him.
4 He told the woman to stop.
5 The woman told him to mind his own business and said some rude words.
6 She stormed off, screaming at the poor boy.

Situation 3

1 At home.
2 The woman's neighbour.
3 The neighbour lets his dog do his business right by the woman's front door and she always has to clean it up.
4 The woman asked the neighbour to take the dog somewhere else to do its business, or to pick it up.
5 The neighbour was horrible, and said he would put it through the letter box.
6 The woman will carry on picking it up.

Situation 4

1 On the bus.
2 A couple of kids (teenagers).
3 The teenagers had their feet on the seat in front of them.
4 The man asked them to put their feet down.
5 The teenagers pushed the man to the floor and started kicking him. He's got bruises everywhere!
6 He's only just been able to walk again!

Situation 5

1 In the street at about 10 p.m.
2 A man with a knife.
3 The man held the knife against the man's nose and demanded his wallet and phone.
4 He didn't say anything. He handed over the wallet and phone.
5 The man ran away.
6 He was trembling for ten minutes and couldn't move. He had never been so frightened in all his life.

T 9.5

A social conscience

1 I was in the bank the other day, and waiting in a queue. I'd **just reached** the front of the queue when this guy jumped in front of me and said, 'I just need to ask a quick question.' I wasn't very happy and I hate making a scene, so I let him. But then it started taking ages. He looked back at me, and grinned. He was so pleased with himself and I **was just furious**! What could I do? I said nothing.

2 I was in the park, right, and there was this woman with three kids. She'd obviously had a bad day, yeah, **she'd just been shouting** at the kids for messing around. One of the kids, the eldest boy, about eight, bumped into his little sister and knocked her over. The mother turned on this kid, the boy, and she hit him really hard. I went over to her and told her to stop. She told me to mind my own business, and said some very rude words and stormed off, screaming at the poor boy. He was **just a kid**!

3 My neighbour always lets his dog do his ... you know ... business right by my front door, and I always clean it up, day after day, because **it just stinks**! So the other day I asked him if he could get his dog to do its business somewhere else, or could he pick it up because I didn't like it right by my front door. He was absolutely horrible, and said he'd put it in my letter box from now on! So I suppose **I'll just carry on** picking it up. What else can I do?

4 I was on the bus the other day. **There was just me** and a couple of kids. These two kids had their feet on the seat in front of them, so I asked them to put their feet down. These kids, they must have been about sixteen or seventeen, came over to me, pushed me onto the floor, and started kicking me. I've got bruises everywhere! **I've only just been able** to walk again!

5 I was walking down the street coming home from work about ten at night, it was dark, and this guy jumped out of nowhere and said, 'Gimme your wallet and phone!' He had a knife, which he had right

up against my nose. I didn't say anything. I was **just terrified**! I thought he was going to kill me. I **just handed over** both and he ran away. I was trembling for ten minutes. I couldn't move. I've never been so frightened in all my life.

Talking about you

3 Briefly review the form of *would have* + past participle in relation to situation 1, e.g. *I would have asked the man to go to the back of the queue, I wouldn't have let the man go first.* Elicit other possible answers for situation 1, drilling the weak form /əv/ for *have* if necessary.

Put students in groups of three or four to discuss the situations in the recording. Monitor and check for accurate use of *would/wouldn't have.* Make a note of any common errors and feed back on them at the end of the section, or in a subsequent lesson.

SPOKEN ENGLISH – *just*

1 Students will be familiar with the use of *just* to mean a *short time ago/before*, but may not be aware that it has other meanings and that it is very common in spoken English. Focus attention on the examples. Students do the matching task, working individually. Check the answers.

Answers
*I'd **just** reached the front of the queue ...* – a short time before
*I **just** need to ask a quick question.* – only/simply
*... I was **just** furious!* – really

2 Refer students to the tapescript on SB p128 to find further examples of *just*. (See bold examples in **T 9.5** above.)

3 **T 9.6** **[CD 3: Track 9]** Focus attention on the example and the position for *just*. Give students time to read the sentences. Check students understand that *go to the loo* is informal for *go to the toilet.* Get students to complete the task, then play the recording so that they can check their answers.

Play the recording again and get students to repeat. If necessary, ask students to give the meaning of each use of *just*, following the wording in exercise 1 (see bracketed text in *Answers*).

Answers and tapescript

T 9.6

1 Alice isn't here. She's **just** gone. (a short time before)
2 I'm sorry I'm in a bad mood. I'm **just** tired, that's all. (only/simply)
3 I **just** love your new coat! (really)
4 I've **just** finished the most wonderful book. You must read it! (a short time before)
5 I don't want any wine. **Just** a glass of water, please. (only/simply)
6 John's so generous. I think he's **just** amazing! (really)
7 **A** Who's coming tonight?
B **Just** me. (only/simply)
8 Hold on a minute. I'm **just** going to the loo. (only/simply)

READING AND SPEAKING (SB p74)

The victim meets the burglar

ABOUT THE TEXT
The crime theme continues in this section with a newspaper article about a real meeting that took place between a burglar and his victim as part of a process called Restorative Justice. This gives victims the chance to tell offenders about the real impact of their crime, to get answers to their questions, and to receive an apology. It gives offenders the chance to understand the real impact of what they have done, and to do something to repair the harm. Supporters of Restorative Justice say that it holds offenders to account for what they have done, personally and directly, and helps victims to get on with their lives. The Restorative Justice Consortium, mentioned in exercise 2, is the independent umbrella organization for Restorative Justice in England and Wales.

This is the fourth jigsaw reading in the course. Students discuss crimes they have experienced or heard about in a pre-reading task. They then make predictions about Restorative Justice and about the text based on the headlines and introduction to the article. Students read about either the victim or the burglar, answer comprehension questions, and then exchange information. The section ends with a general discussion on crime and punishment.

The article recycles some of the target structures from the start of the unit. Encourage students to use the context to guess the meaning of new vocabulary or allow them to use dictionaries if appropriate. With weaker classes or if you are short of time, be prepared to pre-teach/check these items:

Introduction: *an encounter*

The victim: *scruffy, passer-by, to register* (to realize), *to smash, stitches* (in a wound), *purpose* (the point of something), *dysfunctional, heroin addict, to ruin, stunned, relieved*

The robber: *to rehabilitate, to bump into someone* (to meet by accident), *a sense of relief, to hit rock bottom, ashamed, rehab* (short for *rehabilitation*), *over the moon* (very happy).

1 Lead in to the topic by giving an example of a crime you experienced or that you know about. You could use an example from a recent news story if you prefer.

Discuss the questions as a class, eliciting a range of short accounts of different crimes. Again, give students the option of talking about crimes in the news if they prefer. Use this as an opportunity to assess students' knowledge of the topic vocabulary. If necessary, feed in key words that also appear in the newspaper article, e.g. *burglar, burglary, to break into, to be jailed, fraud, to be given a sentence, to release (a prisoner), to commit a crime.*

2 The questions in this exercise give students an opportunity to predict the effects of Restorative Justice before they read about them in the article. Check the pronunciation of *Restorative Justice*: /rɪˈstɔːrətɪv ˈdʒʌstɪs/. Read the notes and questions as a class and elicit one or two ideas. Students discuss the questions in groups of three.

Elicit possible answers in a short feedback session.

Possible answers

Restorative Justice hopes to: make the criminal understand the effect of his/her crime; stop him/her doing it again; give the victim the opportunity to ask questions and get an apology

The victim might say: *You have ruined my life. Why did you do this to me? Do you understand how I feel? Do you think you will commit crime again?*

The criminal might learn that crime has a real effect on the victim and that it takes a long time to get over it; that the victim deserves and explanation/apology; that people can be forgiving.

3 Focus attention on the headlines and get students to read the introduction through quickly. Elicit a range of answers to the prediction question. Encourage students to use *might/could have* in their answers.

Possible answers

Peter might have written to Will to say he was sorry.

Will might have visited Peter in prison and they might have talked about the effect of the burglary.

The Restorative Justice Consortium could have introduced them and might have helped them to understand each other.

4 Divide the class into two groups, A and B. With larger classes, you will need to sub-divide the students into more than one group A and more than one group B. Ask all the A students to read about the victim, Will, and all the B students to read about the robber, Peter. Students read through the text and answer the questions, working in their groups. Remind them to underline key information in their text or make brief notes to refer to when they do exercise 5. Encourage them to help each other with any new vocabulary (see *About the text* above). Monitor and help as necessary.

Check that students in each group are confident of the answers before moving on to exercise 5, but don't do a whole-class check at this stage.

5 Ask students to work in A/B pairs, with one group A student and one group B student in each pair. Elicit information for question 1 as an example.

Give students time to exchange their information and answer the questions. Monitor and help as necessary. Make sure students are exchanging the information to help them answer the questions and not simply reading from the text. Check the answers with the class.

Answers

1 Will Riley is 50, he's married and he has a daughter. He's a businessman from north London. Before the burglary, he appears to have enjoyed a normal life with his family.
Peter Woolf is also 50. He is married to Louise and he now works as a counsellor to rehabilitate criminals. He came from a dysfunctional family. He started using drugs at 10 and became an addict at 14. He'd been in and out of prison for 18 years. Stealing was the only thing he knew.
2 Will was getting ready to go to the gym. Peter was coming downstairs after taking some jewellery and money.
3 Will was shocked. He asked, 'What are you doing here?' He realized who Peter was and then he felt scared. He thought, 'If he's got a knife, he could kill me.'
Peter also felt frightened. He thought, 'He's a big guy. If he wanted to, he could hurt me.'
4 Will hadn't realized that Peter had smashed a flower pot on his head. A policeman asked Will if he was OK. He put his hand to his head and felt blood. All the bits of the pot were on the ground. Will had to go to hospital and have stitches.
Peter didn't want to hit him, but he did what he had to do. He feels that he isn't a violent person.
5 Will became too frightened to open his front door. He kept wondering if Peter would have attacked his daughter if she had been at home.
Peter felt relieved because he was going back to prison, which was a place he knew well.
6 Will wasn't sure what the purpose was but he went because he was curious.
Peter couldn't see the point either, but agreed to meet Will because he was bored.
7 Peter referred to the burglary as 'Last time we met ...' Will thought this made the crime sound like a social meeting and got very angry. He screamed questions at Will about why he had been chosen as the victim.
8 It made Peter realize that the burglary had affected Will very badly. Peter was shocked, and Will realized that he was an ordinary man and he wanted to help him.
9 Will is delighted that he's been able to help Peter get his life back. Peter is also delighted because the process helped him to get his life sorted out. He thinks that if he hadn't met Will, he would be dead by now.

What do you think?

Give students time to read through the questions and think about their answers. Elicit a range of responses in a whole-class discussion. In larger classes, students can work in groups and then report back.

Ask students if there is a system of Restorative Justice in their country and what they think of it.

Possible answers

2 The statistic suggests that prison doesn't stop people committing crime.
3 Other forms of punishment include: community service or unpaid work in the local area, returning stolen goods to the owner, curfews and electronic tagging, attending counselling and anger management programmes.

WRITING (SB p112)

Pros and cons – Arguing for and against

1 Ask students the question and discuss the answer as a class. Elicit both advantages and disadvantages of childhood.

2 Check understanding of *pros and cons*. Get students to read the text and then work in pairs to replace the underlined words and phrases in the text with those in the box.

Answers
Childhood – the best time of your life
Some people say that childhood is the best time of your life. However, being a child has both pros and cons.

One advantage is that you have very few responsibilities. For instance, you don't have to go to work, pay bills, or do the shopping, cooking, or cleaning. This means you have plenty of free time to do whatever you want – watch TV, play on the computer, go out with friends, play sports, or pursue other hobbies. Another point is that/Moreover, public transport, cinema, and sports centres cost much less for children. All things considered, being a child is an exciting, action-packed time in life.

However, for every plus there is a minus. One disadvantage is that you have to spend all day, Monday to Friday, at school. Studying usually means you have to do homework, and you have to take exams. Another point is that/Moreover, you may have a lot of free time, but you are rarely allowed to do whatever you want. You usually have to ask your parents if you can do things, from going shopping in town to staying out late or going to a party. Finally, although there are often cheaper prices for children, things are still expensive – and parents are not always generous with pocket money. There's never enough to do everything you want. In fact, sometimes there's not enough to do anything at all!

In conclusion, although some people see childhood as the best time in life, in my opinion children have no real choice, independence, or money. Nevertheless, it is true that choice, money, and independence all bring responsibilities and restrictions – which increase with age.

3 Put students in pairs to look at the paragraphs and decide on their purpose.

Answers
Paragraph 1: to introduce the argument
Paragraph 2: to present the advantages
Paragraph 3: to present the disadvantages
Paragraph 4: to conclude and give the writer's opinion

4 Put students in pairs to match the pros with the cons.

Answers

Pros	Cons
1 don't have to go to work	have to go to school Monday to Friday
2 can go out to parties with friends	need to ask your parents' permission
3 don't have to cook and clean	have to do homework and take exams
4 pay less for things	are never given enough pocket money

5 Read the list of subjects with the class. Put students in pairs to choose one of the subjects and discuss the pros and cons. Tell them to note down the pros and cons they think of. Elicit examples of pros and cons for each subject from the class.

6 Students work in their pairs to complete the phrases with their own ideas. Elicit possible endings for each phrase from a range of students.

7 Ask students to use their notes to write four paragraphs. Remind them of the purpose of each paragraph, and remind them that they should express their own opinion in the last paragraph. Set this for homework. Students can read their essays to the class and discuss each other's conclusions.

VOCABULARY (SB p76)

Words with similar meaning

This section focuses on synonyms and near-synonyms and recycles vocabulary from the article on pp74–5 and from across the unit. Raising awareness of words with similar meanings helps to enrich students' vocabulary and also provides them with a way of avoiding repetition in both writing and speaking. As an introduction to the topic, focus on the pictures of a robber and a burglar. Elicit that the meanings are very similar (both words refer to someone who steals something) but they are slightly different (a burglar breaks into people's houses to steal things; a robber steals money from a bank or shop, or from someone in the street).

1 Focus on the example. Students continue to match the words, working in pairs.

Check the answers with the class, dealing with any pronunciation problems as you go.

Answers

prison – jail	angry – furious
burglar – robber	shocked – stunned
scared – frightened	ordinary – normal
purpose – point	delighted – over the moon
meet – bump into	totally – completely

2 This exercise practises some of the words from exercise 1 in context. Elicit the answers for the first pair of sentences. Check comprehension of *to brainstorm* (to suggest a range of ideas as a group and discuss them) and *to bother* (to take the time/effort to do something). Students complete the task, working individually. Give them time to check their answers in pairs before checking with the class. Students practise reading the sentences in their pairs.

Answers
1 'Did you **meet** anyone you know in town?'
'Yes, I **bumped into** Alice as I was coming out of a shop.'
2 'Aren't you **delighted** with your exam results?'
'You bet. I'm **over the moon**. It's great!'
3 'The **purpose** of this meeting is to brainstorm ideas.'
'Sorry, but I don't see the **point**. Why bother?'
4 'You must be **angry** with Tim for crashing your car.'
'I'm absolutely **furious** with him.'
5 'I was **shocked** when I heard that Joe had died. Weren't you?'
'I was **stunned**. He was only 48.'

6 'I'm **scared** of dogs. I was bitten once.'
'I'm not **frightened** of them. They're usually really friendly.'

3 This exercise highlights words that have subtle differences in meaning or slightly different uses/collocations. Elicit answers to the first pair of examples. Focus attention on the second pair and point out that the adjectives *big* and *great* can be used with some of the nouns in both groups, but the correct answer in each case is the adjective that can be used with all three of the nouns in the group. Students continue the task individually. Allow students to refer to a dictionary for any answers they are unsure of. Allow students to compare answers in pairs before you check with the class.

Answers
1 live **alone** happily
feel **lonely** and unhappy
2 **big** house/mistake/feet
great artist/Wall of China/party
3 **tall** person/building/trees
high mountain/wall/ceiling
4 **little** old lady/boy/finger
small room/glass of wine/dress size
5 **fast** car/train/food
quick drink/worker/thinking

4 This exercise highlights verbs that are easily confused. Students should be familiar with most of the words, but are likely to confuse them, often due to interference from their own language. Look at the example with the class. Students work in pairs to continue the task. Allow them to refer to a dictionary for any answers they are unsure of. Explain if necessary that *talk* and *speak* are very similar in meaning, and both could be used in the second context *talk/speak to my bank manager*. However, *speak* cannot be used with the meaning of *chat informally*, so cannot be used in the first context *talk to my mates for hours*.

Check the answers with the class.

Answers
win the championship / beat Arsenal
make a mess / do you best
talk to my mates for hours / speak to my bank manager
buy someone a present / pay at the cash desk
clean the flat / wash my hair
listen to music / hear a noise
rob a bank / steal some jewellery
borrow money from someone / lend money to someone

SUGGESTION

Encourage students to create a 'confusables' section in their vocabulary records (see TB p14 and p15). They can add in the examples from exercises 3 and 4 and any other items they often get wrong. Remind them to write personalized examples where possible to help them remember the words/phrases.

To give students more practice with the verbs in exercise 4, get them to write pairs of gapped sentences to pass to another student to complete. Students could also have a competition to write and perform a sketch including as many of the phrases as they can.

EVERYDAY ENGLISH (SB p77)

Dealing with money

This section includes the language used to pay a restaurant bill with a card, ask for the price of a room in a hotel, request an account balance, pay for tickets with a credit card, and query the amount of change when paying for drinks.

Students will need to discuss exchange rates at the end of this section, so ask them to find these out before the lesson.

Lead in to the topic by brainstorming vocabulary related to money. Make sure students are familiar with the following: *service* (in a restaurant), *PIN number*, *press enter*, *receipt*, *VAT* (value added tax; a tax that is added to the price of goods and services), *a (cleared) balance* (amount of money in a bank account), *account (number)*, *in credit*, *MasterCard*, *expiry date*, *security number* (a set of figures that appear on the back of a credit/debit card), *a (£20) note*, *change* (money you get back when you pay for something and give too much).

1 **T 9.7** [**CD 3: Track 10**] The recording in this exercise contains the first few lines of each of the main conversations in exercises 2 and 3. There is enough information in each one for students to be able to match the conversations to the photos. Read the instructions and the questions with the class. Play conversation 1 and elicit possible answers.

Play the rest of the recording and get students to complete the matching task and answer the questions about each conversation. Check answers to the matching task, but don't check answers to the questions at this stage.

Answers and tapescript
1 a 2 d 3 b 4 e 5 c

T 9.7
1 **A** Here's your bill.
B Thank you. Is service included?
A No, it isn't. I hope you enjoyed your meal.
2 **A** How much is a standard room?
B £55 per night.
A Does that include everything?
3 **A** I'll pay for the tickets with my MasterCard.
B Can you give me your number?
4 **A** Could you give me the balance on my account?
B Sure. Tell me your account number.
5 **A** Can I have a gin and tonic and two glasses of white wine, please?
B Sure. That's £14.50.
A Thank you.
B And here's your change. 50p.

2 **T 9.8** [**CD 3: Track 11**] Play the recording and get students to check their answers to the questions in exercise 1. Play the recording again and ask them to note down any extra questions that they hear (see questions in brackets in the *Answers* below). Check the answers with the class.

Answers and tapescript

1 a waiter and a customer; they are talking about paying the bill; questions: *Is service included?* (*Can you enter your PIN number?*)
2 a receptionist and a customer; they are talking about the cost of a room; questions: *How much is a standard room? Does that include everything?* (*That's extra, is it?*)
3 a customer services operator and a customer; they are talking about paying for tickets; questions: *Can you give me your number?* (*What's the expiry date? And the start date? And the three digit security number on the back?*)
4 a bank clerk and a customer; they are talking about the customer's account balance; question: *Could you give me a balance on my account?*
5 a barman and a customer; they are talking about paying for drinks; questions: *Can I have a gin and tonic and two glasses of white wine, please?* (*How much did I give you? Oh, did you?*)

T 9.8

1 **A** Here's your bill.
B Thank you. Is service included?
A No, it isn't. I hope you enjoyed your meal.
B It was lovely, thank you.
A Can you put in your PIN number, and then press ENTER? And here's your card and your receipt.
B Thanks. That's for you.
A That's very kind of you. I hope to see you again soon.
B Bye!

2 **A** How much is a standard room?
B £55 per night.
A Does that include everything?
B That includes the room for two people, but it doesn't include breakfast.
A That's extra, is it?
B Yes, I'm afraid it is. But the £55 does include VAT.

3 **A** I'll pay for the tickets with my MasterCard.
B Can you give me your number?
A 5484 6922 3171 2435.
B What's the expiry date?
A 09/12.
B And the start date?
A 10/07.
B And the three digit security number on the back?
A 721.

4 **A** Could you give me the balance on my account?
B Sure. Tell me your account number.
A 4033 2614 7900.
B Bear with me one moment. The current cleared balance on that account is £542.53 in credit.

5 **A** Can I have a gin and tonic and two glasses of white wine, please?
B Sure. That's £14.50.
A Thank you.
B And here's your change. 50p.
A Thanks. Er ... how much did I give you? I think you've made a mistake!
B Sorry?
A I think you must have made a mistake. I gave you £20, but you've given me change for fifteen.
B No, I don't think so.
A Well, I'm pretty sure I gave you a twenty-pound note.
B Oh, did you? Er ... sorry about that. Here you are.
A Thanks.

3 This exercise gives students the opportunity to roleplay the conversations in this section, with the support of conversation skeletons and key word prompts.

Focus attention on the conversation skeletons and on the prompts. The conversations recycle numbers and prices from *Everyday English* in Unit 8 and so students should be able to read the numbers aloud without much difficulty. You might want to review the intonation on account and credit card numbers (see TB p97) and check the pronunciation of *VAT* /viː eɪ ˈtiː/.

Give students a few moments to think about the wording for conversation 1. Choose two confident students to roleplay it for the rest of the class. Encourage them to improvise where they need to, rather than rely on you to give them the actual wording.

Put students into pairs to continue roleplaying the conversations. Monitor and help as necessary.

If you have time, let pairs of students perform one or two conversations for the rest of the class.

4 **T 9.8** [**CD 3: Track 11**] Play the recording, then refer students to the tapescript on SB p128 and let them compare the wording with their roleplays.

5 Check comprehension of: *overdrawn*, *to economize*, *store card*, and *credit limit*. Read and discuss the questions as a class. Don't push students to give details about their financial situation if they seem reluctant or if money is a sensitive subject in their culture. With larger classes, students can discuss the questions in small groups and then feed back.

SUGGESTION

You can recycle the language in this section by getting students to think about recent transactions/enquiries they have made outside the classroom and roleplaying them in English. This can include buying things, asking what's included in a price, ordering currency, paying with a credit/store card, etc.

Don't forget!

Vocabulary revision
Units 7–9 (TB p155), with answers (TB p159)

Workbook Unit 9

Exercise 9 Pronunciation – Linking in connected speech (1)

Exercise 11 Vocabulary – *make* and *do*

Exercise 12 Listening – Scams

Word list

Refer students to the Word list for Unit 9 (SB p156). They could translate the words, learn them at home, or transfer some to their vocubulary notebook.

10

Noun phrases
Compound nouns
I need one of those things ...

All things high tech

Introduction to the unit

This unit looks at various aspects of the theme of technology. It starts with a text on microprocessors that provides the context for language work on noun phrases.

The topic of *Listening and speaking* is *What do you do on the Net?* and the theme of technology is carried through with a *Reading and speaking* section on the new St Pancras Station in London. The *Vocabulary and speaking* section builds on the language work on noun phrases with a focus on compound nouns. The unit ends with an *Everyday English* section on the language used for describing the appearance and use of different objects.

The *Writing* syllabus continues with a description of a famous town or city and the skill of writing notes up into connected text.

Language aims

Grammar – noun phrases This unit covers the words that can be used before and after a noun to form noun phrases. These include articles (*a/an*, *the*) and the number *one*, possessives (*my*, *mine*, etc.), *all* and *everything*, and reflexive pronouns (*myself*, *yourself*, etc. and *each other*).

POSSIBLE PROBLEMS

The rules for the use of *a/an* and *the* can appear complex, and students whose first language doesn't have articles often miss them out altogether. Some students may overuse the number *one* instead of *a/an*. Speakers of Latin languages can often overuse *the* due to interference from their own language.

Possessive adjectives and pronouns are easily confused, as is the use of the apostrophe to indicate possession. Students may also have problems with the difference between *all* and *everything*, as in some languages these are translated by the same word.

Common mistakes

**I come from big city.* (missing indefinite article)
**I'm journalist.* (missing indefinite article with professions)
*It's a horrible weather. (incorrect use of *a/an* with an uncountable noun)
**The modern life is very fast.* (incorrect use of *the* with abstract nouns when talking in general)
*I love London. *It's galleries are brilliant.* (confusion of *its* for possession with *it's* (meaning *it is/has*))
**All was stolen from my bag.* (confusion of *all* with *everything*)
** They speak to themselves every day.* (confusion of *themselves* with *each other*)

Vocabulary The vocabulary focus in this unit is compound nouns. Students focus on the main stress in compound nouns, work with dictionary extracts, and practise building compound nouns. Make sure students have access to a dictionary for the final exercise in this section.

Everyday English This is a functional lesson in which students practise the language of describing objects they don't know the name of.

Notes on the unit

STARTER (SB p78)

1 This task aims to review the parts of speech that can be used in noun phrases. Focus attention on the sentences. Students complete the task in pairs.

Answers
Nouns: *brother, computer, world, laptop*
Definite article: *the*
Indefinite article: *an*
Possessive adjective: *my*
Possessive pronoun: *mine*

In a brief review session, elicit the other indefinite article (*a*), other possessive adjectives (*your, his, her*, etc.), and possessive pronouns (*yours, his, hers*, etc.). If students seem to have problems with these parts of speech and terms, refer them to Grammar Reference 10.1 on SB p143.

2 Focus attention on the sentences. Elicit the reflexive pronouns.

Answers
Mike programs his computer **himself**.
I live by **myself**, which suits me fine.

Point out that we use reflexive pronouns when the subject and the object of the verb are the same.

CHIPS WITH EVERYTHING (SB p78)

Noun phrases

ABOUT THE TEXT
The text introduces the theme of technology with an overview of one of the most important developments in computer technology: the microprocessor, also called a microchip, or chip. The text also provides the context for the study of noun phrases and the different types of words they can consist of: articles, possessives, *all/everything*, and pronouns (see the *Grammar Spot* on SB p79 for examples.)

As you would expect, there is some technical language in the text, but most of this is explained or exemplified in context. However, if you are short of time, or with weaker classes, you could pre-teach/check the following: *silicon, transistor* (a small piece of electrical equipment that can control an electrical signal), *complex, device, to diagnose, microscopic, decade, to fix, to double, capacity, micron* (one millionth of a metre).

1 Focus attention on the title of the text. Ask students what they know about microprocessors. Elicit a range of answers, then get students to read the first two sections *What are they?* and *What do they do?* to check their answers.

Give students time to read the rest of the text and answer the questions in pairs.

Check the answers with the class.

Answers
1 Microchips are huge in importance (the biggest thing since the invention of the wheel). Physically, they are tiny. The smallest are just a few mm^2.
2 Microchips are found in: personal computers, calculators, cameras, radios, ovens, fridges, washing machines, DVDs, watches, cars, TV remotes, mobile phones, medical equipment, CD players.
3 They either say *Yes* or *No* using a simple code with the numerals 0 and 1 to represent the on and off states of a transistor.
4 It takes months, and involves more than 250 manufacturing steps.
5 Because they want to show that the processors are theirs.
6 There are many more things that we could do with microprocessors. Soon they'll be able to fix themselves and even make themselves.

2 Refer students back to the text, and elicit the end of the first sentence (see *Answers* below).

Put students in pairs to complete the rest of the sentences.

Answers
Microprocessors are the biggest thing since the invention of the wheel.
A microchip is a small piece of silicon that has been printed with transistors.
The smallest microchips are just a few mm^2.
The microprocessor is the most complex product that has ever been made.
Microprocessors control everything in our lives.
They are used in all digital devices.
We couldn't text each other on our mobiles without microchips.
Doctors and surgeons wouldn't be able to diagnose, treat, or operate. Nearly all of their equipment contains microchips.
It takes months to make a microprocessor.
Microprocessors will be able to fix themselves and even make themselves.

3 Put students into pairs or small groups to discuss the facts. Get some students to report back to the class.

GRAMMAR SPOT (SB p79)

This *Grammar Spot* highlights the type of words that can be used in noun phrases. Read the notes with the class. Then get students to look for other examples in the text.

Refer students to Grammar Reference 10.1–10.5 on SB pp143–5.

PRACTICE (SB p79)

Articles – *a/an/the*/no article/*one*

This section aims to review the use of the definite article (*the*), indefinite articles (*a/an*), no article, and the number *one*.

1 Discuss the use of the indefinite article in the first sentence. Students continue the task, working in pairs. Monitor and help as necessary. With weaker students, you could allow them to use their own language if appropriate.

Discuss the answers with the class. If students have problems understanding the articles, refer them back to Grammar Reference 10.2 on SB pp143–4.

Answers

I bought **a** laptop and **a** printer on Saturday. (*laptop* and *printer* referred to the for the first time)

The laptop has **an** *Intel* microprocessor. (*laptop* referred to for the second time; *Intel microprocessor* referred to for the first time with *an* used because *Intel* starts with a vowel sound)

Intel is **the** largest manufacturer of computer chips in **the** world. (definite article used with a superlative and to refer to *the world* – the only one there is)

One chip contains millions of transistors. (*one* used to specify number)

I don't understand **(-)** computers. (no article used to refer to computers in general)

ABOUT THE TEXT

This text aims to consolidate the use of the articles discussed in the introductory section. The context is a description of the work of Charles Babbage /bæbɪdʒ/, one of the early designers of computers.

2 **T 10.1** [**CD 3: Track 12**] Ask students to read the text through quickly to get an idea of what it is about. Elicit the answer for the first gap. Students then complete the text. Remind them that some answers don't require an article.

Play the recording so that students can check their answers.

Answers and tapescript

T 10.1

The first computer

Charles Babbage (1791–1871) was (1) **a** scientist and (2) **an** engineer. He had the idea for (3) **the** first programmable computer. He wanted to build (4) **a** machine that could do (5) **(-)** calculations without making the mistakes that human 'computers' made.
He designed a machine called the Difference Engine, and (6) **the** British Government provided funds. (7) **The** machine was never completed because Babbage ran out of (8) **(-)** money.
In 1991, (9) **a** team of engineers from (10) **the** Science Museum in London built one of Babbage's machines, using his original designs, and it worked perfectly.

3 This exercise gives further practice of the articles and also the use of the number *one*. Elicit the answers to the first sentence. Students complete the task, working individually.

Give students time to check their answers in pairs, before checking with the class. If necessary, ask students to explain the use of each article (see bracketed answers below). Deal with any areas of disagreement, again referring back to back to Grammar Reference 10.2 on SB pp143–4.

Answers

1 'Where's Jane?' In **the** kitchen cooking **(-)** lunch. (*the* used when it is clear which kitchen we mean; usually no article with meals)
2 Washington, DC is **the** capital of **the** United States. (definite article used to refer to *the capital* – the only one there is – and in the place name *the United States*)
3 We had **(-)** dinner in **the** best restaurant in **the** world. (usually no article with meals; definite article used with a superlative; definite article used to refer to *the world* – the only one there is)
4 **One** day I'm going to be **a** rich man. (*one day* used to refer to an indefinite time in the future; indefinite article to say what somebody will be)
5 Jake's in **(-)** hospital. He's had **an** operation. (no article in the expression *in hospital* when referring to the institution rather than a specific hospital; *operation* referred to for the first time)
6 Certainly **(-)** computers have changed **(-)** modern life. (no article to refer to computers and modern life in general)
7 'How do you like your coffee?' 'Black with **one** sugar, please.' (*one* used to specify number)
8 I have two daughters. **One** daughter is **a** teacher; **the** other works in **(-)** advertising. (*one* used to specify number; *a* + a profession; *the* used to refer to the daughter a second time; no article + sectors of work)
9 Today is **the** first day of **the** rest of your life. Enjoy it. (*the* + superlative; definite article used to refer to *the rest of your life* – the only one there is)

Speaking

T 10.2 [**CD 3: Track 13**] This activity gives students the opportunity to practise articles in a personalized way. Tell students there are 10 questions in the recording for them to reply to. Focus attention on the examples in the Student's Book and play question 1. Elicit other possible answers, checking the use of articles carefully.

Put students into groups of three. Play the rest of the recording, pausing after each question so that students can exchange answers.

Play the questions again and elicit a range of answers from the class (see possible answers in brackets). Highlight any mistakes with articles and give students the opportunity to self-correct.

Possible answers and tapescript

T 10.2

1 Where did you have lunch today? (I had lunch at home/in a restaurant/at a friend's house.)
2 Where's your mother at the moment? (She's at work/in town/at the shops.)
3 Do you prefer tea or coffee? (I prefer coffee.)
4 What's the name of the river in London? (It's the River Thames.)
5 Have you got a pet? What's its name? (I've got a cat. Its name is Sylvester.)
6 What's your father's job? (He's a salesman/an engineer./He works in manufacturing.)
7 How do you get to school? (I come by bus/by car./I walk to school.)
8 What's the name of the Christian holy book? (It's called the Bible.) And the Islamic holy book? (It's called the Koran/Qur'an.)
9 Who's sitting nearest the window? (Adam is sitting nearest the window.) Next to the teacher? (I'm sitting next to the teacher.)
10 Where are you going after the lesson? (I'm going home/to the cinema/to the library.)

Possessives

This section aims to consolidate the use of possessive adjectives and pronouns (exercise 4), and review the use of the apostrophe for possession (exercise 5).

4 Focus attention on the examples and check the answers with the students as a class.

> **Answers**
> I'm very proud of **my** children. (possessive adjective)
> Don't touch that! It's **mine**! (possessive pronoun)
> James is an old friend of **ours**. (possessive pronoun)

Focus attention on the sentences.

Elicit the answers for the first sentence. Students complete the exercise, working individually.

Check the answers. If students have made mistakes, review the use of possessive adjectives and pronouns, referring to Grammar Reference 10.3 on SB p144. Also check the difference between *it's/its* and *who's/whose*:

it's = it is/has
its = possessive adjective (third person)
who's = who is/has
whose = the question word/relative pronoun for possession

> **Answers**
> 1 'Is that **her** book?' 'Well, it isn't **mine**.'
> 2 '**Whose** is that car?' 'It's **ours**. Nice, huh?'
> 3 Microsoft owes **its** success to Windows. That's why **it's** the biggest software company in the world.
> 4 Those aren't **your** socks. These blue ones are **yours**.
> 5 Mary, this is Pete. Pete's an old friend of **mine**.
> 6 My sisters borrow **my** clothes, and I borrow **theirs**.

5 Focus attention on the two sentences with apostrophes. Give students time to compare the examples and work out the rule.

> **Answers**
> *'s* is used with singular nouns.
> *s'* is used with plural nouns.

Elicit the position for the apostrophe in sentence 1. Students complete the exercise, working individually. Give them time to check in pairs before checking with the class. If students have problems with sentence 4, remind them that *child* has an irregular plural *children* and so the possessive is *children's*.

Point out that the answer to sentence 5 could also be ... *my brother's girlfriends* if there is only one brother and he has more than one girlfriend.

> **Answers**
> 1 I've borrowed my dad's car.
> 2 My parents' new house is great.
> 3 I like Alice's boyfriend.
> 4 The children's room is upstairs.
> 5 I really like my brothers' girlfriends.

its or *it's*

6 **T 10.3** **[CD 3: Track 14]** This is a short activity to help students recognize possessive adjectives and pronouns, and distinguish them from other words that sound the same. Play the first sentence and elicit the answer.

Play the rest of the recording, pausing at the end of each sentence. Students underline the correct words.

Check the answers with the class.

> **Answers and tapescript**
> **T 10.3**
> 1 Living in London has **its** disadvantages.
> 2 To start with, **there's** a lot of traffic.
> 3 Londoners like **their** parks and open spaces.
> 4 For them **it's** important to escape from busy city life.
> 5 London's full of kids, and **they're** always on the move.
> 6 The grown-ups have got their parts of town, and the kids have got **theirs**.

all and *every* ...

This section highlights the difference between *all* and *everything*. With weaker students, elicit and revise the ways of using *all*:

All (of) + noun – *All (of) my friends* ...

All of + pronoun – *All of us* ...

Subject pronoun + *all* + verb – *We all go* ...

All + subject pronoun + verb – *All I eat* ... (this structure is used to give emphasis and means *The only thing(s)* ...).

Point out that we use *everything/everyone*, rather than *all*, on its own.

7 Elicit the mistake in the first sentence. Students discuss the mistakes in the other sentences, working in pairs. Check the answers with the class.

> **Answers**
> 1 I buy **all my** clothes in the market.
> 2 **Everything** was stolen in the burglary.
> 3 'Did they take any of your CDs?' '**All of them**.'
> 4 In my family **we all like** football.
> 5 **Everyone** enjoyed the party.
> 6 **All of the students** in my class work hard.

8 Elicit the answer for sentence 1. Students complete the sentences, working individually.

Check the answers with the class.

> **Answers**
> 1 Everybody/Everyone
> 2 All
> 3 Everything
> 4 all
> 5 everybody/everyone; everyone/everybody

Reflexive pronouns and *each other*

This section uses simple graphics to highlight the difference between reflexive pronouns (*myself*, etc.) and *each other*.

9 Give students time to read the examples and match the graphics. Remind students that we use reflexive pronouns when the subject and the object are the same.

Answers
I cut **myself** shaving. ⮌
They send **each other** Christmas cards. ⇆

Elicit the answer for sentence 1. Students complete the sentences, working individually.

Check the answers with the class, making sure students understand the meaning of *make yourself at home* (make yourself comfortable, as if you were in your own home) and *help yourself* (serve yourself food).

Answers
1 We love **each other** and we're going to get married.
2 He's crazy! He could have killed **himself**!
3 Do you like the cake? I made it **myself**.
4 'Can you make me a cup of tea?' 'No. Do it **yourself**.'
5 My kids get on well with **each other**.
6 Please make **yourself** at home.
7 We're very different, but we understand **each other**.
8 Her kids are good. They know how to behave **themselves**.
9 The food's all ready, so help **yourself/yourselves** to whatever you want.

Mime

This activity gives students the opportunity to practise reflexive pronouns and *each other* in an active and fun way. Demonstrate the activity by miming one of the actions that can be done alone. Students guess what you're doing. Choose individual students or pairs to mime an action for the class.

With larger classes, students can work in groups of four to do the activity.

ADDITIONAL MATERIAL

Workbook Unit 10
Exercise 1 Noun phrases
Exercises 2–5 Articles
Exercises 6–7 Possessives
Exercises 8–9 *all* and *every*
Exercise 10 Pronouns – *myself/each other*

LISTENING AND SPEAKING (SB p81)

What do you do on the Net?

ABOUT THE LISTENING

This section continues the theme of technology with a focus on how people use the Internet (often abbreviated to *Net*). It also refers to *the web* (short for *World Wide Web*). People often use these terms interchangeably but they are not strictly the same thing: the Internet is the computer system that allows people in different parts of the world to exchange information; the web is the huge collection of documents, pictures, sounds, etc. in different places that are connected through the Internet.

There are a number of references to online services and businesses in the pre-listening work and the recording:

Google – the largest search engine on the Internet. The verb *to google* has moved into spoken English, e.g. *I googled the subject and found a really good website.*

Facebook/MySpace – social networking sites

eBay – an online auction site

YouTube – a video sharing website

Wikipedia – a free online encyclopaedia

BBC Bitesize – the BBC's free online study resource for school-age students in the UK

Amazon – an American electronic commerce company which sells books and other products

Hotmail – one of the oldest free email services

Friends Reunited – a social networking site based on the theme of reunion with former friends

The listening task consists of five people of different ages talking about how they use the Internet. Students listen and decide who does what. There is a *Spoken English* feature on the words *also*, *as well*, and *too*. In the pre- and post-listening exercises students discuss some true/false statements about the Internet and discuss their own use of the Internet.

Students should be able to do the listening tasks without much vocabulary help. However, if you feel your students need help with some of the topic-related vocabulary, do a brief review of the following items: *website, webpage, a profile, a (bank) balance, to transfer money, to log onto, to click on, to trace your ancestors, to download music, to update, satellite navigation system.*

As a lead-in to the topic, ask *What's the common abbreviation for Internet?* (*Net*). Then ask the question in the section title. Elicit a range of answers from the class, writing the main uses and services on the board.

1 Give students time to read the statements. Deal with any vocabulary queries (see *About the Listening* for information about the services/businesses mentioned). Put students into groups of three or four to discuss the statements. Monitor and help as necessary.

Check the answers with the class.

Answers
All the statements are true.

2 Elicit the correct order for sentence 1. (All the sentences are taken from the **T 10.4**). Students complete the task, working individually.

Check the answers.

Answers
1 I go onto websites about sport.
2 I use the Net mainly for *Facebook*.
3 I just log onto my bank and click on *Pay Now*.
4 I do nearly all my shopping online.
5 I download music onto my MP3 player.

3 **T 10.4** [CD 3: Track 15] Allow students time to read the task. Play the recording about Tom and elicit the answers. Play the rest of the recording and get students to complete the task, working individually.

Students compare their answers in pairs/small groups before checking with the class.

Answers and tapescript
Tom: watch videos, talk to friends, buy and sell things
Monica: do social networking, look for work, see what's on
Justin: pay bills, watch sport, book and buy things
Daisy: send emails, get news and weather
David: research family history, practise languages, download music

T 10.4

1 Tom
I go onto websites about sport. I'm into skateboarding, so I go onto skateboarding websites. I watch a lot of skateboarding videos on *YouTube*.

I go on things like *MySpace*, where I can talk to friends from school.

Er ... if I'm doing school work, I use *Google* and *Wikipedia*, which can be really useful. And *BBC Bitesize* helps with revision, and there are tests so you can practise.

I do quite a lot of shopping – clothes, shoes and stuff. I go to *Amazon* for DVDs, games, CDs. And *eBay* for all sorts of things. I'm trying to buy some tickets for a gig on *eBay*. I'm also selling some of my old stuff on it.

2 Monica
I use the Net mainly for *Facebook*. You post a photo and a profile of yourself. You can say what you want – biography, hobbies, interests, music, films.

You control who can see your profile. Other people search for friends, people who share common interests. When you identify someone on the site you'd like to meet, you can ask to become a friend.

I also use the Net to look for jobs and flats, and to see what's on at the weekend.

3 Justin
I use Internet banking. It's good 'cos I can get my balance any time of day or night, I can transfer money instantly. So I like paying bills online. I just log onto my bank and click on *Pay Now*, and the bill is paid immediately. Easy!

I'm into American baseball, so I watch live baseball games from the US. And ... what else? I book restaurants, cinema tickets, holidays. Oh, I get traffic reports, too. Oh, yes! I do nearly all my shopping online. I do my weekly supermarket shop, and it's all delivered. Clothes, birthday presents, Christmas presents, books, music – the lot!

4 Daisy
I don't like reading onscreen, and I don't like watching DVDs, either, but I do use the Net for three things. I email a lot with *Hotmail*. I get the news every day on *The Guardian* website. And I also check the weather every day. I get up in the morning and get a weather forecast for my town for early morning, mid-morning, early afternoon, and evening. Then, and only then, I get dressed!

5 David
I've gone onto a website called *Friends Reunited*, and I've met up with people from my school days. And I've researched my family history, and traced my ancestors back over two hundred years. I'm retired, so I have lots of time to do these things.

I like to keep up my languages, so I watch the news in Spanish and in French, too. And I download music onto my MP3 player. And I update my satellite navigation system, as well.

4 **T 10.4** [CD 3: Track 15] Put students into pairs and give them time to choose a person. Play the recording again. Students listen and take notes about the person they have chosen. Ask some students to tell the class about the person they chose.

SPOKEN ENGLISH – *also, as well*, and *too*

This section helps students work out the word order with these common words in spoken English.

1 Read the examples as a class. Ask students to note the position of the highlighted words in each sentence. You could refer students to the tapescript on SB pp128–9 and get them to find more examples (see underlining in **T 10.4** above).

2 Read the first sentence with the class and elicit the same sentence three times, with the different expressions added. Point out the use of the comma before *too*. Students complete the task individually Check the answers.

Answers
I **also** go onto social networking sites. / I go onto social networking sites **as well**. / I go onto social networking sites, **too**.
I **also** download music and videos. / I download music and videos **as well**. / I download music and videos, **too**.
I **also** go onto websites to get the weather. / I go onto websites to get the weather **as well**. / I go onto websites to get the weather, **too**.

3 Elicit the answer to the first example. Students continue the task, working individually. Check the answers and remind students that both *as well* and *too* are used at the end of a sentence, but *also* is not possible in this position.

Answers
'Dave's nice.' His sister is **as well/, too.**
'I'm going home now.' 'I am **as well/, too.**'
Don't forget your coat. And take your umbrella **as well/, too.**
Buy some bread. And some coffee **as well/, too.**

4 Students complete the task individually. Allow students to compare their answers in pairs before you check answers with the class.

Answers
'I like Harry.' 'Me, **too.**'
'I'm thirsty.' 'Me, **too.**'

What do you think?

Give students time to read the questions. Put students into groups to discuss the questions. Elicit a range of answers from the class in a feedback session.

SUGGESTION
If your students make use of online learning help in studying English, ask them to recommend the best websites. Write them in a list or on a handout that can be added to over the course.

EXTRA IDEA
Technology questionnaire TB p156
If you would like to continue with the theme of technology, you can photocopy this questionnaire. You will need one sheet for each student. The questionnaire is intended to provide a review of key vocabulary and to be a light-hearted springboard for discussing gadgets. The answers to questions 5 and 6 appear on TB p159.

READING AND SPEAKING (SB p82)

Architecture old and new

ABOUT THE TEXT
The technology theme is carried through in a text about the new St Pancras /pæŋkrəs/ International Station in London. Located in central London and originally built in the 1860s, the station has undergone major redevelopment and was reopened in 2007. Passengers can now catch the Eurostar there (the service between London and France/Belgium, using the tunnel under the English Channel). Other railway references in the text include: TGV (*train à grande vitesse*, French for 'high-speed train'), Grand Central (a terminus station in Midtown Manhattan in New York City, the biggest station in the world, with 44 platforms), Gare du Nord (one of the six large terminus stations of the Paris main line network, and the busiest station in Europe, with around 180 million travellers per year).

The text takes the form of an article about the changes to St Pancras station and what it can now offer to passengers and the local area. Much of the new vocabulary can be worked out from the context, but you might want to pre-teach/check the following items:

Words used to refer to the station/area: *stunning, regeneration, thriving, a masterpiece, a feat of engineering, to restore, a triumph*

Construction words/areas of the station: *basement, storage, unsupported, a span, escalator, brasserie* (an inexpensive restaurant serving French food), *Gothic* (a style of building common in western Europe between 12th–16th centuries), *revolving door, laundry lift, plumbing* /plʌmɪŋ/, *penthouse.*

Lead in to the topic by eliciting a description of the train station in the students' capital city. Ask them if travelling from there is a positive or negative experience.

1 Give students time to rank the features in order. Students compare their ideas with a partner, and then with the rest of the class. Establish if there is a feature which is important to everyone in the class, and if there is a difference of opinion between men/women and different ages in the group.

2 Focus attention on the photos of the station, and elicit some descriptions. Feed in any vocabulary students need.

Possible answers
The station has a curved glass roof, and looks very modern.

3 Students read through the questions. Set a time limit of 2–3 minutes for them to find the answers. Tell them not to worry about new vocabulary at this stage but just to find the answers to the questions. With weaker students, pre-teach/check the items related to the glass roof: *unsupported, a span.*

Answers
1 It opened in 2007.
2 You can travel across the UK, and to Paris, Brussels, and Lille.
3 Between 1863 and 1868.
4 It was 240 feet (75m) wide and appeared to float without supports across all five platforms in a single span.

4 Focus on the chart. See *About the text* above for notes on vocabulary. Give students time to read the article again and find the information to complete the chart.

Allow students to check their answers in pairs before checking with the class.

Answers

Original STATION	New STATION
Cost £436,000	**Cost £800 million**
Took five years to complete	Took three years to restore
Basement used for storage	**Basement is check-in and departure lounge**
Five platforms	Fifteen platforms

5 Students work in pairs to answer the questions. Remind them that they must correct the false sentences.

Answers
1 ✗ The escalators lead up to the **platforms**.
2 ✗ The glass roof has been **restored**.
3 ✓
4 ✗ Farmers bring in fresh produce from **Europe**.
5 ✓
6 ✗ The hotel was advanced for its time because it had **a lift and revolving doors**.
7 ✓
8 ✗ The best place to meet at St Pancras is the **statue called 'The Meeting'**.

6 **T 10.5** [CD 3: Track 16] This exercise reviews the work on numbers that students did in Unit 8. Elicit the meaning of the abbreviations *m* (million), *kph* (kilometres per hour), and *ft* (feet – a unit of measurement equivalent to about 30cm). Encourage students not to go back to the text, but to discuss from memory what they think the numbers refer to. Play the recording and get students to check their answers in pairs. Ask students to read the first number aloud and then to continue the task in pairs.

Answers and tapescript

T 10.5
1 The new station handles fifty million passengers a year.
2 Eurostar travels at 300 kilometres per hour, or 186 miles per hour.
3 Six thousand men built the original station.
4 The roof is 240 feet, or 75 metres, wide.
5 The new station opened in the twenty-first century.
6 A Eurostar train is a quarter of a mile, or 400 metres, long.
7 The champagne bar is 300 feet long.
8 The Midland Grand Hotel opened in 1873.
9 It closed in 1935.
10 The statue 'The Meeting' is 9 metres tall and weighs 20 tons.

What do you think?

Give students time to read through the questions and think about their answers. Elicit a range of responses in a whole-class discussion. In larger classes, students can work in groups and then report back.

WRITING (SB p114)

A famous town or city – from notes to writing

This section shows students how they can use an ideas map to prepare the information they need for a piece of writing. Students get practice in building the information in the ideas map into connected text. There is also an exercise on words and expressions that link ideas together.

1 Focus attention on the photo and elicit information about New York from the class. Students work in pairs to exchange other ideas/information.

Collate students' answers on the board.

2 Divide students into pairs. Get them to read the information in the diagram. Deal with any vocabulary queries. Students compare the information on the board with the diagram, working in their pairs.

3 Pre-teach/check the following: *nickname*, *to found*, *skyscraper*, *commuter*, *24/7* (= 24 hours a day, seven days a week), *bagel*. Focus attention on the paragraph headings in the text. Point out that they correspond with the categories in the diagram. Elicit the missing words for number 1. Students complete the task, working individually. Monitor and help as necessary.

Check the answers.

Answers
1 'The Big Apple'
2 Hudson River
3 Naples and Madrid
4 New Amsterdam
5 1664
6 immigration
7 boom
8 September 11th, 2001
9 densely populated
10 170
11 foreign born
12 1.4 billion
13 12,000
14 37,000 runners
15 baseball
16 40 million
17 shopping
18 variety
19 hotdogs
20 'The city that never sleeps'

4 Elicit an example of extra information in the text. Students continue the task, working in pairs.

Answers

New York City's influence is seen throughout the world.

The nickname 'The Big Apple' was given to it by early immigrants because the city seemed so huge and full of promise.

The city grew in importance and was the capital until 1790.

From the early 20th century it became a world centre for industry, commerce, and communication.

3,000 people died in the attacks on the World Trade Center.

Five of the largest ethnic groups are: Puerto Ricans, Italians, West Indians, Chinese and Irish.

One in three New Yorkers uses public transport to get to work, whereas in the rest of the US 90% of commuters go by car.

The subway is open 24/7.

The marathon is held annually on the first Sunday of November. It's the largest in the world.

Many New Yorkers jog round Central Park.

The two most popular baseball teams are the New York Yankees and the New York Mets.

Major tourist attractions include the Metropolitan Museum of Art, Times Square, and Central Park.

Places to eat include diners with burgers, bagels and pizza, and the Grand Central Oyster Bar.

5 Refer students to the first word of the text *Although* and elicit why it is used (to introduce a contrast). Students continue the task, working in pairs.

Check the answers with the class.

Answers
Although – introduces a contrast
its – refers back to New York City
However – introduces a contrast
distinctive – a descriptive adjective which makes the text more interesting
two of which – refers back to the skyscrapers
whereas – introduces a contrast
is home to – more interesting alternative to 'has'
with (so much to do) – refers back to all the things that New York has

6 In this task, students reuse the vocabulary from exercise 5 in new contexts. Elicit the answer for sentence 1. Students continue the task, working in pairs.

Check the answers with the class.

Answers

1 Its	5 Although
2 two of which	6 distinctive
3 is home to	7 whereas
4 However	8 With

7 Set the planning and research for the writing for homework. Ask students if they need any help with their notes and then get them to write their description. If appropriate, ask students to exchange their first drafts and make suggestions as to how to improve them. Students' final drafts can be displayed on the classroom walls.

VOCABULARY AND SPEAKING (SB p84)

Compound nouns

Students will be familiar with compound nouns from their earlier learning and have already focused on compound adjectives in Unit 6. They will need to have access to a dictionary to do exercise 6 in this section.

1 Read the notes with the class and focus on the examples. Point out that compound nouns can be spelt as one word, two words, or with a hyphen, e.g. *air-conditioning.*

Get students to say the words out loud and establish where the stress falls.

Answer
The stress is usually on the first syllable, apart from in *departure lounge*:
railway station
art gallery
masterpiece
departure lounge

2 Focus attention on the dictionary extracts. Elicit which base word is used (*head*). Briefly review the different types of information given in the extracts (pronunciation, word type, definition, example(s), cross-references to other words, help with usage). Refer students to the phonetics for each word and elicit the pronunciation.

3 This activity gives students the opportunity to practise the words in exercise 2. Ask a pair of students to ask and answer question 1. Check what *RIP* /ɑːr aɪ ˈpiː/ stands for (*rest in peace*). Point out that for question 4 students should use one of the words from exercise 2 and try to think of other types of lights on a car, too. Students continue the activity in pairs. Monitor and check students' pronunciation and drill the words again as necessary. Students are often reluctant to stress compounds on the first part, so it's worth repeating this until they get it right.

Answers
1 To cure a headache.
2 On a headstone.
3 Use/Wear headphones.
4 Headlights, side lights, fog lights, and reversing lights.
5 The headlines.
6 In New York City.
7 Students' own answers.

4 **T 10.6** [**CD 3: Track 17**] Elicit the first false compound noun with *sun*. Students work in pairs to complete the task.

Elicit the answers for the rest of the compound nouns. Then play the recording of the true compound nouns and get students to repeat.

Answers and tapescript
sunpool parking card tea table money case

T 10.6

sunglasses	suncream	sunset
credit card	birthday card	business card
tea bag	teacup	teatime
briefcase	suitcase	bookcase

5 Elicit the base word for set 1. Students work in pairs to complete the task. Remind them to decide on the spelling of the words (one word, two words, or hyphenated). If you are short of time, you could write the base words on the board in jumbled order for students to match.

Check the answers with the class, eliciting the spelling as one or two words, or hyphenated. If students have had problems with stressing the compound nouns, drill a selection of the answers with the class.

Answers
1 dining **room**/waiting **room**/changing **room**
2 **traffic** lights/**traffic** warden/**traffic** jam
3 antique **shop**/second-hand **shop**/shoe **shop**
4 Spider-**Man**/post**man**/chair**man**
5 **hair**brush/**hair**dresser/**hair**cut
6 news**agent**/travel **agent**/estate **agent**
7 **motor**way/**motor**bike/**motor** racing
8 wrapping **paper**/toilet **paper**/wall**paper**

6 Focus attention on the examples in the Student's Book. Put students into pairs to do the dictionary work. With larger classes, or if you are short of time, allocate one or two base word(s) to each pair and then get students to pool their research.

Students work in groups of four to describe the compound nouns to each other. Monitor and check for accuracy of the definitions and for pronunciation of the compound nouns. Feed back on any common errors after the activity or in a later lesson.

Possible answers
hand: handbag, handbrake, handcuffs, handful, handgun, hand luggage
foot: football, footbridge, footpath, footprint, footstep
finger: fingermark, fingernail, fingerprint, fingertip
fire: fire alarm, fire brigade, fire door, fire engine, fire escape, fireman
air: air bag, air bed, air force, airport, airmail
water: water cannon, watercress, waterfall, water level, watermelon, waterski

EVERYDAY ENGLISH (SB p85)

I need one of those things ...

This section gives students the language they need to describe or define an object they don't know the name of. There is also a *Music of English* box to highlight sentence stress. Remind students they can use the target language in this section in the classroom when asking to use/borrow something, or to ask the name of something.

1 **T 10.7** [CD 3: **Track 18**] Focus attention on the objects in the photos but don't name them at this stage. Read the instructions with the class and then play the first recording. Students point to the correct object.

Play the rest of the recording. Students select the other four objects and then check in pairs.

Answers and tapescript
1 d (a corkscrew)
2 j (dental floss)
3 g (chopsticks)
4 c (fly swatter)
5 a (oven gloves)

T 10.7
1 I need **one of those things you use** when you want to open a bottle of wine. You know, you pull and it goes pop.
2 I'm looking for **some of that stuff you use** when you want to clean between your teeth. It's **like** string. It's white. You use it like this.
3 They're **long and thin**, and the Chinese **use them** to pick up food.
4 It's **made of plastic**, and it's used **for killing** flies.
5 They're **things you use when** you're cooking and you want to pick up something that's hot.

2 **T 10.7** [CD 3: **Track 18**] This exercise highlights the key language students are going to use. Play the first recording again and elicit the missing words.

Play the rest of the recording. Students complete the sentences, then check their answers in pairs.

When checking the answers, highlight the use of the word *stuff* /stʌf/ to mean 'a substance or material'. Point out that we use this word in speaking when we don't know the exact word for something.

Answers and tapescript
See words in **bold** in **T 10.7** above.

MUSIC OF ENGLISH

1 **T 10.8** [CD 3: **Track 19**] Play the recording and tell students to just listen to the sentences. Play it again and ask students to focus on the main stresses. Get students to practise the sentences. If they have problems, play the recording again and drill the sentences chorally.

2 Students practise the other sentences in exercise 2. Monitor and check for accurate pronunciation. Be prepared to model the examples yourself for different students to repeat.

Answers and tapescript
T 10.8
I need one of those things you use to open a bottle of wine.
I'm looking for some of that stuff you use when you want to clean between your teeth.
They're long and thin, and the Chinese use them to pick up food.

3 Elicit a description of another of the objects on p85. Students work in groups to continue the activity – one student describes and the others guess, and then they change roles. Encourage students to use expressions from exercise 2 in their answers.

Answers
b It's in the shape of a stick, and rub it on bits of paper so that you can stick them together.
e You use it when you want to fix something. It's got a handle, and you put it in and then turn it to make something looser or tighter.
f You stick it on your skin when you've cut yourself. It covers the cut and keeps it clean.
h It's a coloured liquid, and you put it on your finger nails to make them look nice.
i You use it when your finger nails are long. It's hard and rough, and you rub it on the ends of your nails to make them a bit shorter, and to make them a nice shape.

4 **T 10.9** [CD 3: **Track 20**] Tell students they are going to hear nine descriptions and they should try to guess what is being described. Play the first description as an example and get students to guess the item being described.

Play the rest of the recording. Students note down their ideas and then compare their answers in pairs.

Refer students to SB p151. Play the recording again. Students look at the pictures, identify the objects, and record. Elicit the names of the items and check the pronunciation.

Answers and tapescript

1 e a washing-up sponge
2 h knitting needles
3 c a remote control
4 b washing powder
5 j Blu-tak®
6 o drawing pins
7 g tape measure
8 n padlock
9 i a light bulb

T 10.9

1 It's one of those things you use in the kitchen. You use it to do the washing-up.
2 It's long and thin and sharp at one end. Usually you have two, one in each hand. You can make things out of wool with them.
3 It looks like a mobile phone; it has buttons you push, but you use it to change channels on the TV.
4 It's the stuff you wash clothes with. You put it in the washing machine. It's a powder. It smells ... aaaah!
5 It's used for sticking things on the wall, like pictures or posters. It's soft and sticky.
6 They're made of metal. You can also use them to stick things on the wall, but they're sharp. They make a hole. You use them on a notice board.
7 It's a kind of ruler. You use it to measure things that are very long, like a room. It's made of metal, usually.
8 It's something you use when you're travelling. You put it on your suitcase so no one can get into it. You have a key to open it, to take it off.
9 You know! It's got a round, metal bit at one end, and the other end is made of glass. You put it in a lamp to make light.

5 **T 10.10** **[CD 3: Track 21]** Focus attention on the sentence stems. Play the recording and get students to complete the sentences.

When checking the answers, make sure students are getting the main stresses right in the sentences. If not, play them again and get students to repeat.

Answers and tapescript

T 10.10

1 It's one of those things you **use in the kitchen**.
2 It's long and thin and **sharp at one end**.
3 It looks like **a mobile phone**.
4 It's the stuff you **wash clothes with**.
5 It's used for **sticking things on the wall**.
6 They're made of **metal**.
7 It's a kind of **ruler**.
8 It's something you use when **you're travelling**.
9 You know! It's got a **round, metal bit at one end**.

6 Put students into new pairs for this activity. Refer them back to the pictures on SB p151. Elicit a description of one of the objects, and get the rest of the class to identify it.

Students continue the activity in their pairs. Remind them to change roles each time. Monitor and check for accurate use of the target language and for the main stresses in the pronunciation. If students have serious problems, drill the target language again and then get them to continue.

7 **T 10.11** **[CD 3: Track 22]** Tell students they are going to hear two longer conversations in a shop, and they must identify what each customer is asking for. Remind students it doesn't matter if they don't know the names of the objects!

Play the recording once and check the answers. Encourage students to describe the object and its function before you tell them the name of each thing. Remind students of the work they did on compound nouns and elicit the main stress on each word.

Answers and tapescript

1 a dustpan and brush
2 a cheese grater

T 10.11

Conversation 1

A Yes, madam. How can I help you?
B I'm looking for a thing you use in the house ...
A Yes, now what do you do with it exactly?
B Well, it's not one thing. It's two things. And they're usually made of plastic.
A Uh huh.
B You know if you make a mess, like you drop bread or smash a glass, and there are bits all over the floor ...?
A And you need to pick them up?
B Yes! You go like this ... SHUP! SHUP!
A What you're talking about is ...

Conversation 2

A Can I help you, sir?
B Yes. I don't know how you say this in English. I'm looking for a thing you use in the kitchen ...
A OK.
B It's like a thing with, you know, holes ...
A Uh huh. What's it for?
B Well, it's for cheese or vegetables like carrots.
A And what do you do with it?
B If you don't want a big piece of cheese, or a whole carrot, but you want little pieces, you can push ... you can move ... I don't know how you say it. Like this!
A Ah! OK! What you mean is ...

8 Refer students to the tapescript on SB p129 as a model for their conversation. Remind them to choose an object that they don't know the name of. Students work in their pairs to write their conversation. Monitor and help as necessary.

Students act out their conversations to the class and get them to guess the objects. This can be done in a later lesson, or across a series of lessons, if you are short of time.

Don't forget!

Workbook Unit 10

Exercise 11 Vocabulary – *a suitcase/luggage*
Exercise 12 Pronunciation – Diphthongs
Exercise 13 Phrasal verbs – Phrasal verb + noun (2)
Exercise 14 Listening – Lost and found

Word list

Refer students to the Word list for Unit 10 (SB p156). They could translate the words, learn them at home, or transfer some of them to their vocabulary notebook.

Modals of probability
Phrasal verbs (2)
Expressing attitude

Seeing is believing

Introduction to the unit

The title of this unit is *Seeing is believing*, and the content covers the broad topics of evidence and crime. These topics provide the context for the language work on modals of probability, both present and past. The *Reading and listening* section is a Sherlock Holmes detective story called *The Three Students*. The *Vocabulary* section continues the coverage of phrasal verbs with a focus on verbs with *out* and *up*. *Everyday English* looks at common adverbs and expressions for expressing attitude. This is continued in the *Writing* section with a focus on joining ideas using adverbs and expressions.

Language aims

Grammar – modals of probability This is the second unit on modal verbs. Unit 4 dealt with modals of advice, permission, and obligation, and their use in requests and offers. If necessary, remind students of the introduction to modal and related verbs in Grammar Reference 4.3 on SB p137.

In this unit the focus is on *must/may/could/might/can't* for probability. The language work is divided across two presentations. The first covers present modal forms *must/could/might/can't* + infinitive. It also highlights the continuous infinitive form, e.g. *She might be waiting outside* and the use of the verb *look like*. The second presentation covers the past modal forms *must/may/could/might/can't* + *have* + past participle. Students will have already met the perfect infinitive forms *might/could/should have* + past participle in Unit 9 (see Grammar Reference 9.5–9.6 on SB p143). Although they will be familiar with the form, they are still likely to make mistakes.

POSSIBLE PROBLEMS

Students may be confused that, when expressing probability, the negative of *must be/must have been* is *can't be/can't have been*, not *mustn't/mustn't have been*.

Many languages don't have a direct equivalent of *may/might/could* and so students tend to approximate the meaning by using *perhaps* or *maybe*, sometimes as a direct translation from their own language.

Students often have problems producing the more complex perfect modal forms. It's worth briefly revising common past participles to help them. Students also tend to overstress *have* in these forms instead of making it weak: /əv/. There is a pronunciation section on SB p89 to help students with this key area.

Common mistakes:	Corrections:
**No answer. She mustn't be at home.*	*She can't be at home.*
**He looks as his mother.*	*He looks like his mother.*
**She might working today.*	*She might be working today.*
**They must have leave early.*	*They must have left early.*
**She can't have went out.*	*She can't have gone out.*

Vocabulary The vocabulary focus in this unit is phrasal verbs with *out* and *up*, e.g. *work out*, *make up*. Students analyse dictionary extracts, and then work on a range of phrasal verbs and their meanings in context.

Everyday English This lesson highlights the use of common adverbs for expressing attitude in speaking, e.g. *obviously*, *hopefully*, etc.

Notes on the unit

STARTER (SB p86)

This section sets up the theme of the unit with a series of optical illusions. Your students may well recognize some of them, but should still enjoy working with a partner to see what they make of the images. Check comprehension of *parallel lines*. Give students a few moments to look at the images and decide what they can see before putting them into pairs. Students discuss the optical illusions, exchanging information about what they can see and trying to find the things and people in the list across the range of images.

Monitor and check the language students use to discuss the images. They are unlikely to use the modal verbs or *look like* completely correctly, but it will give you an indication of the areas students need to focus on.

Discuss the answers with the class. Encourage individual students to point out where the 'hidden' images are. Tell students not to worry if they couldn't find all the things in the task – different people are able to see different things.

Answers
eight people – picture 4 (x3), 6, 7 (x2), 8 (x2)
three animals – picture 2, 5 (x2)
an old lady – picture 7
five young ladies – picture 4 (x3), 7, 8
a word – picture 6 (liar)
the colour red – picture 1
parallel lines – picture 3 and 9
a musical instrument – picture 8

OPTICAL ILLUSIONS (SB p86)

must be/can't be/looks like

This section focuses on the present form of the modals of probability, along with the verb *look like.*

1 Read the instructions with the class. Pre-teach/check *candlestick, a feather, wobbly, jelly, dots.* Students match the sentences to the illusions, working in their pairs.
Check the answers with the class.

Answers
a 8 b 4 c 1 d 7 e 2 f 5 g 9 h 6 i 3 j 3

2 **T 11.1** [CD 3: Track 23] Play the first three speeches in the recording. Elicit the number of the illusion (number 1) and the reason for it. (When the pink's next to the green, it looks red.)
Play the rest of the recording and get students to point to the illusion that is being discussed each time. Elicit the order from the class. If necessary, play the recording again so that students can listen for the reason behind each illusion and identify which two the woman can't see.
Check the answers with the class.

Answers and tapescript
Order of images discussed: 1, 4, 8, 6, 7, 6, 2, 5, 3, 9.
1 When the pink's next to the green it looks red.
4 You can see one girl behind a candlestick or two girls looking at each other.
8 You can see another girl if you look in the shadows.
6 It looks like someone wearing glasses but you can also see the word 'liar'.
7 There is an old lady with a feather in her hat and also a *young* lady with a feather and a fur coat.
2 The elephant appears to have five legs.
5 The picture could be a duck or a rabbit.
3 The lines are all straight and parallel if you look at them line by line. The dots must be creating the illusion.
9 The lines are the same length if you measure them.
The woman can't see the young lady with the feather and the fur coat, or the word 'liar'.

T 11.1
Optical illusions
T = **Ted** **B** = **Bridget**
T How many colours can you see?
B Er, three, if you don't include white, – er green, pink, and red.
T No, look again. There's only two, pink and green When the pink's next to the green it looks red.
B Really? I don't think so. They can't be the same colour. Well, er, maybe. What about this one, the girl? That must be a candlestick in front of her face.
T Yes, you can see one girl behind a candlestick or two girls looking at each other.
B Oh yes, amazing, three girls then! And that one, it looks like a man playing the saxophone.
T Or ... another girl. Look, in the shadows ...
B Oh yes, I can see her now – she's wearing a hat and lipstick.
T Do you think so? Can you see any more people?
B Yes, that looks like someone wearing glasses and that one is an old lady, and, I'm not sure, but I think she might be wearing a feather in her hat.
T I can also see a young lady with a feather and a fur coat. And I can see the word 'liar'.
B Really? I can't see either of those.
T OK. Try this. Count the legs on that elephant.
B One, two, three – er, it can't have five legs. That's a clever drawing. So is that one; it could be a duck or a rabbit. It depends how you look at it.
T The square looks strange, don't you think?
B Yeah, it looks wobbly, like a jelly.
T But the lines are all straight and parallel.
B No, they can't be.
T Well, they are. If you look line by line, you'll see.
B I suppose. The dots must be creating the illusion.
T And the last one. Which line's longer?
B Well, the one on the left must be longer.
T Get your ruler and measure.
B Agh. They're the same size – of course. I should have known!
T Interesting, isn't it, the tricks your eyes can play?

GRAMMAR SPOT (SB p86)

1 Read the sentences as a class and elicit the answers to the concept questions.

Answers
most sure: *It must be a duck.*
less sure: *It could be a duck./It might be a duck.*

2 Students discuss the meaning in pairs before checking with the class.

Answer
It can't be a duck. = I'm sure it isn't a duck.

3 Give students time to do the tasks in their pairs. Check the answers and remind students that we can't say *look as*: **She looks as a businesswoman.*

Answers
We use *look like* + noun (= resemble/look similar to)
We use *look* + adjective (= seem to be/appear)

4 Give students time to do the tasks in their pairs. Check the answers.

Answer
The dots **must be creating** the illusion.

If necessary, refer students to Grammar Reference 11.1–11.2 on SB p145.

PRACTICE (SB p87)

Fact or fiction?

This section gives students the opportunity to practise the modals of probability in response to widely-held beliefs on a range of subjects.

1 Give students time to read the statements. Check comprehension of *to have a higher pain threshold* (to bear pain better), *to reflect*, *a penny*, *bird-brained* (silly/stupid), *snowflake*, *a bat*.

Get two students to read out the examples for sentence 1. Check the main stresses on the responses, drilling chorally and individually as necessary:

That must be true.
It could be true but I'm not so sure.

Divide the class into pairs to discuss the statements. Monitor and check for accurate use of the modals and correct pronunciation. Check students are using the negative form *can't be* correctly, rather than *mustn't be*.

Students discuss the statements as a class. Then feed back on any errors in the use of the modals and correct them carefully.

2 **T 11.2** [**CD 3: Track 24**] Play the recording and let students check their ideas. Play the recording again if students have missed any of the facts in the explanations. Elicit which facts students found most surprising.

Answers and tapescript

T 11.2

Fact or fiction?

1 A **Lightning never strikes in the same place twice.**
B This is completely untrue. Lightning often strikes in the same place over and over again – high trees, tall buildings, mountain tops. In fact the purpose of lightning conductors is to be struck time and time again.

2 A **Hurricanes always have ladies' names.**
B This used to be true. From 1953 to 1979 only female names were used but now both men's and women's names are used. One name for each letter of the alphabet. The same lists are reused every six years. These are the first six names for 2012: Alberto, Beryl, Chris, Debby, Ernesto, Florence.

3 A **Women have a higher pain threshold than men.**
B Some research suggests the opposite, but most people still believe this to be true because women have to give birth. We will never know how men would cope with this experience.

4 A **The sea is blue because it reflects the sky.**
B This is true in a way. The white light from the sun is a mixture of all the colours of the rainbow but the air reflects blue light more than other colours so we see a blue sky. Then, when the sky is brilliant blue, the sea is also, because the water reflects the blue of the sky.

5 A **A penny dropped from a skyscraper can kill a person.**
B Not true. It might give you a cut or a bruise but it's not likely to kill you.

6 A **Hair and nails continue to grow after death.**
B Not true. This is an optical illusion. After death the body quickly dehydrates and the skin shrinks, which gives the illusion that both nails and hair are still growing.

7 A **Birds are bird-brained and stupid.**
B Not true. Some birds are the cleverest animals known to science. For example, crows are smarter than chimpanzees, and some parrots don't just mimic but understand human speech.

8 A **No two snowflakes are the same.**
B This could be true. No one has yet found two identical snowflakes, but out of all the zillions that fall it is likely that two may be the same.

9 A **Bats are blind.**
B Not true. Bats have excellent eyesight. People think they must be blind because they have a sound radar, which means they can hunt insects at night. But it doesn't mean that they can't see.

SUGGESTION
Students can research other widely-held beliefs and urban myths for homework. Get them to write statements and then test other students in pairs/small groups.

Grammar and speaking

3 **T 11.3** **[CD 3: Track 25]** This exercise gives practice of the modals in a statement and response activity.

Focus attention on the prompts for the example and elicit the main stresses in the sentence:

You must be very worried.

Put students into new pairs to continue the task. Point out that students will need to use continuous infinitive forms in some of the responses. If necessary, refer the class back to exercise 4 in the *Grammar Spot* on p86.

Monitor and check for accurate use of the modals and correct pronunciation. Note down any common errors and highlight them after the listen and check stage.

Play the recording so that students can check their answers. Put students in new pairs to practise the sentences again. Make sure students are using the modals correctly, including the continuous infinitives.

Answers and tapescript

T 11.3

1 **A** I think I've lost my passport.
B You must be very worried.
2 **A** Your phone's ringing!
B It might be Jane.
3 **A** Paul's taking his umbrella.
B It must be raining.
4 **A** Harry and Sally never go on holiday.
B They can't have much money.
5 **A** Hannah's not in class.
B She could be in the coffee bar.
6 **A** Look! Three fire engines!
B There must be a fire somewhere.
7 **A** Tom hasn't seen Zoë for ages.
B They can't be going out together any more.
8 **A** Whose jacket is this?
B It might be John's.
9 **A** You got top marks in the test!
B You must be joking!

What are they talking about?

4 **T 11.4** **[CD 3: Track 26]** This exercise consolidates the target modal verbs with a series of situational dialogues. Focus attention on the questions for conversation 1. Play the recording and get students to listen and read. Ask two students to read and complete the responses to the questions.

Give students time to read the questions for conversations 2–5. Play the recording, pausing after each conversation to give students time to discuss the questions in pairs.

Elicit students' conclusions and reasons in a feedback sessions.

Possible answers and tapescript

1 They can't be at home because they are paying for the drink. They could be in a restaurant but they aren't ordering food. They must be in a pub because they pay for the drinks when they order them.
2 They can't be talking about a TV because one of them suggests taking out the battery. It might be a mobile phone but they talk about a screen. It must be a laptop computer because the screen is frozen.
3 It can't be a driving test because she has to wait a couple of days for the result. It could be an exam but she doesn't talk about 'passing' or 'failing', It must be a job interview because she talks about 'getting it'.
4 They must be brother and sister because they talk about 'mum and dad'. They can't be talking about a wedding present because they talk about '25 years'. It could be a birthday present but it is for both parents. It must be an anniversary present because their parents have been married for 25 years and they suggest something in silver.
5 They can't be watching a film because one of the speakers shouts. They could be drinking at a bar but they don't offer each other a drink. They must be dancing because they talk about 'going clubbing'.

T 11.4

1 **A** A glass of white wine and a mineral water, please.
B Still or sparkling?
A Sparkling, please.
B Do you want ice and lemon with that?
A Just ice, thanks. How much is that?
2 **A** I can't believe it. My screen's frozen again.
B Unplug it and take the battery out. Then start it up again. That sometimes works for me.
A OK. Here goes.
3 **A** So how did it go?
B Not too bad, thanks.
A Were you very nervous?
B Yeah, but I tried not to show it.
A Oh. When will you hear?
B In a couple of days. They said they'd phone me at the end of the week and let me know if I'd got it.
4 **A** Have you any idea what to get them?
B Not really, but it should be something special.
A Yeah, 25 years is a long time.
B It would be nice to get something silver.
A Yeah. Why don't we club together and get something from both of us, then we can afford something really nice?
B Good idea. Mum and Dad would love that.
5 **A** Do you come here a lot?
B What?
A I said DO YOU OFTEN COME HERE?
B Yeah, me and my friends come every Saturday night. This your first time?
A Yeah, here. We usually go clubbing at the Zanzibah.
B Wow – I've heard the Zanzibah's legend.
A Yeah, how'd you like to try it with me next Saturday?

ADDITIONAL MATERIAL

Workbook Unit 11

Exercises 1–3 Modal verbs of probability – present

Exercise 5 Continuous infinitive

WHAT ON EARTH HAS HAPPENED? (SB p88)

must have been/can't have been

This section introduces and practises modal verbs of probability in the past, in the context of two friends talking about a burglary over the phone. Students hear only one side of the conversation at first and this provides a natural context for them to use modals of probability to talk about what must/might/could or can't have happened. Students are given the opportunity to check their ideas when they listen to the complete conversation in exercise 4.

1 **T 11.5** [CD 3: Track 27] Focus attention on the photos of the two women. Ask:

   Which one is Christina? (the one looking upset)
   Which is Rachel? (the one lying on her bed)
   What do you think they are talking about?

   Don't pre-teach any of the vocabulary related to the burglary as this will give away the answer to the question in exercise 1.

   Play the recording. Students read and listen, then discuss with a partner what they think has happened. Monitor and help, dealing with any vocabulary queries as you go.

   Elicit a range of possible ideas as to what has happened but do not confirm or reject answers at this stage.

2 This is a recognition task to check that students understand the use of the modal verbs. Tell students that there is one more likely answer in each pair. Elicit the answer to question 1 as an example. Encourage students to give reasons for their answers. Students continue the task, working in pairs. Monitor and help as necessary. Do not check answers with the class until after exercise 4.

What do you think?

3 Focus attention on the example and then elicit a summary of students' ideas for each question from different pairs. Monitor students' use of the modal verbs and note down any common errors. Deal with these when focusing on the *Grammar Spot* after exercise 4.

4 **T 11.6** [CD 3: Track 28] Play the recording and get students to check their answers. Establish if the students had worked out the story correctly and if there were any surprises.

Answers and tapescript

1 They must be friends.
2 Christina's flat must have been burgled. (It's clear that she's very upset. Rachel asks *What else is missing? Have you called the police? Is there much mess? Did they ransack the place?*)
3 It may have happened while she was at work. (Rachel says *They must have known no one was at home.*)
4 She must be Christina's flatmate. (Rachel mentions Ella's leather jacket and asks *Does she know?* Ella goes to lectures and has exams so she must be a student.)
5 Christina's laptop computer could have been taken. (Rachel asks *Had you saved everything?* so they might be talking about her laptop.)
6 She can't have told her. (Rachel says *She's going to get such a shock when she gets back.*)
7 She must have done. (Rachel says *Good. Have they any idea who might have done it?*)
8 They must have been thrown onto the floor. (Rachel says *Oh how awful! Your lovely clothes.* and ... *it must be really difficult to see exactly what's missing.*)

T 11.6

R = Rachel C = Christina

R Hello.
C Rachel? It's me, Christina. Something dreadful's happened.
R Hi, Christina, what on earth's wrong? Tell me.
C My flat's just been burgled.
R Oh, no! That's terrible. When?
C Well, I discovered it when I came in from work, two hours ago. The door was wide open.
R They must have known no one was at home. What did they take?
C My laptop, of course, with all my work, and my photos on it.
R Had you saved everything?
C Yes, fortunately, I'd put my work and most of my photos on CD.
R Thank goodness. What else is missing?
C My camera, and a whole load of Ella's jewellery, and her new leather jacket.
R Not your camera! Well, at least you still have your photos. Oh, and Ella's expensive leather jacket! Does she know?
C No, she doesn't. She's not back from college yet.
R She's going to get such a shock when she gets back – and she's got her final exams soon.
C I know, but at least she had her laptop with her so they didn't get that.
R Yeah, that's good. I know she always takes it with her to lectures. Have you called the police?
C Oh, yes, they're here now.
R Good. Have they any idea who might have done it?
C Well, they say there've been quite a few burglaries in the area and the flat above me was also done.
R So, it wasn't just *your* flat then? Is there much mess? Did they ransack the place?
C The mess is terrible. Whoever did it emptied out all my drawers and my clothes are all over the bedroom floor.
R Oh how awful! Your lovely clothes. Did they take any of them?
C I don't know. I haven't checked. The police have told me not to touch anything.
R Yes, of course, and anyway, it must be really difficult to see exactly what's missing.
C Oh, it is. Oh, Rachel, *(crying)* it's just chaos here.
R Look, Christina you're obviously really upset. I'm coming round. I'll help you tidy up. I'll be there in 15 minutes.
C Oh, Rach. You're a great friend. Thanks so much.

SPOKEN ENGLISH – *What on earth ...?*

1 **T 11.7** **[CD 3: Track 29]** Ask students if they can remember what Rachel asks when Christina says something dreadful has happened (... *what on earth's wrong?*) Read the notes and examples as a class.

Play the recording and get students to repeat, imitating closely the stress and intonation. If students have problems, drill the sentences chorally and individually.

> **T 11.7**
>
> What on earth has happened?
>
> Where on earth have you been?
>
> Who on earth left the window open?

2 **T 11.8** **[CD 3: Track 30]** Read through the cue sentences with the class. Elicit possible responses to sentence 1. Students then work in pairs to continue the task. Monitor and check for accurate stress and intonation.

Play the recording and get students to check their answers. If students had problems with the pronunciation, drill the sentences using the recording as a model. Then put students into new pairs to practise again.

> **Answers and tapescript**
>
> **T 11.8**
>
> 1 **A** I can't carry all these shopping bags.
> **B** What **on earth have you bought**?
> 2 **A** Tom's broken his arm in three places.
> **B** How **on earth did he do that**?
> 3 **A** There's someone at the door!
> **B** Who **on earth could it be at this time of night**?
> 4 **A** My aunt left all her money to a cats' home.
> **B** What **on earth did she do that** for?
> 5 **A** I can't find my car keys.
> **B** Where **on earth have you put them**?

GRAMMAR SPOT (SB p89)

This section highlights the past modal forms, building on the present modals in the *Grammar Spot* on p86. At this stage, you can focus on helping students get the form right, as pronunciation is practised in the section that follows.

1 Read the notes as a class and then get students to work out the present forms.

> **Answers**
> They must be friends.
> They might catch the burglar.
> It can't be my jacket.

Point out that these forms can also have future meaning, e.g. the police might catch the burglar soon/some time in the future.

2 Give students time to formulate the sentences and then check the answers.

> **Answers**
> He must have loved her very much.
> She can't have been at home.

3 Read the notes as a class and then get students to work out the past form. Emphasize that *must* in this context is a modal verb of obligation, not of probability.

> **Answer**
> I had to call the police.

Refer students to Grammar Reference 11.3 on SB p145.

PRACTICE (SB p89)

Grammar and pronunciation

This section helps students with the pronunciation of the weak form /əv/ in forms like *must have*. This should help to consolidate the forms and give students confidence in producing them.

1 **T 11.9** **[CD 3: Track 31]** Elicit the modal form that matches with number 1. Students continue the task, working individually.

Play the recording. Students repeat chorally and individually.

> **Answers and tapescript**
>
> **T 11.9**
>
> 1 must have
> 2 can't have
> 3 could have
> 4 might have
> 5 may have

2 **T 11.10** **[CD 3: Track 32]** This exercise practises the past modal forms at sentence level. Play the sentences and get students to repeat. If students have problems with the weak forms, refer them to the stress shading on the sentences. Also refer them to the phonetic transcriptions in exercise 1 to show how /əv/ follows on directly from the modal verb, e.g. /mʌstəv/

Students repeat the lines as a class. Play the recording again if students have problems with the pronunciation.

> **Tapescript**
>
> **T 11.10**
>
> 1 It must have been stolen.
> 2 I can't have lost it.
> 3 He could have taken it.
> 4 I might have dropped it.
> 5 She may have found it.

3 **T 11.11** **[CD 3: Track 33]** Ask a pair of students to read out the cue sentence and response for number 1. With weaker classes, briefly review the past participles students will need to use in the responses. Students take it in turns

to read and respond. Monitor and check for accurate formation of the past modals and for the correct stress. Note any common errors and correct them carefully with the class after the listen and check stage.

Play the recording and get students to check their answers. If necessary, play the recording again as a model and get students to repeat. Put students in new pairs to practise again.

Answers and tapescript

T 11.11

1 **A** I can't find my ticket.
  B **You must have dropped it.**
2 **A** John didn't come to school yesterday.
  B **He must have been ill.**
3 **A** Why is Isabel late for class?
  B **She might have overslept.**
4 **A** I can't find my notebook.
  B **You must have left it at home.**
5 **A** The teacher's checking Maria's exercise.
  B **She can't have finished already!**
6 **A** Why is Carl looking so happy?
  B **He may have done well in the test.**

Discussing grammar

4 This exercise reviews modals of obligation and ability, *shall* for suggestions and certainty, and also the modals of probability from this unit. If you are short of time, ask students to complete the sentences for homework and then do the discussion stage in the next lesson.

Elicit possible answers for sentence 1. Students complete the exercise, working individually. Then discuss the answers as a class.

Answers

1 He **can't/could/might/must** have been born in the 1960s. (*can't* = impossibility; *could/might* = possibility; *must* = certainty)
2 **Can/Could** you help me with the washing up, please? (requests)
3 You **can/can't/could/must/should** see the doctor immediately. (*can* = possibility; *can't* = impossibility; *could* is possible if part of a conditional sentence, e.g. *You could see the doctor immediately if it was an emergency*; *must/should* for obligation/advice)
4 **Can/Can't/Could/Must/Should/Shall** we go out for a meal tonight? (*Can/Could* = permission/request; *Can't we ...* expresses a strong desire; *Must* (obligation) expresses that the speaker doesn't want to go; *Should* = advice; *Shall* = a suggestion)
5 **I can/can't/could/must/might/should/shall** stop smoking. (*can/can't* = ability; *could* is possible if part of a conditional sentence, e.g. *I could stop smoking if I wanted to*; *must* = strong obligation; *might* = possibility; *should* = obligation; *shall* = a strong intention)
6 **I can/can't/could/must/might/shall/should** learn to speak English. (*can/can't* = ability; *could* is possible if part of a conditional sentence, e.g. *I could learn to speak English if I had more time*; *must* = strong obligation; *might* = possibility; *should* = obligation; *shall* = a strong intention)

SUGGESTION

You can give further practice of the past modals with the use of interesting photographs that are open to interpretation of what has happened. These can often be found in magazines and put into different categories, e.g. people, places, weather, etc. Bring in a selection of images to the class and get students to use them as a prompt for *must have/can't have/might have*, etc. Students can also bring in their own images or photos they have taken if appropriate.

ADDITIONAL MATERIAL

Workbook Unit 11

Exercises 6–7 Modal verbs of probability – past

Exercise 8 Tense review

READING AND LISTENING (SB p90)

The Adventures of Sherlock Holmes

ABOUT THE TEXT

The theme of crime and evidence is carried through with *The Three Students*, an adaptation of a story by Sir Arthur Conan Doyle. Sherlock Holmes is one of the most famous and popular detectives in English literature. The character first appeared in 1887. In 1893 when Conan Doyle tried to kill Holmes off in a story so that he could concentrate on other writing, there was such an outcry that he wrote *The Adventure of the Empty House*, which explained how Holmes cheated death and returned to detective work in London. Holmes is famous for his intellectual prowess and astute observation when solving difficult cases. Dr Watson is the fictional friend and biographer of Sherlock Holmes. According to the stories, Holmes and Watson lived at 221b Baker Street in London between1881–1904.

Conan Doyle wrote four novels and fifty-six short stories that featured Holmes. *The Adventure of the Three Students* is one of 13 stories in a collection known as *The Return of Sherlock Holmes* from 1904.

Encourage students to use the context to help them with new vocabulary. With weaker classes or if you are short of time, you could pre-teach the following:

Part 1: *tutor, valuable* (*time*), *servant, mud*
Part 3: *to gamble away money*

Don't check the words which are highlighted in the text, as students will work out their meaning in *Language work* exercise 1.

1 Lead in to the topic by brainstorming vocabulary related to crime. Make sure students are familiar with the following: *detective, investigation, to look for clues, a suspect, to solve a mystery, intruder, motive, to deny doing something, culprit, to make someone suspicious.*

Focus attention on the picture on p90 and ask what students know about Sherlock Holmes /ˌʃɜːlɒk ˈhəʊmz/. Elicit a range of information, including the correct answers to statements 1–3.

Ask students which Sherlock Holmes stories they have read/seen in films and what they thought of them.

Answers
1 London 2 19th century 3 Dr Watson /ˈwɒtsən/

2 Refer students back to the picture and ask them to look at the section headings in the story. Elicit a range of predictions about the content of the story but don't confirm any answers at this stage.

3 See *About the text* above for notes on vocabulary. Check the pronunciation of the names in this section: Hilton Soames /ˈhɪltən səʊmz/ and Bannister /ˈbænɪstə/. Set a time limit of 2–3 minutes for students to read Part 1.

Allow students time to discuss their answers in pairs before checking with the class. For question 1, ask students which towns the story could be set in (probably Oxford or Cambridge).

Answers
1 In one of England's most famous university towns; to do some research.
2 An old acquaintance and tutor at one of the colleges.
3 The papers for the Greek translation exam.
4 Some of the exam papers.
5 He didn't want to have a scandal at the college.
6 Mr Soames' servant.
7 A broken pencil, a cut in the leather top of his desk, and a small lump of black mud.
8 Someone must have copied the exam questions.

4 Ask students what information the picture gives about the story. Set a time limit of 2–3 minutes for students to read Part 2. Students discuss the statements in pairs. Remind them to correct the false sentences.

Check the answers with the class.

Answers
1 False. The three students lived on the floor above.
2 True.
3 False. The clues (the cut leather and the mud) were on the desk.
4 False. They were next to the window because the intruder wanted to see when Doctor Soames was returning.
5 True.
6 False. The intruder didn't see Doctor Soames because he returned through the side door.
7 False. He must have escaped through the bedroom window.

5 This task gives students the opportunity to 'play detective' and discuss the prime suspect. It's also a good way of recycling the past modals from earlier in the unit.

See *About the text* for notes on vocabulary. Check the pronunciation of the names in this section: Gilchrist /ˈgɪlkrɪst/, Daulat Ras /ˈdaʊlət rɑːs/, and Miles McLaren /maɪlz məˈklærən/. Set a similar time limit of 2–3 minutes for students to read Part 3. Check the motives of each of the students in the story (see *Answers* below). Focus attention on the example sentences in the Student's Book and elicit possible endings. Remind students of the use of the weak form /əv/ in the pronunciation of the past modals forms.

Students discuss Part 3 of the story in pairs. Remind them to give reasons for their deductions.

Set up a whole-class feedback stage to elicit students' ideas of who the culprit is and why.

Answers
Gilchrist was short of money so might have wanted to sell copies of the exam papers.
Ras is a good student but Greek translation is his weakest subject. He might have been tempted to cheat.
McLaren is very intelligent but he's been lazy. He might have been worried about the exam and so might have been tempted to cheat.

Listening

6 **T 11.12** **[CD 3: Track 34]** This is the final part of the story in which Holmes reveals the culprit.

Pre-teach/Check the following items from the recording: *spikes (on a running shoe), sole (of a shoe), to lock a door, to scratch*. Give students time to read through the questions quickly.

Play the recording through once. Establish who the culprit is (Gilchrist) and who in the class guessed correctly.

Students answer the questions in pairs. Play the recording again if they have missed any of the information.

Answers and tapescript
1 When Holmes learnt that Gilchrist was an athlete and a long jumper, he became suspicious.
2 He went to the sports ground and collected some mud. It was the same black mud as on Hilton Soames' desk.
3 Gilchrist was returning from doing some sport and carrying his shoes, which had spikes on their soles. He passed his tutor's window and saw the examination papers on his desk. He tried the door and it opened. He entered the room, put his shoes down on the desk and moved to the window to copy the papers and watch for Soames. He heard Soames coming in at the side door, so he picked up his shoes, scratched the top of the desk with the spikes on his shoes, and left a lump of black mud. He ran into the bedroom and didn't notice another lump of mud on the floor from the shoes.
4 'Brilliant, Holmes! Just brilliant.'
'Elementary, my dear Watson.' (This phrase is often associated with Holmes when explaining how he has made deductions and solved mysteries.)
5 Because he left Soames' door unlocked and so Gilchrist was able to get in.
6 The examinations can take place because the other students haven't seen the exam papers. Gilchrist isn't going to take the examination and he is going to leave the university and England for Africa. There won't be a scandal at the college.

T 11.12
SH = Sherlock Holmes
HS = Hilton Soames
G = Mr Gilchrist
W = Dr Watson
B = Bannister
HS Holmes! Watson! At last! Tell me. What have you found out? Can the Greek examination take place?

SH Absolutely, the mystery is solved.
HS Really? But who ...? Which student ...?
SH Dr Watson, can you please ask Mr Gilchrist to join us?
W Of course. Mr Gilchrist? Mr Gilchrist? Can you join us, please?
G What is it? What's happened?
SH Close the door, Mr Gilchrist. Now, sit down and tell me honestly, why did you do it? How did you do it?
G What! Oh, no! How did you find out? I'm sorry, so sorry.
SH Come, come Mr Gilchrist, perhaps it's easier if I speak. You see, when I learnt that you were an athlete and a long jumper, I worked it out immediately.
HS How? I don't understand.
SH Let me continue. This is what must have happened. Yesterday afternoon you, Mr Gilchrist, were returning from practising your sport. You were carrying your jumping-shoes, which, as we all know, have spikes on their soles. You passed your tutor's window and because you are over six feet tall you could see into his room. You couldn't help but notice the examination papers on his desk. As you passed the door, you tried it. Amazingly, it opened ...
HS What? How ...?
SH Yes, Bannister had forgotten to lock it. Is that not true, Bannister?
B Oh dear, Mr Holmes. Mr Soames, sir, I'm sorry sir. Mr Holmes could be right, I was in a hurry.
SH So, Gilchrist, you entered the room, put your shoes down on the desk and moved to the window to copy the papers and watch for your tutor. Am I right so far?
G Yes, yes.
SH Suddenly you heard your tutor coming in at the side door. Quickly, you picked up your shoes, scratching the top of the desk with the spikes in your haste and leaving a lump of black mud. You ran into the bedroom. You didn't notice that another lump of mud fell to the floor from your shoes. This morning at 6 a.m., I went to the sports ground and collected a sample of mud. It was the same black mud.
W Brilliant, Holmes! Just brilliant.
SH Elementary, my dear Watson. Is this all correct, Mr Gilchrist?'
G Absolutely correct. I feel so bad, so guilty and ashamed. But can I just show you this, Mr Soames?
HS What is it?
G It's a letter. I wrote it in the middle of the night. Read it, please. In it I say how sorry I am for what I did.
HS Ah yes. And you say you're not going to take the examination. Oh, and you're going to leave the university and the country.
G Yes, I am. I'm going to work in Africa.
HS Gilchrist, I am really pleased to hear that.
B Oh, Mr Soames. Mr Gilchrist. It's all my fault. I'm so sorry.
G Absolutely not your fault, Bannister. I am the guilty one.
SH Well, Mr Soames, Mr Gilchrist, time for Watson and myself to have breakfast, I think. I hope the exams go well, Mr Soames. Good luck in Africa, Mr Gilchrist. Goodbye.
HS Thank you, Mr Holmes. It was such a lucky chance that you were staying in town at this time.

What do you think?

Give students time to read through the questions and think about their answers. Elicit a range of responses in a whole-class discussion. In larger classes, students can work in groups and then report back.

Possible answers
Modern detectives would work in a bigger team with access to a range of tools and tests, e.g. fingerprints, DNA /diː en ˈeɪ/ testing, CCTV /siː siː tiː ˈviː/ camera footage, handwriting analysis.

Language work

1 Focus attention on the first highlighted word *acquaintance*. Elicit the meaning and then get students to continue the task, working in pairs.
Elicit a range of answers from the class.

Answers
acquaintance – a person you know but not a friend
agitated – anxious/upset
irritably – in an annoyed way
disturbed – moved from their original place
lump – a piece (without a regular shape)
stand on tiptoe – to stand with your heels raised off the ground

2 This activity reviews the present and past modal forms that students practised at the beginning of the unit. Elicit the answer for sentence 1.
Students rewrite the sentences, working individually. Give them time to check their answers in pairs before checking with the class. If students enjoy roleplay, get them to deliver the sentences as if they were Sherlock Holmes talking to Watson about the case.
Check students get the main stresses in the sentences right. If they have problems, drill the sentences as a class.

Answers
1 One of the students must be the culprit.
2 Bannister can't have done it.
3 The lump of mud could be a clue.
4 The leather might have been cut by a knife.
5 He can't have escaped through the study window.
6 The culprit may still be hiding in the bedroom.
7 He could have jumped out of the bedroom window.
8 Gilchrist must have done it.

Telling the story

This activity gets students to retell the story in their own words. Focus attention on the examples in the Student's Book. Students read them aloud and then continue the story. Be prepared to prompt and encourage other students to feed in if anyone gets parts of the story wrong or misses anything important out. With weaker classes, you could write key words from each part of the story on the board.

VOCABULARY (SB p92)

Phrasal verbs (2) with *out* and *up*

This is the second focus on phrasal verbs in the course. If necessary, refer students back to Unit 4 and remind them that phrasal verbs can be literal or idiomatic, and separable or inseparable.

1 Focus attention on the dictionary extracts. Point out that they show different uses of two phrasal verbs. Put students in pairs to answer the questions.

Answers
1 *work out*; *make up*
2 *sth* = something; *sb* = somebody
3 separable: *work sth out* with the meanings, 'find the answer, solve, calculate'; *make sth up* with the meanings 'invent; form'
inseparable: *work out* with the meanings 'progress in a good way, do physical exercise'; *make up (with sb)* with the meaning 'become friends again after an argument'

2 Elicit the phrasal verb students need to use for sentence 1, and the correct tense and form of the verb. Remind students to use the context to work out the correct tense and form of the phrasal verbs in the rest of the exercise.

Students complete the sentences, working individually. Check the answers with the class.

Answers
1 Sherlock Holmes **worked out** who committed the crime.
2 That's a lie. You **made** that **up**, didn't you?
3 I know we argue a lot, but we always kiss and **make up** afterwards.
4 Don't worry, things will **work out** in the end. They always do.
5 He's determined to lose weight. He **works out** at the gym every day.
6 Woman **make up** 56% of the students in this university.
7 Can you **work out** this bill for me? I don't understand all those figures.
8 You must have **worked out** the answers by now.

3 This exercise introduces more examples of phrasal verbs and the nouns and noun phrases that can follow them. Elicit the answer for number 1 before students complete the task, working individually.

Allow students time to check their answers in pairs before checking with the whole class.

Answers
1 find out what time the train leaves
2 break up with a boyfriend/girlfriend
3 break out of jail
4 eat up all your greens and you'll be healthy
5 eat out in a Chinese restaurant
6 save up to buy a new car
7 sort out all my CDs
8 take up golf
9 fall out with a friend after a row about money
10 come up with a good idea

4 **T 11.13** [CD 3: **Track 35**] This exercise consolidates the meaning of the phrasal verbs in exercise 3. Elicit the phrasal verb for sentence 1. Students complete the task, working in pairs. Remind them to use the same form as the verbs in the original sentences.

Play the recording so that students can check their answers.

Answers and tapescript

T 11.13
1 You need to learn to relax. Why don't you **take up** yoga?
2 He's just **come up with** a brilliant plan to save the business.
3 There's no dessert until you've **eaten up** all your meat and vegetables.
4 Anne and Tony aren't talking to each other. They must have **fallen out**. They may even have **broken up**.
5 Did you hear the news? Three dangerous prisoners have **broken out of** the local prison.
6 You must learn to **sort out** your washing into coloureds and whites.
7 We're **saving up** so we can buy a house.
8 Have you **found out** why you didn't get the job?

5 **T 11.14** [CD 3: **Track 36**] This gives students the opportunity to use the phrasal verbs in a more personalized way. Elicit a possible ending to sentence 1. Students work in pairs to complete the rest of the sentences.

Ask pairs of students to read their sentences to the rest of the class and compare ideas.

Play the recording to give students a further set of answers to compare with. Elicit the responses speaker B makes each time, playing the recording again as necessary.

T 11.14
1 **A** I've just found out that I've won the lottery!
B Congratulations!
2 **A** I never eat out because I can't really afford to.
B Me neither.
3 **A** I don't ever fall out with my husband.
B What, never? I can't believe that.
4 **A** I can't work out if I feel warm or cold today.
B Yeah. It's one of those days.
5 **A** I'm saving up to take my grandma on holiday.
B That's kind.
6 **A** I need to sort out my life. I've got problems at work and I've got problems with my boyfriend.
B Poor you. Come on, let's go out for a drink. Take your mind off things.
7 **A** I've just come up with a fantastic idea.
B Uh! I'll believe it when I hear it.
8 **A** It's important to make up after an argument.
B Yeah, kiss and make up. Never let the sun go down on an argument.

EVERYDAY ENGLISH (SB p93)

Expressing attitude

In this section, students focus on key adverbs and phrases that express a speaker's attitude and link sections of conversation, e.g. *Personally*, *Apparently*, *Anyway*, etc. These are very common in spoken English and provide valuable 'extra' information on what has been said or what is going to be said.

1 **T 11.15** [**CD 3: Track 37**] Focus attention on the photo and where the people are (in class/a lecture theatre). Read the instructions as a class and then play the recording through once. Check the answers to the questions.

Answers
The two people in the conversation are students at the same school/college. One of the other students/their friends has been accused of cheating in a Maths exam.

2 **T 11.15** [**CD 3: Track 37**] Students read the conversation again, focusing more closely on the words in bold.

Check comprehension of some of the target words and expressions which may be new. Ask *Which word/expression means …?*

- from what I have heard about the situation (*apparently*)
- I find that hard to believe (*No kidding!*)
- in fact (*Actually*)
- in addition to what I've just said (*anyway*)
- I think it's probably true that … (*Presumably*)

It's worth pointing out to speakers of Latin languages that *actually* doesn't refer to time and is not a synonym for *at the moment* or *currently*.

Play the recording and get students to repeat chorally and individually. Encourage correct stress and intonation, exaggerating the voice range if students sound rather 'flat'.

3 **T 11.16** [**CD 3: Track 38**] Students read the first two lines of the speech. Establish the context (a person who works in an office talking about one of their colleagues).

Elicit the correct adverb for number 1. Students complete the task, working individually. Play the recording so that they can check their answers. Highlight the use of *Anyway* in the context of this conversation (= I'm going to change the subject).

Students work in pairs and take turns to read the lines aloud. Monitor and check. If they have problems with the pronunciation, play the recording again as a model and get students to repeat.

Answers and tapescript

T 11.16
Did you hear about Marcus? You know, the guy who works in my office. Well … **apparently**, he's going to be promoted. **To be honest**, I don't understand why. **Personally**, I think he's hopeless at his job. He never does any work. **In fact**, all he does all day is chat to his friends on the phone and drink coffee. **Unfortunately**, his desk is next to mine. **Presumably**, he'll move to another office now, so **hopefully** I won't have to work with him any more. **Anyway**, enough about me. How's your work going? Are you still enjoying it?

4 **T 11.17** [**CD 3: Track 39**] This exercise gives students the opportunity to practise the adverbs and phrases in a personalized way. Elicit a possible ending for the first exchange. Students work in pairs to complete the task. Monitor and help as necessary.

Play the recording and get students to compare their answers.

Ask two students to read out their version of number 1 and continue the conversation. Students work through the rest of the activity in their pairs. Monitor and help as necessary.

You will need to review these expressions in subsequent lessons. Encourage students to try to use them in their conversations in and outside the classroom.

T 11.17
1 **A** Hi! You're Pete, aren't you?
B Actually, no, I'm not. Pete's over there talking to Robert.
2 **A** What did you think of the film? Great wasn't it?
B Personally, I thought it was rubbish. I just don't like all that blood and fighting.
3 **A** What's the latest gossip about Clara and her boyfriend?
B Apparently, she's going to dump him. She's met someone else.
4 **A** What's the weather like in spring?
B Generally, it's warm during the day but you still need to wear a jumper or cardigan in the evening.
5 **A** What time will we arrive?
B Hopefully, in the next hour, unless there's another traffic jam.
6 **A** I've phoned and left messages for them but no reply.
B Presumably, they're away on holiday. Try them on their mobile.
7 **A** What did you do when you saw the accident?
B Obviously, we called 999 immediately. Then we went to see if we could do anything to help.
8 **A** How did you feel when they offered you the job?
B To be honest, I was amazed. I didn't expect to get it but of course I was delighted. It'll be a challenge.

WRITING (SB p116)

Expressing attitude – joining ideas

This section builds on the language covered in *Everyday English* and recycles some of the words from that lesson. The exercise focuses on linking words and expressions in writing, firstly at sentence level and then at text level in the context of a letter to a friend.

1 Students will be familiar with the linkers in this exercise but should find it useful to review how each one is used. Elicit how sentence 1 can be joined with *but*. Students then continue the task, working individually. Tell them there are four possible versions of sentence 1. Give them time to check their answers in pairs before checking with the class.

Answers
1 George was rich, but he wasn't a happy man.
George was rich, although he wasn't a happy man.
Although George was rich, he wasn't a happy man.
George was rich. However, he wasn't a happy man.
2 Jo rang me from a phone box because she's lost her mobile.
Jo's lost her mobile, so she rang me from a phone box.

2 Read the pairs of words and expressions and their meanings as a class. Elicit a possible ending for the first sentence. Students complete the task, working individually.

Elicit a range of answers from the class. Highlight pronunciation of the linking words and expressions as you go.

Possible answers

1 Actually, we're getting married soon.
2 Naturally, when I was a child I didn't know anything about the world of work.
3 She stood and waited for over an hour, but unfortunately, the bus didn't come.
4 Nevertheless, he became a very successful businessman.
5 Anyway, you've heard enough about me? What have you been doing recently?

SUGGESTION

As an extension to exercise 2, get students to write their own sentences using the linking words. Alternatively, they can work in pairs to write a short sketch using a selection of the words and phrases.

3 Students read the first four sentences. Elicit the correct word for the first gap. Students continue the task, working in pairs.

Check the answers with the class, giving students time to discuss any points of disagreement.

Answers

1 so
2 Unfortunately,
3 but
4 However
5 of course
6 Actually
7 but
8 although
9 because
10 In fact
11 Anyway

SUGGESTION

Students write their own letter to a friend, giving their most recent news and using the words and expressions in this section.

Don't forget!

Workbook Unit 11

Exercise 4 Pronunciation – Linking in connected speech (2)

Exercise 9 Vocabulary – adjectives to nouns

Exercise 10 Prepositions – Verb + preposition

Exercise 11 Listening – Shaksper?

Word list

Refer students to the Word list for Unit 11 (SB p157). They could translate the words, learn them at home, or transfer some of them to their vocabulary notebook.

12

Reported speech
Ways of speaking
You know what they say

Telling it how it is

Introduction to the unit

This last unit focuses on reporting – both as the language aim of reported speech and via a range of contexts linked to newspapers and the press. Reported speech also provides a way to pull together and revise aspects of the tense system, providing a useful overview at the end of the course.

Vocabulary and speaking practises verbs that relate to ways of speaking, and *Reading and speaking* highlights a range of influential people across history in a section called *People who changed the world*. The *Listening and speaking* section is based on the theme of the press and accuracy in reporting, with an interview with a singer who feels he has been misrepresented. There are opportunities for revision and extension of reported speech throughout the skills sections. *Everyday English* brings the final unit to a close with a light focus on clichés in conversation.

The *Writing* syllabus ends with the second focus on correcting mistakes and the task of writing a thank-you email.

Language aims

Grammar – reported speech The language presentation covers reported statements and questions, and also commands and requests in the context of two newspaper articles. The *Practice* section reviews and extends students' knowledge of reporting verbs. Although most students will not have studied this target language before, students usually find the tense changes in reported speech (the 'one tense back' rule) quite straightforward and logical, and there may be similar patterns in their own language. The concept is easy to grasp, so any initial mistakes are likely to be based on form, rather than meaning.

POSSIBLE PROBLEMS

Reporting questions can present a few problems, mainly with word order and the lack of auxiliary *do/does/did*. Having spent time getting used to forming questions with *do/does/did*, it may seem strange to some students to leave out the auxiliary in reported questions. Students tend to overuse *that* when reporting commands, often due to interference from their own language. The difference between *say* and *tell* also causes problems for some students.

Common mistakes:	**Corrections:**
**He asked where was I working.*	*He asked where I was working.*
**They wanted to know where is he.*	*They wanted to know where he was.*
**He asked me where did I work.*	*He asked me where I worked.*
**She asked do you like Indian food.*	*She asked if I liked Indian food.*
**They asked that I call them back.*	*They asked me to call them back.*
**She said me that she was happy.*	*She said that she was happy.*
**He told that he'd got the job.*	*He said that he'd got the job./He told me that he'd got the job.*

Vocabulary The vocabulary focus links to the language work with a series of exercises on verbs that describe ways of speaking, e.g. *argue*, *admit*, *whisper*, etc.

Everyday English The final section focuses on clichés that are often used to end a conversation, e.g. *Better safe than sorry.*

Notes on the unit

STARTER (SB p94)

1 Check that students understand the basic terms *direct speech* and *reported speech*. If necessary, write two simple examples on the board to illustrate the difference:

'I'm tired,' said Sue. (the original words/direct speech)
Sue said that she was tired. (reported speech)

Focus attention on the first sentence and elicit the original words. Students write the girl's words for the other examples.

Answers
I'm a student.
What are you doing in London?
I arrived on Monday.

2 This exercises highlights the fact that reported thoughts behave in the same way grammatically as reported speech. Focus attention on the first reported thought and elicit the original words. Students write the thoughts for the other examples.

Answers
I think she works in an office.
I know I've seen her somewhere before.
I wonder if she'll phone me.

I READ IT IN THE PAPERS ... (SB p94)

Reported speech

ABOUT THE TEXT
The text in this section is adapted from a newspaper article about a three-year-old boy who managed to get onto the Internet auction site *eBay* and buy a car. The story, which is true, is humorous and typical of the 'human interest' stories that often appear in newspapers. The article serves as a realistic context for the target language, as it contains many examples of reported speech based on the journalist's interview with the family. Their surname is pronounced /niːl/ and the car /ˈnɪsæn ˈfɪgərəʊ/. Students should be able to understand most of the vocabulary from context, but you may need to check *a bid* (an amount of money someone offers to buy something online) and *password*.

1 Get students to read the article and then answer the questions.

Answers
Jack Neal is a three-year-old boy. He bought a car on *eBay*.
Jack's father contacted the seller, who agreed to readvertise the car.

2 **T 12.1** [CD 3: Track 40] Focus attention on the first example of direct speech and the equivalent in reported speech in the article. Students continue reporting the words and thoughts, working in pairs.

Play the recording and get students to check their answers. If they have made mistakes, remind them of the 'one tense back' rule. Elicit reactions to the text and to Jack's activities online.

Answers and tapescript

T 12.1

Look, Mum! I've bought a car on *eBay* for £9,000!
A three-year-old boy used his mother's computer to buy a £9,000 car on the Internet auction site *eBay*.
Jack Neal's parents only discovered their son's successful bid when they received a message from the website.
The message said they (1) **had bought** a pink Nissan Figaro.
Mrs Neal, 36, said that they (2) **couldn't understand** it. She explained that she (3) **had been** on the Net the day before, but she (4) **hadn't bought** anything.
'Jack kept telling us that he (5) **was** so happy, and that we (6) **would** soon get a big surprise.'
Mrs Neal, from Sleaford, Lincolnshire, thought Jack (7) **was joking.** He often used the computer, and she was pretty sure that he (8) **knew** her password.
Her husband, John, 37, phoned the seller of the car, and explained that there (9) **had been** a mistake.
'Fortunately he saw the funny side and said he (10) **would advertise** the car again.'
Mr Neal has told Jack to be more careful, and he has asked his wife to change her password.

3 This exercise focuses on how we report commands and requests. Give students time to find the wording in the article and then check the answers.

Answers
Mr Neal has told Jack to be more careful.
He has asked his wife to change her password.

4 **T 12.2** [CD 3: Track 41] This exercise gives further practice in reporting statements and commands/requests in the context of the story about Jack. Ask a pair of students to read out the direct speech and the reported equivalent in number 1. Point out that sometimes other words also change when we report speech, e.g. *My Jack – her son, his mother – Mrs Neal.*

Students complete the task, working individually. Give them time to check their answers in pairs before checking with the class.

Answers and tapescript

T 12.2

1 Mrs Neal said her son was very clever.
2 She told me he usually played computer games.
3 His father explained that he had bought the computer for his work.
4 Mrs Neal decided that she wouldn't use *eBay* any more.
5 Jack said he didn't know how it had happened.
6 He told reporters that he had always liked computers.
7 His mother asked Jack to tidy his room.
8 His father told him to go and play football.

Reported questions

ABOUT THE TEXT
This section contains a further newspaper article to contextualize reported questions. The article, a true story, is about a man who threw £20,000 into the air in a town in mid-Wales. When questioned later, he said that he wanted to 'spread a little sunshine'.

Aberystwyth is a market town and holiday resort on the west coast of Wales. Dyfed-Powys /'dəfɪd 'paʊɪs/ Police is the force responsible for a large number of counties in Wales.

Students should be able to understand most of the vocabulary from context, but you may need to check the following: *to start a riot* (in this context, to create noise and confusion), *to hurl something into the air*, *to grab*.

5 **T 12.3** **[CD 3: Track 42]** Focus attention on the newspaper article. Get students to read it through quickly, and elicit what it is about. Focus attention on the direct questions and the example answer in the article. Students then work in pairs to match the direct questions and thoughts to the gaps in the article, and then report them.

Play the recording and get students to check their answers. Play the recording again, pausing after each reported question and getting students to repeat chorally and individually.

Elicit some reactions to the article.

Answers and tapescript

T 12.3

Man throws away £20,000 in town centre

A mystery man started a riot in a busy town centre yesterday by hurling £20,000 in banknotes into the air.

Traffic was stopped at 11.00 a.m. in Alexandra Road, Aberystwyth, mid-Wales, as money rained down from the sky.

Local shopkeeper Anthony Jones, 55, said, 'I couldn't understand it, so I asked my neighbour (1) **what was happening**.' They saw people on their hands and knees grabbing money. 'No one knew (2) **where the money came from**,' he said. 'They were just stuffing it in their pockets.'

Passer-by Eleanor Morris said, 'I wondered (3) **if there had been a road accident**, because the traffic was at a complete standstill.'

Flower seller Cadwyn Thomas saw the man, who was wearing a red Welsh rugby shirt. 'I asked him (4) **why he was giving away** all his money, but he didn't answer. He just laughed.'

Police asked Cadwyn if she (5) **knew the man**. 'I told them I'd never seen him before. He certainly wasn't from around here.'

Dyfed-Powys Police later confirmed that a forty-year-old man from Aberystwyth had been questioned. 'He refused to tell us (9) **why he'd done it**,' a spokesman said, 'so it's a complete mystery. He wanted to know if we (7) **were going to** arrest him, but giving away money isn't against the law.'

GRAMMAR SPOT (SB p95)

1 Read the notes and the example sentence as a class. Students complete the reported speech in the other sentences. Point out that *that* is optional in reported sentences.

Answers
She told me she **had seen the film before**.
She was sure that **I would like it**.

2 Students read the sentences and answer the question. Allow students time to check their answers in pairs before checking with the whole class.

Answers
In the first sentence *tell* means *say*; in the second sentence it means *order*.

3 Read the notes and examples as a class. Focus on the other two direct questions with the class and elicit the reported questions. Write the reported questions on the board and underline *if*. Highlight that in reported questions we repeat the question word if there is one; if there isn't a question word, we use *if* or *whether*.

Answers
She asked me **how long I was staying**.
She wanted to know **if I knew Mike**.

Refer students to Grammar Reference 12.1–12.3 on SB p146.

6 **T 12.4** **[CD 3: Track 43]** This exercise gives further controlled practice of reported questions. Read the instructions and the example as a class. Students report the rest of the questions, working individually. Play the recording and get students to compare their answers. Refer students to the tapescript on SB p131. Students practise the conversation in pairs.

Answers and tapescript
They asked me where I was going.
They asked me where I had been.
They wanted to know if I lived in the area.
They wondered how old I was.
They wanted to know if I had been with friends.
They demanded to know if I had been drinking.
They asked if I could remember what time I had left home.

T 12.4

A I was coming home from the club the other night and I was stopped by the police.
B Were you? Did they ask you lots of questions?
A They certainly did. They asked me where I was going and where I'd been, and they wanted to know if I lived in the area.
B Were you scared?
A You bet!
B What else did they ask?
A Well, they wondered how old I was, and they wanted to know if I'd been with friends.
B Huh! I'm glad *I* wasn't with you.

A Then they demanded to know if I'd been drinking.
B And had you?
A No, not much, anyway. They also asked if I could remember when I'd left home.
B Do you know why they were asking all this?
A No idea. They wouldn't tell me.

PRACTICE (SB p96)

But you said ...!

1 **T 12.5** [CD 3: **Track 44**] Ask two students to read out the example conversation. Students complete the conversations, using their own ideas. Monitor and help as necessary. Play the recording and let students compare their answers.

Play the recording again and get students to practise the conversations in pairs. If necessary, refer them to the tapescript on SB p131. If you think students need more practice, put them in new pairs to practise their own versions of the conversations.

Possible answers and tapescript

T 12.5

1 **A** Bill's coming to the party tonight.
  B Really? I thought you said **he wasn't feeling well**.
2 **A** Have you got a cigarette?
  B I didn't know you **smoked**!
3 **A** Oh, no! I've spilt tomato ketchup on my white shirt!
  B I told you to be careful. I knew **you'd do that**.
4 **A** Did you get me a drink?
  B Sorry. I didn't realize **you were here**. What would you like?
5 **A** I'm 25 today!
  B Are you? I didn't know **it was your birthday**. Many happy returns!
6 **A** Oh, no! It's raining!
  B Really? But the weather forecast said **it was going to be a nice day**.
7 **A** You left the doors and windows of the flat open this morning.
  B I'm sorry. I was pretty sure **I'd closed** everything.
8 **A** Where did Tom go last night?
  B I've no idea **where he went**.

The interview

2 Focus attention on the job advert and the examples. Elicit a few more possible questions and then let students continue the task in pairs.

Collate students' questions on the board/an OHT under a series of headings, e.g. *qualifications*, *previous experience*, *salary*, etc.

Possible answers

What qualifications do you have?
Do you have any computing skills?
Do you speak any foreign languages?
What are your main strengths and weaknesses?
Have you ever managed a team?
What is your current salary?
Why did you leave your last job?
Did you travel a lot in your last job?

3 **T 12.6** [CD 3: **Track 45**] Read the instructions and examples as a class. Students report other possible questions, using the ideas from exercise 2 and any other questions they think relevant to a receptionist.

Play the recording and let students compare their ideas.

Tapescript

T 12.6

They wanted to know how old I was.
They asked me what I was doing at the moment.
They asked me how much I was earning.
They asked where I'd worked before.
They asked me if I liked working in a team.
They wanted to know when I could start!

SUGGESTION

If you have time, you could get pairs of students to roleplay an interview between Julia and the interviewer, using a range of questions. Students then work with a new partner and report the questions asked and answers given.

Reporting verbs

This section introduces and practises a range of reporting verbs with the following patterns:

verb + infinitive
verb + sb + infinitive
verb + *that* + clause

4 Students should be familiar with the meaning of the verbs in the box and should be able to match them to the direct speech fairly easily. Focus attention on the example, then let students continue the task in pairs. Check the answers.

Answers

2f 3d 4a 5h 6g 7b 8c

5 **T 12.7** [CD 3: **Track 46**] Focus attention on the example. Students report the sentences in exercise 4, using the appropriate verbs. Give students time to check in pairs before playing the recording. If there are any areas of disagreement, write the numbers of the relevant sentences on the board.

Play the recording. Students check their answers. Highlight the verb pattern of any sentences that students got wrong.

Answers and tapescript

T 12.7

1 She asked me to help her.
2 He reminded her to post the letter.
3 She promised to work hard for her exams.
4 He invited me to his party.
5 She encouraged me to go travelling.
6 He offered to give me a lift to the airport.
7 He persuaded me to apply for the job.
8 She explained that she'd been very busy.

SUGGESTION

Encourage students to record the reporting verbs in their notebook according to the pattern that they follow:
verb + infinitive: *promise*, *offer*

verb + sb + infinitive: *ask*, *remind*, *encourage*, *persuade*, *invite* (in **T 12.7** the pattern is *invite* + sb + *to* + noun, but it can also be used with the infinitive, e.g. *They invited me to spend the summer with them.*)

verb + *that* + clause: *explain*

Students can add more verbs to each list as they come across them.

She didn't say that!

6 **T 12.8** **[CD 3: Track 47]** Explain that students are going to hear five short conversations with speakers in different situations. There is at least one mistake in the reported speech shown in the Student's Book. Play the first conversation and then focus on the example showing the mistake.

Play the recording once and get students to note down the mistakes in numbers 2–5. Put them in pairs and give them time to formulate the corrections to the mistakes, following the example for conversation 1. Remind them to use the reporting verbs in exercise 4 where possible.

Play the recording again if necessary to allow students to complete/confirm their answers. Check the answers with the class.

Possible answers and tapescript

2 He didn't say he'd got the job as manager. He said he'd got the job of assistant manager.
3 Caroline didn't say Mike couldn't have a turn. She told Ben to let Mike have a turn. She explained that he had to learn to share his toys.
4 Sally didn't ask James to meet her outside the cinema at 6.45. She asked him to meet her inside the cinema at 7.45.
5 Tom didn't offer to mend Sally's computer. He said he wasn't an expert. He didn't ask for £75. He said he would do it for nothing.

T 12.8

1 Merinda is phoning to talk to Jenny.
A Can I speak to Jenny, please?
B I'm afraid she isn't here at the moment. Who's calling?
A This is Merinda, from work. Could you give her a message?
B Sure.
A Can you ask her to ring me as soon as she's back? It's quite important.
B I'll pass on your message.

2 Peter is talking to his boss.
A At the moment we can only offer you the job as assistant manager. I hope that's acceptable. The salary is £20,000 a year.
B That's fine. I'll take the job.
A There's a possibility of promotion in the next six months, if everything works out.
B Great!

3 Caroline is talking to her son, Ben.
A Now Ben, you can play on the bike for a bit, but then you must let Mike have a turn. OK? You have to learn to share your toys.
B OK, mum.

4 Sally is leaving a message for James.
This is a message for James. It's Sally here. I've booked the cinema for 8.00, so I'll see you inside the cinema at about 7.45. Hope that's OK. See you later.

5 Tom is talking to Sally.
A I'll look at your computer for you, but I can't promise to mend it. I'm not an expert.
B Will you charge me for it?
A Don't be silly. Of course not. I'll do it for nothing.

ADDITIONAL MATERIAL

Workbook Unit 12
Exercises 1–4 Reported speech
Exercise 5 Reporting verbs – Verb + infinitive
Exercise 6 Reporting verbs – *ask* and *tell*

WRITING (SB p117)

Correcting mistakes (2)

This final writing section reviews a range of target language from the course in an error correction task. The text type is a thank-you email written by Kati, the same character who appeared in *Writing* Unit 1, to her host family in Dublin. Students go on to write their own thank-you email to someone they have stayed with.

1 Focus attention on the photo of Kati and ask what students can remember about her from *Writing* Unit 1. Refer them back to her letter on p103 and remind them of the symbols they used to correct it. Read the instructions with the class and elicit the mistakes in the first sentence of the email (see *Answers* below).

Students continue the task, working individually. Remind them to use the correction symbols on p103 wherever they can. Monitor and help as necessary.

2 Put students in pairs to compare the mistakes they have found and correct the email. Monitor and help as necessary. If students can find only 20 mistakes or fewer, discuss the remaining errors with the whole class, isolating the key parts of the text on an OHT if possible.

Check the corrected wording with the class. Again, mark the corrections on an OHT if possible.

Answers

To: GillandBobKendall@lightspeed.net **Attachment:** GoodbyeDublin.jpg
Subject: Hello from Kati

Dear Mr and Mrs Kendall

I've been home now **for** two weeks, but I **had** to start work immediately, so this is the first time **that it's been** possible for me to write. How are you all? Are you busy as usual? **Is** Tim **still working** hard for his exam next month? I ~~am~~ **miss** you a lot and also all my friends from Dublin. :-)

Yesterday I~~'ve~~ received an email from my **Spanish** friend, Martina, and she told me about some of the other people I met. She **said** that Atsuko and Yuki **are going to** write **to** me from Japan. I am lucky because I made so many good **friends while** I was in Ireland. It was really interesting for me to meet people from so many different countries. I think that we not only improved our English (I hope **so**!) but we also **got to know/met** people from all over the world and this is important.

My family are fine. They had a good summer holiday by the lake. We are all very **excited** because my brother **is getting/going to get** married just before Christmas and we like **his girlfriend very much**. They have **been looking** for a flat near the city centre but it is **not** easy to find one. If they **don't** find one soon, they will have to stay here with us.

Please can you check something for me? I can't find my red scarf. I think **I might have left** it in the **cupboard** in my bedroom.

Please write soon. My family send best wishes to you all. I hope I can come back next year. **Staying** with you was a **really** wonderful experience for me. Thank you for **everything** and excuse my mistakes. **I've** already **forgotten many/a lot of** words.

Love and best wishes to you all,
Kati XX

P.S. I hope you like the attached photo. It's nice, isn't it? It's the one you took when I was leaving!

3 Ask students to think about the time they stayed with someone. Put them in small groups to discuss the visit and say if they enjoyed it.

Give students time to make brief notes about their stay, referring to Kati's email as a model for ideas.

Students write their email for homework. Students can exchange their first drafts and make suggestions as to how to improve them, using the correction symbols on p103. Students then hand in their final drafts, or email them to you for checking.

VOCABULARY AND SPEAKING (SB p97)

Ways of speaking

This section builds on the language work done on reported speech with a range of verbs used to describe ways of speaking. Many of these can be used as reporting verbs, e.g. *persuade, promise*. Students categorize verbs according to their meaning, practise preposition use after verbs, do a sentence-building task, and then write and act out conversations, using the verbs.

1 Focus attention on the diagram. Explain that it shows a good way of categorizing the verbs and recording them in a visual way. Elicit another example from the box to add to one or two of the categories. Students complete the task, working in pairs.

Check the answers with the class, dealing with any pronunciation problems as you go.

Answers
good idea: *suggest*, advise, recommend
disagreeing: *argue*, row, quarrel
social: *talk*, chat, gossip
volume: *shout*, whisper, scream
in a court of law: *admit*, accuse, deny
expressing dislike: *complain*, protest, criticize
giving commands: *tell*, order, demand

SUGGESTION
Encourage students to use diagrams to record sets of related words, e.g. topic-based lexical sets, verbs with different patterns, or vocabulary from reading/listening tasks that they want to remember.

2 This task practises common verb + noun phrase collocations. Elicit possible verbs for number 1. Students complete the task, working in their pairs. Remind them to look carefully at the words that follow the gaps, especially prepositions, to help them choose possible verbs.

Possible answers

1 chat, talk	5 complain
2 row, argue, quarrel	6 scream
3 shout	7 protest
4 admit, deny	8 suggest, recommend

3 Elicit the missing prepositions for number 1. Students complete the task, working individually. Give students time to check in pairs before checking with the class.

Answers
1 I talk **to** my kids **about** everything.
2 My boss criticizes – me **for** my work.
3 I agree **with** you **about** most things, but not politics.
4 I discuss – everything **with** my wife.
5 People love gossiping **about** celebrities.
6 The teacher accused me **of** cheating in the exam.

4 Look at the example with the class, then elicit one or two possible sentences beginning *My mother advised me to*. Students complete the task, working in pairs. Elicit some answers from the class and make sure that students have used the correct pattern for each verb.

Possible answers
My mother advised me to think carefully before I made a decision.
The teacher told the students to work harder.
My doctor persuaded me to do more exercise.
My friends suggested that I should go home.
I admitted that I'd been stupid.
My brother complained that the teacher was boring.

5 Read the instructions as a class. Ask students to read out the example conversation and the summary. Put students into new pairs to write their conversation. Give them time to decide which verbs they want to illustrate. Suggest that they group verbs that can easily be integrated into a context, e.g. *complain / criticize / promise*; *chat / invite / accept*; *invite / refuse / persuade*, etc.

Give students time to write their conversations. Monitor and help as necessary. Explain that students are going to act out their conversations and other students must give a summary of what is happening. Focus on the example summary in the SB, and point out that we use present tenses to report something that is being said right now. Students act out their conversations and the rest of the class give a summary. With larger classes, students can work in groups for this stage. Note down any common errors and feed back on them after the activity/in a later lesson.

Don't highlight errors as students are acting out their conversations, as this is intended to be freer practice.

SUGGESTION
You can give regular further practice with the verbs in this section by asking students to summarize conversations they have heard, both in their own language and in English. This can be a 'warmer' activity at the start of any lesson.

ADDITIONAL MATERIAL

Workbook Unit 12
Exercise 7 Vocabulary – Ways of speaking
Exercise 8 Vocabulary – Other reporting verbs

READING AND SPEAKING (SB p98)

People who changed the world

ABOUT THE TEXT
This final *Reading and speaking* section focuses on five people who have had a huge influence on different areas of life, from science to music and entertainment, across the centuries. The title of the text, *Movers and shakers*, is an informal expression meaning 'people who are powerful or have a lot of influence'.

Charles Darwin /tʃɑːlz 'dɑːwɪn/ was a British scientist who developed the theory of evolution by natural selection – the process by which plants and animals that are well adapted to particular environments will survive, while others will die. His 1859 book *On the Origin of Species by Means of Natural Selection* caused great controversy because his ideas were seen as an attack on the account of the origins of life in the Bible.

Galileo Galilei /gælɪ'leɪəʊ gælɪ'leiiː/ was an Italian astronomer, mathematician, and physicist, who studied the movements of the planets and believed that the sun, not the earth, was the centre of the universe. Copernicus (1473–1543), also mentioned in the text, was a Polish astronomer who first suggested that the earth and other planets moved round the sun. The Church considered Galileo a dangerous heretic and he was punished for his beliefs in the 1630s.

Emmeline Pankhurst /'eməliːn 'pæŋkhɜːst/ was the founder of the Women's Social and Political Union (WSPU), which was known as the 'suffragettes'. The suffragettes fought for women's rights, especially the vote, in the early 1900s. Pankhurst's daughters, Christabel and Sylvia, were also suffragettes and worked for the rights of poor women.

Sigmund Freud /'sɪgmənd frɔɪd/ was an Austrian doctor who developed psychoanalysis, a new way of understanding the human mind and treating mental illness. He believed that we have an unconscious mind where there are thoughts and feelings that we do not know we have, and that bad experiences as a child can affect a person's mental health as an adult.

Elvis Presley /'elvɪs 'prezli/ was a US singer and guitar player who became one of the most successful and popular singers ever. As a young man he was known as 'Elvis the Pelvis' because of the way he moved his hips when he performed. He also became known as 'The King' and, although he died in 1977, his popularity still continues.

The text consists of an introduction and five short profiles, which summarize each person's work and their influence. Each one also has two short quotations illustrating how each person saw the world and what others said about him/her. This gives further practice in reported speech. In the tasks, students discuss their own heroes/heroines as a lead-in, then pool what they know about the five people shown in the photos. They answer pre-reading questions, and then read and exchange the key information about the people. In the final stages, students summarize the influence of the five people and answer general discussion questions.

Encourage students to use the context to help them with new vocabulary, but you may need to pre-teach/explain the following:

Charles Darwin: *creationists* (people who believe that the universe was created exactly as the Bible describes it), *to evolve*, *Adam and Eve* (the first man and woman according to Jewish, Christian, and Islamic religions), *to be descended from*, *insoluble* (can't be solved or explained), *agnostic* (a person who is not sure whether or not God exists).

Galileo Galilei: *to rotate* (to move in a circle around a fixed central point), *an axis* (an imaginary line through the centre of a planet), *fantastic* (in this context, *not practical or sensible*), *heresy* (an action/belief that opposes the official beliefs of a religion; adj = *heretical*), *to pave the way* (to create a situation which will allow sth to happen), *Holy Scriptures* (the Bible).

Emmeline Pankhurst: *rational, militant, tactics, to slash, railings, force-feeding, to go on hunger strike, hysterical, to abandon your duty.*

Sigmund Freud: *motivations, unaware, to deny* (in this context *to refuse*), *notion, to undermine, bulk, unverifiable.*

Elvis Presley: *adolescent* (adj), *shake your hips, to mesmerize, to alienate, indifferent* (in this context, *of rather low quality*) *mediocre, obituary.*

1 Give an example of your own hero/heroine. Give students a few moments to think of their own examples and then discuss their ideas as a class. Establish which area of life most of the students' heroes/heroines come from, e.g. sport, science, etc.

2 Students read the introduction to the text. Check comprehension of *not always so* (in this context, *not always believed*). Focus attention on the photos and the names of the people. Put students in pairs to exchange ideas about each person and make brief notes. Tell them not to worry if they can't say much, as they will find out more later in the lesson.

3 Check comprehension of *equality* and *shook the world* (shocked and upset public opinion). Students discuss the answers to the questions in their pairs, without reading the texts. Students then read the texts quickly and find the information to check their answers. Make sure students understand that they don't need to read every word, but just scan the texts to find the relevant information.

Answers
1 Elvis Presley
2 Emmeline Pankhurst
3 Galileo Galilei
4 Charles Darwin
5 Sigmund Freud

4 Put students in new pairs. Focus attention on the questions and let students choose the text they want to read. If most pairs choose the same one, you may need to assign different texts to some pairs so that all five of the texts are covered. In smaller classes, students may have to read more than one text.

See *About the text* above for notes on vocabulary. Give students time to read the text and answer the questions, working in their pairs. Encourage them to use the context to help them with new vocabulary, and to help each other. They can use dictionaries if appropriate. Monitor and help as necessary. Encourage students to use their own words to report what each person said about his/her ideas, rather than copying directly from the text.

Put students into groups of five, with one student who has read each text. Students compare and exchange information. Encourage them to use their own words, rather than quoting directly from the text.

Answers
Charles Darwin
1 Science.
2 1859, when his book *On the Origin of Species by Means of Natural Selection* was published. It shocked the world.
3 His ideas were opposed because they contradicted the religious beliefs of the time.
4 He said that the origins of life couldn't be explained and that he had to remain agnostic.
His opponents said that people were not descended from monkeys and there was no point in a world without God.

Galileo Galilei
1 Science.
2 1633, when he was found guilty of heresy. He spent the last years of his life imprisoned in his own home.
3 His ideas were opposed because they were considered dangerous by the Church.
4 He said that the truth is easy to understand when you have found it, but the point is to discover the truth yourself.
His opponents said that his ideas were wrong, ridiculous, and against the Bible.

Emmeline Pankhurst
1 Politics.
2 1908–9, when she was sent to prison three times. She went on hunger strike and was force-fed. In 1918 the government changed the law on voting rights. In 1928, women got equal voting rights to men.
3 Her ideas were opposed because people believed that a woman's place was in the home.
4 She said that the suffragettes weren't law-breakers, but they wanted to be law-makers.
Her opponents said that the suffragettes were hysterical and unreasonable, and were not doing their duty as wives and mothers.

Sigmund Freud
1 Science/Psychology.
2 1900, when his book *The Interpretation of Dreams* was published.
3 His ideas were opposed because they were not scientific enough.
4 He said that the mind is like an iceberg because most of it is hidden.
His opponents said that it isn't possible to prove whether his ideas are right, and his attitude to scientific research was irresponsible.

Elvis Presley
1 Popular music.
2 1956, when he arrived on the pop scene, and changed attitudes to music, sex, language, and fashion.
3 His ideas were opposed because he made teenagers want to be different from their parents, and parents thought this was dangerous.
4 He said that he couldn't help moving to rock and roll when he heard it.
His opponents said that he wasn't a very good singer or musician, and he would soon be forgotten.

5 Check that students understand *prevailing ideas* (ideas that were accepted at a particular time). Students continue working in their groups of five to discuss the questions. Elicit a range of responses in a whole-class feedback session.

Answers
Charles Darwin
1 He made people think about how the Earth and different types of animals and plants had been created.
2 The idea that God created the Earth and everything on it.
3 Modern ideas about evolution became accepted.

Galileo Galilei
1 He encouraged people to think in a scientific way.
2 The idea that the earth was the centre of the universe, and the sun revolved around it.
3 People started to look at the world in a more scientific way.

Emmeline Pankhurst
1 She helped get women the right to vote.
2 The idea that women cannot think rationally, and should stay at home.
3 Women got the vote and began to achieve other rights.

Sigmund Freud
1 He created the science of psychology.
2 The idea that something is only true if it can be proved by scientific methods.
3 People became interested in the unconscious mind and how it works.

Elvis Presley
1 He made rock 'n' roll music popular.
2 The idea that teenagers should be just like their parents.
3 The modern teenager was born, and other rock 'n' roll singers and groups became popular.

What do you think?

Give students time to read through the questions and think about their answers. Elicit a range of responses in a whole-class discussion. In larger classes, students can work in groups and then report back.

LISTENING AND SPEAKING (SB p100)

What the papers say

ABOUT THE LISTENING

This section continues the theme of reporting with a focus on the accuracy of news reports in the press. The context is an interview with a singer called Jamie Seabrook. He is a fictitious character, but the interview highlights problems that are typical of high-profile entertainers.

The interview and tasks are divided into three parts: introducing Jamie and talking about the press in general; examples from Jamie of what he sees as mis-reporting; changes that Jamie has made to his life and his overall opinion of himself.

In terms of vocabulary, you may need to pre-teach/check the following before the task for each part:

Part 1: *sell-out concerts, be in trouble with the law, rehab* (rehabilitation (assisted recovery) from drug or alcohol addiction)
NOTE: *Clinic* in Part 1 of the recording refers to a private health clinic where wealthy people and celebrities go to rest and recover from various mental and emotional problems. Such clinics are often known informally as *rehab clinics* because the assumption is that people spend time in them to recover from drug or alcohol addiction.

Part 2: *to fall out* (have an argument), *prescription drugs, migraines, do drugs* (informal for 'take drugs'), *drink driving, exhausted, exhaustion.*

Part 3: *to become a Buddhist, to meditate, to deserve attention*

The section also deals with opinions about the press in general and differences in styles of reporting. In the UK, there are broadly two main categories of newspaper. The tabloids, e.g. *The Sun, The Daily Star*, tend to focus on less serious content, especially celebrities, sports, and sensationalist crime stories. These newspapers are also called 'red top' papers, on account of the colour used under their main title. The newspapers associated with higher-quality journalism, e.g. *The Times, The Independent*, are called 'broadsheets' because traditionally they used a larger format. This is changing, however, as many of these newspapers are now adopting a more compact format. They are often referred to as 'quality newspapers'.

If possible, bring in two or three British newspapers to help set up the topic. Choose a mixture of tabloids and broadsheets/serious newspapers. Use the papers to review/introduce key vocabulary: *reporters, the press, headlines, scandal, celebrities, press attention, the facts of a story, to tell the truth, neutral/factual reporting, angles on a story, column inches, to make up/invent stories.*

1 Focus attention on the headlines and allow students time to read them. Ask students to contribute information and ideas about newspapers in their country.

2 Discuss the questions as a class, elicit a range of answers and examples from the students. This should lead to some interesting discussion, especially in multilingual classes.

3 **T 12.9** [**CD 3: Track 48**] Focus attention on the photo of Jamie. Ask students what sort of lifestyle they think he has.

See notes about vocabulary in *About the listening.* Give students time to read the questions, then play Part 1 of the recording. Let students discuss their answers in pairs before checking with the class.

See notes about vocabulary for Part 2 in *About the listening.* Focus attention on the chart. Explain that Barbara James was Jamie's PA (personal assistant). Play Part 2 of the recording once. Students complete the chart and answer question 6. Encourage them to pool their knowledge and exchange answers. Play the recording again if students have missed any of the information, before checking with the class. This will give students the opportunity to get further practice in reported speech.

See notes about vocabulary for Part 3 in *About the listening.* Give students time to read the questions, then play Part 3 of the recording. Let students discuss their answers in pairs before checking with the class.

Answers and tapescript

Part 1

1 He's been in the music business for 20 years; he performs sell-out concerts to 50,000 people. He's had problems with his family; he's been in trouble with the law.
2 He was in a rehab clinic.
3 Most of the time he doesn't mind press attention. He says it's nice that people want to know all about him, but he doesn't like it when it gets too much.
4 He says that some reporters try to tell the truth, but most of them make up stories to sell their newspapers.

Part 2

5

	What did they say about him?	What did *he* say?
reporters	his career was finished; he'd never sing again	he's just recorded a new album
ex-friends	his marriage was breaking up; he had fallen out with his brother about money and they weren't speaking to each other	his marriage is fine; he and his wife have just celebrated their fifteenth wedding anniversary; he gets on fine with his brother
people in clubs	they'd seen him taking drugs	he takes prescription drugs for migraines, but never illegal drugs; he only drinks alcohol on special occasions

police officers	they thought he'd been drinking and arrested him for drink driving	he'd been working all day and he was exhausted
Barbara James	he hadn't paid her for six months, and he made her work seven days a week without a break.	It broke his heart when Barbara said those things. He treated her like family. When he met her she was nothing, and he gave her everything. None of what she says is true.

6 He says he checked into a clinic for a month because he was suffering from exhaustion.

Part 3

7 He has become a Buddhist, and stopped eating meat. He spends four hours a day meditating. He's going to give half his future income to charity.

8 He's decided that life is too short, and he's getting old. He doesn't care what people think. He's made up his mind to do something useful with his life.

9 He/She refused to read the story about Jamie's lifestyle change, because there were much more serious stories that deserved attention, and Jamie was just a celebrity.

10 He can't control what the press says about him. He has to be true to himself. He lives his life as honestly as he can, and he tries to be nice to everyone. If you're in the public eye, then you have to be prepared to have bad things said about you. He knows what's true about him and what's a lie, but he can't change what is in the newspapers and on TV.

T 12.9

An interview with Jamie Seabrook.
I = Interviewer J = Jamie

Part 1

I And now for my final guest. He's a singer and songwriter who's been in the music business for twenty years. He still performs sell-out concerts in front of fifty thousand people. But his life hasn't all been easy. He's had problems with his family and he's been in trouble with the law. And he's just completed a month's rehab in a clinic in Texas. He's never out of the headlines ... Please welcome Jamie Seabrook!

J Hello, good evening.

I Now Jamie, you're in the newspapers and magazines every day. You're photographed wherever you go. Tell me, what do you think of the press?

J Well, it's kind of nice to have people want to know all about me. Sometimes it gets to be too much, but most of the time I don't mind the press attention. I'm sure there are some reporters who really try to tell the truth, but I'm afraid that most of them make up stories to sell their newspapers.

I Are you saying that the stories aren't true at all?

J That's right! They're completely invented!

I Can you give us an example?

J Sure I can! I can give you hundreds!

Part 2

J Two years ago, reporters said my career was finished, and that I'd never sing again. Some friends, who are now ex-friends, said that my marriage was breaking up, and that my brother and I had fallen out and had an argument about money and weren't speaking to each other. Not one word of that was true!

I And in fact your career is on a high ...

J I've just recorded a new album, and my marriage is fine. Sally and I have just celebrated our fifteenth wedding anniversary ...

J ... and my brother and I get on just fine.

I But things haven't all been easy for you. You spent a month in rehab because it was said that you had a drug and alcohol problem ...

J All that's just lies! I've never had a drug or alcohol problem. People in clubs said they'd seen me taking drugs, but it's simply not true. I take prescription drugs for migraines, that's all. I don't do illegal drugs. And I only drink alcohol on special occasions, like my birthday.

I But you were arrested for drink driving just a few months ago!

J Not so! Police officers thought I'd been drinking, but I was driving home from the recording studios and it was two o'clock in the morning and I'd been working all day and I was exhausted. I fell asleep at the wheel. I checked into a clinic for a month because I was suffering from exhaustion.

I Now, you had another legal problem recently. Your personal assistant, Barbara James, said you hadn't paid her for six months, and you made her work seven days a week without a break. Is that true?

J It broke my heart when Barbara, my PA, said those things about me. I treated her like my own family. When I met her she was nothing, and I gave her everything. None of what she says is true.

Part 3

I I read that you have become a Buddhist, that you have stopped eating meat, that you spend four hours a day meditating, and that you are going to give half your future income to charity. Is this true?

J Yes, it is. I've decided that life is too short, and I'm getting old. I don't care what people think. I made up my mind to do something useful with my life.

I Now when this story broke a few days ago, the news presenter on MBC's Morning News refused to read the story, saying that there were much more serious stories that deserved attention, and that you were just a celebrity. What do you say to that?

J I can't control what the press says about me. I have to be true to myself. I live my life as honestly as I can, I try to be nice to everyone around me. If you're in the public eye, then you have to be prepared to have some pretty terrible things said about you. I know what's true about me and what's a lie, but I can't change what is said about me in the newspapers and on the television.

I Well, sadly our time has run out and we've come to the end of the show. A big thank you to my guest, Jamie Seabrook, and good luck with the new album!

J Thank you. It's been a pleasure.

SPOKEN ENGLISH – *don't mind / don't care*

1 Read the notes and examples as a class. Point out that *I'm easy* is a more informal way of saying *I don't mind*. Also point out that *don't care* can easily sound rude – this depends largely on intonation, so students should be very careful when using it.

2 Students work individually to complete the short conversations with *I don't care / I don't mind*.

Answers

1 I don't mind.
2 I don't care.
3 I don't mind.
4 I don't care.

What do you think?

Give students time to read through the questions and think about their answers. Elicit a range of responses in a whole-class discussion. In larger classes, students can work in groups and then report back.

SUGGESTIONS

- If your students are interested in the press and media, you could get them to compare the treatment of a news story in a broadsheet/quality newspaper with the same story in a tabloid. Ask students to look at aspects like headlines, photos, number of column inches, use of language, and opinion vs fact.
- Students could do a ranking task with a list of news stories/features, e.g. a celebrity wedding, news of a financial recession, a bank robbery, a sporting achievement, a political scandal, etc. Students put them in order according to their importance and the order in which they should be reported in a newspaper/on TV or radio.

EVERYDAY ENGLISH (SB p101)

You know what they say ...

This final *Everyday English* section of the course focuses on the use of clichés to bring a conversation to an end. Students look at a pair of examples and then match common clichés with lines from conversations.

NOTE

A cliché /ˈkliːʃeɪ/ is a comment or saying that is used very often, and can be seen as overused. Clichés are very common in spoken English because they allow the speaker to sum up a situation without having to think too hard. Students should enjoy working with these expressions, which are intended mainly for recognition. Correct stress and intonation on the expressions is crucial to the listener interpreting the meaning in the correct way. 'Flat' intonation or the wrong stress can make the speaker sound insincere or even sarcastic. It's worth pointing out that clichés should be avoided in writing, especially in a more formal style.

The example in *And finally ...* is taken from a play by William Shakespeare, probably written in the middle part of his career, between 1601 and 1608. It is both the title of the play and a line used in it.

1 Read the introduction as a class. Focus attention on the examples and ask students to identify the cliché in each one. (*You win some, you lose some. You learn something new every day.*) Ask students if they have ever heard these expressions in everyday conversation.

2 Give students time to read the lines in **A**. Check comprehension of *fed up, anti-malaria, to reverse, right-wing*. Explain that the matching lines in **B** sit directly opposite **A**, but sometimes in jumbled order. Elicit the matching lines for the first pair of sentences (see *Answers* below).

Put students in pairs to continue the task. Remind them to use the context to help them.

3 **T 12.10** [CD 3: **Track 49**] Play the recording so that students can check their answers.

Ask students to use the context to explain the following expressions: *Never mind* (= don't worry/it doesn't matter); *Cheer up!* (= don't be sad); *Great minds think alike* (used to emphasize a coincidence; or two people reaching the same conclusion at the same time); *It takes all sorts to make a world* (= people vary a lot in their character and abilities); *It's all right for some* (used to say you think that someone is very lucky); *Time's a great healer* (= you will feel better over time).

Answers and tapescript

T 12.10

1 **A** I'm so fed up! I lost my mobile yesterday!
B Cheer up! It's not the end of the world.
A I got the time wrong, and I missed my plane.
B Never mind. We all make mistakes.

2 **A** I forgot her birthday, so I sent her a text.
B Well done. Better late than never.
A So you like Russian novels, do you? So do I!
B Great minds think alike.

3 **A** Tim's strange. He's not like me at all.
B It takes all sorts to make a world.
A I worked so hard for that exam, and I still failed.
B You did your best. You can't do any more.

4 **A** I've got ten exams in the next two weeks.
B Rather you than me.
A I've got three months' holiday!
B It's all right for some.

5 **A** I'm going to pack some anti-malaria tablets.
B Good idea. Better safe than sorry.
A I haven't heard from my kids for weeks!
B No news is good news.

6 **A** That party was awful. I hated it.
B You can say that again. I couldn't stand it.
A I reversed into a wall and broke a tail light.
B It could be worse. You could have hurt someone.

7 **A** She's been so sad since her husband died.
B I'm sure it's tough, but time's a great healer.
A I wonder if their marriage will last.
B Only time will tell.

8 **A** Our neighbours are extreme right-wing.
B Live and let live. That's what I say.
A I trusted Peter, and he stole all my money!
B Oh, well. You live and learn.

And finally ...

Focus attention on the quotation from Shakespeare. Point out that *All's well that ends well* has been adopted into modern English and is considered a cliché. Ask students how they think it is used (it is often used after a situation has ended in a positive way, or to indicate that things have turned out well after a period of difficulty). Ask students if they think it is a good expression to use at the end of the course. If appropriate, ask students if they can think of any others. These don't need to be clichés, just expressions students think are fitting, e.g. *It's been great working with you. I really hope to see you again next term. Don't forget to keep in touch*, etc.

Don't forget!

Vocabulary revision
Units 10–12 (TB p157), with answers (TB p159)

Workbook Unit 12

Exercise 9 Phrasal verbs – Phrasal verbs in context (2)

Exercise 10 Pronunciation – Ways of pronouncing *ou*

Exercise 11 Listening – *You weren't listening!*

Word list

Refer students to the Word list for Unit 12 (SB p157). They could translate the words, learn them at home, or transfer some of them to their vocabulary notebook.

Photocopiable materials

Unit 1

Understanding meaning from context

1 Read texts 1–3 on p146 quickly and match them to the text types (a–e). There are two text types that you don't need.

a a review
b a travel guide
c a story
d an information leaflet
e an article

2 Read text 1 again more slowly and look at the underlined words. Choose the correct information for each word.

1 This word comes after *more* and before *than*, so it's *an adjective* / *a noun*.
It must mean '*easy* / *difficult* to find' because people don't know who Bansky is.
2 This word follows *most* so it's *a verb* / *an adjective*.
It must mean *awful* / *famous* because of the contrast following *but*.
3 This expression must mean *to know* / *not to know* because Bansky is a mystery man.
4 This word must mean *loved* / *hated* his images, because Banksy's book has sold a lot of copies.
5 This word follows *to* so it's a *verb* / *preposition*.
It must mean to *buy* / *clean off*, because the context is negative about graffiti.

3 Read text 2 again more slowly. What type of words are 6–10?

6 ____________ 8 ____________ 10 ____________
7 ____________ 9 ____________

4 Complete the sentences about words 6–10 with the correct words in the box. There are three words that you don't need.

proud selection pay sad divides side argue cover

6 This word must mean '____________' because the text says the city stands on both sides of the river.
7 This word must mean 'to have something to be ____________ of' because the overall context is positive.
8 This word must mean 'to go from one ____________ to the other' because the text is talking about bridges across the river.
9 This word must mean a '____________' because the text gives examples of the food you can buy.
10 This word must mean 'negotiate or ____________' because the text refers to getting the best prices.

5 Read text 3 again more slowly. Complete the sentences about words 11–15.

11 This word is a(n) ____________. It must mean ____________
because ____.
12 This word is a(n) ____________. It must mean ____________
because ____.
13 This word is a(n) ____________. It must mean ____________
because ____.
14 This word is a(n) ____________. It must mean ____________
because ____.
15 This word is a(n) ____________. It must mean ____________
because ____.

Compare your answers with a partner.

1

Mystery Man of Art

His work sells for thousands of pounds, but he is more (1) elusive than Dracula on a summer's day.

The mystery man of graffiti, Banksy, is one of Britain's most (2) renowned artists, but we don't know for sure who he is. Even his parents are said (3) to be in the dark about his artistic identity.

Banksy's art has been covering public walls for more than 10 years, but little is known about him. His name is said to be Robert Banks and he is thought to have been born in Bristol in 1974.

Banksy's fans love his work because it is open to all people and is often very funny. Even people who don't collect art have (4) lapped up his images. His latest book has sold more than 250,000 copies.

But Banksy also has critics. Some think his work is vandalism, not public art. Many local councils have promised to clean off his images.
A London councillor said, 'Graffiti is a crime. It costs thousands of pounds (5) to remove it every year.'

Despite this criticism, Banksy …

2

Hungary –
tradition, culture, and fun

Right now the coolest city in Europe has to be **Budapest**. The River Danube actually **(6)** splits the city into two places, with Buda on the left and Pest on the right. Both Buda and Pest **(7)** boast spectacular buildings, including Buda Castle, and the Parliament building on the Pest side.

Budapest's streets are safe and getting around is easy. You can take the clean and quick metro system, a bus, tram, or trolleybus. It's also a great city for walkers, with wide avenues, green parks, and a clear layout. There are seven city bridges that **(8)** straddle the gently flowing Danube.

After enjoying a morning of sightseeing, be sure to try one of the old-fashioned coffee houses that sell creamy coffee and wonderful cakes. Food is never very far away, with **Budapest**'s restaurants offering local dishes and markets selling an **(9)** array of sausages, meats, cheese, fruits, and vegetables.

There are plenty of opportunities to buy souvenirs, but in the markets be prepared to **(10)** haggle to get the best prices.

3

The latest books for the summer **BOOK CORNER**

The Lighthouse

(11) Set in the south-west of England in the 1980s, this is a story of the Spencer family, who want to fulfil their dream of living by the sea. Moving to Cornwall after leaving London for a new, stress-free life, the Spencers start (12) renovations of an old, empty lighthouse in the hope of making it a family home. But the Spencers soon regret their decision as they realize that the building and the area around it hold dark and mysterious secrets. Why did the old lighthouse keeper leave so suddenly, never to be seen again? And who is the woman who (13) gazes at the lighthouse from a distance every day but never comes near? When going to the police for help proves useless, the family (14) turns detective to find out what happened in the lighthouse and why no one wants to talk about it. What follows is a series of events that will test their relationships to the limit. Full of powerful descriptions, this story is (15) intriguingly written and will keep you guessing right to the very end.

Song Matthew and Son

1 Write the aspects of work in the correct lists.

~~earning money~~ commuting every day job insecurity learning new skills low salaries job satisfaction lack of free time working as a team a big workload being promoted

Pros	Cons
earning money	

2 **[CD 1: Track 19]** Cover the words of the song. Listen and tick (✓) the problems that the singer mentions in the cons list in exercise 1.

3 Work with a partner. Write the lines of the song in the correct place. Use the content and rhyme to help you.

There's a five-minute break and that's all you take, Even though they're pretty low and their rent's in arrears And the eight-thirty train to Matthew & Son. The files in your head, you take them to bed, you're never ever through. (x2) for Matthew & Son, he won't wait.

4 **[CD 1: Track 19]** Listen to the song again and check.

5 Choose the correct information.

1. Matthew & Son must be the name of *a company / an employee.*
2. 'The work's never done' and 'you're never ever through' means the work is never *good enough / finished.*
3. In the line 'Watch them run down to platform one', 'them' refers to *the commuters / Matthew & Son.*
4. People are too *old / afraid* to ask for a pay rise.
5. The singer complains that *rents are very high / people get behind with the rent.*

6 Imagine you work for Matthew & Son and you are travelling home with other commuters on the train. Work with a partner. Tell him/her about your working life and what you do each day.

MATTHEW AND SON

Up at eight, you can't be late

(1) ______________________________

Watch them run down to platform one

(2) ______________________________

Matthew & Son, the work's never done, there's always something new.

(3) ______________________________

And they've been working all day, all day, all day!

(4) ______________________________

for a cup of cold coffee and a piece of cake.

Matthew & Son, the work's never done, there's always something new.

(5) ______________________________

And they've been working all day, all day, all day!

He's got people who've been working for fifty years

No one asks for more money coz nobody dares

(6) ______________________________

Matthew & Son, Matthew & Son, Matthew & Son, Matthew & Son,

And they've been working all day, all day, all day!

Unit 2

Making small talk

♀ 1

Name: Maria Fuentes
From: the suburbs of Bilbao, northern Spain
Job: marketing manager | **Work for:** the Spanish wine industry
Arrived: two days ago | **Staying at:** the Park Inn
Reason for trip: to promote Spanish wine
Sights visited in the city: the modern art exhibition; planning to do a city tour
Opinion of city: You haven't seen a lot, but it looks interesting

♂ 2

Name: Carlo Ponti
From: Milan, northern Italy
Job: furniture designer | **Work for:** a design company
Arrived: a few hours ago | **Staying at:** the City Hotel
Reason for trip: attending a conference on computers in design
Sights visited in the city: You haven't had time to see anything yet
Opinion of city: none yet – ask others for suggestions

♂ 3

Name: Ben Sakamoto
From: born in Kyoto, but you live outside Tokyo
Job: IT developer | **Work for:** a new independent IT company
Arrived: yesterday | **Staying at:** the Inn on the River
Reason for trip: to recruit bilingual staff
Sights visited in the city: You took photos at the cathedral; bought presents in old part of the city
Opinion of city: small but attractive; people seem friendly

♂ 4

Name: Frans Hantelmann
From: the Netherlands, just outside Rotterdam
Job: garden designer | **Work for:** a range of clients as a freelance
Arrived: two days ago | **Staying at:** Brown's Hotel
Reason for trip: researching gardening styles for a book
Sights visited in the city: the city park; you're looking forward to visiting gardens in the area
Opinion of city: set in a lovely area

♂ 5

Name: Santiago Puerta
From: born in La Plata, but you now live in Buenos Aires
Job: chef | **Work for:** a five-star hotel
Arrived: last night | **Staying at:** the Kingsbridge Hotel
Reason for trip: a working holiday to experience cooking in a UK restaurant
Sights visited in the city: just the river area by the hotel
Opinion of city: pretty but perhaps a bit small; you would like to visit a bigger city – ask others for suggestions

♀ 6

Name: Suzanne Leclerc
From: born in Strasbourg, but you live outside Lyons
Job: lecturer | **Work for:** Lyons university
Arrived: a week ago | **Staying with:** local family
Reason for trip: to set up a student exchange programme
Sights visited in the city: You've done the bus tour of the city; visited the library and art gallery
Opinion of city: lots of facilities for quite a small city

♀ 7

Name: Anita Nagy
From: the suburbs of Budapest
Job: tourism consultant | **Work for:** tourist office
Arrived: 10 days ago | **Staying at:** the Abbey Court
Reason for trip: attending an English course
Sights visited in the city: You've been on a river cruise; no time to do anything else – ask others for suggestions
Opinion of city: very attractive but you wish you could practise your English more

♀ 8

Name: Angelika Kohl
From: born in south Germany, you now live in Berlin
Job: translator | **Work for:** a range of clients as a freelance
Arrived: last week | **Staying with:** English friends in the city
Reason for trip: attending a conference on translation
Sights visited in the city: new art gallery; want to go hill-walking outside city
Opinion of city: You love it; you visit your friends every year

Vocabulary revision

Crossword Unit 1 (SB pp10–11)

1 Use the clues to complete the grid.

1 She is loved and ______ by her family.
2 He's always ______ about work.
3 He's 96 now, and he's in a special home for the ______.
4 They don't live in the city centre. They live in the ______.
5 I get on well with my brothers and sisters – we're a very ______ family.
6 They're very poor and they live in a ______.
7 My great-grandmother is very old and ______ now.
8 You can't use that cup – it's ______.
9 Those buildings are unsafe and due for ______ soon.
10 Oxford University is very ______ in the academic world.

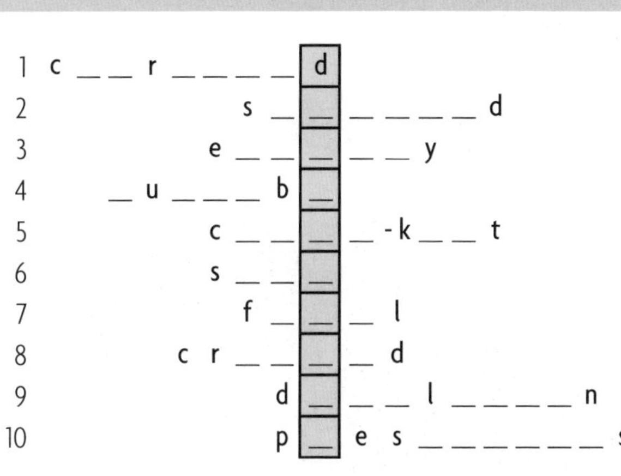

2 Write the letters from the boxes to discover the mystery job

____

Crossword Unit 2 (SB pp18–19)

Use the clues to complete the puzzle with the adjectives.

ACROSS

5 Someone who is **e**______**c** is slightly strange. (9)
6 Someone who is **b**___-______**ed** is often in a bad mood. (3, 8)
7 If you feel **f**______**ed**, you feel angry because you can't do or get what you want. (10)
8 Someone who is **s**______**t** is used to always getting exactly what they want. (6)
9 Someone who is **o**___-______**ed** doesn't like modern things. (3, 9)
10 If you are **d**______**ed** to someone, you love them a lot. (7)

DOWN

1 Someone who is **s**______**l** has done well and achieved a lot. (10)
2 Someone who is **w**___-______**ed** always tries to do the right thing. (4, 11)
3 Someone who is **c**______**ve** doesn't like change. (12)
4 Someone who is **p**______**te** about something has strong opinions about it. (10)

Definitions Unit 3 (SB pp26–27)

1 Use the definitions to complete the words from the story of *Romeo and Juliet*.

1 lasting for ever (7)
2 something you do to make someone suffer because they made you suffer (7)
3 to send someone away from a place for ever (6)
4 to bring people together (5)
5 a feeling of very great sadness after someone has died (5)
6 a quarrel that goes on for a long time (4)
7 to say goodbye and leave each other (4)
8 to ask someone very strongly to do something (3)

1 e
2 r
3 b
4 u
5 g
6 f
7 p
8 b

2 Rearrange the highlighted letters to answer the question.

What did Juliet use to kill herself?

Unit 4

Song Our house

1 Work with a partner. Choose the correct words in the song. Use the grammar, context, and rhyme to help you.

2 **[CD 2: Track 2]** Listen to the song and check.

3 Who in the song …?

1 remembers happy times spent playing *the singer*

2 has some housework to do ______________

3 is very tidy ______________

4 is in a hurry because he's seeing his girlfriend ______________

5 is dreaming ______________

6 says they won't be separated ______________

7 is being a bit naughty ______________

8 wears smart clothes at the weekend ______________

4 Work with a partner and answer the questions.

1 What image of childhood is given in the song? Choose the three most appropriate adjectives.

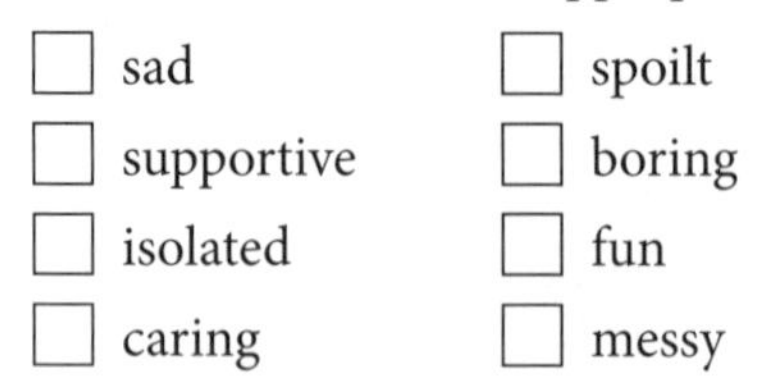

2 Do you think this image is true for most children today? Why/Why not?

3 Why do you think the songwriter wrote the song?

4 What other images of childhood do you know from books/songs/films/paintings?

Our House

Father wears his (1) Sunday / Monday best
Mother's tired, she needs a (2) sleep / rest
The kids are playing up downstairs
Sister's sighing in her sleep
Brother's got a date to (3) keep / make
He (4) must / can't hang around

Our house, in the middle of our street
Our house, in the middle of our …

Our house it has a (5) crowd / group
There's always (6) nothing / something happening
And it's usually quite loud
Our mum she's so house-proud
Nothing (7) ever / never slows her down
And a mess is not (8) allowed / aloud

Our house, in the middle of our street
Our house, in the middle of our …

Our house, in the middle of our street
Our house, in the middle of our …
Something tells you that you've got to get away from it

Father gets up late (9) for work / today
Mother (10) has / must to iron his shirt
Then she sends the kids to school
Sees (11) him / them off with a small kiss
She's the one they're going to miss
In lots of (12) days / ways

Our house, in the middle of our street
Our house, in the middle of our …

I remember way back then when everything was true and when
We (13) would / used have such a very good time such a fine time
Such a happy time
And I remember how we'd play, simply waste the (14) time / day away
Then we'd say nothing would come between us two dreamers

Repeat verse 1 and chorus

Unit 6 Describing people and things **Student A**

1 Answer your partner's questions about Katie and her flat.

Katie	
Age	late 20s
Personality	quiet, very hard-working
Looks	quite small; attractive
Hair	long, fair, and curly
Height	about five foot two
Clothes	well-dressed, designer labels
Hobbies	reading and walking

Katie's flat	
General description	quite old-fashioned, comfortable and with lovely views
Floor	6th
Size	pretty big, $80m^2$
Number of rooms	5, living room, kitchen, bathroom, two bedrooms
Size of living room	3m by 4m
Which part of town	near the park
How far to shops	about 10 minutes

2 Now ask your partner information questions about Martin and his flat. Complete the chart.

Martin	
Age	
Personality	
Looks	
Hair	
Height	
Clothes	
Hobbies	

Martin's flat	
General description	
Floor	
Size	
Number of rooms	
Size of living room	
Which part of town	
How far to shops	

3 Tell your partner about someone you know and where he/she lives. Give the same information as in the chart.

Unit 6 **Describing people and things** **Student B**

1 Ask your partner information questions about Katie and her flat. Complete the chart.

Katie	
Age	
Personality	
Looks	
Hair	
Height	
Clothes	
Hobbies	

Katie's flat	
General description	
Floor	
Size	
Number of rooms	
Size of living room	
Which part of town	
How far to shops	

2 Now answer your partner's questions about Martin and his flat.

Martin	
Age	late 40s
Personality	very nice, good fun and very sociable
Looks	slim and good-looking
Hair	curly and dark
Height	about 1m 80
Clothes	casual; has his own style
Hobbies	travelling, cooking, spending time with friends

Martin's flat	
General description	spacious and well-decorated; some interesting objects
Floor	3rd
Size	big, $90m^2$
Number of rooms	7, living room, kitchen, bathroom, two bedrooms, office
Size of living room	5m by 3m
Which part of town	right in heart of the city
How far to shops	2 minutes

3 Tell your partner about someone you know and where he/she lives. Give the same information as in the chart.

Vocabulary revision

Phrasal verbs Unit 4 (SB pp34–35)

Solve the phrasal verb anagrams in the box to complete the sentences.

~~ogcbak~~	pugid	niveig	etspu	pugribn
novile	shpupu	puvige	ketaup	puwrog

1 Would you like to ***go back*** in time to the 1920s?

2 Adding another room will ____________ the value of your house.

3 He decided to ____________ his own business.

4 He ____________ in London, with his grandparents.

5 They have to ____________ just £40 a week.

6 I want to do more sport, so I've decided to ____________ golf.

7 You really ought to ____________ smoking!

8 Children are always asking for new toys, but you shouldn't ____________ to them all the time.

9 It's very tiring to ____________ children on your own.

10 We went to ____________ some vegetables from the garden.

Wordsearch Unit 5 (SB pp42–43)

Find words in the word search to complete the sentences.

A	U	T	O	M	A	T	I	C	A	L	L	Y
C	O	P	L	D	C	X	V	E	A	P	D	R
E	G	H	L	K	T	I	O	N	Z	R	S	P
C	O	N	S	C	I	O	U	S	N	E	S	S
S	T	I	O	P	V	A	E	L	D	D	Y	R
P	I	P	A	R	A	L	L	E	L	I	O	E
B	N	G	O	O	T	E	D	X	L	C	W	V
F	R	A	L	I	E	N	G	T	S	T	E	U
R	T	O	U	B	D	T	W	E	K	I	F	L
R	I	O	Y	R	C	S	E	N	S	O	R	S
S	M	T	R	E	N	U	D	D	E	N	T	I
A	R	J	E	M	F	P	O	U	K	S	W	O
T	E	R	R	E	S	T	R	I	A	L	G	N

1 These are my **predictions** for the future!

2 Scientists will discover a **p**_ _ _ _ _ _**l** universe where everything looks the same as here.

3 We will meet **a**_ _ _**n** life from other planets.

4 Doctors will be able to **e**_ _ _ _**d** our lives so that we live to be much older.

5 Everyone will be a vegetarian because they will feel **r**_**v**_ _ _ _ _ _**n** at the thought of eating meat.

6 We will understand a lot more about **c**_ _**sc**_ _ _ _**n**_**ss** and the human mind.

7 We will discover that there is extra-**t**_**r**_ _ _ _ _ _ _ _**l** life.

8 We won't have to switch machines on, because they will be **ac**_ _ _ _ _**ed** by our voices.

9 We won't have to go shopping, because our fridge will order food **a**_ _ _**m**_ _ _ _ _ _ _ _**y**.

10 We will have **s**_ _ _ _ _**s** in our rooms to detect when we come in.

Word formation Unit 6 (SB pp48–49 and 108)

Complete the sentences with the correct form of the word in brackets.

1 The magazine was full of the ____________ styles in hair and clothes. [LATE]

2 She was ____________ at how much her nephews had grown. [AMAZE]

3 He wasn't the most exciting man, but he loved her ____________. [PASSION]

4 Bored with doing the same old thing, she decided to apply for a more ____________ job. [CHALLENGE]

5 Although her broken wrist was ____________, she carried on working. [PAIN]

6 The journey was long and ____________. I was glad when I finally arrived home. [TIRE]

7 It was over a hundred years old – ____________ down through generations from mother to daughter. [PASS]

8 No one saw four-year-old Aitor ____________ behind the door. [HIDE]

9 Grandma is in the kitchen ____________ a celebration dinner for the whole family. [COOK]

10 Do you want to see the photos ____________ at my 21st birthday party? [TAKE]

Unit 7

Song Somewhere only we know

1 Choose the correct words to complete each part of the song.

2 **[CD 2: Track 37]** Listen to the song and check.

3 Find words and expressions in the song that match these meanings.

1 under *beneath*
2 to find by accident ______
3 the spoken version of *going to* ______
4 parts of a tree that have leaves ______
5 to depend on ______
6 to know something really well ______

4 Match the sentence beginnings and endings.

1 The song is about a place [e]
2 Going to the place gave him [ ]
3 He regrets that life [ ]
4 He's feeling old and tired [ ]
5 He found a fallen tree [ ]
6 At the end of the song, [ ]

a and he wants to feel more certain.
b he invites another person to join him in the special place.
c and wondered if he'd been there before.
d a sense of belonging.
e that is important to the singer.
f is getting complicated.

5 Change/Complete the sentences to make them true for you.

1 I think/don't think the place in the song is real because …
2 I like/don't like the song because …
3 The song makes me feel …
4 A place that I feel passionate about is …

Compare your ideas with a partner.

Somewhere only we know

I **(1)** *walked* across an empty land,
I **(2)** ______ the pathway like the back of my hand.
I **(3)** ______ the earth beneath my feet,
Sat by the river and it **(4)** ______ me complete.

~~walked~~ felt made knew

Chorus
Oh, simple thing, where have you **(5)** ______ ?
I'm **(6)** ______ old and I need something to rely on.
So **(7)** ______ me when you're gonna let me in,
I'm getting tired and I need somewhere to begin.

tell getting gone

I **(8)** ______ across a fallen tree,
I felt the branches of it **(9)** ______ at me.
Is this the place we **(10)** ______ to love?
Is this the place that I've **(11)** ______ dreaming of?

been looking came used

Repeat chorus

So if you **(12)** ______ a minute, why **(13)** ______ we go,
Talk about it somewhere only we know?
This **(14)** ______ be the end of everything.
So why don't we go, somewhere only we know,
Somewhere only we know?

could don't have

Repeat chorus and verse 3

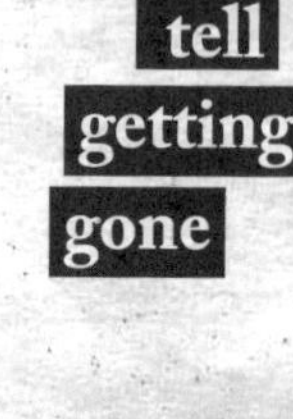

Vocabulary revision

Definitions Unit 7 (SB pp58–59)

1 Use the clues to complete the grid.

2 Rearrange the highlighted letters to find the mystery word.

a very famous sportsman, musician, film star, etc.

_ _ _ _ _ _ _ _ _

1 Someone who teaches people how to play a sport. _ o _ _ _
2 another name for football s _ _ _ _ _
3 very rich _ e _ _ _ _ y
4 a pause in the middle of a football game _ _ _ _ t _ _ _
5 land that is not used for anything w _ _ _ _ _ r _ _ _ d
6 a private school in Britain _ _ _ _ _ _ s _ _ _ _ l
7 happening all over the world w _ r _ _ w _ _ _
8 a feeling of strong competition between two teams r _ _ _ _ _ _ y
9 a great ability to do something well t _ _ _ _ _
10 very good at something _ i f _ _ _

Adjective Anagrams Unit 8 (SB pp66–67)

Solve the adjective anagrams and match the words to their definitions.

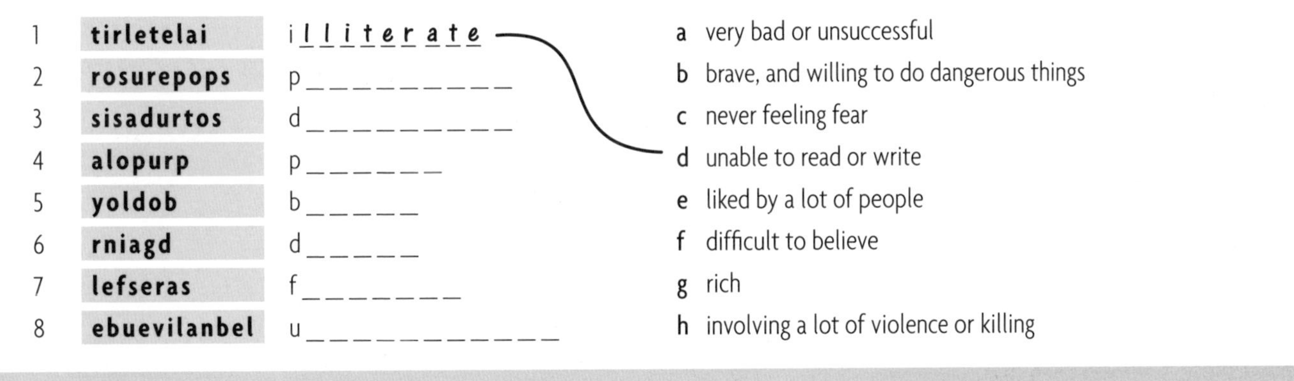

1 **tirletelai** i l l i t e r a t e
2 **rosurepops** p _ _ _ _ _ _ _ _ _
3 **sisadurtos** d _ _ _ _ _ _ _ _ _
4 **alopurp** p _ _ _ _ _ _
5 **yoldob** b _ _ _ _ _
6 **rniagd** d _ _ _ _ _
7 **lefseras** f _ _ _ _ _ _ _
8 **ebuevilanbel** u _ _ _ _ _ _ _ _ _ _ _

a very bad or unsuccessful
b brave, and willing to do dangerous things
c never feeling fear
d unable to read or write
e liked by a lot of people
f difficult to believe
g rich
h involving a lot of violence or killing

Crime Unit 9 (SB pp74–75)

Use the clues to complete the puzzle.

ACROSS

2 ______ crime happens in cities, not the countryside.
4 Criminals ______ crimes.
5 ______ clothes are not very smart.
7 A ______ family is one with a lot of problems.
10 Many famous celebrities go into ______ to stop taking drugs.
11 ______ is the crime of stealing.

DOWN

1 To ______ someone means to send them to prison.
3 ______ justice is when criminals meet their victims and say sorry.
4 When you have ______, you talk to someone about all your problems.
6 A drug ______ is someone who cannot stop taking drugs.
8 The police try to ______ criminals.
9 A ______ is someone who is walking past.

Unit 10

Technology questionnaire

1 Read the questionnaire and tick (✔) your answers. Then check your score at the bottom of the page.

Technophile or technophobe?

1 How many of these do you use regularly?

- ☐ CD player
- ☐ computer/laptop
- ☐ digital radio
- ☐ recordable DVD player
- ☐ flat screen TV
- ☐ *iPod*
- ☐ webcam
- ☐ satellite navigation

2 You need to contact a friend quickly. Do you …?

- ☐ **a** send him/her a text message
- ☐ **b** write him/her a letter
- ☐ **c** try to find a phone box
- ☐ **d** phone him/her on your mobile

3 You'd like to try on some clothes you saw in a magazine. Do you …?

- ☐ **a** try to find something similar in the local shops
- ☐ **b** order them online
- ☐ **c** post your completed order form to the company
- ☐ **d** travel 75 km to the nearest shop

4 How many of these have you used in the last two weeks?

- ☐ Internet banking
- ☐ *eBay*
- ☐ email
- ☐ *Facebook*
- ☐ *Google*
- ☐ *MSN Messenger*
- ☐ *Wikipedia*
- ☐ *YouTube*

5 How many of these terms can you explain?

- ☐ blog
- ☐ spam
- ☐ cookies
- ☐ podcast
- ☐ emoticon
- ☐ broadband

6 How many of these abbreviations do you recognize?

- ☐ Cc
- ☐ DAB
- ☐ FAQs
- ☐ GPS
- ☐ HD
- ☐ ISP
- ☐ SMS
- ☐ www

7 Which of these have you never managed to do?

- ☐ bookmark a webpage
- ☐ chat on the Internet
- ☐ download an MP3 file
- ☐ follow satellite navigation
- ☐ install software
- ☐ print photos taken on a digital camera
- ☐ set the timer on a recordable DVD player
- ☐ take a photo on a mobile

8 Which new invention would make your life complete?

- ☐ **a** a robot that does all the housework
- ☐ **b** a portable super-computer that replaces every other gadget
- ☐ **c** a dream projector that records your dreams while you sleep
- ☐ **d** an automatic dog walker

1 one point for each tick (✔)
2 a 3 b 0 c 1 d 2
3 a 1 b 3 c 2 d 0
4 one point for each tick (✔)
5 one point for each tick (✔)
6 one point for each tick (✔)
7 minus one point for each tick (✔)
8 a 2 b 3 c 0 d 1

0–13 Why are you a technophobe? There's nothing to be scared of. Gadgets can make your life easier, and they can be fun! Go on, have a go!

14–27 You have a healthy attitude to technology. You use gadgets to make things easier but you don't let them dominate your life.

28–39 You live in high-tech heaven! You are very comfortable with technology and you love new gadgets. But don't let them rule your life. It's good to talk face-to-face sometimes!

Score

2 Compare your score with a partner. Then discuss these questions.

1. Which invention or gadget could you not live without?
2. What invention or gadget have you bought and never used?
3. Gadgets in general – essential for modern life or a waste of money?

Vocabulary revision

Buildings Unit 10 (SB pp82–83)

Write the words from the box in the correct place, then use some of the words to complete the sentences.

iron	stunning	revolving doors
basement	extend	crystal
outdated	arches	bronze
platform	escalator	vast
roof	glass	restore

materials used in buildings	parts of buildings
adjectives to describe buildings	**verbs to describe work done to buildings**

1 They have decided to ____________ the old theatre to its original state.
2 There is a huge ____________ underneath the hotel.
3 The roof is held up by large stone ____________.
4 Statues are often made of ____________.
5 The building seems quite ____________ and old-fashioned now.
6 The house isn't very big, so they are going to ____________ it.

A mystery Unit 11 (SB pp90–91)

1 Complete the police officer's crime report with the correct words from the text *The three students*.

I entered Miss Baxter's room. There were (1) **s**[_] _ _ _ that someone had climbed through the window. I knew this because there were some photographs on the windowsill, and they had been (2) **d** _ _ _ _ _ _ _ _. I looked around, hoping to find some (3) **c** _ _ [_] _. I noticed a small piece of paper on a shelf. The shelf was quite high, and I had to stand on (4) **t** _ _ _ _ [_] to reach it. I picked it up and (5) **e** _ _ _ _ _ _ [_] it carefully. It was part of a letter, and at the bottom was the name 'George.'

'Who is George?' I asked Miss Baxter, and she immediately became very nervous and (6) **a** _ _ _ _ _ _ [_]. 'He's just someone I know,' she said, 'just an old (7) **a** _ _ _ _ _ _ _ _ [_] _ **e**.'

2 Look at the highlighted letters and rearrange them to find the final word.

When I asked George if he had been in the room, he (8) _ _ _ _ _ _ it.

Reporting verbs Unit 12 (SB pp96–97)

Read the clues and complete the crossword with the correct reporting verbs.

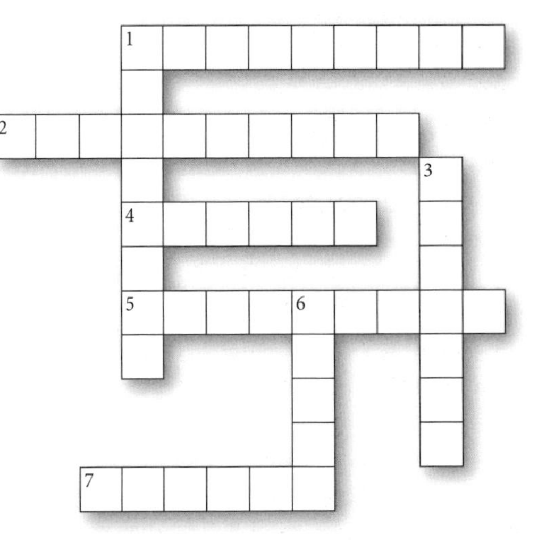

ACROSS

1 I wasn't going to take the job, but Maria ____________ me to accept it. (9)
2 When I was at school, my parents always ____________ me to do my best. (10)
4 Matt didn't ____________ me to his party. (6)
5 Sara ____________ that she was late because the bus had broken down. (9)
7 Can you ____________ me to post this letter? It's really important and I mustn't forget! (6)

DOWN

1 He borrowed £10 from me, but he ____________ to pay it back next week. (8)
3 I didn't have any money, so Tim ____________ to buy me a drink. (7)
6 I ____________ Mark to give me lift to the station, and he said he would. (5)

Answers

Photocopiable materials

Extra ideas Unit 1

Understanding from context

1 1 e 2 b 3 a

2 1 difficult
2 an adjective; famous
3 not to know
4 past; positive
5 a verb; clean off

3 6 adjective (past participle used as an adjective)
7 verb
8 verb
9 noun
10 verb

4 6 divided
7 proud
8 side
9 selection
10 argue

5 11 an adjective (past participle used as an adjective); 'located in place and time'; the text gives the place and date
12 a noun; 'building work'/ 'improvements'; they want to make the lighthouse into a home
13 a verb; 'look at'; the woman is interested in the lighthouse but she doesn't go near it
14 a verb; 'becomes'; the family have to do the investigation because it was useless to go to the police
15 an adverb; 'in an interesting way'; the reader will be guessing what happened until the end of the story

Extra ideas Unit 2

Song *Matthew and Son*

1 **Pros:** earning money, learning new skills, job satisfaction, working as a team, being promoted

Cons: commuting every day, low salaries, lack of free time, a big workload, job insecurity

2 commuting every day, low salaries, lack of free time, a big workload

3 1 for Matthew & Son, he won't wait.
2 And the eight-thirty train to Matthew & Son.
3/5 The files in your head, you take them to bed, you're never ever through.
4 There's a five-minute break and that's all you take,
6 Even though they're pretty low and their rent's in arrears

5 1 a company
2 finished
3 the commuters
4 afraid
5 people get behind with the rent

6 Students' own answers.

Vocabulary revision Units 1–3

Unit 1

1 1 cherished
2 stressed
3 elderly
4 suburbs
5 close-knit
6 slum
7 frail
8 cracked
9 demolition
10 prestigious

2 Mystery job: dressmaker

Unit 2

ACROSS
5 eccentric
6 bad-tempered
7 frustrated
8 spoilt
9 old-fashioned
10 devoted

DOWN
1 successful
2 well-intentioned
3 conservative
4 passionate

Unit 3

1 1 eternal
2 revenge
3 banish
4 unite
5 grief
6 feud
7 part
8 beg

2 The boxed letters make the word *dagger*

Extra ideas Unit 4

Song *Our house*

2 1 Sunday
2 rest
3 keep
4 can't
5 crowd
6 something
7 ever
8 allowed
9 for work
10 has
11 them
12 ways
13 would
14 day

3 2 mother
3 mother
4 brother
5 sister
6 the singer
7 the kids
8 father

4 1 supportive / fun / caring
Students' own answers

Vocabulary revision Units 4–6

Unit 4

2 Adding another room will **push up** the value of your house.
3 He decided to **set up** his own business.
4 He **grew up** in London, with his grandparents.
5 They have to **live on** just £40 a week.
6 I want to do more sport, so I've decided to **take up** golf.
7 You really ought to **give up** smoking!
8 Children are always asking for new toys, but you shouldn't **give in** to them all the time.
9 It's very tiring to **bring up** children on your own.
10 We went to **dig up** some vegetables from the garden.

Unit 5

1 predictions
2 parallel
3 alien
4 extend
5 revulsion
6 consciousness
7 terrestrial
8 activated
9 automatically
10 sensors

Unit 6

1 latest
2 amazed
3 passionately
4 challenging
5 painful
6 tiring
7 passed
8 hiding
9 cooking
10 taken

Extra ideas Unit 7

Song *Somewhere only we know*

2 2 knew
3 felt
4 made
5 gone
6 getting
7 tell
8 came
9 looking
10 used
11 been
12 have
13 don't
14 could

3 1 beneath
2 come across
3 gonna
4 branches
5 rely on
6 to know sth like the back of your hand

4 2 d 3 f 4 a 5 c 6 b

5 Students' own answers

Vocabulary revision Units 7–9

Unit 7

1
1 coach
2 soccer
3 wealthy
4 half time
5 waste ground
6 public school
7 worldwide
8 rivalry
9 talent
10 gifted

2 Mystery word: superstar

Unit 8

1 illiterate
2 prosperous
3 disastrous
4 popular
5 bloody
6 daring
7 fearless
8 unbelievable

Unit 9

ACROSS	DOWN
2 urban	1 jail
4 commit	3 restorative
5 scruffy	4 counselling
7 dysfunctional	6 addict
10 rehab	8 arrest
11 theft	9 passer-by

Extra ideas Unit 10

Technology questionnaire

5 **blog** – short for 'web log', an online personal diary with thoughts and opinions on life as well as links to other websites

spam – junk email sent to many people at once, usually involving advertising or offering services

cookies – small files which websites place on your computer's hard disk so they can recognize you the next time you use their site

podcast – an audio or video file that can be downloaded to a portable player or a computer

emoticon – a face made up of text, e.g. winking ;-) or smiling :-) which can be used to add meaning

broadband – a high-speed Internet connection

6 **Cc** – an email instruction to copy/send your message to additional addresses as well as the main recipient

DAB – Digital Audio Broadcasting, usually just called 'digital radio'

FAQs – Frequently Asked Questions, a list of standard answers to questions which newcomers to a topic or website may have

GPS – Global Positioning System, a system of satellites and receivers that allows people and devices to pinpoint their precise location and navigate routes

HD – High Definition, a high-quality TV standard that makes the most of large screens

ISP – Internet Service Provider, a company that provides Internet connections to private and business customers

SMS – Short Message Service, usually known as 'text messaging'

www – World Wide Web, the system of connected documents on the Internet, which often contain colour pictures, video, and sound

Vocabulary revision Units 10–12

Unit 10

materials used in buildings: iron, crystal, glass, bronze
parts of buildings: basement, platform, roof, arches, escalator, revolving doors
adjectives to describe buildings: outdated, stunning, vast
verbs to describe work done to buildings: extend, restore

1 restore
2 basement
3 arches
4 bronze
5 outdated
6 extend

Unit 11

1
1 signs
2 disturbed
3 clues
4 tiptoe
5 examined
6 agitated
7 acquaintance

2
8 denied

Unit 12

ACROSS	DOWN
1 persuaded	1 promised
2 encouraged	3 offered
4 invite	6 asked
5 explained	
7 remind	

OXFORD
UNIVERSITY PRESS
Great Clarendon Street, Oxford OX2 6DP
Oxford University Press is a department of the University of Oxford. It furthers the University's objective of excellence in research, scholarship, and education by publishing worldwide in
Oxford New York
Auckland Cape Town Dar es Salaam Hong Kong Karachi Kuala Lumpur Madrid Melbourne Mexico City Nairobi New Delhi Shanghai Taipei Toronto
With offices in
Argentina Austria Brazil Chile Czech Republic France Greece Guatemala Hungary Italy Japan Poland Portugal Singapore South Korea Switzerland Thailand Turkey Ukraine Vietnam
OXFORD and OXFORD ENGLISH are registered trade marks of Oxford University Press in the UK and in certain other countries

First published 2009
2013 2012 2011 2010 2009
10 9 8 7 6 5 4 3 2 1

ISBN: 978 0 19 476877 1 Teacher's Pack
ISBN: 978 0 19 476873 3 Teacher's Book
ISBN: 978 0 19 476876 4 Teacher's Resource Disc

Printed in Spain by Orymu S.A.

ACKNOWLEDGEMENTS

The authors and publisher are grateful to those who have given permission to reproduce the following extracts and adaptations of copyright material: p47 *I Believe* Words and Music by Ian Dury and Michael Gallagher © Templemill Music and Mute Song. All rights on behalf of Templemill Music administered by Warner/Chappell Music Ltd, London W6 8BS. Reproduced by permission; p59 'Rocket Man, Steve Bennett' BBC Saturday Live, 10 March 2007. © BBC Radio. Reproduced with kind permission of Steve Bennett and BBC Radio; p92–93 'Don't panic, It's only a Fish' by Lucy Elkins, *Daily Mail*, 17 April 2007. © Daily Mail 2007; p147 *Matthew and Son* Words & Music by Cat Stevens © Copyright 1966 Cat Music Limited. Used by permission of Music Sales Limited. All Rights Reserved. International Copyright secured; p150 *Our House* Words and Music by Christopher Foreman and Cathal Smyth © 1982 EMI Music Publishing Limited. EMI Music Publishing Limited, London W8 5SW. Reproduced by permission of International Music Publications Limited (a trading name of Faber Music Ltd). All Rights Reserved; p154 *Somewhere Only We Know* Words & Music by Tim Rice-Oxley, Tom Chaplin & Richard Hughes © Copyright 2004 Universal Music Publishing MGB. Used by permission of Music Sales Limited. All Rights Reserved. International Copyright secured.

Although every effort has been made to trace and contact copyright holders before publication, this has not been possible in some cases. We apologize for any apparent infringement of copyright and if notified, the publisher will be pleased to rectify any errors or omissions at the earliest opportunity.

We would also like to thank the following for permission to reproduce the following photographs: Alamy p147; iStockphoto pp150, 154, 156 (laptop), (figure/ emmgunn)